Frontiers in Sociology and Social Research

Volume 7

Frontiers of Sociology and Social Research is a cutting-edge social science book series focusing on new directions in sociological and broader social science research. These new directions could be novel theoretical paradigms, developing topical areas of research, innovative methodologies, and/or substantive findings that exemplify and anticipate trends in subfields. The series is predicated on the observation that any field of knowledge in contemporary times is a dynamic rapidly changing body of perspectives and understanding that continuously builds upon the foundation of extant scholarship. The series encourages manuscript submissions from both new and established scholars of sociology, anthropology, social policy, and other allied disciplines.

Francesca Comunello • Fabrizio Martire •
Lorenzo Sabetta
Editors

What People Leave Behind

Marks, Traces, Footprints and their Relevance to Knowledge Society

Springer

Editors
Francesca Comunello
Department of Communication and Social Research
Sapienza University of Rome
Rome, Italy

Fabrizio Martire
Department of Communication and Social Research
Sapienza University of Rome
Rome, Italy

Lorenzo Sabetta
Department of Communication and Social Research
Sapienza University of Rome
Rome, Italy

This work was supported by Sapienza-University of Rome

ISSN 2523-3424 ISSN 2523-3432 (electronic)
Frontiers in Sociology and Social Research
ISBN 978-3-031-11755-8 ISBN 978-3-031-11756-5 (eBook)
https://doi.org/10.1007/978-3-031-11756-5

This Springer imprint is published by the registered company Springer Nature Switzerland AG
The registered company address is: Gewerbestrasse 11, 6330 Cham, Switzerland

Acknowledgments

This work was financially supported by Sapienza - University of Rome Conferences funding program and the PhD in "Communication, Social Research, and Marketing." The Sapienza Department of Communication and Social Research (CoRiS) also provided invaluable support. We express our sincere gratitude to Antonio Fasanella (then Coordinator of the PhD program) and Alberto Marinelli (Director of the Department).

Contents

Editors and Contributors

About the Editors

Francesca Comunello Department of Communication and Social Research, Sapienza – University of Rome, Rome, Italy

Fabrizio Martire Department of Communication and Social Research, Sapienza – University of Rome, Rome, Italy

Lorenzo Sabetta Department of Communication and Social Research, Sapienza – University of Rome, Rome, Italy

Contributors

Stefano Agostini Department of Communication and Social Research, Sapienza – University of Rome, Rome, Italy

Maria Romana Allegri Department of Communication and Social Research, Sapienza – University of Rome, Rome, Italy

Francesco Amato Department of Social Science, University of Naples Federico II, Naples, Italy

Enrica Amaturo Department of Social Science, University of Naples Federico II, Naples, Italy

Biagio Aragona Department of Social Science, University of Naples Federico II, Naples, Italy

Laura Arosio Department of Sociology and Social Research, University of Milano-Bicocca, Milan, Italy

Silvia Barbotto Forzano Department of Philosophy and Education Sciences, University of Turin, Turin, Italy

Andrea Borghini Department of Political Sciences, University of Pisa, Pisa, Italy

Arianna Calderamo Department of Communication and Social Research, Sapienza – University of Rome, Rome, Italy

Gaia Casagrande Department of Social and Political Sciences, University of Milan, Milan, Italy

Ciro Clemente De Falco Department of Social Science, University of Naples Federico II, Naples, Italy

Thomas P. Flynn Department of Behavioral Sciences, Winston-Salem State University, Winston-Salem, NC, USA

Emma Garzonio Department of Communication and Social Research, Sapienza – University of Rome, Rome, Italy

Giovanna Gianturco Department of Communication and Social Research, Sapienza – University of Rome, Rome, Italy

Tilo Grenz Bertha von Suttner Private University, St-Pölten (Lower Austria), Austria

Giovanna Leone Department of Communication and Social Research, Sapienza – University of Rome, Rome, Italy

Laurent Licata Université Libre de Bruxelles, Brussels, Belgium

Tatiana Lysova University of Milano-Bicocca, Milan, Italy

Alessia Mastropietro Department of Psychology, Sapienza – University of Rome, Rome, Italy

Peter Mechant Department of Communication Sciences, Ghent University, Ghent, Belgium

Stefano Migliorisi Department of Communication and Social Research, Sapienza – University of Rome, Rome, Italy

Anne Monier ESSEC Business School, Cergy, France

Mariella Nocenzi Department of Communication and Social Research, Sapienza – University of Rome, Rome, Italy

Maria Patsarika Social Design Institute, University of the Arts, London, UK

Gabriella Rava Charles University, Prague, Czechia

Keith Robinson Griffith University, School of Humanities, Chelmer, QLD, Australia

Vincenzo Romania Department of Philosophy, Sociology, Education and Applied Psychology, University of Padua, Padua, Italy

Daniel J. Rose Department of Behavioral Sciences, Winston-Salem State University, Winston-Salem, NC, USA

Aluminé A. Rosso IIAEC, Buenos Aires, Argentina

Vincenzo Scalia Department of Political and Social Sciences, University of Florence, Florence, Italy

Isora Sessa Department of Communication and Social Research, Sapienza – University of Rome, Rome, Italy

Barbara Sonzogni Department of Communication and Social Research, Sapienza – University of Rome, Rome, Italy

Emanuela Susca Department of Economics, Society, Politics, University of Urbino 'Carlo Bo', Urbino, Italy

Daniela Tafani Department of Political Sciences, University of Pisa, Pisa, Italy

Scott Townsend Department of Graphic Design, North Carolina State University, Raleigh, NC, USA

Chapter 1
Toward a Sociology of Traces

Francesca Comunello, Fabrizio Martire, and Lorenzo Sabetta

What We Talk About When We Talk About Traces

The use of traces and footprints in social sciences can be seen at once as providing an imperfect, feet-of-clay foundation, or instead as omnipresent and inevitable, or even as a trailblazing approach. Indeed, addressing this topic may lead to a situation similar to "the classic stages of a theory's career" ironically outlined by William James: it is first "attacked as absurd; then it is admitted to be true, but obvious and insignificant; finally it is seen to be so important that its adversaries claim that they themselves discovered it" (in Merton, 1968: 22). Ultimately, traces are a type of evidence. Related to a "family of terms such as 'remains,' 'relics,' 'fragments,' 'traces,' 'vestiges', and 'residues'" (Lucas, 2012: 12), these data represent a record of past activities and events we can no longer directly interact with. Haunted by arbitrariness (the entropy of what has reached us), absence (the potential significance of what has not reached us), impermanence (traces duration can well be ephemeral, also endangered by the very act of investigating them), and hesitancy (the original authors have no say in confirming or disproving such information), the notion of traces apparently points to a subpar and vicarious strategy. Actually, *the* quintessential strategy of archaeology and history, disciplines that turn to traces through force of circumstances, and not without lamentation:

> Most human affairs happen without leaving vestiges or a record of any kind behind them. The past, having happened, has perished with only occasional traces. To begin with, although the absolute number of historical writings is staggering, only a small part of what happened in the past was ever observed (. . .). And only a part of what was observed in the past was remembered by those who observed it; only a part of what was remembered was recorded; and only a part of what was recorded has survived; only a part of what has survived

---

F. Comunello · F. Martire · L. Sabetta (✉)
Department of Communication and Social Research, Sapienza University of Rome, Rome, Italy
e-mail: francesca.comunello@uniroma1.it; fabrizio.martire@uniroma1.it; lorenzo.sabetta@uniroma1.it

F. Comunello et al. (eds.), *What People Leave Behind*, Frontiers in Sociology and Social Research 7, https://doi.org/10.1007/978-3-031-11756-5_1

has come to historians' attention; only a part of what has come to their attention is credible; only a part of what is creditable has been grasped; and only a part of what has been grasped can be expounded or narrated by the historian. (Gottschalk, 1950: 46)

Sure, paleontologist and historians can make a virtue out of necessity (see, e.g., Muir, 1991; Zemon Davis, 2010: 5–6; Peltonen, 2012; Bassi, 2016), but the commonsensical assumption is that immediate observation and interrogation of phenomena in their entirety are preferable—time travel would be more effective.[1] However, the recourse to traces is getting more frequent not only for studying the human past, which we are forced to access through the small and dilapidated gate of its remnants, but also for making sense of our contemporaneity, which could be observed first-hand and freely questioned.[2] The list of disciplines varies, also in terms of the specific meaning attributed to traces, and includes, unsurprisingly, semiotics (Eco & Sebeok, 1983; Galinon-Mélénec, 2016; Olteanu et al., 2019) and forensics (Wiltshire, 2019; Servida & Casey, 2019; Burnier & Massonnet, 2020), but also anthropology (Napolitano, 2015; Dragojlovic & Samuels, 2021), philosophy (Heil, 1978; MacDonald, 1991; Bouton, 2020), sociology (Gómez-Barris & Gray, 2010; Heiskala, 2021), psychology and neuroscience (De Brigard, 2014), literary criticism (Orgel, 2015), digital humanities (Bardiot, 2021), evaluation studies (Brahim & Lotfi, 2020), and urbanism (Johung & Sen, 2013).[3] This stunning variety also elevates the risk of conflating traces with other kind of information, and then it is but a small step to an all-encompassing view that would see traces everywhere: a dynamic reminiscent of the so-called "law of the instrument" or "Maslow's hammer."

[1] Analogous arguments induced Lazarsfeld (1950) to spell out our obligations to future historians, who might reproach us for not having given enough thought to what they will want to know about our epoch. Similarly, time capsule initiatives are intended to preserve fragments of our culture for posterity purposes, sealing deliberately certain items and scheduling their future retrieval (Jarvis, 2003). Not to mention technical issues, the cultural/hermeneutical problem is still there: "today the contents of time capsule x are unremarkable because they are commonplace; in three thousand years, x might vaguely suggest the gestalt of a vanished civilization, although precisely what this might mean is unclear; in deep time, however, the contents of time capsule x—assuming they survive relatively intact—would almost certainly require another Champollion or Ventris to decipher what, thousands of years previously, were its commonplace and transparently meaningful artifacts and signs" (Matuozzi, 2004: 242; see also Zerubavel, 2003, and Ferraris, 2012).

[2] This is a simplification. As a matter of fact, the problem of gathering empirical evidence of otherwise unobservable phenomena is not more pressing for analysts of no-longer-existing subjects than it is for analysts of still-existing ones: nowadays contemporary (say) populism, colorblind discrimination, or social mindscapes are (almost) as directly unobservable as ancient Egypt civilization or Renaissance cities.

[3] So-called hard sciences are not unaffected by the concept of trace either. In analytical chemistry, "trace analysis" designates the determination of very small amounts of elements and compounds present as admixtures in the major components of the sample under examination (see Hulanicki, 2016). Perhaps more pertinently, it should be noted that medicine (diagnostic procedures and symptomatology in particular) has always relied on traces in the process of determining pathological conditions: "the model of medical semiotics that makes it possible to diagnose diseases not recognizable through a direct observation and is based on superficial symptoms sometimes irrelevant to the layman" (Ginzburg, 1979: 280). In this sense, it has also been argued (Pape, 2008) that traces do connect sciences and humanities.

After all, the following three questions examined by Tilly actually apply to any form of scientific research: "how does the phenomenon under investigation leave traces? How can analysts elicit or observe those traces? Using those traces, how can analysts reconstruct specified elements, causes, or effects of the phenomenon?" (Tilly, 2002: 252). Indeed, there is hardly any evidence which has not been considered, at one time or another, as the trace of something else one would like to explain.[4]

The last sentence is distinctively Lazarsfeldian, pinpointing a problem, however, characteristic of any empirical science: how to establish a connection between a series of observations and a more fundamental state of affairs/property (the actual main focus of interest) that has given rise to those indicators (see Lazarsfeld, 1958; see also Swedberg, 2018)—"and this is also what men have tried to do over the centuries when they have asked their sweethearts: 'Do you *really* love me?'" (Lazarsfeld, 1953: 352). Although his terminology often evokes parallels with traces (he talks indifferently of "indicators," "symptoms," "clues," and "signs"), Lazarsfeld stoutly championed a statistical "model of convergence" (see Fasanella, 2022): the higher number of data sets which go in the same direction and the greater the correspondence among those data, the more confidently scholars can consider their interpretations reliable and trustworthy. Traces, though, suggest a different orientation toward data (and their relation to the underlying "quality" they can be traced back to). Historiography, trace-based discipline par excellence, might come to the aid of those who would like to grasp the peculiar payoff of heuristic strategies based on traces interpretation. The tenth (and last) of what Arnaldo Momigliano defined "the rules of the game in the study of ancient history" reads:

> The historian is not an interpreter of sources, even in the very act of interpreting them. He is, rather, an interpreter of that reality of which his sources are telling signs or fragments. The historian encounters an author in a text, and in a decree he perceives the legislative body that issued it under specific circumstances; inside an ancient house, he finds the person who inhabited it, and in a tomb he finds the beliefs of the group to which the deceased belonged. The historian interprets his documents as traces of individuals who have vanished. He finds the meaning of a text or object in front of him because he understands how it belonged in that situation of which it was a product and part. The historian transfers what survives to a world that is no longer present. What ultimately makes a historian is the ability to read the document as if it were not a document, but an actual event of past life. (Momigliano, 2016 [1974]: 45)

Typical of interpretations of traces is the spirit of Peircean abduction (see Timmermans & Tavory, 2012; Atkinson, 2018): the use of conjectural inferences to explain some enigmatic experience by linking specific materials with theoretical generalizations via hypothesis construction (see also Misak, 2013: 47–50). Most importantly, far from taking data at face value, researchers confronted with traces are pushed to go (even wildly) beyond their surface and apparent meaning (this is Momigliano's lesson). A trace in itself is neither precious nor worthless but, almost

[4]It holds true for social phenomena in general what judge Giovanni Falcone said about Sicilian Mafia in particular: "everything is a message, everything is full of meaning in the world of Cosa Nostra, no detail is too small to be overlooked" (in Stille, 1995: 6).

tautologically, appraisable only for what it can be traced back to—turning data into substantial interpretations, traces might constitute "strategic research materials" (Merton, 1987).[5] Excellent theories can do almost everything, granted. But why are traces supposed to enable this abductive theoretical surplus? It is not just that they are essentially more informative than standard evidence; if footprint-like clues are insightful, it is because they are often left without awareness. A key point of trace-like evidence is that they are *evidence that did not expect to possess evidential character*: actually, they are seen as evidence only from the perspective of the analyst, while those who produced the trace did not envisage its potential. In this sense, traces are informative not only because they did not intend to inform anyone, but mostly because they were usually unintended in the first place (actually, intentionality might have changed them or made them faded out[6]). Allowing "unauthorized inference" (Gibbs, 1999: 115) to take place, traces convey intelligence and insight not only about elements unbeknownst to their producers but also about aspects they might rather not want to declare altogether (see Sabetta, 2020)—and this is what makes them useful also for studying current phenomena and actors who have not yet vanished.

The idea of appreciating the involuntary component of traces (conceiving them primarily as clues rather than statements), bracketing off the overt intentionality in their production in order to get at something more profound, is what lies behind Ginzburg's evidential paradigm, a method of interpretation that recurs throughout many chapters included in this volume. Ginzburg's approach is too famous to need to be scrupulously repeated here, but the core of his method is more than pertinent to our concerns, based as it is precisely on traces, "on debris, on marginal data, considered as detectors. This way, details usually considered unimportant or even trivial, 'low', could provide the key for understanding the highest product of human spirit" (Ginzburg, 1979: 280). If these kinds of data seem trivial and marginal is because they were so, originally, to their producers/authors (actually, it may be assumed that they were not even recognized as potential information or data). But seemingly marginal matters can be transmuted into fundamental theoretical matters and, actually, as Merton put it (1987: 16–19), the "trivial" is a prime example of strategic research materials: there is no necessary relation between the socially ascribed significance of empirical data under examination and their significance for analytical purposes—"the scientific and the human significance of those materials can be (…) poles apart" (Merton, 1987: 18). Therefore, traces allow researchers

[5]This approach is altogether different from the idea that information should be tackled in their totality ($N =$ all) or statistically representative fractions thereof (random sample) because they are envisioned as formally equivalent, interchangeable, and one piece of evidence is as good as any (see Fasanella and Sabetta 2022: 122–123).

[6]Animals, too, are obviously capable of throwing their predators off the scent by covering their own tracks and footsteps—but they can do even better: for example, Australian magpies outsmarted ornithologists by purposefully removing GPS trackers placed on them for studying their movements [see Crampton et al. (2022)].

to probe and go beyond the accounts that collective and individual actors offer of themselves:

> At least three fourths of the lives of the saints of the high Middle Ages can teach us nothing concrete about those pious personages whose careers they pretend to describe. If, on the other hand, we consult them as to the way of life or thought peculiar to the epoch in which they were written (all things which the biographer of the saint had not the least intention of revealing), we shall find them invaluable. Despite our inevitable subordination to the past, we have freed ourselves at least to the extent that, eternally condemned to know only by means of its "tracks", we are nevertheless successful in knowing far more of the past than the past itself had thought good to tell us. Properly speaking, it is a glorious victory of mind over its material. (Bloch, 1992[1954]: 52–53)

It is through the interpretation of the analyst that a trace speaks, not through the intention of its original protagonist; indeed, as Bloch put it (1992[1954]: 61), one reads a trace in spite of what its producer intended.[7] And this perspective does not get less rewarding when applied to modern-day phenomena: "even in the present, who among us would not prefer to get hold of a few secret chancellery papers or some confidential military reports, to having all the newspapers of 1938 or 1939?" (Bloch, 1992[1954]: 62. See also Ginzburg, 2017).

True, False, Fictive

Traces are not less or more subject to inaccuracy or unreliability than any other kind of evidence. Indeed, they open a threefold understanding of social reality, connected to the triad of what is "true, false, and fictive"—here we are quoting the subtitle of an essay collection by Ginzburg (2012), titled indeed *Threads and Traces*. We have (–) truthful, genuine traces that allow reliable inference; (–) fallacious, invalid traces that bring about false results; and (–) deliberately misleading traces that seem to be authentic but are actually not, plausible but deceptive traces left behind on purpose. Arguably, the latter are the trickiest ones: the false that advertises itself as true. How to work out the fine (and crucial) line between what's false and what's fictive?[8]

---

[7]The tension between subjectivism and objectivism in social science is long-lasting and venerable and cannot be thought through thoroughly here. However, it should be observed that even dealing with artifacts intentionalism is not the only interpretative option: interestingly enough, criticizing rigidly intentionalist explanations of material culture, Eaton notes that "makers are not infallible guides to the functions of artifacts they themselves have made (...) Sometimes artifacts' first functions are not even anticipated or endorsed by their makers. (...) In the case of hermeneutically complex artifacts—like artworks—the maker may not even be the best interpreter of the artifact; in some cases, she may not even understand it. Indeed, artists are notoriously poor interpreters of their own work. The fact that the maker's intention is often a reliable indicator to an artifact's function (...) does not mean that intentions are constitutive of function" (2020: 41).

[8]Of course, this affects not only the topic of what has been (hopefully true, real facts and events) or what might have been (possible, different alternatives), that is, the retrospective dimension of "what

Erasing one's own tracks and producing false ones: the ability to "pretend to pretend, which implies the calculation of a subject in relation to another subject able to calculate" (Eidelsztein, 2018: 105) is distinctively human. And so is the reaction to the realization of having been examined: previously inadvertent traces can well become deliberately occasioned once their producers perceive their informative potential—individuals might then communicate intentionally what will appear unintentionally transpired (see Lombardo & Sabetta, 2021).

Data are at the core of definitions of contemporary society. Van Dijck et al. (2018: 9), for instance, when defining the *platform society*, highlight that platforms constitute a global online ecosystem "that is driven by algorithms and fueled by data." *Datafication* processes (Mayer-Schoenberger & Cukier, 2013) can be defined as the ability to translate into data several aspects of the world (and of people's lives) that were never quantified before. Currently, personal behavior, business processes, cities, private lives (Mulligan, 2014), and even beauty (Elias & Gill, 2018) are being quantified. What emerges from datafication and "self-tracking cultures," which have been deeply transformed and enhanced by digitization processes, is a *quantified self* (Lupton, 2016). "Personal digital data" are generated continuously, and they are "fundamentally about the lives of humans" (Lupton, 2016: 5): indeed, "they have begun to play a significant role in influencing people's behaviors, sense of self, social relationships and, increasingly, their life chances and opportunities" (ivi).

An important share of personal digital data can be considered as traces, inadvertently left by users as they interact with digital tools and services (ranging from search engines to social media platforms, from smartphones to wearable devices). Through the datafication, commodification, and selection processes performed by online platforms (Van Dijck et al., 2018), these inadvertent behaviors retroact on user (and usage) online experiences, as platforms select the most relevant content or services to offer, creating *personalized* experiences.

Scholars have framed such ecosystems in terms of a "black box society" (Pasquale, 2015), since platforms generally operate through ways that appear opaque to most of their users (Gillespie, 2014) and only partially known to the general public. While most users are unaware of the specific algorithmic mechanics that regulate social media platforms, search engines, and other digital tools and services, there is also a growing development of "algorithmic imaginaries," which are ways "in which people imagine, perceive and experience algorithms" (Bucher, 2017). Indeed, digital media users create mental models of how algorithms operate, and some of them rearrange their behaviors and interactions accordingly. In Bucher's research, for instance, some Facebook users have reported their efforts to "train" the algorithm, in order to get more suitable information on their social media feeds, while other referred to have modified their posting behaviors to better suit the algorithms, thereby gaining more visibility on the platform (Bucher, 2017). Indeed,

---

has been left behind." It also affects the predictive dimension of traces, the use of trace-like information to forecast and make predictions.

users show a growing tendency to mention (their understanding of) algorithms, when addressing digital tools and services usage, expressing their evaluation over their mechanisms, and sometimes expressing a playful attitude toward the exploration of these dynamics, including intentionally changing their activities in order to tame the algorithm and unlock a better online experience (for an exploration of algorithmic imaginaries, as emerged among dating app users, see Parisi & Comunello, 2020).

A large share of personal digital data can be considered as truthful, genuine traces, which are left inadvertently by users. Even in those cases, nevertheless, platform affordances and imagined affordances (Nagy & Neff, 2015) enable specific behavioral strategies and tactics, encouraging some behaviors while discouraging (or constraining) others. Users figure out the appropriate behaviors that should be performed on each digital platform by negotiating with affordances and by collectively developing socio-cultural usage norms that tend to be platform-specific, generating so-called media ideologies (Gershon, 2010). This understanding of the appropriate manner of acting on digital platforms emerges at the intersection between platform affordances and socio-cultural considerations, and it tends to vary over time as well as across different social groups, with strong differences emerging, for instance, between different generations, but also at an individual level (Fernández-Ardèvol et al., 2020).

Therefore, we need to question the very notion of "truthful and genuine" traces, if the aim is translating the meaning of traces into different environments (including the offline world). Furthermore, as illustrated by the aforementioned users' experimentations in exploring and training the algorithms, personal digital data can also constitute deliberately misleading traces, aiming at retroacting of platform's mechanics themselves and on the overall platform usage experience.

Platform Society and Its Footprints: What People Leave Behind in the Digital Age

There is something essential to online platforms that activates the production of "data that did not require a special effort to collect, [being] the digital by-product of the routine operations of a large capitalist institution" (Savage & Burrows, 2007: 887). As van Dijck, Poell, and de Waal point out, the datafication process is closely intertwined with *commodification*, as platforms are constantly engaged in processes that transform the collected data into economic value. The global platform ecosystem is, indeed, "overwhelmingly corporate" (van Dijck et al., 2018: 4), while platforms are "formalized through ownership relationships and business models" (ibid.: 9). While a thorough analysis of the *corporate* nature of the contemporary online environment, and its dealing with data and traces, is out of the scope of this Introduction, it is worth mentioning that such a context has given birth to what has been defined as "surveillance capitalism" (Zuboff, 2019), an economic system which deploys and commodifies human experience for extracting (information), predicting (behaviors), and selling/making profit.

In such a context, power relations are at the core of the struggles between users and digital artifacts and between citizen/consumers and corporations. Digital technologies, as cultural artifacts, can be considered as *battlefields*, where different social groups confront each other (Oudshoorn & Pinch, 2003). In the 1990s, Kline and Pinch highlighted the need to consider "the social structure and power relations within which technological development takes place" (1996: 767). Power is embedded in technological objects, while different social groups have different abilities "to shape the development of an artifact" (ivi), and they are, in turn, differently shaped by it. A similar mutual shaping approach can be observed with regard to algorithms and to the ways they deal with our digital traces: while it is true that "algorithms certainly do things to people, people also do things to algorithms. The social power of algorithms—particularly, in the context of machine learning—stems from the recursive 'force-relations' between people and algorithms" (Bucher, 2018, p. 42). Nevertheless, different social groups have different levels of agency and exert different power in these negotiation processes, by being, for instance, included or excluded in the design and technology definition, as well as in data gathering and elaboration processes, which tend to operate (paradoxically, if we consider the unprecedented amount of data circulating in contemporary societies) by following the representation of an "ideal user" which is far from being inclusive, in terms of gender, age, ethnicity, etc.

Early *cyberfeminists*, by focusing on digital technology's production, development, and adoption, highlighted how technology was essentially designed by men and for men, as most digital artifacts produced an ideal user that was far from being neutral: it was, indeed, male (Haraway, 1985). More recent discussions about *ageism* in digital technology (considering both the design process and the symbolic level) highlighted how socio-cultural views and designers' backgrounds converge, as digital technologies are generally thought of as addressing "young" people, consistent with the backgrounds and standpoints shared by computer scientists (Rosales & Svensson, 2021). These views tend to consider older people as "unexpected users" of digital tools and services (Rosales & Fernández-Ardèvol, 2020), based on (often hidden) assumptions and power dynamics.

This also seems to apply to the ways in which artificial intelligence systems and social media platforms algorithms deal with personal digital data. Critical algorithm studies (Gillespie, 2016; Kitchin, 2017), as well as journalistic accounts (Allen, 2016), have underlined the widespread of biases in such systems. Indeed, it is in the complex interactions between digital artifacts and socio-cultural considerations that such phenomena emerge. As highlighted by Airoldi (2021), for a better understanding of these dynamics, we need to focus on both "culture in the code" and "code in the culture," as the mechanics of algorithmic systems are shaped not only by designers (and influenced by their standpoints) but also by the data with which these systems are fueled, data that are generally produced by users. As Noble points out, by focusing on search engines indexing and ranking criteria, "the algorithms used to produce the results of searches perpetuate the reinforcement of an oppressive power towards people of color and women in particular, highlighting how racism and sexism have become, often unconsciously part of the language and technological infrastructure that we use every day" (2018: 1). Similarly, when addressing artificial intelligence, Chu et al. highlight that "predictive models in AI systems amplify inequity, privilege, and power in society" (2022). Following this perspective, Klinger and Svensson (2018) "deresponsibilize" algorithms as a computer construct, clarifying how their influence can be understood only if considered in the complex dialectical relationship between media logic, technology, and economy, which is needed to understand how algorithms work and how they impact on some representations of reality.

Consistently, we believe that digital traces, when consisting of personal digital data, should be observed from a multidimensional and mutual-shaping perspective, with emphasis on power relations. This, considering how traces generated by individual and collective online behaviors are enabled (and shaped) by the affordances and constraints of digital environments (which are in turn influenced by the complex dynamics of design, adoption and personal domestication) and also filtered by users' negotiations with such affordances. Such approaches can also interpret how socio-technically situated traces retroact within digital systems, fueling algorithms and predictive models, thus reinforcing (or questioning) the systemic power relations.

Structure and Logic of the Volume

This volume contains a selection of the papers presented at the international conference "What People Leave Behind: Marks, Traces, Footprints and their Significance for Social Sciences," held online on June 15–16, 2021, and hosted by the Department of Communication and Social Research at Sapienza-University of Rome.[9] The initial set of research questions that drove us to organize this conference was heterogeneous, almost erratic (indeed, otherwise we would not put a conference together). How does Google predict flu peaks before public health authorities do? Why are these predictions wrong at times? How did Walmart link a spike in the sales of Pop-Tarts to hurricane forecasts? Why are people's inadvertent little gestures more revealing of their authentic character than any formal posture they may carefully construct? How can a single piece of unintentional information be infinitely more informative than thousands of public records? What kind of data does Netflix use to profile its customers? What did Marc Bloch mean by *témoignages involontaires*? Considering that no systematic analysis exists regarding social traces

[9]Traces of this event can still be found on the Internet: https://web.uniroma1.it/whatpeopleleavebehind/. Vital (and economically generous) help was provided by the PhD Program in "Communication, Social Research, and Marketing" then coordinated by Antonio Fasanella: we are grateful and indebted.

and footprints, even basic points were open to discussion—what have to be considered traces and footprints main characteristics, as well as their epistemological significance, ontological status, and the use (or lack thereof) of these concepts in classical social theory. These questions, however, have been answered in different ways during the conference. Eventually, the debate came to center on four main lines of reasoning: the spatial and interactional dimension of traces, their modern algorithmic and social media-induced nature, the political stakes they carry and raise, and their methodological/epistemological implications. This volume is split accordingly across four parts.

Traces are inherently embedded into certain spatial configurations of our environment and tied to its partitioning, categorization, density, perception, and representation (basically, its complexity). Such spatial structures, of course, are not kept in an artificial void, but crowded by endless series of actions and reactions, resembling Bruegel's paintings rather than de Chirico's; this topologically enacted, relational, back-and-forth processual iteration greatly affects traces production, bearing upon both their display and their understanding. Part I (titled "Traces Between Space, Interaction, and Symbols") is composed of five essays that focus on this interplay of factors: significantly, all are empirical analyses, providing as many case studies (remarkably conceived, in four out of five cases, as cross-contextual examinations). Monier's chapter tries to puzzle out a peculiar kind of mark, the donor plaques exhibited by recipient institutions like museums for expressing appreciation to their (mostly financial) contributors. Instead of simply betokening innocent generosity and dispassionate philanthropy, these plates epitomize the result of a process of negotiation, documented by Monier through ethnography and interviews conducted in both Paris and NYC, symbolizing otherwise invisible power relations. The following chapter, authored by Townsend and Patsarika, also carries out a transnational comparison (between Greece and the USA) regarding the role played by traces, here intended as indexical forms of representation, in sensemaking processes performed within local communities. Special attention is given to researcher-participant interactions, public ethnography, and so-called cultural probes, in their shaping actors' experiences of design community projects: in these situations, traces are what give flesh (and social substance: history, identity, relations, desires, and struggles) to formal structures. In Chap. 4, Grenz and Robinson reconsider the debate on the epistemological dimension of traces and tracing confronting Western approaches with non-Western ones (Aboriginal "First Australians" in particular). Rather than opposing Indigenous and non-Indigenous perspectives, they demonstrate how traces imply different cultural notions of social binding, thus conceiving interpretative tracing as a cosmopolitical tool of analysis. Chapter 5 continues the emphasis on spatial and interactional features of traces, exploring the process of *avant la lettre* gentrification of a former neighborhood in Winston-Salem, North Carolina, and the displacement of its African American, working-class residents. Rose and Flynn guide the reader through the residues of what (and who) this process has left behind, identifying historical patterns of conflict and succession in urban areas: in this case, traces are also what avoid the complete cultural erasure of the black community. Symbols, interactions, and spaces of traces are also highlighted in the last chapter of the first part, in which Rosso puts into use the physical and virtual footprints of museum visitors in four different settings (Buenos Aires, London, Paris, and NYC). Taking into account several dimensions (the experientiality of visits and their trajectories, visual performances, architectural organizations, online feeds), Rosso shows how selfies, hashtags, and gift shops have re-shaped the form of modern museums; such subsequent aftereffects are now actively triggered.

We already underscored that online communication, interactive technologies, and automated digital agents took the game to another level, basically unfolding a new "socio-technical order" (Law, 1990: 10; see also Airoldi, 2021) in which traces play an even more significant role. They are simply more ubiquitous, sought-after, and inspectable than it was in Internet-less societies. Part II, titled "Algorithms, Social Media, and Online Footprints," specifically addresses this Internet-mediated system and its peculiarities in terms of traces. In the chapter that opens the section, Agostini, Gianturco, and Mechant mix offline ethnography, netnography, and interviews for delving into the microcosm of virtual communities. The trail of digital traces unintentionally left behind by groups of users is, at once, indispensable for making sense of the feeling of belonging that community members have and conducive to forms of mutual surveillance, peer-to-peer monitoring, and reciprocal adjustments; interestingly enough, as the authors claim, it would have been hard to spot many indicators of these dynamics without using qualitative methods.

Digital traces might also prove valuable in opening the black box of algorithmic culture: in Chap. 8, Amato and Aragona discuss four empirical cases that show how digital footprints can be used for exploring (i.e., auditing, testing, and parsing) algorithms' models and outcomes. For example, the automatization of inequality and discrimination, both gender- and race-wise, is perfectly disguised and invisible at the surface level, becoming more perspicuous and comprehensible only through the study of side effects and by-product information. Algorithms, however, are personally interpreted and re-interpreted too, thanks to a process of individual meaning-making that impacts actors' decisions of sharing (or refraining from doing so) sensitive data—this is the main focus of Casagrande's contribution. Relying on data regarding young wannabe journalists, she distinguishes between intentionally disseminated and unintentionally exuded traces, underlining the entanglement of self-branding and self-tracking practices (i.e., how and why "digital self" and "quantified self" overlap). Part II ends with another analysis of the interaction between traces and algorithms: in Chap. 10, Garzonio dissects the European legal framework for AI, examining not only its strengths and weaknesses but also the current opposition of self-regulation laissez faire with more binding injunctions. Quite incisively, digital traces are considered are full-fledged means of production, whose consequality can be underappreciated by both people and legislators.

Legal conundrums, economic revenues, individual and collective agency, power differentials among actors and rectors (see Reed, 2020), and gray areas of various sorts—the topic of this volume could hardly be more politically charged. If anything, stimulating interpretations at odds with actors' intentional meanings, the analysis of social traces is often on a slippery slope. Part III, broadly titled "Traces and Political Sphere: Capitalism, Surveillance, Personal Rights, and Moral Concerns," is intended to account for the numerous political ramifications of traces and footprints;

unsurprisingly, the majority of chapter here included tend to adopt a critical stance toward late capitalism. The opening chapter, authored by Borghini, Scalia, and Tafani, revolves around the typical predicament of "watching the watchers" and "guarding the guards." Authors examine how the nexus of digital traces production relates to the issues transparency and surveillance, which are currently reinforcing each other on an arguably unprecedented scale. The case of WikiLeaks founder Julian Assange, and his mission for total transparency, aptly illustrates how surveillance cultures can cultivate new forms of power actually concealed; to expose these and pockets of secrecy, therefore, is consistent with emancipatory purposes of Enlightenment-inspired political principles. Another angle on political principles is provided by Chap. 12, which is devoted to clarify a momentous example of social traces, i.e., the impact of human (and carbon) footprints on the environmental crisis. Calderamo and Nocenzi put unsustainable traces at the center stage of climate change, key to understanding and then envisioning effective solutions for avoiding worst potential consequences; accordingly, they claim that traces should play a pivotal role in new sociological theories of sustainable development. In Chap. 13, Leone, Licata, Mastropietro, Migliorisi, and Sessa present yet another distinctive frame of traces' political relevance: the colonial legacy of European imperialism, with special attention to fascist colonial policy in East Africa. Bringing this debate (far less widespread in Italy than abroad) to a more sophisticated level, the authors argue that previously marginalized, if even noticed, rests of colonialism are still not entirely devoid of political import; the ambiguous effects of racialized advertising in particular are gauged using qualitative interviews. In Chap. 14, traces are linked to video surveillance, CCTV culture, and security space. Drawing on Foucault's work on disciplinary power, Lysova tries to keep together theories on surveillance society and the notions of security and governmentality; using the concept of traces, she proves how these two different strategies of implementation of surveillance might coexist. The intertwinement of traces and personal freedom is addressed also in Allegri's chapter, focused on the right to be forgotten—the erasure of what one has left online in order to protect her/his own identity. Minor past oversights and imprudent emotional manifestations can hunt their protagonists long after they have already forgotten about them, continuing to affect people's reputation; Allegri takes into account the legal debate (and the decisions made by the European Convention for the Protection of Human Rights and Fundamental Freedoms) on such issues for opening up new interpretative possibilities and policy-making strategies. In the final chapter of Part III, Susca engages with Bauman's and Zuboff's theories regarding visibility, surveillance, and capitalism. Traces, here, are examined in a new and original perspective: why do social actors keep leaving traces of even intimate actions that made them easier to be profiled and oriented? Susca unravels the tradeoff between personal autonomy and selective advantages, offering perceptive sociological considerations on future developments.

The fourth and last part of this volume is Mertonianly titled "Traces as Strategic Research Materials." We have already clarified that the concept of traces is rather close to Merton's idea that some facts are better suited than others to construct hypotheses and, basically, to make social science out of data (see Swedberg, 2019). This final part features some epistemological and empirical arguments aimed at advancing such a heuristic claim. In Chap. 17, Rava analyzes matters of significance and meaninglessness, intentionality, and unawareness, in terms of a semiotics investigation. Using the prism of Internet trolling, she argues that even apparently trivial and inconsequential footprints of provocative online behavior might end up being fully significant indicators, semiotically investigable using the paradigm of traces. The stress on traces as distinctive social facts of study, strategic for grasping many nuances of contemporary digital culture, continues in Amaturo's and De Falco's chapter. They specifically focus on the panoply of geographic traces resulting from GPS technologies and the so-called social Internet of things: geomediatization and digital economy are examined, originally, within the framework of actor-network theory. In Chap. 19, the sociology of traces is usefully fertilized with the work of classical social scientists, drawing in particular on the Katz-Lazarsfeldian tradition of empirical research on personal influence, still central in digital methods. Breaking down several methodological strategies (web sentiment analysis, text mining, and social network analysis among others), Sonzogni tries to hold traditional and modern approaches together, underscoring both their differences and analogies. Chapter 20 combines methodological and epistemological reflections too, in this case for reaching a more precise understanding of virtual footprints' different shades; Arosio distinguishes online found data (digital traces), online retrieved data (web-mediated documents), and online captured data (online behaviors). She also offers meticulous distinctions as for the inadvertent vs. deliberate character of traces as well as for more or less unobtrusive measures of digital activities. In Chap. 21, Barbotto embarks on a journey through traces that allows the reader to acquire a panoramic perspective on the semiosphere, including issues regarding contemporary art, everyday life, and physiognomy; several techno-aesthetic variations of action and perception are addressed, and the possibility of generating new traces via elimination/interpolation of previous ones is explored. In the last chapter, Romania adopts a Goffmanian perspective for making sense of what he defines as "shameful traces"—the trail of marks left behind by image-based sexual abuses. Romania picks the story of Tiziana Cantone (an Italian woman who committed suicide in 2016 after the nonconsensual dissemination of her intimate images) as a case study, which is then articulated within a broader symbolic interactionist framework carefully constructed around the concept of trace.

A Call for (More) Research

This volume is not self-explanatory (or, if you will, reflexive) enough to be considered itself as a trace—it is a signal more than a sign (Bacharach & Gambetta, 2001). Still on what this volume is not, rather than describing a supposedly full-fledged area of studies, it aims at opening up new possibilities. Focusing on the role of traces in contemporary societies points to new methodological and conceptual challenges. The critical questions for big "data", raised by boyd and Crawford (2012) more than a decade ago, remain largely unanswered; by questioning the "era of big data" and considering the wide variety of digital traces left behind by people, they asked: "will large-scale search data help us create better tools, services, and public goods? Or will it usher in a new wave of privacy incursions and invasive marketing? Will data analytics help us understand online communities and political movements? Or will it be used to track protesters and suppress speech? Will it transform how we study human communication and culture, or narrow the palette of research options and alter what 'research' means?" (boyd & Crawford, 2012: 662). When it comes to the design of digital tools and services, with specific concern to social media environments, the tension between the public good and invasive marketing strategies is still strong, while social media platforms are growingly gaining momentum and power over their users. Data analytics is surely helping us better understand online civic and political engagement, while they are also employed to track protesters and orchestrate global dis- and misinformation campaigns, let alone cyberwar initiatives, often relying on bots. We still need to figure out, doubtlessly, how big data (and digital traces) will transform the ways in which we study human communication and culture. On the one hand, over the last decade, several big data-driven research on social and cultural problems seem to have failed even asking appropriate and relevant questions or adopting solid frameworks for interpreting data. On the other hand, some social scientists, by refusing to dig deeper into these unprecedented amounts of data, seem to have missed the chance of contributing solid methodological and conceptual models to an ever-growing line of research.

This book collects contributions from several sub-fields of social sciences, proposing different methodological and conceptual approaches to the study of online and offline traces. We do believe this sample constitutes a call for further involvement, by social scientists, in such an important stream of scholarship. From both a conceptual and a methodological perspective, traces and footprints represent a promising research field—they are extremely good to think with and yet underappreciated by scholars. From both a scholarly and a societal perspective, it is of utmost importance that boyd and Crawford's questions (2012) do not remain unanswered.

References

Airoldi, M. (2021). *Machine habitus: Toward a sociology of algorithms*. Polity.

Allen, A. (2016). The 'three black teenagers' search shows it is society, not Google, that is racist. *The Guardian*, June 10.

Atkinson, P. (2018). The spirit of abduction. *Contemporary Sociology, 47*(4), 415–417.

Bacharach, M., & Gambetta, D. (2001). Trust in signs. In K. S. Cook (Ed.), *Trust and society* (pp. 148–184). Russell Sage Foundation.

Bardiot, C. (2021). *Performing arts and digital humanities: From traces to data*. Wiley.

Bassi, K. (2016). *Traces of the Past. Classics between history and archaeology*. University of Michigan Press.

Bloch, M. (1992). *The historian's craft*. Manchester University Press.

Bouton, C. (2020). The privilege of the present: Time and the trace from Heidegger to Derrida. *International Journal of Philosophical Studies, 28*(3), 370–389.

boyd, d., & Crawford, K. (2012). Critical questions for big data: Provocations for a cultural, technological, and scholarly phenomenon. *Information, Communication & Society, 15*(5), 662–679.

Brahim, B., & Lotfi, A. (2020). A traces based system helping to assess knowledge level in e-learning system. *Journal of King Saud University - Computer and Information Sciences, 32*(8), 977–986.
Bucher, T. (2017). The algorithmic imaginary: Exploring the ordinary affects of Facebook algorithms. *Information, Communication and Society, 20*(1), 30–44.
Bucher, T. (2018). *If… Then: Algorithmic power and politics*. Oxford University Press.
Burnier, C., & Massonnet, G. (2020). Forensic analysis of condom traces: Chemical considerations and review of the literature. *Forensic Science International, 310*(110255), 1–14.
Chu, C. H., Nyrup, R., Leslie, K., Shi, J., Bianchi, A., Lyn, A., et al. (2022). Digital ageism: Challenges and opportunities in artificial intelligence for older adults. *The Gerontologist*, online first.
Crampton, J., Frère, C. H., & Potvin, D. A. (2022). Australian Magpies *Gymnorhina tibicen* cooperate to remove tracking devices. *Australian Field Ornithology, 39*, 7–11.
De Brigard, F. (2014). The nature of memory traces. *Philosophy Compass, 9*(6), 402–414.
Dragojlovic, A., & Samuels, A. (2021). Tracing silences: Towards an anthropology of the unspoken and unspeakable. *History and Anthropology, 32*(4), 417–425.
Eaton, A. W. (2020). Artifacts and their functions. In I. Gaskell & S. A. Carter (Eds.), *The Oxford handbook of history and material culture* (pp. 35–53). Oxford University Press.
Eco, U., & Sebeok, T. (Eds.). (1983). *The sign of three: Dupin, Holmes, Peirce*. Indiana University Press.
Eidelsztein, A. (2018). *The graph of desire: Using the work of Jacques Lacan*. Routledge.
Elias, A. S., & Gill, R. (2018). Beauty surveillance: The digital self-monitoring cultures of neoliberalism. *European Journal of Cultural Studies, 21*(1), 59–77.
Fasanella, A. (2022). The Unmarked and the Methodology of Social Research. In C. Lombardo & L. Sabetta (Eds.), *Against the background of social reality. Defaults, commonplaces, and the sociology of the unmarked*. Routledge.
Fasanella, A., & Sabetta, L. (2022). Theory as an option or theory as a must? The bearing of methodological choices on the role of sociological theory. In C. Crothers & L. Sabetta (Eds.), *The anthem companion to Robert K. Merton* (pp. 107–131). Anthem.
Fernández-Ardèvol, M., Belotti, F., Ieracitano, F., Mulargia, S., Rosales, A., & Comunello, F. (2020). "I do it my way": Idioms of practice and digital media ideologies of adolescents and older adults. *New Media and Society, 24*(1), 31–49.
Ferraris, M. (2012). *Documentality. Why it is necessary to leave traces*. Fordham University Press.
Galinon-Mélénec, B. (2016). From "traces" and "human trace" to "human-trace paradigm". In P. Bourgine, P. Collet, & P. Parrend (Eds.), *First complex systems digital campus world e-conference 2015* (pp. 337–349). Springer.
Gershon, I. (2010). *The breakup 2.0: Disconnecting over New Media*. Cornell University Press.
Gibbs, R. W. (1999). *Intentions in the experience of meaning*. Cambridge University Press.
Gillespie, T. (2014). The relevance of algorithms. In T. Gillespie, P. J. Boczkowski, & K. A. Foot (Eds.), *Media technologies: Essays on communication, materiality, and society* (pp. 167–193). MIT Press.
Gillespie, T. (2016). Algorithm. In B. Peters (Ed.), *Digital keywords: A vocabulary of information society and culture* (pp. 18–30). Princeton University Press.
Ginzburg, C. (1979). Clues: Roots of a scientific paradigm. *Theory and Society, 7*(3), 273–288.
Ginzburg, C. (2012). *Threads and traces: True false fictive*. University of California Press.
Ginzburg, C. (2017) *Unintentional revelations: Reading history against the grain*, in Id. *Exploring the boundaries of microhistory*, "The Fu Ssu-nien Memorial Lectures 2015" (pp. 41–81). Academia Sinica.
Gómez-Barris, M., & Gray, H. (2010). Toward a sociology of the trace. In M. Gómez-Barris & H. Gray (Eds.), *Toward a sociology of the trace* (pp. 1–15). University of Minnesota Press.
Gottschalk, L. (1950). *Understanding history: A primer of historical method*. Knopf.
Haraway, D. (1985). A manifesto for cyborgs: Science, technology, and socialist feminism in the 1980s. *Socialist Review, 15*(80), 65–107.
Heil, J. (1978). Traces of things past. *Philosophy of Science, 45*(1), 60–72.
Heiskala, R. (2021). *Semiotic sociology*. Palgrave.

Hulanicki, A. (2016). Characteristics and specificity of trace analysis. In I. Baranowska (Ed.), *Handbook of trace analysis: Fundamentals and applications* (pp. 3–16). Springer.
Jarvis, W. E. (2003). *Time capsules. A cultural history*. McFarland and Co.
Johung, J., & Sen, A. (Eds.). (2013). *Landscapes of mobility: Culture, politics, and placemaking*. Routledge.
Kitchin, R. (2017). Thinking critically about and researching algorithms. *Information, Communication and Society, 20*(1), 14–29.
Kline, R., & Pinch, T. (1996). Users as agents of technological change: The social construction of the automobile in the rural United States. *Technology and Culture, 37*(4), 763–795.
Klinger, U., & Svensson, J. (2018). The end of media logics? On algorithms and agency. *New Media and Society, 20*(12), 4653–4670.
Law, J. (1990). Monsters, machines and sociotechnical relations. *The Sociological Review, 38*(1), 1–23.
Lazarsfeld, P. F. (1950). The obligations of the 1950 pollster to the 1984 historian. *Public Opinion Quarterly, 14*(4), 617–638.
Lazarsfeld, P. F. (1953). A conceptual introduction to latent structure analysis. In Id (Ed.), *Mathematical thinking in the social sciences* (pp. 349–387). The Free Press.
Lazarsfeld, P. F. (1958). Evidence and inference in social research. *Daedalus, 87*(4), 99–130.
Lombardo, C., & Sabetta, L. (2021). The appearance of nothingness: Concealed strategic actions. In W. Brekhus, T. DeGloma, & W. R. Force (Eds.), *The Oxford handbook of symbolic interaction* (pp. 1–21). Oxford University Press. (online first).
Lucas, G. (2012). *Understanding the archeological record*. Cambridge University Press.
Lupton, D. (2016). *The quantified self*. John Wiley & Sons.
MacDonald, M. J. (1991). "Jewgreek and Greekjew": The concept of the trace in Derrida and Levinas. *Philosophy Today, 35*(3), 215–227.
Matuozzi, R. N. (2004). Review of time capsules: A cultural history by William E. Jarvis. *Libraries and Culture, 39*(2), 241–243.
Mayer-Schoenberger, V., & Cukier, K. (2013). *Big data. A revolution that will transform how we live, work, and think*. Eamon Dolan.
Merton, R. K. (1968). *Social theory and social structure*. The Free Press.
Merton, R. K. (1987). Three fragments from a sociologist's notebooks: Establishing the phenomenon, specified ignorance, and strategic research materials. *Annual Review of Sociology, 13*, 1–28.
Misak, C. (2013). *The American pragmatists*. Oxford University Press.
Momigliano, A. (2016)[1974]. The rules of the game in the study of ancient history. *History and Theory, 55*(1), 39–45.
Muir, E. (1991). Introduction: Observing Trifles. In E. Muir & G. Ruggiero (Eds.), *Microhistory and the lost peoples of Europe* (pp. 7–28). The Johns Hopkins University Press.
Mulligan, C. E. A. (2014). *The impact of datafication on strategic landscapes*. Ericsson Working Paper.
Nagy, P., & Neff, G. (2015). Imagined affordance: Reconstructing a keyword for communication theory. *Social Media+ Society, 1*(2), 1–9.
Napolitano, V. (2015). Anthropology and traces. *Anthropological Theory, 15*(1), 47–67.
Noble, S. U. (2018). *Algorithms of oppression*. New York University Press.
Olteanu, A., Stables, A., & Borţun, D. (2019). *Meanings & Co.: The interdisciplinarity of communication, semiotics and multimodality*. Springer.
Orgel, S. (2015). *The reader in the book: A study of spaces and traces*. Oxford University Press.
Oudshoorn, N., & Pinch, T. (2003). *How users matter: The co-construction of users and technology (inside technology)*. MIT Press.
Pape, H. (2008). Searching for traces: How to connect the sciences and the humanities by a Peircean theory of indexicality. *Transactions of the Charles S. Peirce Society, 44*(1), 1–25.
Parisi, L., & Comunello, F. (2020). Dating in the time of "relational filter bubbles": Exploring imaginaries, perceptions and tactics of Italian dating app users. *The Communication Review, 23*(1), 66–89.
Pasquale, F. (2015). *The black box society: The secret algorithms that control money and information*. Harvard University Press.

Peltonen, M. (2012). The method of clues and history theory. In S. Fellman & M. Rahikainen (Eds.), *Historical knowledge: In quest of theory, method and evidence* (pp. 45–76). Cambridge Scholars Publishing.
Reed, I. A. (2020). *Power in modernity. Agency relations and the creative destruction of the king's two bodies*. University of Chicago Press.
Rosales, A., & Fernández-Ardèvol, M. (2020). Ageism in the era of digital platforms. *Convergence, 26*(5-6), 1074–1087.
Rosales, A., & Svensson, J. (2021). Perceptions of age in contemporary tech. *Nordicom Review, 42*(1), 79–91.
Sabetta, L. (2020). Ethnography (and social research) between words and deeds. *Etnografia e Ricerca Qualitativa, 3*(2020), 483–495.
Savage, M., & Burrows, R. (2007). The coming crisis of empirical sociology. *Sociology, 41*(5), 885–899.
Servida, F., & Casey, E. (2019). IoT forensic challenges and opportunities for digital traces. *Digital Investigation, 28*, S22–S29.
Stille, A. (1995). *Excellent cadavers. The Mafia and the death of the First Italian Republic*. Random House.
Swedberg, R. (2018). On the near disappearance of concepts in mainstream sociology. In H. Leiulfsrud & P. Sohlberg (Eds.), *Concepts in action* (pp. 23–39). Brill.
Swedberg, R. (2019). How do you make sociology out of data? Robert K. Merton's course in theorizing (Soc 213–214). *The American Sociologist, 50*(1), 85–120.
Tilly, C. (2002). Event catalogs as theories. *Sociological Theory, 20*(2), 248–254.
Timmermans, S., & Tavory, I. (2012). Theory construction in qualitative research: From grounded theory to abductive analysis. *Sociological Theory, 30*(3), 167–186.
Van Dijck, J., Poell, T., & De Waal, M. (2018). *The platform society: Public values in a connective world*. Oxford University Press.
Wiltshire, P. (2019). *Traces. The memoir of a forensic scientist and criminal investigator*. Bonnier.
Zemon Davis, N. (2010). *A passion for history. Conversation with Denis Crouzet*. Truman State University Press.
Zerubavel, E. (2003). *Time maps: Collective memory and the social shape of the past*. The University of Chicago Press.
Zuboff, S. (2019). *The age of surveillance capitalism: The fight for a human future at the new frontier of power*. Profile books.

Francesca Comunello (PhD) is a Full Professor at the Department of Communication and Social Research, Sapienza University of Rome. Her research and publications focus on the intersections between digital technology and society, including digitally mediated social relations, ageing and digital communication, gender and ICT, civic engagement, digital platforms and disaster communication. She has been a member of several national and international research projects and research networks (including European Commission-funded projects); she has also been the PI of several research projects focusing on digital media. She has held a 2-year fellowship at the Internet Interdisciplinary Institute, Universitat Oberta de Catalunya (Barcelona, Spain), and was awarded a 5-week "Media and Communication Fellowship" by the School of Languages, Social and Political Sciences (LSAP), University of Canterbury, New Zealand. Her work has been published in highly ranked journals such as: *New Media and Society*, *Information Communication and Society*, *Media Culture and Society*, *The Sociological Review*, *The Communication Review*, *Ageing and Society*, *American Behavioral Scientist*, *Violence Against Women*, and *International Journal of Press/Politics*. She has authored 3 books: the most recent one (with Simone Mulargia) is *Social Media in Earthquake-Related Communication* (Emerald, 2018).

Fabrizio Martire (PhD) is Professor of Sociology at the Department of Communication and Social Research, Sapienza University of Rome. Among his main scientific interests: sociological theory, history of sociology and social researches, methodology of social researches (with a specific focus on data collection strategies and techniques), public opinion analysis, evaluation (with a specific focus on quality of social research outputs). On these issues he has organized and supervised several scientific projects, publishing almost 70 essays (monographs, edited volumes, articles in Italian and international journals, chapters). He has attended several international and Italian conferences, giving seminars in a number of foreign universities (Spain, Republic of Korea, Chile, Colombia). He is member of the Advisory Board of the Research Network—Quantitative Methods (RN21) of the European Sociological Association (since 2019); partner of the "Global Center of Spatial Methods for Urban Sustainability", Berlin, Technische Universität; Member of the Scientific Committee of the Editorial Series "Methodology of Human Sciences", official series of the Section of Methodology of the Italian Sociological Association (since 2017); and member of the Teaching Board of the doctoral course in communication, social research and marketing, Department of Communication and Social Research, Sapienza University of Rome. Since 2021, he is the Director of the BA program in "Communication, technologies and digital cultures" at Sapienza University of Rome.

Lorenzo Sabetta (PhD) is a postdoctoral researcher at the Department of Communication and Social Research, Sapienza University of Rome, and Adjunct Professor of Sociology at Luiss University. Previously, he was a postdoc fellow in the USA, at the Department of Sociology at the University of Missouri/Columbia (2017–2018), and in Sweden, at the Institute for Analytical Sociology at Linköping University (2019–2020). He was also invited visiting researcher at Nuffield College at the University of Oxford (January–February 2022) and EkSoc Fellow at the Faculty of Economics and Sociology at University of Lodz (February–June 2022). He works at the intersection of sociological theory, cultural-cognitive sociology, sociology of knowledge, and methodology of social sciences. His recent publications include: *The Anthem Companion to Robert K. Merton* (Anthem Press, 2022, with C. Crothers); *Against the Background of Social Reality. Defaults, Commonplaces, and the Sociology of the Unmarked* (Routledge, 2022 forthcoming, with C. Lombardo); *Appearance of Nothingness. An Analysis of Concealed Strategic Actions* (in W. Brekhus, T. DeGloma, and W.R. Force, eds., *The Oxford Handbook of Symbolic Interaction*, 2021).

Part I
Traces Between Space, Interaction, and Symbols

Chapter 2
Leaving a Trace: Donor Plaques as Material Evidences of Generosity?

Anne Monier

Introduction

The Key Role of Donor Recognition

Philanthropy comes from the Greek word "philanthropia," composed of "phil" (to love) and "anthropos" (the human). Philanthropy, in its etymology, can be understood as the "love of humanity." More concretely, philanthropy is also a practice of voluntary giving. It has been defined as "the voluntary giving and receiving of time and money aimed (however imperfectly) towards the needs of charity and the interests of all in a better quality of life" (Van Til, 1990). If generosity has existed since the birth of mankind, modern philanthropy, i.e., institutionalized philanthropy in its contemporary form, was born in the USA after the Civil War (Zunz, 2012), increased a lot during the twentieth century, and became an important element of civil society not only in the USA but also in Europe (in particular from the 1980s).

If philanthropy has been thought to be an act of simple generosity, scholarship has shown the complexity of this act and of the meaning it can have. In particular, studies show that giving comes with strings attached: people expect something in return. The anthropologist Marcel Mauss already conceived philanthropy as an exchange between a gift and a counter-gift (Mauss 2007[1925]). Modern philanthropy relies on a similar process, as a person making a donation receives benefits for it, mostly financial (tax deductions) or symbolic (recognition). In this sense, donor recognition is an important part of philanthropy.

A. Monier (✉)
Essec Business School, Cergy, France
e-mail: Anne.monier@ens-lsh.org

F. Comunello et al. (eds.), *What People Leave Behind*, Frontiers in Sociology and Social Research 7, https://doi.org/10.1007/978-3-031-11756-5_2

The Traces of Philanthropy: Donor Plaques

Donor recognition comes in many forms. Indeed, there are different ways for recipient institutions to express their gratitude to donors, through public or private acknowledgments—from speeches to letters or press releases. But donor recognition can also be expressed through donor plaques—on walls, signs, or objects/buildings. Three forms in particular can be seen at institutions: a "donor wall," which is a collective plaque with all the names of donors of an institution (as you can see in most American museums); a "donor sign," which is a plaque under the work of art that was given or financed or on a part of the project that was funded (e.g., "this painting was given by Mr. X" or "this chapel was restored thanks to the generosity of Mrs. Z"); or a "naming plaque," which is the naming of a material object or a building (a bench, a statue, a theater, etc.), and it usually comes with a plaque as well, to mention the new name and the gift. If "naming" usually refers to this last practice (naming an object or building), it is important to underline that donor recognition is always done by mentioning the name of the donor—except for anonymous donors. Naming—in a broader sense, i.e., as all the traces of recognition that have the name of the donor on them—is an important part of modern philanthropic practices.

What is interesting here to us is that these practices of donor recognition that rely on donor plaques in their different forms are all "traces" of philanthropy. This means that these plaques are material evidence of generosity, i.e., what is concretely left behind once the gift is made, and it can stay for a long time, as we will see. Giving is not a one-time practice that fades into the unknown after the gift is made; it is a social and political practice that leaves a trace. This chapter aims at understanding the practices and meanings around these traces of philanthropy that are donor plaques.

An Understudied Topic

The questions of donor recognition and of naming are very present in the gray literature: a large number of philanthropy professionals have taken an interest in it and integrate it into their strategies. There are countless articles, posts, or reports on the importance of this practice and the best strategies.

However, donor recognition and donor plaques are not well researched by academics. On plaques more generally, there is an important body of literature in history, archeology, or semiotics, but almost nothing on donor plaques more specifically. The question of naming is also understudied, and, when it is studied, it is mainly by researchers in philanthropy studies or in law. Examples include John K. Eason's article, "Private motive and perpetual conditions in charitable naming gifts: when good names go bad," published in Eason (2005), by the UC Davis Law Review and William A. Drennan's publication, "Where generosity and pride abide: charitable naming rights."

The social sciences literature has done very little to address the issue. Some scholars mention it when discussing the motivations of donors, such as Francie Ostrower in her introduction to *Why the Wealthy give*:

> Buildings, programs and even entire institutions are named for wealthy benefactors. The playbills of many performing arts organizations offer long lists of their donors. In Museums, placards next to works of art identify the men and women by whom they were donated. Hospital wings and endowed university chairs carry the names of large contributors.

A few rare French works also evoke it ["In the case of very large donations, this attention goes as far as giving the name of the donor to a room or dedicating a commemorative plaque to him" (Tobelem, 2010)]. Despite a few mentions, the practice of naming would benefit from being analyzed in depth, notably by using the tools of anthropology and sociology. Indeed, naming refers to the idea of filiation, of perpetuation, of identity—the question of naming carries a large number of issues (Martin de La Soudière, 2004).

An Important Phenomenon

Why is it important to study these traces of philanthropy that are donor plaques? First, because philanthropy is a growing phenomenon all around the world, and in particular in many European countries, where the welfare state is slowly losing its key role. In France, for example, philanthropy has grown a lot since the 1980s and in particular since the 2000s with the 2003 law on tax deduction for philanthropic giving and the 2008 law enabling the creation of endowments ("fonds de dotation"). This growing phenomenon goes along with the increase of donor plaques on buildings, monuments, and cultural institutions, all around the urban landscape, where it is now easy to spot a donor plaque.

It is also important because examining these traces of philanthropy gives us the opportunity to analyze a material object: a plaque, with an inscription on it. The study of philanthropy through its very concrete aspects (an object) is quite unusual. It is important to give particular attention to the object itself (what does it look like, where is it on the wall or on the object/building), but also to the inscription (what is written, how, etc.). These material traces of philanthropy also have a specific timeline, as they cannot last forever, like any other object (the plaque can be broken or suffer from the weather, etc.).

Last, focusing on donor plaques helps us get a better understanding of the symbolic aspects of philanthropy by looking at how generosity is transcribed concretely and visually. It is about examining not only the concrete aspect of the plaque but also the meaning behind this particular object and practice. Studies on philanthropy usually focus on the practice of giving itself, more than on the benefit that is given in return and on the meaning it conveys. Looking at "what remains" once the donation is made is also a way to ask broader questions, as we will see.

Traces of Philanthropy and Sociology of Elites

These traces of philanthropy as benefits that are donor plaques are mostly given to big donors. Small donors do not receive such recognition—with some exceptions. This is why we are developing this analysis within the sociology of elites. In particular, this practice of donor plaques and naming says a lot about elites' relation to time and space.

First, donor plaques reveal a special relation to space: it is interesting to take into account where the plaque is placed, in which part of the institution, which part of the wall, how people walk by it, if the place is changed over time, etc. Second, they also relate to time and more precisely on the way elites project themselves into the future: it is key to examine the duration of the plaque, the evolution of the object over time, etc. Last, it also says a lot about the relation of private individuals to public institutions: how they negotiate to get what they want, how fundraising professionals accept or refuse their demands, and how the plaques are appropriated by the public by using the new names (or not).

In this sense, our work is quite original in three ways. It combines an analysis of the relation of elites to time but also space, which is quite unusual. It examines their relation to the future, while many studies on elites and time are about their relation to the past. It furthers our understanding of the relation between these elites and public institutions, as their names appear in public places.

Methodology

This work is based on two qualitative research, which are both at the crossroads between different disciplines (anthropology, sociology, political science).

- The first research is part of my Ph.D. dissertation on elite transnational philanthropy, where I analyzed how French cultural institutions raised funds in the USA, through the example of American Friends groups of French cultural institutions (American Friends of the Louvre, American Friends of the Paris Opera and Ballet, etc.). American Friends groups are American organizations that allow American donors to make donations to foreign institutions while still receiving tax deductions. The study is based on a qualitative survey conducted during 3 years (2011–2014) in France (Paris) and in the USA (New York), using four main methods: ethnography (participatory observations), interviews, document and press analysis, and archives.
- The second one is a new research project that I began in 2018 with Nicolas Duvoux[1] (University Paris VIII) on the donor plaques, to question the material

[1] I would like to specifically thank Nicolas Duvoux as some of these thoughts were inspired by a text we wrote together for a conference.

traces of philanthropy. It was supposed to rely mostly on ethnography, interviews, and document and press analysis. This second research has unfortunately been paused due to the Covid pandemic, but we were able to do some exploratory interviews and some analysis of donor plaques' pictures.

Donor Plaques in Philanthropic Giving: When Elite Donors Leave Something Behind

As donor recognition is an important part of philanthropy, donor plaques are growing on the walls, objects, and buildings of institutions receiving gifts from major donors. Donor plaques are particular objects that reveal elites' relation to space and time.

Donor Plaques: A Particular Object

Donor plaques are a particular object that can take different forms. The appearance of the plaque is symbolic, i.e., it means something beyond its mere appearance: the size, the location, the material, and the color can have different meanings. To frame these forms, institutions usually have a "plaque policy" or a "naming policy" that describes the way these practices are undertaken. Plaques are also the evidence that showing the name of donors is important in the philanthropic world. Here are the key questions to ask when analyzing a donor plaque:

- *How?*

  How is it? The size and dimensions of the plaque can vary depending on the space available on the wall or the object/building for the plaque and on the amount of the donation, but depends also on the number of names that have to be mentioned—that is, for example, for collective plaques, it can be quite big. The materials are also different: wood, stone, aluminum, plastic, etc. Last but not least: How is it inscribed (long message, short message, golden letters, small black letters, etc.)?
- *What?*

  What does it say? What is written on it? It varies from one plaque to another. For collective plaques, it is usually a quick line of introduction (e.g., "the institution is grateful to its generous donors") and the list of the names of the different donors, following the alphabetical order or the amount category. The messages on signs under a work of art are usually quite short ("This painting has been acquired thanks to the generous gift of Mr and Mrs. X."). Those on objects/buildings can be a little longer. The analysis of the typeface and of the words that are used is key to understand the esthetic and symbolic aspect of the plaque.

- *Where?*

  Where is it placed? Donor plaques, as we mentioned, can be on different places. First is the type of place in the institution: it can be a wall or a sign under a work of art or in a hall or corridor. Another interesting aspect is the specific place within the institution: Is it at the entrance, in the main hall, or in a specific room? A last question relies on the position of the plaque on the wall: high up, in the middle, in a corner, etc.
- *How long?*

  How long do these plaques stay on the walls of recipient institutions? This is a key question to understand donor plaques. Do these plaques stay forever on the walls? What happens when the donor dies? For collective plaques, they can usually last a long time. For individual plaques, it depends on the gift and on the agreement that was passed between the parties. In particular, in the case of naming practices, the duration of the naming is part of the contract and depends on the amount of the gift.
- *Who?*

  Who are the actors? There are usually different actors involved. First, of course, it is a relationship between a donor and an institution, usually the head of development or of fundraising, and sometimes the director of the institution. But there are also other actors involved like the craftsman who creates the plaque. For individual plaques, what is interesting is that donor plaques are a social contract between two parties (donor/recipient) and the plaque (and its form) is usually an object of negotiation, as we will see.

These particular objects that are donor plaques take different forms but are also revealing of a specific relation of elites to space and time.

Donor Plaques: A Relation to Space

Donor plaques as concrete objects reveal a specific relation that elites have to space. There is an important body of literature on this topic and on the way elites think about space.

Given the high residential concentration of elites and their increasing segregation (McCammack, 2014), studies of the most privileged groups are often anchored in an analysis of elites' relation to space. This relation to space appears in different ways in the recent literature on elites. The search for control and enclosure of a space is one of the crucial mechanisms of their capacity to reproduce their advantage over time (Pinçon & Pinçon-Charlot, 2007). For these categories, but also for broader groups, which have in common that they constitute the most internationalized segments of a highly skilled workforce, it is the articulation of several spaces that constitutes a form of advantage (Andreotti et al., 2016).

This relation to space can also be analyzed through representations of self and others, of the drawing of social and symbolic boundaries that it induces. Thus, the new boundaries of distinction come with an important presence of elites in central and dynamic urban areas (Prieur & Savage, 2013) that were not the prerogative of the traditional bourgeoisies who had an exclusive relation to "highbrow" culture. The naturalization of poverty is also made possible by a specific relation to space (Cousin, 2017).

Finally, far from being (only) an object of analysis, space is very often constitutive of the definition of the perimeters of research on elites, in particular because certain cities concentrate wealth—the case of New York being of course exemplary in the USA (Sherman, 2017). Very often, the urban scale is still too large in relation to numerically small groups, and it is in places of work (Godechot, 2007) or education (Khan, 2011) that the samples of respondents are constituted.

Donor plaques obey the same logic and reveal the way elites define and manage their presence in space and choose their own space, separated from other social categories. Having a plaque on a wall at a public institution is a way for these elites to take up the space, to position themselves in a public space. Moreover, by staking claim to an important spot in an institution (like a hall or an entrance), donor plaques symbolically reveal their capacity to occupy a space in a particularly meaningful manner.

Donor Plaques: A Relation to Time

Donor plaques are also revealing of a specific relation of elites to time. Scholarship in sociology of elites has also addressed this issue of their relation to time.

Muriel Darmon (2015) has shown, in her work on socialization to preparatory classes, that the acquisition and mastery of a specific relation to time is a central dimension of these elite studies. From the top to the bottom of the social hierarchy, from the mastery of time—one's own and others'—enjoyed by dominant groups to the temporal expectation and heteronomy suffered by the dominated, this dimension (time) is central to the analysis of relations between social groups (Darmon et al., 2019).

The question of elites' relation to the past is present in several works. Scholarship on this matter insists on the importance of roots, of the inscription in the long term through a lineage as an element of distinction between elite groups. There is also some research on elites' relation to the future, mentioning their strategies of heritagization, filiation, and inheritance (Pinçon & Pinçon-Charlot, 1996). One way for these elites to leave a more important trace than that left with their family (often understood in the broad sense) is to make a donation. The gift is an investment that allows the donor to leave, engraved in stone, a proof of his/her generosity and altruistic action.

However, the capacity for subjective projection and objective control of the future should be among the central elements of any analysis of social stratification. As the relation to the future can be inscribed in present material resources, focusing on objects—which must be understood in its material sense—offers an indication of the position of the donor in the internal stratification of elites (the more "luxurious" and well placed is the plaque, the higher the elite). Our approach, in this sense, articulates the objectivity and even the materiality of the trace with the subjectivity of an individual projection that is reflected in a choice, a negotiation, a realization, and an inscription on the plaque, as a benefit of a philanthropic donation. In this way, it is possible to look back, hypothetically and with an important analytical gain, on the social relations that can be revealed through the different traces of philanthropy.

Moreover, since philanthropic donations are subject to significant tax deductions, it is important to study the link between private wealth and public affairs. From this point of view, it seems important to consider this research on the material traces of philanthropy as the manifestation of a projection into the future, but also as a benefit being made possible with the help of the citizens (tax deduction being the citizens' money). It relates to the economic frameworks of the transmission of wealth (Piketty, 2013) but also to the political and institutional frameworks where the preferences of the elites are privileged (Gilens and Page, 2014; Cagé, 2018).

In this relation to time, several elements have to be taken into account to analyze it: the dating of the plaque, the evolution in time of these material objects, the duration of the plaque (as we said, some objects and buildings may be named for a certain period of time), the strategy behind the timeframe, and how they project themselves into the future. These plaques can be seen as a privilege to leave something behind—not everyone does—but also something that is visible to many people, not just the family or the relatives, but all the people entering the institution and even beyond (if there are press articles about the gift). One key question is: what do these donors wish to leave behind (as well as the possible gap between their wish and the actual trace they leave)?

The Traces of Philanthropy: A Political Subject?

Donor plaques are a way for elites to leave a trace, revealing their relation to time and space, but they are also a reflection of the values that characterize a society or even a nation, as we can see with the difference between the USA and France regarding this practice.

Traces and Values: Who Deserves to Leave a Trace?

France and the USA do not have the same practices in terms of plaques and naming, which reflects different values. This difference is also linked to the history of philanthropy in both countries, as its development is more recent in France.

Many of my French interviewees who were living in the USA underlined the importance of this practice that is widespread in the USA and follows a certain number of rules ("In the United States, all of this (. . .) is very formalized"). A French diplomat emphasizes the central role of naming in American philanthropy:

> Americans love that, they have rooms in their name, they even have benches in Central Park in their name, when you go to Central Park, you can buy a bench, you go to a theater, you can buy a seat, so basically it's very important this recognition ... all the amphitheaters in the universities, all the buildings are named after someone, who is a donor.

Many of the French people living in the USA who were interviewed insisted on this aspect: American donors pay great attention to these forms of recognition ("They are very specific about this (...) they want their name to be inscribed").

In France, it is not a common practice, as several respondents explained to me ("Yes, putting up plaques for donors is not part of the republican tradition ... it's not our culture, we don't have the same culture of visibility"; "It's very American, not so common in France"). A French curator explained to me that naming exists in certain cases, when a "collection" is donated (such as the Salle Personnaz at the Musée d'Orsay, named after the donor, Antonin Personnaz), but what is new is naming for a "financial donation."

Indeed, in France, traditionally, only the "grands hommes" (the great men) get to have their names on the walls or get to have a building/street named after them: great writers, painters, sculptors, politicians, doctors, researchers, etc. These are people who contributed to the "greatness of the Nation." France even has a monument dedicated to these "great men" (the Panthéon, in Paris): the inscription on the front says "aux grands hommes, la patrie reconnaissante"—to these great men, from their grateful homeland. This particularity is revealing of the values that are supported—more about honor, patriotism, and greatness than about wealth.

Donors Leaving Traces: An Ongoing Debate

However, practices are evolving within institutions, and naming is becoming more and more common in France, but with different modalities than in the USA: this question remains an open debate.

Indeed, if putting a plaque with the names of donors is now usual in many French institutions, naming a room after a donor still raises problems, as the head of a cultural institution puts it:

> There is naming on a wall, a general wall (...) you will see on the wall the name of lots and lots of donors ... but on the other hand there is no Barbara or Albert something room ... contrary to the American Museums/Ah yes, it's still a bit different ... /Very!! But [such Museum] ... (...) they are doing it ...

As it is a sensitive issue, the naming of rooms is a practice adopted in a differentiated manner. It depends first on the field. Thus, while it may be delicate for a museum to name a gallery after a donor, performing arts institutions may do so more easily when it is a small room, which is not, as in the case of the museum, the main place where art is practiced (a salon, an auditorium, and not the performance hall). Indeed, we saw this for one of them:

> [The American Friends received] a gift from the Beauregard Foundation to fund various operations, supplementing previous grants of $500,000. In appreciation of this gift and for having supporting [the institution] for many years (. . .), the [institution's] salon is renamed the "Beauregard Salon."

Another notable difference distinguishes large institutions with international outreach from smaller ones, where this issue is still being debated, primarily for ethical reasons:

> • A: It's true that (. . .) attributing the name of a donor or a Friend to a room has already been raised once or twice, while I've been here for a very short time (. . .). I think it's something in any case that French museums refuse to do for the moment, but really for ethical reasons I would say, well deontology . . . curatorial . . .
>
> • B: Well, larger French museums . . .
> • C: The Louvre, are they doing it?
> • B: Oh well . . . [meaning: oh well yes].
> • A: Yes, they've been there, yes, and Orsay too . . .

The adoption of naming practices is thus differentiated within institutions, leaving them a certain amount of freedom as to how to implement this practice.

Finally, this question of naming is also debated in other European countries with American Friends associations, which are confronted with the same difficulties, as mentioned by the head of an English association ("Yes, actually in the UK we have the same reticence for names being bashed over . . . but now they come around because the government funds are getting cut down. It is easier with Foundations, but they don't want to have the 'Barclay's Theater' (she laughs)"). It seems that, as in France, setting up donor plaques is no longer a real problem, but the naming of rooms and buildings is more contested.

What is at stake here with the proliferation of donor plaques is not only the question of values but also the occupation of public spaces. Indeed, these plaques that represent private donations are present in public spaces. Allowing public spaces to be used for private reasons changes the meaning given to these places. Scholarship in the sociology of elites has shown how elites tend to reappropriate public spaces for themselves: donor plaques show concretely this idea. It makes us ask the question of the meaning that philanthropy can have when it conquers public spaces, by leaving new traces.

Negotiating the Visibility of the Trace

While donor plaques are increasingly present on the walls of institutions, the question of their visibility is key. Plaques can be more or less visible. Thus, this visibility is negotiated between the two parties.

It is the responsibility of the recipient institution to negotiate the type of recognition the donor will receive—specifically, the framework and form the donor plaque will take. Many times, as it was explained to me by interviewees, donors want big plaques so that their name and gift can be well seen by visitors. The heads of the institution have to be very clear about what they can and cannot accept. Some institutions have guidelines or a chart of ethics, drawing red lines to define what is possible or not, because it is known that the relationship between donors and recipients is an asymmetrical one (Ostrander & Schervish, 1990; Ostrander, 2007). The power struggle is even stronger when the amount of the donation is very high. It is difficult to refuse a big and beautiful donor plaque to someone who made a million-dollar gift. A lot relies on the social and diplomatic skills of the people in charge of negotiating at the institution.

The visibility is also staged and showed off. Often, when a plaque is being made, there is an "unveiling ceremony." This is a ceremony to offer the plaque publicly, revealing the importance of its visibility. I attended one of these ceremonies at a prestigious Parisian cultural institution. It was for the restoration of one part of a monument. The fundraising team had raised 800,000 € (for a total budget of one million euros), thanks to the gifts of eight couples or individuals. There was a press release announcing the ceremony. At this ceremony, many important people were present—among them the president of the institution, the president of the board, a former minister (very well known), and the ambassador of the UK in France (because one of the donors was from the UK). There were speeches, they "unveiled" the plaque, and then there was a cocktail.

While most donors want a lot of visibility, certain donors do not want to have as much (or any) visibility. When John D. Rockefeller Jr. made his million-dollar donation in May 1924 to the Château of Versailles in France, it was expected that something like a plaque would be in the negotiation. When a plaque was offered, he actually refused at first. He even insisted that his name not be mentioned, preferring to highlight the generous gesture from the USA to France. Similarly, when the heads of Versailles offered to name one of the largest boulevards in the city of Versailles (Boulevard Saint-Antoine) after him, he preferred to choose a small street adjacent to the castle, which he felt would be "more relevant." He also wished to be mentioned only as one donor among others when the collection of restorations was published. But when you visit Versailles, you can still see a plaque on a wall, which says:

> Au lendemain de la guerre mondiale, un citoyen des Etats-Unis d'Amérique, John D. Rockefeller Jr. a contribué par ses magnifiques libéralités à restaurer le château et le parc de Versailles, le Palais de Trianon et leurs jardins, la Cathédrale de Reims, le Château de Fontainebleau. En inscrivant ici le nom de John D. Rockefeller, le gouvernement de la République a voulu lui témoigner la gratitude du people français. (1924–1936)[2]

It is interesting to see that it is inscribed in golden letters and that it mentions all the other institutions, but also that it underlines the gratitude not of the institution but of the people of France, making it a national recognition.

---

[2] "In the aftermath of the World War, a citizen of the United States of America, John D. Rockefeller Jr., contributed with his magnificent generosity to the restoration of the Palace and Park of Versailles, the Palace of Trianon and its gardens, the Cathedral of Reims, and the Castle of Fontainebleau. By inscribing here the name of John D. Rockefeller, the government of the Republic wanted to show him the gratitude of the French people" (1924–1936).

Power Relations Around the Traces: Resisting Donor Plaques and Naming

Donor plaques and naming also reveal the power relations taking place in philanthropy. While these practices are increasing, some people are resisting in different ways, in particular by drawing red lines or adapting new practices.

Drawing Red Lines

As they are facing the proliferation of these traces in their institutions, the heads of these institutions try to resist a feeling of being invaded by these plaques.

In this sense, charts of ethics can play an important role. For example, the chart of ethics of the Louvre Museum mentions the question of naming and its limits in the section "practices for granting compensation and naming rooms":

> Some of the Louvre's rooms have time-honored names, which means that their names were fixed more than fifty years ago (e.g., Galerie d'Apollon, Salle du Manège, etc.). The Musée du Louvre will not rename a space in the museum after an individual donor in recognition of a particularly important gift. If a space does not have a historical name, the President-Director may propose to the Museum's Board of Directors that it be named after a donor in recognition of a particularly important gift. The naming of a room will be for a limited period of time, depending on the amount and nature of the donation, in accordance with the policy for granting compensation validated by the Board of Directors on October 10, 2003.

It is interesting to see that they mention their limits. Thus, naming and plaques become an adopted practice, but red lines are being drawn to resist the power that donors can exert with their gift.

Resistance can also be expressed by refusing to use a new name. I experienced this with one of my interviewees, who was an important person working in the arts in New York. This relates to a well-known example of naming. In July 2008, American billionaire David H. Koch donated $100 million over 10 years to renovate the building. The theater was then named the "David H. Koch Theater," a name it would have to bear for at least 50 years (after which it can be renamed). As I expressed my surprise that this Lincoln Center building was named the David Koch Theater, my interviewee got angry:

> Oh please, don't call it that !!!! I'm gonna tell you the story. The building was called the New York State Theater, because it was the New York State and the government who worked in order to give the city the theater, it was built thanks to Rockefeller, and the State really helped. And [a friend] and I were so ashamed to see that liberal guys just erase all the work of the State and put his name. It's really a shame !! Actually, we still call it the 'New York State Theater'.

His reaction shows that even if the name changes, and there is a reappropriation of the monument by the donor, people can still resist by using the former name. Some interviewees in Paris also told us that naming was sometimes a failure as people do not use the new name—because they do not want to or they forget to.

Adapting Practices: A Political Act to Avoid Becoming "a Museum of Plaques"

Beyond drawing red lines, recipient institutions can also resist by adapting the practices. In France in particular, they adapt US practices in terms of donor plaques. One of the practices in the USA is for institutions to categorize donors on the plaque depending on the amount of the donation:

> This is something that I have never seen done in France . . . in the US they list every year . . . the Museum of Modern Art for instance . . . every major institutions lists its contributors, by name, unless you wanna be anonymous. Most people don't wanna be anonymous because somebody will go ask them: 'why aren't you on the list ?', so they might as well show they're on the list . . . and it's divided: those people gave a million dollars, these people give 5000 and these people gave 500. And there is a lot . . . in smaller communities, not in NY, there's people that expect that their friends will be giving at the same level if they can, if they have the same means, it's very systemically organized in the US.

One of the non-cultural American Friends associations, which is linked to a hospital, has even thought about naming the hospital's rooms according to the amount of donations. The manager's speech appears particularly technical and calculated as to the value of each room:

> So that's why I am trying to make a list of 6 or 8 projects where we can put their names on . . . in the emergency room, in the pediatrics room . . . and we put a dollar figure, so maybe $1 million for the emergency room, and $.5 million dollars for the pediatric suite . . . and for the rooms, because you know the hospital is a private hospital, so on the 5th Floor, like here in NY in the Presbyterian Hospital on the 23rd . . . you have amenities, a terrace, a bar and the rooms are more . . . more elegant than the other rooms . . . So we have 120 rooms and some are nice than the others, so we could put a price on these rooms, maybe $100,000 for the biggest, and $50,000 for the others.

Faced with the demands of the Americans, who calculate the amount of their donations according to the compensation that will be offered, a certain number of French institutions refuse to engage in this kind of practice and prefer to offer a common plaque, where the differentiation is not as rationalized and calculated. The idea is to emphasize the equal treatment of donors, who have all made a gesture toward the institution, and to offer a "global recognition":

> Ah yes, we constantly have the American Friends saying: tell us how many rooms you have. Because they translate it into plaques (*laughs*) and . . . we refuse to answer these questions, because we don't want to become a museum of plaques, basically, and we prefer to put a recognition element at the entrance of the museum, in a place of value, but then we are confronted with something that is more complicated, because when you have paid for the elevator, you have your name on the elevator, when you have paid for the large room, well . . . well . . . so visually it is very simple. We want to try to mark a global recognition and if

> we apply the financial scales, we are in ... in something that is cruel and unfair, because it is not the same economic scale, because ... so it is not simple.

The heads of these institutions thus went against the desires of some American donors, because it was against their values. They preferred to offer an alternative, more in line with their values and their vision of what a cultural institution is.

Adapting Practices: A Less Visible Trace

Recipient institutions in France also adapt the US practices around the visibility of the traces left by donors. American donors have a different approach to visibility than French institutions. The terms of application offered to American donors are thus adapted and redefined, as the head of development at one of the institutions explained to me:

> They pay a lot of attention to this visibility and recognition ... (...) Beyond the traditional visits or evenings in the museum, for the Americans, it is naming. Naming is crucial for them. But it's getting a bit complicated, because it's difficult to name the rooms, especially since we have a strict charter. And there we feel the weight of the cultural differences. They want big plaques, and their name in huge golden letters, whereas we only propose a small grey plaque in the corner, so we feel a disappointment on their part when they react. The visibility here is not staged in the same way. And we're not allowed to name anything anywhere. So they always ask us for simulations, we send them the simulations so that they can see what it will look like.

This question of visibility appears to be an adjustment variable that is very much used. Some non-French American Friends associations also use it, as the head of one of the English associations explained to us: "No problem with that, we're good with naming ... although the plaques are not as big as in the U.S."

This adaptation is carried out in a particularly consensual way while being careful in still satisfying the donors. The recipient institutions are indeed particularly careful not to offend the donors and are constantly trying to satisfy all parties—and all the more so when the donors are Americans, which requires the recipients to be particularly "diplomatic":

> Naming, that's it ... and likewise ... something that could actually, that could have been very shocking (...), we try to frame things (...) to pay tribute to donors as it should be, while framing the way it's done, and respecting rules that are ... (...) more precise, and that allow everyone to ... to be satisfied.

The practices are gradually adopted and integrated, giving rise to new forms of naming, hybrid forms, halfway between American philanthropic practices and the context of the French cultural world. Leaving a trace that is the result of a negotiation between donors and recipients is also about building bridges and a "shared world."

References

Andreotti, A., Le Galès, P., & Javier Moreno Fuentes, F. (2016). *Un monde à la carte: Les villes européennes des cadres supérieurs*. Presses Universitaires de France.

Cagé, J. (2018). *Le prix de la démocratie*. Fayard.

Cousin, B. (2017). Refounded neighbourhoods and spatial justice: The inhabitants' attitudes towards urban segregation. In G. C. Lelandais & Y. Sentürk (Eds.), *Identity, justice and resistance in the neoliberal city* (pp. 63–83). Palgrave Macmillan.

Darmon, M. (2015). *Classes préparatoires: La fabrique d'une jeunesse dominante*. La Découverte.

Darmon, M., Dulong, D., & Favier, E. (2019). Temps et pouvoir. *Actes de la recherche en sciences sociales, 226–227*, 6–15.

de La Soudière, M. (2004). Lieux dits: nommer, dé-nommer, re-nommer. *Ethnologie Française, 34*, 67–77.

Eason, J. K. (2005). Private motive and perpetual conditions in charitable naming gifts: When good names go bad. *U.C. Davis Law Review, 38*(2), 375–463.

Gilens, M., & Page, B. (2014). Testing theories of american politics: Elites, interest groups, and average citizens. *Perspectives on Politics, 12*(3), 564–581.

Godechot, O. (2007). *Working rich: Salaires, bonus et appropriation du profit dans l'industrie financière*. La Découverte.

Khan, S. (2011). *Privilege: The making of an adolescent Elite at St Paul's School*. Princeton University Press.

Mauss, M. (2007 [1925]). *Essai sur le don, Forme et Raison de l'échange dans les sociétés Archaïques*. Presses universitaires de France.

McCammack, B. (2014). Global Elites' power over urban space: The long history and bleak future of segregating and selling the city. *Journal of Urban History, 40*(6), 1161–1167.

Ostrander, S. (2007). The growth of donor control: Revisiting the social relations of philanthropy. *Nonprofit and Voluntary Sector Quarterly, 36*(2), 356–372.

Ostrander, S., & Schervish, P. G. (1990). Giving and getting: Philanthropy as social relation. In J. Van Til (Ed.), *Critical issues in American philanthropy: Strengthening theory and practice* (pp. 67–98). Jossey-Bass.

Piketty, T. (2013). *Le capital au XXIe siècle*, Seuil, Coll. « Les livres du nouveau monde »

Pinçon, M., & Pinçon-Charlot, M. (1996). *Grandes fortunes. Dynasties familiales et Formes de richesse en France*. Payot.

Pinçon, M., & Pinçon-Charlot, M. (2007). *Les Ghettos du Gotha. Comment la bourgeoisie Defend ses espaces*. Le Seuil.

Prieur, A., & Savage, M. (2013). Emerging forms of cultural capital. *European Societies, 15*(2), 246–267.

Sherman, R. (2017). *Uneasy street. The anxieties of affluence*. Princeton University Press.

Tobelem, J-M. (2010 [2005]). *Le Nouvel Âge des musées. Les Institutions culturelles au défi de la gestion*. Armand Colin.

Van Til, J. (1990). *Defining philanthropy*. Jossey Bass.

Zunz, O. (2012). *La philanthropie en Amérique. Argent privé, affaires d'Etat*. Fayard.

Anne Monier, Ecole Normale Supérieure Alumna, holds a Ph.D. in social sciences (ENS/EHESS) and is a Researcher at the ESSEC Business School Philanthropy Chair (France). A specialist in philanthropy, she has published two books on this topic—*Nos chers Amis Américains* (PUF, 2019) and, with Sylvain Lefèvre, *Philanthropes en démocratie* (PUF/VDI, 2021)—as well as several scientific articles in academic journals like *Genèses*, *Politix*, and the *Socio-Economic Review*. Her research interests are philanthropy, sociology of elites, cultural policies, transnational relations, inequalities, mobilizations, and environment. She is now working on a new project on climate philanthropy. She also teaches at the School of Public Affairs at Sciences Po. She has been a Visiting Scholar at Columbia University, Harvard University, and New York University and has presented her work in several international conferences, colloquia, and workshops in different countries—from the USA to Japan, Italy, or Switzerland.

Chapter 3
Rethinking Cultural Probes in Community Research and Design as Ethnographic Practice

Scott Townsend and Maria Patsarika

Introduction

As interdisciplinary collaborators that combine research with application directly, we are interested in enlarging on methods that "make the everyday world its problematic" (Smith, 1990: 28), "...where the body, emotions, and senses are viewed phenomenologically, together with an increased focus on representation" (Liebenberg, 2009: 443). How can methodologies, tools, and methods support "data" and interpretation of how the world is experienced and understood by social actors, and how does their participation become part of their interventions in their communities? Specifically, we are interested in examining precedents from participatory design of "cultural probes," acknowledging their ambiguous position in design and research, along with other methods and methodologies that help to identify, unfold, and build on the traces that researchers and community members "leave behind."

In this chapter, we explore these questions first by means of a brief review and assessment of the ideologies and application of design methods and tools in participatory, social design, with a particular focus on cultural probes. We then present two case studies from design research that takes place in Greece and the United States and led by one of us (Townsend). In these two case studies, "cultural probes" are applied as enablers of dialogue and sensemaking between researcher and community member in open-ended public practices. Our intention is to draw attention to the participatory design "trail" that researcher-participant interactions reveal,

S. Townsend (✉)
Department of Graphic Design, North Carolina State University, Raleigh, NC, USA
e-mail: sttwn@ncsu.edu

M. Patsarika
Social Design Institute, University of the Arts, London, UK
e-mail: m.patsarika@arts.ac.uk

F. Comunello et al. (eds.), *What People Leave Behind*, Frontiers in Sociology and Social Research 7, https://doi.org/10.1007/978-3-031-11756-5_3

specifically the possibilities for understanding community members' social, cultural, and historical identities that underlie their sense of place, desires, and perceptions of change and can support reflexive dialogue and design co-creation with researchers.

Exploring the social world through the lens of culture and representation may be less analytically precise than sociology's or anthropology's focus on "structures." And yet, traces allow us to "fill" social structures with history and identity, relations, desires, and struggles—what arguably makes up the "social." From our interdisciplinary perspective, therefore, traces open up possibilities for understanding the coproduction of the social world and individual actors' intentions, needs, and aspirations (Banet-Weiser, 2010).

Design and "Social Worlds"

Social Inclusivity Within Design Discourse

Published in 1971, designer Victor Papanek's *Design for the Real World* introduced critiques ostensibly about consumption and green politics. More recently, Clarke argues that Papanek contributed to notions of ". . . a holistic design approach that embraced design inclusivity . . . premised on a broad recognition of social inequality; as summarized by Whiteley, there was no justification for designing trivial and stylish consumer items for the affluent of the advantaged countries, when the majority of humankind was living below subsistence level" (Clarke, 2013: 153). In Clarke and Whiteley's re-evaluation, Papanek's influence on participatory design in the 1960s and 1970s, especially in Northern Europe, has greatly influenced the discourse and practices of contemporary design and social inclusivity. Design is for the most part still complicit with constructing the social for good or ill, and while designers may attempt to address manifold issues of inclusion and representation as these unfold in the "real world," they are part of complex, technocentric, and market-driven systems of governance and production that typically streamline and reduce the complexity of social issues in representations, in what is still broadly perceived as a process of reductive "problem-solving."

"Frameworks of the Social": From Homogeneity to More Diverse Motivated Viewpoints

Contemporary ideas of social design utilize a broader mandate for change through participatory approaches and collective outcomes in addition to market objectives (Armstrong et al., 2014: 15). Rather than shying away from the challenges and power issues inherent in a dialogic modus operandi, these perspectives urge a critical examination of the interplay between design and broader structural and cultural issues (e.g., Björgvinsson et al., 2012). Many scholars exploring social interactions in design can be seen to have moved away from consensus-driven and politically neutral perceptions of design to embrace an approach to design participation rooted in an outlook that sees the struggles and tensions among stakeholder groups as key political acts in democratic contexts of collaboration. This resonates with the early Scandinavian model of participatory design that sought to challenge hegemonic voices and foreground excluded people's voices (Björgvinsson et al., 2012).

Within these often conflicting agendas, how do we approach the representation of others and their participation? From a broader interdisciplinary perspective, the methods and tools employed in design to empower marginalized people and advocate their social histories and needs often escape critique (Harding, 1993).

Media Representations

For example, research on contemporary storytelling employed in truth commissions, advocacy projects, newsfeeds, and social media suggests that people's complex life histories are presented reductively through victim typologies and short, emotional narratives that are stripped of context and history. Storytelling practices of this kind tend to individualize collective struggles, while the structures and politics that determine marginalized people's everyday lives and struggles are set aside (Fernandes, 2017). In other words, while personal testimonies are sought to give voice to those who are powerless and marginal, media representations can be reductive within a simplistic narrative, often silencing other stories and voices. Looking at stories as curated, standalone texts, disembedded from the storyteller's everyday life and social networks, and not as an unfolding dialogical process, is thus likely to compromise both the complexity of people's history and social life and the storyteller's meaning-making, agential capacities.

Instrumentalized Design Methods

While methods in the social sciences are part of an overall research agenda, methods chosen in design practice to understand people and contexts (primarily defined as "users") are often chosen arbitrarily. For example, the highly successful book *Universal Methods of Design: 100 Ways to Research Complex Problems, Develop Innovative Ideas, and Design Effective Solutions* (Martin et al., 2012) gives two-page overviews of various methods extracted from a range of disciplines, including the social sciences. As an overview or series of abstracts, "UMD" introduces students and others, while the authors take pains to provide a conscientious bibliography of original sources. However, designers (as a worst-case example) often choose a particular method from the book to use as a quick exercise with potential "users" to lend validity to a design proposal. This "toolbox mentality" stems from an acceleration and acceptance of instrumentalist values that have become the core of design, business, and education to assert control in response to increasing conflicts in social and cultural realms. Consequently, design interventions and modernist-inspired solution finding continue to be critiqued as abstracting and devaluing lived, material experiences, instrumentalizing community knowledge, and compromising people's agency while potentially exacerbating complex problems (Escobar, 2018).

Methods and "tools" have an embedded "intentionality" in how they, in turn, shape perceptions and experiences of the user (or participant) by their perceived affordance and use in context. While design readily embraces the social with democratic claims, such as "everybody designs" (Manzini, 2015), viewing the world through a mindset of interdependence, it is still governed by a toolbox mentality made manifest in design practices and visual representations of the world (Julier & Kimbell, 2019). A toolbox mentality, we argue, reflects an instrumentalist rather than a more reflexive approach to understanding the social, potentially missing culturally embedded nuances and indexical forms of representation, among other things—what we refer to as "traces"—in the way in which people give meaning and form their social practices and how researchers engage with and interpret these social practices, informed by their disciplinary-led traditions.

The Tie Between Reflexive Research and Design and Social Innovation

Reflexive approaches to qualitative research can help in interrogating discipline-specific assumptions about knowledge and appreciating the inter-relationship between subjective and methodological concerns, leading to more rigorous research (Harding, 1993). This calls for an open, explicit negotiation of the relationship between researcher and participants, starting from a recognition that both parties carry their own cultural, social, professional perspectives and interests and, subsequently, that the outcomes of the research process reflect such a negotiation of cultures and intentions (Palaganas et al., 2017). Ezio Manzini, a professor at Milan Polytechnic and proponent of "design and social innovation," discusses the process of "sensemaking" to eventual "problem-solving" as a co-design process of catalyzing existing context-specific knowledge in communities. This aligns with the greater intent of reflexive research, placing both design and research in the community as dialogical and responsive. The starting point of our research is based on principles of design and social innovation, specifically expanding on Manzini's emphasis on "diffuse" design, where local knowledge is recognized as fundamental and equal to the specialized knowledge of a formally trained researcher and designer (Manzini, 2015) (Fig. 3.1).

"Sensemaking" in local settings is based on examining the "traces" (in the sense of semiotics, i.e., indexical forms of representation) of people/communities. Since

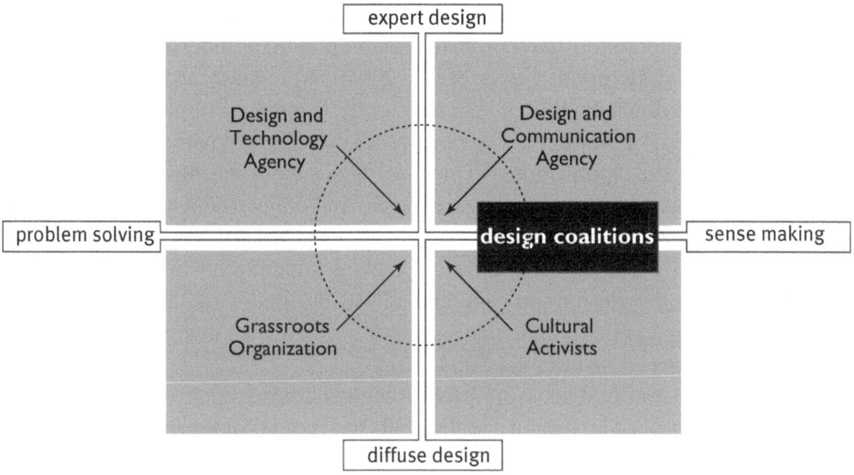

Fig. 3.1 After Manzini (2015), modified

this model implicitly is based on "border crossings" between different groups (cultural, disciplinary), the role of interpretation must be consciously and reflexively constructed (Liebenberg, 2009) to understand attitudes, practices, and experiences. "Problem-solving" in the latter design proposals is most useful where the actual production of a solution is more reliant on the communities' shared expertise and technē. The community/network can become co-authors and influence the ongoing changes and design interventions concretely as adopted changes in practice and developing agency. As design becomes more situated and experience-oriented, a cycle can be created, reminiscent of participant action research (Santos, 2013; Fals-Borda & Mora-Osejo, 2003). For example, sensemaking and problem-solving are reliant upon veridicality and judgment about changes in lived material experiences—does change adequately respond to ongoing issues of people and communities? How do groups and individuals dynamically respond to each other? How do other ideas and resources, through a larger social and economic realm, get synthesized into a local context?

A Participatory Method: Strengths and Weaknesses in "Cultural Probes"

Cultural probes are extensively discussed in design research and practice as enabling users' culturally embedded and contextual understandings and experiences to emerge and inform the design process (e.g., Graham et al., 2007; De Leon & Cohen, 2005; Gaver et al., 1999, 2004). Broadly speaking, probes are shown to invite users' open, informal, inspirational, and playful perspectives and chance observations. They provide a trigger for memories and ongoing dialogue with design participants, while also giving informants control over their use, especially when given to them to autonomously record and reflect upon their understandings and the collectivities they draw upon. Gaver et al. (2004: 56) caution against "scientific" uses of probes, acknowledging that "the returns are layered with influence, ambiguity, and indirection." Elsewhere, Gaver et al. (1999: 24) explain their focus and intentions behind the application of probes: "[. . .] we concentrate on aesthetic control, the cultural implications of our designs, and ways to open new spaces for design. [. . .] trying to establish a role as provocateurs (25)." The above suggests that probes were initially developed as physical packets aimed to encourage participant engagement with the design process and allow designers to take away users' perspectives "while explicitly maintaining room for their own interests, understandings and preferences" (Gaver et al., 2004: 56).

Much of the literature discussing probes neglects, however, to document what happens between probe and design and thus fails to account for the interpretation and implementation process that takes place. Instead, probes tend to be applied as ready-mades with set directions for use, without consideration of contextual, social, cultural, or other factors that may affect researcher-participant communication, understandings, and interpretations. Probes are abstracted representations of researchers' questions and intentions; when applied by community members, the takeaway is a representation, too, of their understandings and responses, which are then given meaning to by designers working solo.

To give an example, Celikoglu et al. (2017) report on the engagement with probes of users (application and generation of data) and designers (data interpretation) in a project that explored tasks associated with ironing. When it comes to the user-participant group, the intention was to understand the situated order in which a chain of tasks unfolds (i.e., washing, drying, collecting the clothes, ironing, and hanging) and the use of related products (iron, ironing board, laundry basket, etc.) The "ironing probes package" included a diary and a task book that was returned with descriptive materials, such as daily narratives, photos, and drawings. The designer-participants were instructed to take the probes packages as a starting point to explain how they make sense of them toward a new ironing board design. The designers engaged with user responses, generating "ideas for a new 'system' or a new 'experience of ironing', rather than for an ironing 'product' as instructed in the design task," and were "highly selective when deciding what mattered among the data contained in users completed probes packages" (92–93). User-participants commented that ". . . the packages [are] 'too structured' in terms of impositions on their daily lives [while the] interaction between the researchers and users during the probing process is lacking" (96). All in all, this example shows how the interpretation of data inevitably goes through several layers of representation, where the negotiation of both party's subjective understandings and the situated nature of the probes' responses may be downplayed in the absence of dialogue (Boehner et al., 2007: 1079–1082).

Critiques (e.g., Boehner et al., 2007; Dourish, 2006; Matthews & Horst, 2008) have problematized the shift from a seemingly open to a more closed interpretation of people's perspectives, typically represented and abstracted through digital or other media, rather than presented and, even, debated within the situated activities in researcher-community member encounters. More broadly, an interrogation of the "virtualism" of design methods is voiced by Julier and Kimbell (2019: 19): "Illustrated outputs of social design, such as personas or user journey maps, can travel through networks of project partners detached from specificity and grounded actuality. Persons are actual, but personas are virtual. Such virtualism masks the reproduction of inequalities by performing change that cannot actually happen." Even when members are encouraged to directly reflect on their ways of being, Collins and Evans (2017: 15) argue, this is not a straightforward process: "descriptions of a social world by its members often draw upon received ideologies or myths, rather than social life as it is lived. Probes must go beyond this [...] to enable participants to make their taken-for-granted assumptions and practices more visible."

Much of the debate on probes and their uses in participatory design derives from associations with ethnographic methods. Probes, however, were not intended to generate data in the first place, whereas ethnography goes beyond data gathering to analyze socio-cultural meaning and practices embedded as they are in specific settings (Boehner et al., 2007: 1083). An analogy between probes and fragments, on the one hand, and ethnographic methods and traces, on the other hand, as we perceive it, might be useful: the first point to inspirational, yet elusive and sporadic, clues that are highly subjective; the second enable traceable associations with cultural, meaning-making practices within community settings. The limitations of cultural probes, as well as their controversial appraisal in relevant literature, have been characterized as a "discount ethnography" technique (Dourish, 2006: 548), symptomatic of a lack of clarity about the role of the researcher and the process of generation and interpretation of data. This challenges designers to capture the "actual" in situated environments, in distinction to the play of mediated symbols, or, more specifically, how the world is experienced and interpreted by social actors and how change manifests itself in people's lives, as well as the potential for design to develop into a socially embedded practice.

Reflexive methodologies suggest interfaces between the researcher and others, while cultural probes function as speculative "black boxes" in design. We would like to extend uses of cultural probes toward amplifying local culture, as intermediaries between the past and the present while encouraging locals to articulate future possibilities. We appreciate the subjective engagement that cultural probes encourage and their idiosyncratic character that highlights participant biographies; however, we also aspire to see them embedded in cultural and social practices providing occasions for enacting social and cultural meaning and articulating complex narratives and dialogical zooming in and out across space and time that brings forward traces of history and social issues, as well as subjective realities and understandings in the here and now.

Case Study 1: Ongoing Design Interventions Kefalonia Greece

"Sensemaking"

As a separate project, one of us (Townsend) originally developed an inquiry into local perceptions of history and community in Southern Europe vis-à-vis EU identity and the role of design and branding. One of these communities was in Greece, originally starting as an inquiry into local perspectives on issues of austerity. The original 2015 interviews were unstructured based on personal biography. Narratives developed out of personal experiences keyed to historical markers, for example, the Civil War era, a devastating earthquake that depopulated the island after 1953, economic development in the 1980s and 1990s, and the current austerity and post-austerity period. Working with a community network in Kefalonia and the Ionian Center for Arts and Culture subsequently developed into a long-term engagement with design and social innovation, where student teams from the United States (College of Design, North Carolina State University) and students from the American College of Thessaloniki (Greece) worked with community stakeholders and networks of academics and government authorities in the Ministries of Education and Culture.

A hybrid research method was developed based on cultural probes and ethnographic methods. From initial interviews, common references were used to develop a "negotiating tool" based primarily on local practices. This combines the fragmentary and ungrounded qualities of a cultural probe with more traceable ethnographic methods that connect back to social practices and shared interpretations between participants and researchers. Second-round interviews took place in the interviewees' suggested location. Participants were encouraged to invite a colleague or friend while following local practices of "coffee and food" brought into the space. The artifact is designed to be cheap and portable and can be placed on a desk or kitchen table, used in mediating and visualizing different experiences and points of view between the two participants. These negotiations are primarily independent of the researcher and take place between the two participants. These discussions build out to shared personal biographies and include negotiating individual and collective values, or experiences as chronological narratives, followed by collective experience sharing, leading to negotiated values. Unstructured group and individual interviews were conducted, and key themes emerged from the gathered data. Later in 2019, archaeological documentation as part of our ongoing collaboration, along with local archive research, helped us to understand historical (archive) and place-based (site photos) references, especially regarding social practices, extended family connections, and key historical recollections (Figs. 3.2 and 3.3).

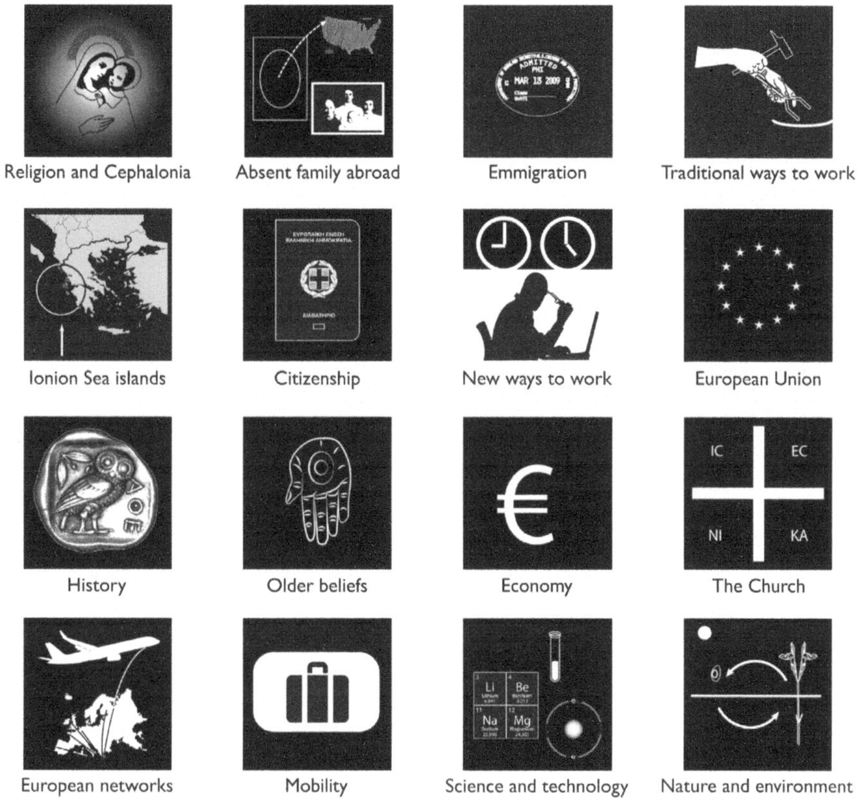

Fig. 3.2 Common references

Common References from Initial Interviews

- **Local Identity**
  - The role and practice of religion
  - Traditional ways to work
  - Nature and environment
- **Regional Identity**
  - The Greek Orthodox Church
  - History
  - Older beliefs and practices
  - The economy
- **Greek Citizenship/Cosmopolitanism**
  - European networks
  - Mobility

Fig. 3.3 Matrix

  - Science and technology
  - The European Union
- **Diaspora Identity**
  - Emigration
  - New ways to work
  - Personal isolation

Ethnographic methods broadened to include more public discussions, where motivated community stakeholders solicited designers in solving immediate problems. Stakeholders included local educators, the 35th Ephorate for Prehistoric and Classical Antiquities, the Focas-Kosmetatos Foundation, and other ongoing community initiatives. Based on a long-term exchange, a common concern centered on preserving place-based local identity while creating a sense of cosmopolitan engagement in the EU and elsewhere. Specific needs of strengthening community engagement in museums and educational activities were discussed. Currently, many local institutions use entrepreneurial strategies working with national and international networks that are combined with local and community resources. The first multi-stakeholder effort is now strategically focused on museum practices, education, as well as more user-centered proposals for connecting with diaspora communities through digital networks. The first design proposal is about the modification of practices in local education in secondary schools as an educational unit in instruction. This shifts museum education directly to educational institutions that have human and capital resources while increasing intergenerational participation through interviews, photo documentation, and historical preservation and archiving as an augmentation to local museums.

Design Proposal

Project 1

Transitioning from participatory research to an actual design project, this design intervention aids in negotiating interpretations of local histories in an educational unit in a high school curriculum. Students at the 2nd Secondary School of Argostoli will interview members of their family and community who experienced and remember key events and social practices in the 1950s. In doing so, they will also document and describe the significance of an object, photo, or other things that holds personal significance to their interviewees and is associated with the era.

The data out of students' initial research will be analyzed and documented in digital templates/archives that the school will maintain for the community to enrich with future community research. The digital template, audio-visual data from students' interviews, and printed examples of the collected artifacts will all be exhibited in a day event co-organized with and intended for the school and the local community. Engagement in the community context helps in negotiating a public, place-based history along with understanding both larger social, cultural, and political connections in local place-making. Photographs based on individuals' objects and spaces will act as a prompt for recorded interviews. Open-ended assessments will then be shared, looking for connections or "thematic" clusters of common community experiences (Fig. 3.4).

Project 2

Project 2 includes augmenting local historical collections in museums. Each recreated object is based on a first-person story within larger historical events. The objects are inspired by the common objects that are displayed in the museum and are similar

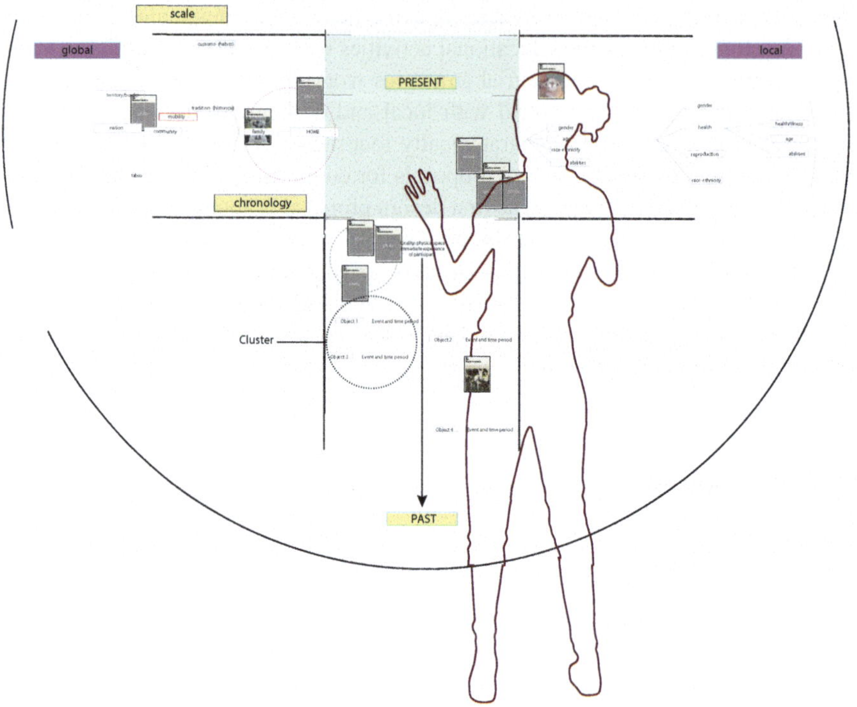

Fig. 3.4 Organizing images and text in "living history" scenarios: individual references in the collection are organized through "scale" (global to personal: horizontal axis) and chronology (vertical axis) using written descriptions, connections, and clustering

to museum interpretative practices. Additional programming can be created through modifying the itinerary to include other settings and locations and can be self-guided with reusable pamphlets or through simple websites optimized for mobile phones or part of a formal tour that can be combined with events in the museum directly. Daily informal encounters with the installations act as a reminder of historical events in the spaces that they occurred in.

Case Study 2: Graduate Research Group, United States

Concurrently in a graduate research group one of us (Townsend) is leading in the Department of Graphic Design, North Carolina State University, students are provided a framework for exploring reflexive methods in communities to ongoing community participation in design solutions, which oft time is about community representation, design of services, and long-term changes in social practices. Conceived as a "making seminar," within the existing course structure of the Master of Graphic Design program at North Carolina State University, the course provides background and experimentation in developing a hybrid series of modest probes equally based on reflexive ethnographic methods (such as Liebenberg) and the legacy of cultural probes from design.

"Sensemaking"

In one two-person team, semi-structured interviews were conducted in the LGBTQ community with stakeholders that are involved in non-profit community organizations, regarding local history and community. Additional methods included site surveys of locations, literature review, and GIS data on support for different initiatives such as state-wide referendums on LGBT issues. Stakeholders include sexual minority elders as an underserved population facing generational differences; healthcare providers who may not all understand fears sexual minority elders have about access and discrimination; sexual minority youths that can benefit from knowing the history and benefit from learning how others deal with trauma and hate; and isolated older adults that may interact with sexual minority elders and may participate in services that can be tapped into.

As LGBTQ rights become law in the United States, some members of the community have begun to consider generational issues and experiences including social isolation of people over 50. The social forces that shaped this generation are now "historicized." The experiences of Stone Wall (1969), HIV/AIDS and the Reagan era of the 1980s, and "don't ask and don't tell" policies of the 1990s, popular culture, and social practices have helped shape a shared identity. For younger people in the community, these circumstances are seen as increasingly remote regarding their sense of community and identity. Secondly, isolation can be understood as social isolation as well as geographic isolation especially in rural areas of the state.

The team's initial discussions centered on the following questions: What are the generational differences within the LGBTQ community? How do elderly sexual minorities seek out community and where is it found? What are the causes of isolation within sexual minorities and what are the barriers to overcoming it? As part of ongoing research leading to participation in the design process for an eventual design proposal, a modified "probe" was created based on ideas that came out of initial interviews and as an extension into ethnographic methods. In these interactions, participants redefined the initial assumptions of the researchers about what constitutes a "neighborhood" to a concept of "social network" that is based on daily and weekly routines of social contact outside of a traditional neighborhood, a fundamental issue in dispersed "exurban" US communities like the "Triangle" region in North Carolina. Follow-up unstructured interviews based on individual maps led to descriptions of activities and valuations given by the interviewee. The nodes on the map led to relational understandings between the different subject matter covered, often including conditional circumstances or "compare and contrast" between things that might be understood as opposition or conflicts by the participant, for example, the relative value of work versus home and family (Figs. 3.5, 3.6, 3.7, 3.8, 3.9, and 3.10).

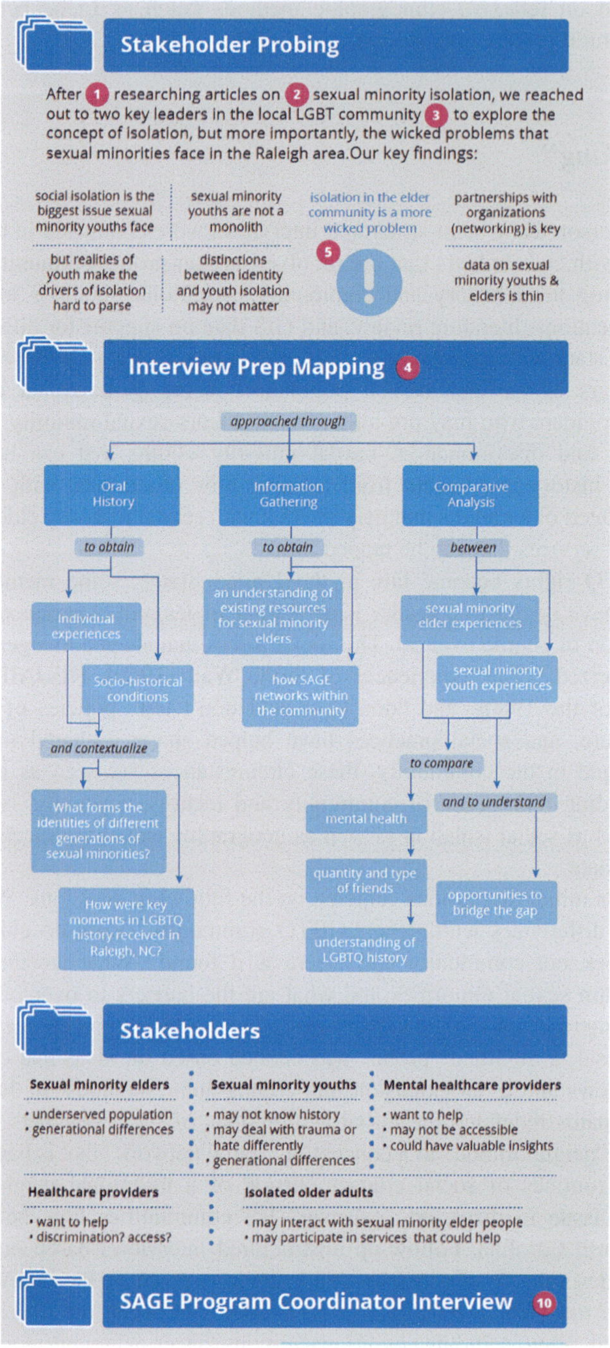

Fig. 3.5 Stakeholder inventory

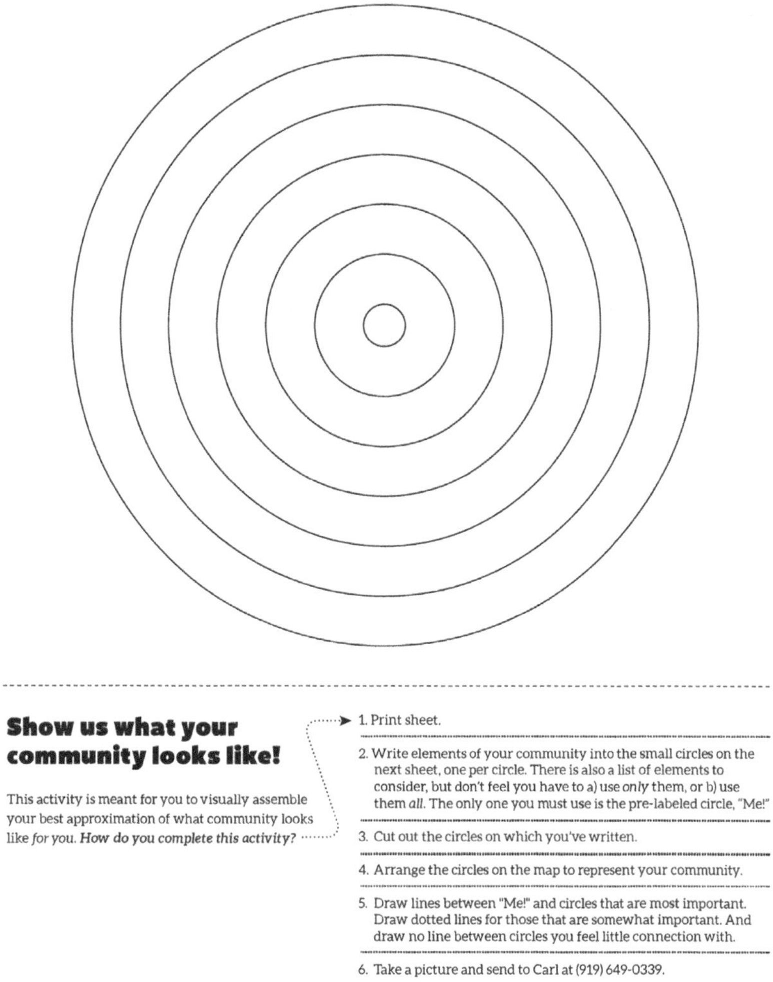

Fig. 3.6 Intro to mapping (online interface and through printable forms)

Design Proposal: "We Are Here—A Pride Raleigh Reclamation Project"

"We are here" is an umbrella term for a locally based project aimed at exploring and supporting 50+ sexual minorities and their concerns. This service design project is part of a larger movement, the Pride Raleigh Reclamation Project. PRRP works to reconstruct and preserve the history of sexual minorities in Raleigh and surrounding areas and partners with the LGBTQ Center of Raleigh and the City of Raleigh to address community needs and lobby for and against legislation to reach equal status and consideration. PRRP will use initial community outreach through the design

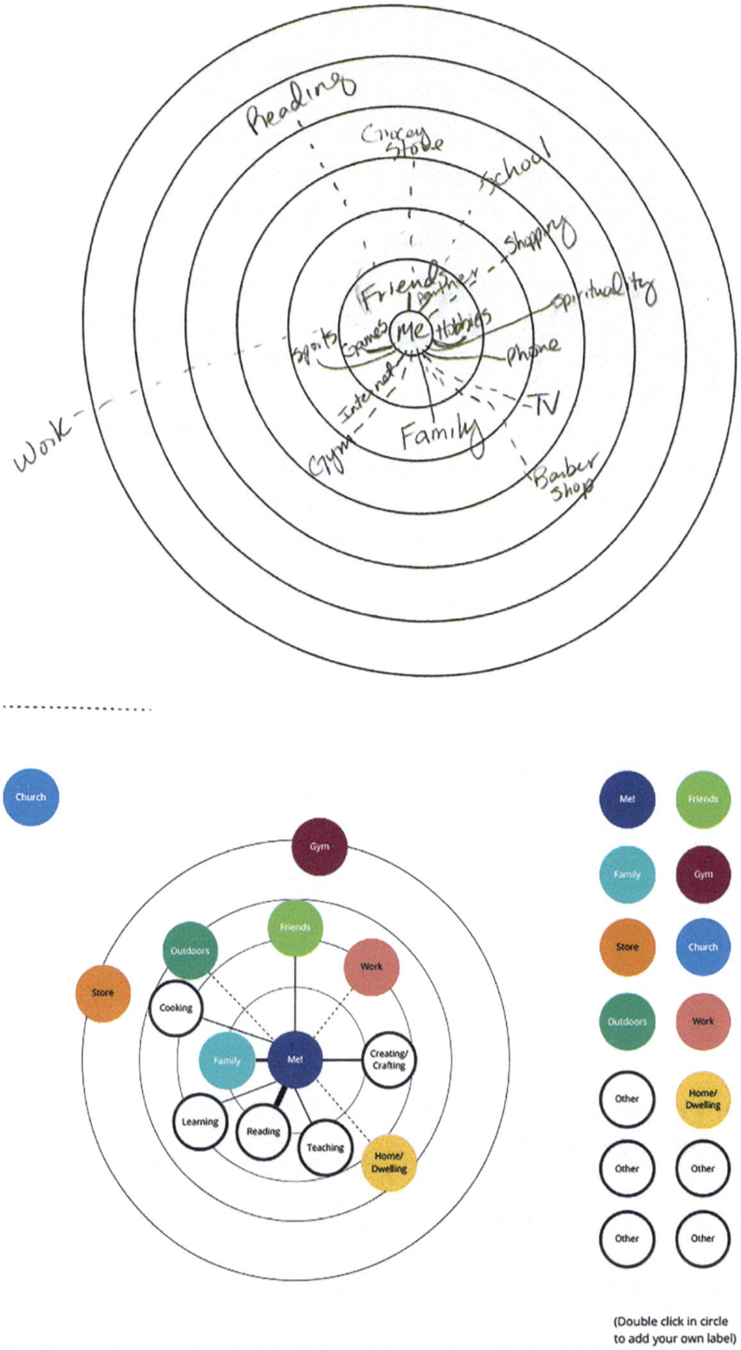

Fig. 3.7 Maps from participants

Fig. 3.8 Maps created by participants

Fig. 3.9 Granular timeline designed to accommodate personal anecdotes within a larger shared history

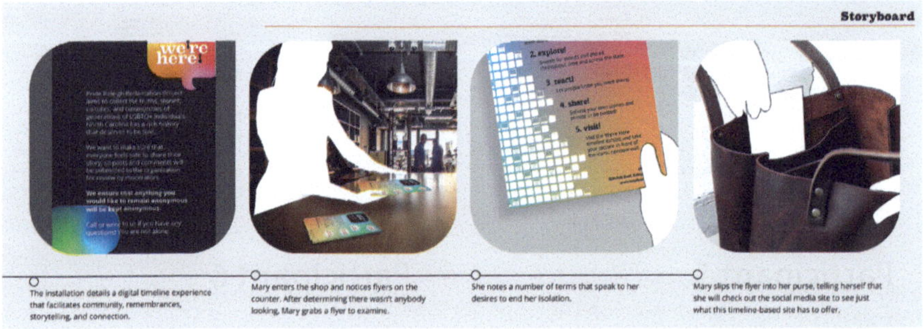

Fig. 3.10 Larger outreach in the community

intervention to hone the concept of "We're Here!" to the point where it can begin funding efforts. The initial proposal centers around a timeline-based website that allows people to record personal, historical, and landmark-based moments for sexual minorities in the Raleigh area over the past century. The concept extends to a Pride Park, with the primary focus being the Community Wall, where people can take selfies and group photos, and a digital wall mirroring the website timeline, where users tap on posts, photos, and news articles over time. Phase 2 builds on the first phase, spreading community to harder-to-reach targets like closeted individuals.

In these examples, the responsive modification of various "probes" in response to discursive discussion and shared interpretations between the researcher and participant creates a dialogical space that can provide a space for participatory design. Objects as design prototypes along with open storylines (or scenarios) of use can lead to a more reflexive design framework through ongoing designing as social practices. Participatory design as an ongoing social practice in the community is processual as an ongoing and evolving "design intervention" rather than a final designed solution, supporting the notion of the designed environment as the interconnections between objects, infrastructures, and "habits of mind" (Willis, 2006).

Conclusions

In this chapter, we have discussed how design methodologies and tools, specifically cultural probes, can fundamentally shape the exchanges between researchers and community members, including their interpretation and presentation of resulting data. We then presented two case studies where cultural probes reflected community members' social and cultural practices as they developed in researcher-participant interactions. In this manner, working in communities can become a form of "public ethnography" as an effort to understand and analyze social practices from multiple knowledge and disciplinary perspectives, define social problems that often go unrecognized, and explore the subjective experiences of individuals without, however, prioritizing them over systemic social problems.

Conceptualizing designing with communities as a form of public ethnography can add social value to design. Design-led and instrumentalized approaches and tools were discussed as potentially standardizing peoples' lived experiences in typified representations and excluding design participants from interpretation, thus rendering them mere informants. Ethnography, however, is "particularly suited for showing complex social relations" requiring that the researcher is in context and discovers extant things, rather than only confirming what one already knows (Vaughan, 2005: 412–413). The analytical strength of the ethnographic process goes beyond statements about community members' experiences and practices, interpreted as they may be by researchers; instead, it is better "understood as the interplay between members and the ethnographer" (Dourish, 2006: 543). In other words, the data that derives from participatory design interventions in the community that claims to be socially inclusive cannot focus solely on how people engage with social practices and culture but also on what new meanings these interventions may acquire when appropriated and embedded in social practice (idem: 546).

Ethnography can benefit, too, from design's problem-solving approach, proactive practice, and interventions, by sustaining a dialogue with the community in ongoing co-creation (Segelström & Holmlid, 2015: 141). Ingold (2014: 388) calls this process *edification* (after Rortry 1980), i.e., the process of keeping the conversation going and responding to community needs with long-term and open-ended commitment and attentiveness. The expansion of design projects in communities is likely to invite critique and novel perspectives on the applicability, relevance, or transferability of design interventions and generate new conversations on change on a social level. We view this process as a fruitful synergy between design and ethnography, moving beyond the dominance of methods in design practice while expanding on the affordance of cultural probes and engagement between researchers and community members as socio-cultural beings in context.

References

Armstrong, L., Bailey, J., Julier, G., & Kimbell, L. (2014). *Social design futures: HEI research and the AHRC*. University of Brighton.

Banet-Weiser, S. (2010). Afterword: Traces in social worlds. In H. Gray & M. Gomez-Barris (Eds.), *Toward a sociology of the trace* (pp. 289–292). University of Minnesota Press.

Björgvinsson, E., Ehn, P., & Hillgren, P. A. (2012). Agonistic participatory design: Working with marginalised social movements. *CoDesign, 8*(2–3), 127–144.

Boehner, et al. (2007, April–May). How HCI interprets the probes. In *CHI proceedings designing for specific cultures*, April 28–May 3, 2007. San Jose, California, USA.

Celikoglu, O. M., Ogut, S. T., & Krippendorff, K. (2017). How do user stories inspire design? A study of cultural probes. *Design Issues, 33*(2), 84–98.

Clarke, A. J. (2013). "Actions speak louder" Victor Papanek and the legacy of design activism. *Design and Culture, 5*(2), 151–168. https://doi.org/10.2752/175470813X13638640370698

Collins, H., & Evans, R. (2017). Probes, surveys, and the ontology of the social. *Journal of Mixed Methods Research, 11*(3), 328–341. https://doi.org/10.1177/1558689815619825

De Leon, J. P., & Cohen, J. H. (2005). Object and walking probes in ethnographic interviewing. *Field Methods, 17*(2), 200–204. https://doi.org/10.1177/1525822X05274733

Dourish, P. (2006, April). Implications for design. In *Proceedings of the SIGCHI Conference on Human Factors in Computing Systems* (pp. 541–550).

Escobar, A. (2018). *Designs for the pluriverse*. Duke.

Fals-Borda, O., & Mora-Osejo, L. E. (2003). Context and diffusion of knowledge: A critique of Eurocentrism. *Action Research, 1*(1), 29–37.

Fernandes, S. (2017). *Curated stories: The uses and misuses of storytelling*. Oxford University Press.

Gaver, B., Dunne, T., & Pacenti, E. (1999). Design: Cultural probes. *Interactions, 6*(1), 21–29 (originally). January/February 1999, from https://interactions.acm.org/archive/view/jan.-feb.-1999/design-cultural-probes1

Gaver, W. W., Boucher, A., Pennington, S., & Walker, B. (2004). Cultural probes and the value of uncertainty. *Interactions, 11*(5), 53–56.

Graham, C., Rouncefield, M., Gibbs, M., Vetere, F., & Cheverst, K. (2007, November). How probes work. In *Proceedings of the 19th Australasian Conference on Computer-Human Interaction: Entertaining User Interfaces* (pp. 29–37).

Harding, S. (1993). Situated knowledges: The science question in feminism and the privilege of partial perspective. *Feminist Studies, 14*(3), 575–599. https://doi.org/10.2307/3178066

Ingold, T. (2014). That's enough about ethnography! *Hau: Journal of Ethnographic Theory, 4*(1), 383–395. https://doi.org/10.14318/hau4.1.021

Julier, G., & Kimbell, L. (2019). Keeping the system going: Social design and the reproduction of inequalities in neoliberal times. *Design Issues, 35*(4), 12–22.

Liebenberg, L. (2009). The visual image as discussion point: Increasing validity in boundary crossing research. *Qualitative Research, 9*(4), 441–467.

Manzini, E. (2015). *Design, when everybody designs: An introduction to design for social innovation*. MIT Press.

Martin, B., Hanington, B., & Hanington, B. M. (2012). *Universal methods of design: 100 ways to research complex problems*. Rockport Publishers.

Matthews, B. & Horst, W. (2008). What can we learn from the probes? The role of interpretation in contributions to knowledge. *Working Papers in Art and Design, Vol. 5.*
Palaganas, E. C., Sanchez, M. C., Molintas, M. P., & Caricativo, R. D. (2017). Reflexivity in qualitative research: A journey of learning. *The Qualitative Report, 22*(2), 426–438.
Rittel, H. W. J., & Webber, M. M. (1973). Dilemmas in a general theory of planning. *Policy Sciences, 4*, 155–169.
Santos, D. (2013). Chapter twenty-four: (Participatory) action research and the political realm. *Counterpoints, 354*, 492–513.
Segelström, F., & Holmlid, S. (2015). Ethnography by design: On goals and mediating artifacts. *Arts and Humanities in Higher Education, 14*(2), 134–149. https://doi.org/10.1177/1474022214560159
Smith, D. E. (1990). *The conceptual practices of power: A feminist sociology of knowledge.* University of Toronto Press.
Vaughan, D. (2005). On the relevance of ethnography for the production of public sociology and policy. *The British Journal of Sociology, 56*(3), 411–416. https://doi.org/10.1111/j.1468-4446.2005.00074.x
Willis, A. M. (2006). Ontological designing. *Design Philosophy Papers, 4*(2), 69–92.

Scott Townsend began work in 2002 examining globalization issues vis-à-vis effects on communities through user interaction and visualization of data. Early projects examined border issues bringing together communities in conflict, often exacerbated by globalization. Exhibitions and related projects have been completed in over 90 national and international group and solo venues in the Czech Republic, Greece, Egypt, Cuba, Mexico, South America, Canada, Germany, Japan, Iran, Italy, Serbia, Venezuela, Cuba, China, and the United States. In 2023, the Center for Design and Material Culture (University of Wisconsin) will host an exhibition of work and processes expanding on principles of design and social innovation. Townsend has authored articles in *Zed*, *Statements*, *Brujula*, *Art Papers*, *Visual Communication*, *Design and Culture*, and *Design Issues* and co-authored for peer-reviewed publications outside the field of design. Dissemination through public venues, conferences, and research network presentations have taken place in Australia, Europe, China, and the United States. http://www.imaginarycountry.org

Maria Patsarika holds a Ph.D. from Sheffield University, Department of Sociological Studies and School of Architecture. Her research is on social learning, children's and young people's participation and place-making, co-design, and community engagement. Indicatively, her published work is included in academic journals, such as: *Children's Geographies, Discourse: Studies in the Cultural Politics of Education*, *Co-Design*, and *International Journal of Urban and Regional Research.*

Chapter 4
Traces of Social Binding: Interpretive Tracing as a Bridging Concept

Tilo Grenz and Keith Robinson

Introduction: Bridging History and Presence

The status of traces as an epistemic resource and tracing as a sociocultural practice that draws from those resources have been the subject of intense debate of late. The value that, for example, media anthropological determinations have in defining tracing (Krämer, 2007) is more decisive than ever. Especially in the context of questions of social and cultural digitalization, which emphasizes data as aggregated data (Big Data), a certain epistemology resonates under critical conditions. Traces appear and afford a special access to (ontological-material) reality: as messengers of truth. Traces, thus, experience a naturalization (Reigeluth, 2014). This naturalization takes various forms, of course, but we would be making it too easy for ourselves if we assigned this naturalization (and consequently ontological mindset) only to the explicit "naïve-realist" positions (consider, for instance, the measurement-regime euphoria in the solutionist mindset of data analysts or voter targeting) and in regard to current data-driven societies.

It is an assumption critical of intentionality, which has primarily gone deep into Western perspectives on traces, that which people do incidentally, that is, casually, what they *leave behind*, and so the assumption eludes the intended communication of what constitutes traces in this perspective. In his seminal work, Rokkan (1966: 4), for instance, understands traces as process-produced data:

> generated through the very processes of living, working, interacting in the societies [. . .]—from plain material evidence through all kinds of artifacts to the varieties of symbolic

T. Grenz (✉)
Bertha von Suttner Private University, St. Pölten, Austria
e-mail: tilo.grenz@suttneruni.at

K. Robinson (✉)
School of Humanities, Griffith University, Nathan, QLD, Australia
e-mail: keith.robinson@griffith.edu.au

F. Comunello et al. (eds.), *What People Leave Behind*, Frontiers in Sociology and Social Research 7, https://doi.org/10.1007/978-3-031-11756-5_4

representations of ideas, activities, and events, whether drawings, tales, messages, or documents.

Quite a similar understanding resonates in what historian Carlo Ginzburg famously introduced as "evidential paradigm" (Ginzburg, 1979). Together with a "growth of disciplines based on reading the evidence" (Ginzburg & Davin, 1980:14), this paradigm influenced the humanities from the second half of the nineteenth century onward. At its core lies the epistemic practice of discovering the merest trace of evidence or indication to reflect on and interpret its reasons. This epistemic practice unites modern criminology as well as, for example, the history of arts and other comparable disciplines. Additionally (cf. section "Tracing and Traces in the Western Digital Realm"), the practice characterizes many of the empirical approaches associated with the emergent architectures of digital technologies.

Intriguingly, the inherent understanding of casualness and ephemerality, with which objectivity (and truth) resonates, is deeply inscribed in the history of Western social science. Indeed, it can be traced to the historiographical debate on the status of "sources" as far back as the century before last. The court of meaning probably goes back to the distinction of Gustav Droysen (1868) and Ernst Bernheim (1908) (first 1889) in their foundation of historical source work:

> If we first divide all source material into the two large groups of the tradition and the remains, then we designate with it the most important difference for the methodical treatment of the sources: Everything that has remained and exists directly from the events, we call remnant (Überrest); everything that has been handed down indirectly from the events, passed through and reproduced by human conception, we call tradition. (Bernheim, 1908: 255) (our translation)

This distinction—though of course not the only—foundation is even more remarkable when one considers historical science and social science have continued to approach each other (especially so in post-war Europe), resulting in the significance of the previously mentioned notion of traces as "process-produced data" (Rokkan, 1966: 4). Additionally, this development led to the quantitative, historical social research that referred mostly to standardized and objective-oriented (mass) data such as official statistics and files monopolizing empirical 'authenticity'. At this point one should consider that the trace in question in the above-described development of the Western, historical epistemology did not represent a fact in itself, but "evidence":

> historians observe certain traces; they pose a hypothesis about what caused them; the traces serve as evidence to confirm or falsify their hypotheses. Since historians, unlike natural scientists, cannot reproduce causes, they must use a model of knowledge acquisition in which causes are inferred from their effects. Like any inductive scientist, the historian's inferences are dependent on prior knowledge of comparable phenomena. (Ahlskog, 2017: 112)

There are many other examples of this hypothesis-led "immediacy motive," based on the latent assumption that expressions are not intentionally oriented to a representation or tradition and are therefore more credible. Apparently, this "motive" also affected more or less inductive approaches as evidenced in Goffman's acclaimed account of interaction, i.e., reciprocal orientation in everyday life (Goffman, 1959:

130): "... the 'true' or 'real' attitudes, beliefs and emotions of the individual can be ascertained only indirectly, (i) through his avowals or (ii) [even more indirectly] through what appears to be involuntary expressive behavior" (brackets in orig.).

Both the naturalization of data—following prior knowledge, i.e., assumptions on the social—and the missing contextuality it implies have been repeatedly criticized in recent years. As we previously stated, the current debate has been and is being further intensified by the digitalization discourse (cf. also Grenz, 2020). Crawford et al. (2014) refer to Reigeluth and argue that digital traces are "being icily naturalized, with its institutional and methodological preconditions being marginalized from discussion." Consequently, the idiom "digital traces in context" (Hepp et al., 2018) reacts to the fact that traces have different statuses in different social contexts, i.e., that what happens to materials (tracing) also differs in sociocultural fields. However, the argument that Reigeluth (2014) initiated earlier goes even further. Namely, in the West, there are different epistemologies with which scientists but also everyday actors access traces. Reigeluth refers to French philosophy (relational ontology) and elaborates on the self-relational quality of traces.

Regarding this debate on the epistemological dimension of traces and tracing, our paper advances this idea further. Following our own preliminary work and—this is the essential—in confrontation with an explicitly non-Western epistemology ("First Australians," cf. section "Bridging Vignettes"), what we propose here is another perspective: interpretive tracing (cf. section "(Com)Posing Interpretive Tracing"), i.e., systematically reflecting about the practices and underlying epistemologies of traces as objects of interpretation. Interpretation in this instance means much more than the Western rational ideal of fathoming and/or artfully laying out materials. It is a perspective that is sensitive to the tacit assumptions of objectivity and linear inferencing that underlie many Western approaches. Further, it is an open perspective that is, as we will show, sensitive to various embedded notions of time and temporality (not just time as a linear approach to the world) in particular. Furthermore, this perspective we advocate can eventually show that trace and tracing entail different social, cultural, and societal notions of social binding. In order to do so, we use an Indigenous, non-Western perspective as productive guideline and basis of orientation. Moreover, it is important to note at the outset that the cultural vignettes that follow are each intended to provide insights into particular epistemologies of tracing. Thus, we do not intend to let the Western and the Indigenous perspectives be seen as opposing each other. On the contrary, we have to understand our contemporary, globally (or translocal) entangled world as "global micro-structures" (Knorr & Bruegger, 2002).

In the following section, we will present vignettes illustrating different understandings of traces and tracing. For simplicity, we will use the juxtaposition of individual and economic principles of a Western-digital realm vice versa of some insights from research on Indigenous Australian cultures (First Australians). We will then briefly introduce our proposed perspective of interpretive tracing and present inherent concepts and practices of materiality and, in particular, temporality oriented to them. Thereupon, we argue that and to what extent different understandings of traces and tracing also convey different conceptions of human social binding (individual, collective, i.e., monochronic, polychronic conceptions of culture). We will highlight how such a perspective on interpretive tracing makes it possible to identify such "splinters" or signatures of such conceptions in the global context. We will reveal how the various tracing practices and understandings evoke certain forms of individualized exploitation and alienation while simultaneously bearing a certain socio-moral protective function. This insight is pointed out in the concluding section.

Bridging Vignettes

Tracing and Traces in the Western Digital Realm

Digital traces play a central role in contemporary digitalization in several respects; we begin by emphasizing two such aspects here. Firstly, the architecture of digital media technology is typically designed to generate attention and be self-evident in order to maximize the time users engage. Secondly, this is linked to economic strategies (Plantin u. a., 2018: 297) that radicalize the principle of user configuration. This is because the general types of users that underpin the architecture of the programs are never fixed, but permanently adapted. However, recent studies show that usage data, such as individual dwell times on pages or frequencies of clicks, are not only stored and sold for revenue purposes. Web-based software applications are now successively being designed to be less irritating based on this data in order to make applications seamless, i.e., seamlessly adaptable to users' everyday situations and practices. Data also serve to gradually expand digital offerings with new incentive elements. It is important to note that the "platform capitalism" (Srnicek, 2016) prominently described is primarily about data—namely Big Data—that is collected en masse, stored, and (automatically) analyzed and distributed in near real time.

Online platforms, with all their promises of communication and especially with their ability for people to become visible to and for each other (cf. on the underlying "regime of visibility" Bucher, 2012: 113), are therefore built in a special way. They represent hypercomplex arrangements that can capture a comprehensive picture (i.e., "user behavior") of users incidentally, so to speak—making them complex *trace generators*. At their center is the rational concept of the individual user, whose behavior can be tracked (hypermedially) across multiple spaces with precision. Because this hypermedial "traceability" is of such exorbitant value, the technologies that enable the tracking of the individual user are so extremely coveted but also extremely criticized—at least after they became known (this applies, e.g., to the UDID, i.e., an unchangeable identifier of each individual iPhone, which, however, was already been sharply criticized since 2010 and replaced by another variant (Grenz & Kirschner, 2018: 619)—at present, as is well known, Apple is again in the headlines about this).

Above all, this image of the user is characterized by the fact that they can be precisely analyzed (and understood) through what they casually leave behind (i.e., their digital traces) and—at least according to the assumption inscribed in the digital architecture—their behavior can be predicted and even controlled. "Profiling" is at the center of the core activities of the economic designers of these digital technologies (and thus all advanced forms of computational analysis even beyond the field of economics, it seems). In short, aggregated trace data are supposed to provide access to the "true innermost" realms of people (Anderson, 2008; Latour, 2007). That this naturalization of traces already described in the introduction is by no means utopian is shown by various social conflicts. One example is the Cambridge Analytica data scandal, in which a Facebook data interface was so strained by third parties that it was able to collect and pass on personal data records of millions of users (friends) by means of a Facebook app, without their knowledge.

Tracing and Traces of Indigenous Cultures, First Australians, Songlines, and Yarning

A recent collaborative study (Robinson, 2020) looking at how the emergent processes of mediatization are adopted and adapted to preserve, maintain, and promote traditional Aboriginal and Torres Strait Islander social and cultural values illustrated another perspective in the epistemology of deciphering traces. To understand the complexity required when interpreting traces that are both ancient and non-linear in nature requires an entirely different mindset form everything so far posited by contemporary Western social sciences. This difference is exemplified distinctly when we observe how the many diverse Indigenous Australian nations engage in a communicative process known simply as *Songlines*.

Visitors to an unfamiliar place might consult *Tripadvisor* on their smartphone for information concerning good places to eat and comfortable and affordable places to spend the night. But what if they have no access to the internet? Without a computerized trail digitally documented by past tourists to refer to, our visitor is left vulnerable and open to chance. The ancient Indigenous *Songlines* affords the Aboriginal traveler a means to access that information without the aid of any contemporary media. This puts a whole new meaning to—singing for your supper. Because no written records were kept by First Australians, much of their communicative knowledge cultures are only traceable aurally and orally. However, some traces have survived the colonization process—*Rock Art*, for example. The sacred moments, the aesthetic symbolism of materiality, and the spiritual meanings expressed in First Australian *Songlines* are another incredible resource for researchers studying ancient traces.

Rhoda Roberts AO[1], a Bundjalung woman, nurse, journalist, broadcaster, actor, producer, writer, art advisor, and artistic director, describes the complex architecture

[1]Rhoda was the Creative Director of the *Awakening* segment of the 2000 Sydney Olympic Games opening ceremony which showcased Aboriginal and Torres Strait Islander cultural heritage.

and properties of Songlines thus. Songlines resemble a vast fishing net extending over Australia. The interconnecting lines of the net represent the vast network of trade routes, while the diamond shapes formed within the net represent the clan groups and their ancestral territories. Songlines include crucial cultural, social, and political information together with details of resources available that a traveler needs to survive. Songlines imply a very special materiality, namely, the voice, or rather the voice that only performs according to the situation, leaving behind collective memories or auditive footprints. Consequently, they invoke a spatial and local signature that re-enacts traces originating some 60,000 years in the past. These ancient Songlines are today being recreated in a digital format. The causality and implications offer opportunities for social sciences research which are essential to the trace debate.

(Com)Posing Interpretive Tracing

The idea of interpretative tracing originally arose in the methodological debate within mediatization research and again in the context of the debate on the contexts of traces (Grenz & Kirschner, 2018; Hepp u. a., 2018). Originally, it was about tracing the negotiations of heterogeneous actors in digital spaces and thus conflicts and tensions on the basis of different kinds of data (in a linear, i.e., also Western, frame of reference), but also to determine what actually are the processes that come into view in "trace data" or "process-produced data." In exchange with other studies and authors and especially between the authors of this chapter, it became apparent to address the underlying presuppositions about the "nature" of the trace, about times, places, and materialities within all these approaches. It also fell and still falls at a time when interdisciplinary and international mediatization research is critically coming to terms with its Western perspective and inherent biases (Kannengießer & McCurdy, 2021).

From Place and Materiality to Temporality

So far, the presented fields above highlight how traces cannot simply be read but require interpretation in certain contexts. Furthermore, the insights demonstrated also show how traces (and, by extension, their interpretation) are always significantly contingent on their materiality. As is well known in the respective debate, traces were and are brought into a close relationship of reference with the materials (substances) that have shaped and/or imprinted them (Krämer, 2007). Consequently, the entire composition of the material world (as "material carriers"), which is not only oriented toward—say—writing, falls into the area of possible analysis (again Rokkan, 1966: 4), in and on which actions that have taken place can leave "imprints."

We have shown that certain forms of materiality are transient (the voice; but one could also say, by extension, smells, for instance), as in the case of auditive Songlines in section ("Tracing and Traces of Indigeneous Cultures, First Australian"). Here, materiality affords the chance for understanding only and solely through a specific, situated locality—and through a knowledge collective that interprets at the right time and place in and through a specific practice (singing)—and in turn establishes a social relationship over time through it. This is contrasted with the Western-rational figure of "capturing," which, incidentally, is also prototypically expressed in modern photography. Traces in the digital, as they are also intentionally created by users, for example, in order to become visible to each other (Bucher, 2017), tend to minimize appresentations[2], i.e., the meaningful and sensual completion of given indications (but there are exceptions, as phenomenological analyses of Snapchat (Schlechter & Grenz, 2021) or filter photography (Eisewicht & Grenz, 2017) show).

In addition, it is the significant different temporal orientations or temporal horizons we want to draw on here as they shape the interpretation of (whatever) things as traces, i.e., that are also folded into the very technologies and techniques of capturing traces. In section "Tracing and Traces in the Western Digital Realm", a linear understanding of time is expressed in the everyday practical epistemes that underlie contemporary "trace generators" (e.g., platforms). Behavior is conceived here by providers or data analysts as something that users have done and as a result, subsequently, has consequences. And, there is an assumption that future actions can be influenced by current interventions (e.g., adapting certain "features"). Even if in the form of incongruent interests, traders, designers, and users are in a linear temporal relationship.

Compared to this hypothesis-guided or, as it were, psychologizing approaches given as examples, the time horizons of the Indigenous perspective presented follow other principles or if you will a different logic: Indigenous Australian relationship with and to time is anything but linear. The concept of *place* is combined with both the temporal and the material, meaning "places" within the realms of knowledge locale can be either ideological, theoretical, or memory centric. For example, when engaging with time, strong foundational philosophies exist within Indigenous frames of reference which privilege notions of cyclic continuity. This concept continually confounds Western scholars, often resulting in gross inaccuracies when engaging with Indigenous temporal spaces. Stanner's (2009) expose of the anthropological misinterpretation exemplified by the Westernization of the Indigenous notion of *The Dreaming*, being reduced to simply a time constructed with a past, present, and future, is a prime example of this significant misunderstanding (Fig. 4.1).

The family motto of the Maharajah of Benares, *Satyan nasti paro dharmah*, which itself is a modified passage from the Mahabharata (Sântiparvan, Chap. 160, stanza 24) proclaims "There is no religion higher than truth." Just as religion is

[2] A term originating from phenomenology for the consciousness that people, when perceiving and interpreting things in their environment, add aspects, such as backsides, sensations, etc.

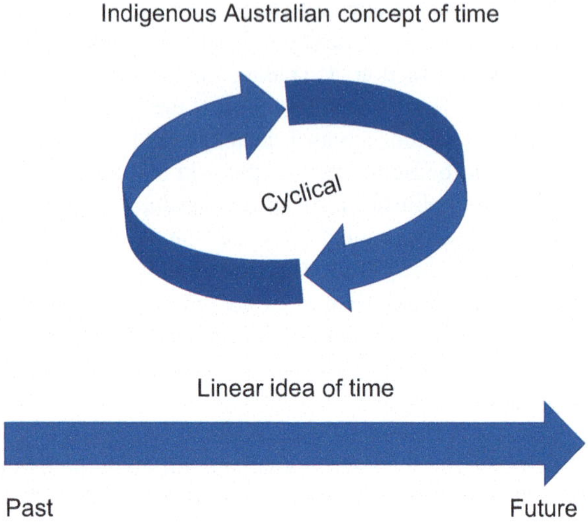

Fig. 4.1 Indigenous Australian concept of time

secondary in terms of importance in this statement, so too is the gaining of knowledge for Indigenous Australians when discussing the methods of knowledge attainment. Truth is always at the forefront. Here truth, in an Aboriginal sense, is anchored in the fundamental notion of inclusiveness. As such, it is a preeminent precept of what it is to *being* an Aboriginal or Torres Strait Islander. A notable aspect of practicing this *Ways of Being* is highlighted by Martin (2008: 77) when she explains how relatedness permits and encourages active participation, thus avoiding "stagnation," "digression," and "dislocation." Consequently, when relatedness is properly "respected in this transformation 'otherness' becomes *'anotherness'*." That is, anotherness encompasses the principles of acceptance, empathy, and generosity, while the Western dichotomous idea of Said's (1979) *otherness* and its malevolent racist undertones demand the transformation to end in replacement. The emphasis attached to the method employed in acquiring knowledge highlights one of the many "fail-safe" precautions embedded in Aboriginal and Torres Strait Islander ancient protocols to ensure individual/group agency and autonomy are never compromised, but this means truth becomes relative.

(World)Society and Social Binding

Traces do not only provide an access or orientation, which is accessed by actors in everyday life. They also frequently provide answers to the sociological question to the hidden ideas of what constitutes society and sociality they refer to.[3] However,

[3] In this regard, one has to keep in mind that digitalization of society is not a new phenomenon. Nassehi (Nassehi, 2019) recently argues that digitization in its core follows the idea of "pattern

this ultimately compels us to ask about inherent forms and conceptions of social binding that are so to say folded into the described conceptions of trace and tracing.

Researchers[4] posit that more time engaging with social media means less face-to-face social interaction and that this reduction or absence of *in-person* social support may be highlighting a correlation between problematic social media use and negative mental health (Shensa et al., 2017). Moreover, in-person social support is considered a protecting factor against negative mental health outcomes, associated with depression and anxiety (Harandi et al., 2017). There is, however, still conjecture among researchers. One cross-sectional study concluded that both offline and online social support were associated with fewer instances of depression-related thoughts and feelings (Cole et al., 2017), whereas other cross-sectional studies established a correlation between in-person social support and reduced depressive symptoms, and emotional-based social support through Facebook was linked to more depressive symptoms (McCloskey et al., 2015; Shensa et al., 2020). Similarly, a longitudinal study argued that only real-life social support produced a tangible sense of wellbeing, while online social support received on social media had no discerning influence on a person's wellbeing (Trepte et al., 2014).

Recent data produced by Primack et al. (2017) declared American teenagers using networked media technologies (NMTs) intensively were three times more prone to feeling socially alienated. Of note, none of these studies examined problematic social media use, only self-reported time spent on social media. The age of deep mediatization is not simply characterized by an abundance of access to NMTs and the distinct processes of production and consumption that surround them; instead, Western perception of the here and now is now defined, first and foremost, by an abundance of digital information (Rey, 2012).

NMTs and in particular the metaverse allow us to construct fictional avatars of ourselves through the use of filters and photo editing software. When used haphazardly, they can proport to extend one's social figurations (see Elias,[5] 1998), but as many have claimed in the preceding studies mentioned, NMTs have a tendency to decrease the frequency, the veracity or conviction, and the overall quality of interactions with real-life people (RLP), which incidentally are three characteristics that are fundamentally sacrosanct to the Indigenous practice of the "ways of being"

---

recognition" that already emerged with modern society, whereby societies had a "digital structure" even before computerization. But, however, modernization brought up particular, new forms and modes of collecting, aggregating, and comparing of (process-produced) data. An important and famous example is the "archival revolution," as described by Rokkan (1969: 63).

[4] As far as we know, all of this research has been completed on Western mainstream populations.

[5] Human figurations are in a constant state of flux, in tandem with shifting patterns of the personality and habitus of individuals. For Elias, the foundation for a scientific sociology rests upon the correction of what he called the *homo clausus* or "closed person" view of humans (the perspective underlying all forms of methodological individualism) and replacing it with an orientation toward *homines aperti* or pluralities of "open people." The nature of any individual's psychology and "way of seeing" emerges out of the figurational matrices in which she/he is a participant. There is resonance here with the Aboriginal concept of the "way of knowing." The emphasis is on the way knowledge is obtained, transferred, and understood.

(see Martin, 2008). NMTs' relative anonymity allows some individuals to falsely create figurations that develop into social groups, the size of which the human brain has neither the time nor the capacity to interact meaningfully with as in a real-life situation. Marx (1920) himself understood that "social relations are closely bound up with productive forces . . . The handmill gives you society with the feudal lord; the steam-mill, society with the industrial capitalist." What social figurations do NMTs give us and are they consistent in characteristics to enable us to accurately track and trace their effects?

According to Krämer (2015: 174), when communicating information, "messengers and traces constitute different dimensions of the transmission" process. The messenger (media) establishes the spatial process, while the trace embodies the temporal process. Further, Krämer states:

> The acts of identification associated with the reading of traces can provide a sense of guidance and transform uncertainty into certainty; the reading of traces is thus a cultural technique of knowledge production. (2015: 178)

It is the cultural technique described here in the production of knowledge that takes on the preeminent role in Indigenous cultures. The technique is not about capturing this time, this place, and this thing; it is more about *flow*. For the Indigenous Australian, everything is in flux. The language reflects that. Their languages are made up of 70% more verbs than those used in the West. For example, *being* a bay gives agency and liberty to the water (in Aboriginal culture, all *things* have agency). It is not that by which the bay is seen but that by which the bay can be seen—so not what we can see and think but that by which we can see and think. The next step in the bay's iteration might be *being* a cloud or *being* a river. It is not about particular thoughts, visuals, and sounds; it is understanding the phenomenon by which they are possible. So, encoding in Indigenous languages constitutes a whole new paradigm.

Indigenous knowledge then is not so much about information as it is method. It is not about state; it is more interested in *process*. Knowledge is not concerned about do this, but rather how to do this. Collectivist groups where children grow up among adults and extended family where time is not a factor encourage high context reasoning (see Hall, 1977) and the foundations of socially distributed cognition (Dcog)[6] (see Hutchins, 1995). However, children of a single- or two-parent family who are reared in a more direct individualistic discipline regime do not experience this and tend to be more characteristic of the "indoor cat." The point we wish to convey here is that individualistic cultures tend to communicate in a more direct fashion, while collectivistic cultures have a tendency to communicate more indirectly. Returning again to the perception of time, high context thinking typically employs a *polychronic* perception of time, while low context cultures understand time as monochronic. Monochronic cultures perceive time as tangible and linear—time is saved or spent; time is reified as money. Because time is seen as money, the

[6]The goal of analysis within DCog is to describe how distributed units are coordinated by analyzing the interactions between individuals, the representational media used, and the environment within which the activity takes place.

West makes and adheres to strict deadlines and focuses on observing, producing, and following sequential patterns in a quest to make their time as financially efficient as possible. Polychronic cultures on the other hand see time as fluid. Consequently, traces take on a socio-moral significance insofar as *non*-Western notions of tracing necessarily require collectivity or community—a modus that is not possible or at least typically not afforded in many current practices of digital tracing.

Reflections and Outlook: Tracing the Social

The juxtaposition of Western and non-Western conceptions of trace and trace interpretation along continental boundaries, as we have undertaken here, is of course a heuristic one. The last 50 years of sociological and, of course, cultural anthropological and social anthropological research have shown that cultures mix globally successively or, in any case, are not fixed along regional containers (Knorr & Bruegger, 2002). We claim that the interpretative tracing approach proposed here can and should make globality an object of reflection. It reacts to the simplifying conception of society (in singular). The term "society," or "societal," has successively fallen into disrepute in recent years because, strictly speaking, it implies uniformity and homogeneity, whereas today's societies are highly differentiated not only rationally (division of labor) but also culturally and socio-morally.

The term "world society" had been offered to respond to this. However, it is important that it is no longer conceived in a totalizing (and homogenizing, e.g., in the sense of an Americanization or McDonaldization) way as a result of the globalization controversies of the 1990s, but emphasizes locally situated, cultural order formations in a global context (Nederveen, 1996; for a "classical" overview, Talbott, 1996). What remains, however, is the notion of a non-determined entanglement of globalization and localization (Robertson, 1992: 100). Robertson (ibid.) describes this relationship as a "mixing of the universal with particular and particular with universal."

Against this global social background, the perspective on interpretative tracing that we have made strong offers us a cosmopolitical instrument of analysis. The point we want to make here in particular is the possibility to trace (sic!) different world-spanning signatures of togetherness—deep-seated conceptions of social binding—that are expressed in global micro-structures. Within different communities, or groups of actors, techniques, and technologies, they act as apparatuses of the social, deeply inscribed in the (historical and very contemporary) practices of tracing.

For the digitization debate of recent years and certain controversies show us that and the notions of the social that underpin them (as they eventually flow into cultural practices and ultimately into the shape and design of today's platform architectures) have again become the subject of a global discussion more than ever. This becomes evident, for example, when we connect the debate on "alienation" with and through digital media described above with critical discourses of today, e.g., with "digital colonialism." The debate there is aimed at Big Data and "data harvesting," which is being pursued especially in the Global South by the major technology corporations of our time. The somewhat broader argument (similar to the critical globalization debate, though significantly more drastic) goes something like this: Data technologies and processing procedures do not only capture the traces (digital trace data) of an enormous mass of people. But this expansive technological regime also transports certain norms and—we would add—subliminal forms of social binding, namely, massive, isolated individuals:

> At the end of the day, you want to find that balance where the perspective of the local expert is respected and it's at the centre of data practices or AI technologies, and you want to see it benefit local communities. (Gorey, 2020)

It becomes even more clear that the persistence of local, cultural ways of dealing with traces and the reading of traces ultimately also function as (often) latent forms of protection and preservation—as we can learn from the Indigenous perspective we have drawn to in this chapter. Thus, the Indigenous concept of strict adherence to social protocols (ways of knowing, being doing) acts as a form of in-built cultural safety valve that inoculates them from cultural erosion. We can follow this route of thought regarding temporality, media, and inherent forms of cultural "safeguarding" even further. Several recent studies within social sciences (e.g., Gibbs u. a., 2015; Grenz & Eisewicht, 2017) contend that platforms like Instagram, App Stores, or Twitter nowadays do not present themselves as "harmonious" orders of people togetherness, but rather as complex and often unmanageable arrangements of diverse groups with equally diverse, often incongruent interests. Consequently, the arbitrary way "friends" are grouped together by Facebook is a situation that is totally foreign to the Indigenous protocols of learning and engaging with "new" acquaintances. This process in Indigenous terms is a fairly long and drawn out process. In this sense, this text is at best a door opener to a significantly broader, cosmopolitan dimension of tracing. It allows us to be systematically sensitive to the often hidden epistemes of today's digital infrastructures and thus to make visible a maybe even "deeper" social layer of "deep mediatization" (Hepp, 2020).

References

Ahlskog, J. (2017). The evidential paradigm in modern history. *Storia della storiografia, 71*(1), 111–128. https://doi.org/10.19272/201711501006

Anderson, C. (2008). *The end of theory: The data deluge makes the scientific method obsolete*. Wired.

Bernheim, E. (1908). *Lehrbuch der historischen Methode und der Geschichtsphilosophie: mit Nachweis der wichtigsten Quellen und Hilfsmittel zum Studium der Geschichte* (6th ed.). Duncker & Humblot.

Bucher, T. (2012). *Programmed sociality: A software studies perspective on social networking sites*. University of Oslo.

Bucher, T. (2017). The algorithmic imaginary: Exploring the ordinary affects of Facebook algorithms. *Information, Communication and Society, 20*(1), 30–44. https://doi.org/10.1080/1369118X.2016.1154086

Cole, D. A., Nick, E. A., Zelkowitz, R. L., et al. (2017). Online social support for young people: Does it recapitulate in-person social support; can it help? *Comput Human Behav, 68*, 456–464.
Crawford, K., Gray, M. L., & Miltner, K. (2014). Big data | Critiquing big data: Politics, ethics, epistemology | Special section introduction. *International Journal of Communication, 8*, 10.
Elias, N. (1998). *On civilization, power, and knowledge: Selected writings*. University of Chicago Press.
Droysen, J. G. (1868). *Grundriss Der Historik*. von Veit & Comp.
Eisewicht, P., & Grenz, T. (2017). App-Fotografie Zur Veralltäglichung Interpretativer Konservierung: Phänomenologische Und Wissenssoziologische Perspektiven. S. 117–32. In herausgegeben von T. Eberle (Eds.), *Fotografie und Gesellschaft. Phänomenologische und wissenssoziologische Perspektiven*. Transcript.
Gibbs, M., Meese, J., Arnold, M., Nansen, B., & Carter, M. (2015). Funeral and Instagram: Death, social media, and platform vernacular. *Information, Communication and Society, 18*(3), 255–268. https://doi.org/10.1080/1369118X.2014.987152
Ginzburg, C. (1979). Clues: Roots of a scientific paradigm. *Theory and Society, 7*(3), 273–288.
Ginzburg, C., & Davin, A. (1980). Morelli, Freud and Sherlock Holmes: Clues and scientific method. *History Workshop, 9*, 5–36.
Goffman, E. (1959). *The presentation of self in everyday life - Erving Goffman - Google Books*. Doubleday.
Gorey, C. (2020). How the rise of 'digital colonialism' in the age of AI threatens Africa's prosperity. *Silicon Republic*. Accessed 10. February 2022 https://www.siliconrepublic.com/machines/abeba-birhane-ucd-digital-colonialism
Grenz, T. (2020). Processualizing Data: Variants of process-produced dat. *Canadian Review of Sociology/Revue Canadienne de Sociologie, 57*(2), 247–264. https://doi.org/10.1111/cars.12280
Grenz, T., & Eisewicht, P. (2017). Variants of interplay as drivers of media change. *Media and Communication, 5*(3), 5–14. https://doi.org/10.17645/mac.v5i3.971
Grenz, T., & Kirschner, H. (2018). Unraveling the App store: Toward an interpretative perspective on tracing. *International Journal of Communication, 12*, 612–628.
Hall, E. T. (1977). *Beyond culture* (pp. 91–131). Anchor Books.
Harandi, T. F., Taghinasab, M. M., & Nayeri, T. D. (2017). The correlation of social support with mental health: A meta-analysis. *Electronic Physician, 9*, 5212–5222.
Hepp, A. (2020). *Deep mediatization: Key ideas in media & cultural studies*. Taylor and Francis, Taylor & Francis Group.
Hepp, A., Breiter, A., & Friemel, T. (2018). Digital traces in context | Digital traces in context – An introduction. *International Journal of Communication, 12*, 11.
Hutchins, E. (1995). *Cognition in the Wild* (No. 1995). MIT Press.
Kannengießer, S., & McCurdy, P. (2021). Mediatization and the absence of the environment. *Communication Theory, 31*(4), 911–931. https://doi.org/10.1093/ct/qtaa009
Knorr, C., & Bruegger, U. (2002). Global microstructures: The virtual societies of financial markets. *American Journal of Sociology, 107*(4), 905–950. https://doi.org/10.1086/341045
Krämer, S. (2007). Was also ist eine Spur? Und worin besteht ihre epistemologische Rolle? Eine Bestandsaufnahme. S. 11–36. In herausgegeben von S. Krämer, W. Kogge, und G. Grube (Eds.), *Spurenlesen als Orientierungstechnik und Wissenskunst*. Suhrkamp.
Krämer, S. (2015). *Medium, messenger, transmission: An approach to media philosophy*. Amsterdam University Press.
Latour, B. (2007). *Beware your imagination leaves digital traces*. | bruno-latour.fr. Accessed 10. February 2022 http://www.bruno-latour.fr/node/245
Martin, K. L. (2008). *Please knock before you enter*. Post Pressed.
Marx, K. (1920). *The poverty of philosophy*. CH Kerr.
McCloskey, W., Iwanicki, S., Lauterbach, D., et al. (2015). Are Facebook "friends" helpful? Development of a Facebook-based measure of social support and examination of relationships

among depression, quality of life, and social support. *Cyberpsychology, Behavior and Social Networking, 18*, 499–505.

Nassehi, A. (2019). *Muster: Theorie der digitalen Gesellschaft*. CHBeck.

Nederveen, P. (1996). Globalisation and culture: Three paradigms. *Economic and Political Weekly: A Sameeksha Trust Publ, 31*(23), 1389–1393.

Plantin, J., Lagoze, C., Edwards, P. N., & Sandvig, C. (2018). Infrastructure studies meet platform studies in the age of Google and Facebook. *New Media and Society, 20*(1), 293–310. https://doi.org/10.1177/1461444816661553

Primack, B. A., Shensa, A., Sidani, J. E., et al. (2017). Social media use and perceived social isolation among young adults in the U.S. *American Journal of Preventive Medicine, 53*, 1–8.

Reigeluth, T. B. (2014). Why data is not enough: Digital traces as control of self and self-control. *Surveillance and Society, 12*(2), 243–254. https://doi.org/10.24908/ss.v12i2.4741

Rey, P. J. (2012). Alienation, exploitation, and social media. *American Behavioral Scientist, 56*, 399–420.

Robertson, R. (1992). *Globalization: Social theory and global culture*. Sage.

Robinson, K. C. (2020). First Australians using mediatisation to preserve, maintain and promote cultural heritage. *Media International Australia, 176*(1), 19–33.

Rokkan, S. (1966). Comparing nations: The use of quantitative data in cross-national research. S. 3–25. In herausgegeben von R. L. Merrit und S. Rokkan (Eds.), *Comparative cross-national research: The context of current efforts*. Yale University Press.

Rokkan, S. (1969). Models and methods in the comparative study of nation-building. *Acta Sociologica, 12*(2), 53–73.

Schlechter, M., & Grenz, T. (2021). Die Sinne im Digitalen: Digital-mediales Zugehörigkeitsmanagement am Beispiel einer Schulethnographie. S. 247–264. In herausgegeben von P. Eisewicht, R. Hitzler, und L. Schäfer (Eds.), *Der soziale Sinn der Sinne*. Beltz Juventa.

Shensa, A., Escobar-Viera, C. G., Sidani, J. E., et al. (2017). Problematic social media use and depressive symptoms among U.S. young adults: A nationally-representative study. *Social Science and Medicine, 182*, 150–157.

Shensa, A., Sidani, J. E., Escobar-Viera, C. G., et al. (2020). Emotional support from social media and face-to-face relationships: Associations with depression risk among young adults. *Journal of Affective Disorders, 260*, 38–44.

Srnicek, N. (2016). *Platform capitalism*. Polity Press.

Stanner, W. E. H. (2009). *The dreaming and other essays*. McPherson's Printing Group.

Talbott, S. P. (1996). *Analysis of corporate culture in the global marketplace*. Case Study of McDonald's in Moscow.

Trepte, S., Dienlin, T., & Reinecke, L. (2014). Influence of social support received in online and offline contexts on satisfaction with social support and satisfaction with life: A longitudinal study. *Media Psychology, 18*, 74–105.

Tilo Grenz, PhD, is a sociologist and currently works at the Bertha von Suttner Private University (Austria). Tilo does research in sociology of knowledge and culture, mediatization and organizational change, and cybersecurity and infrastructural dynamics. His most recent research focuses on non-conventional forms of digital participation in the digital risk society and process-oriented methodologies, i.e., interpretive tracing. Main recent publications are "Processualizing Data: Variants of Process-Produced Data" (Canadian Review of Sociology 57(2), 2019) and "COVID-19, routine dynamics and reflexivity of structure. On the eventful change of Fridays for Future's protest forms" (Austrian Journal of Sociology 46, 2021, with P. Knopp).

Keith Robinson holds a BSc Electronic Engineering. He received his BA double major in Sociology and History from Griffith University in 2015 and a First-Class Honours in Political Science from the University of Queensland in 2016. He completed a PhD with Griffith University in 2021.

Chapter 5
Clues of Displacement: The Gentrification of Silver Hill

Daniel J. Rose and Thomas P. Flynn

Introduction

What people leave behind can provide insights into larger social forces and historical contexts. Physical remnants of older communities can inspire explorations of the past. When traces of previous settlements are located near newer buildings and infrastructure, they suggest a story of social change. Investigating this change can illuminate histories shaped by social structures, power dynamics, and human experiences that reveal much about the people that came before and what led to the neighborhood's present-day state. Such clues of displacement linger today in the spaces of a community formerly known as Silver Hill.

Silver Hill was a settlement that began in the nineteenth century just west of Winston, North Carolina (as the city was known before it merged with the town of Salem in 1913). Although it was overshadowed by larger African American communities in East Winston and other parts of the city, Silver Hill epitomizes many facets of post-Reconstruction history in the Southern United States. Within the enclave, the building of a vibrant African American community, the hardening lines of segregation, the encroachment of a wealthy white community, struggles for racial justice, and eventual displacement can all be found. This displacement, which took place over several decades from the late-nineteenth to mid-twentieth century, was a form of gentrification. As the industrial expansion of Winston-Salem proceeded, the neighborhood became surrounded by wealthy white developments which cut off road access to their homes. African Americans resisted this encroachment and continued living in Silver Hill through the 1970s, but the development of new housing geared toward wealthier buyers eventually replaced the original homes

D. J. Rose (✉) · T. P. Flynn
Department of Behavioral Sciences, Winston-Salem State University, Winston-Salem, NC, USA
e-mail: rosed@wssu.edu; flynnth@wssu.edu

F. Comunello et al. (eds.), *What People Leave Behind*, Frontiers in Sociology and Social Research 7, https://doi.org/10.1007/978-3-031-11756-5_5

and residents. This history serves as an important study because gentrification continues to be a focal point of concern for many communities of color.

This chapter explores the "clues" that illuminate not only the displacement of Silver Hill residents but also the erasure and faulty revision of their history. As in any historical research, the process of discovery can be arduous, with much that is gone and forgotten. But in other meaningful ways, Silver Hill has been misremembered and can be more accurately remembered. History is contested space. This chapter looks at how not only physical clues but also remembrances and contextualization all play roles in how one interprets the significance of Silver Hill.

Physical traces include two remaining houses built during the neighborhood's original settlement period and a cemetery where headstones were removed over 30 years ago. As in most historical research—maps, newspaper articles, property deeds, Census records, city directories, and vital records all contain clues to the history of this former enclave. However, in this instance, the question of "what people leave behind" might be better phrased as "who people leave behind," as the stories of life in Silver Hill cannot be gleaned just from physical traces and historical documents. Descendants of Silver Hill residents provide perhaps the most important details needed to reconstruct an understanding of the life and death of this community.

Background

Beginning in the late 1800s, Winston became a booming industrial city due in large part to its tobacco factories. R.J. Reynolds Tobacco Company, which emerged as the largest employer in the city, was well-known for hiring African American workers and drew many migrants from rural parts of North Carolina, as well as Virginia and South Carolina. Although many African Americans settled near Downtown Winston, Silver Hill began growing just west of the city in the 1880s. By 1900, Silver Hill had about a dozen families living there. However, it was neither exclusively nor predominantly an African American community at that time. Silver Hill was racially mixed in its early years. In fact, as Massey and Denton (1993) have argued, whites and African Americans lived relatively close to each other in most US cities at the turn of the twentieth century. Segregation became a defining feature of the industrial era as both whites and African Americans migrated into places like Winston-Salem. Both de jure and de facto segregation played major roles in Winston-Salem's development. Elizabeth Herbin-Triant (2017) documents the battle over a segregation ordinance passed by the city of Winston in 1912. Even though the ordinance was declared unauthorized by the North Carolina Supreme Court in 1914, whites continued their attempts to enforce segregation through both formal and informal means, such that today Winston-Salem is still one of the most racially segregated cities in the United States (Groeger, 2018).

Theoretical Foundations

This work uses a political economy framework to better understand the traces that the displacement of Silver Hill has left behind. Specifically, the concept of racial capitalism provides key insights into the erasure of this community. Racial capitalism combines the exploitation of African American labor with the second-class citizenship unique to the racialized experience of African Americans in the United States. When situated alongside the particularly avaricious white suburban development of early-twentieth-century Winston-Salem, Silver Hill stands out as an illustrative early example of gentrification. David Harvey's work draws our attention to gentrification's role in the concentration of wealth (1985). He argues that capital accumulation comes from two sources: exploitation of labor and displacement from land. In this case, Silver Hill stood in the way of the expansion of Winston-Salem's wealthy white population and was therefore primed for gentrification.

Silver Hill was a pocket neighborhood—a small enclave that stood out from, but was largely hidden from, the surrounding area. For residents of adjoining neighborhoods, Silver Hill was not a community they normally passed through or interacted with. Frederich Engels (1845) discusses how early industrial Manchester, England, featured a similar separation of middle-class and wealthy residents from working-class communities. Storefronts concealed working-class dwellings from the view of wealthier residents traveling along commercial strips. Bridges were built high above the slums. Poor communities like the one under Ducie Bridge could be accessed only by means of narrow, dirty stairs. Engels sums up the spatial relations in Manchester as follows:

> The town itself is peculiarly built, so that a person may live in it for years, and go in and out daily without coming into contact with a working-people's quarter or even with workers, that is, so long as he confines himself to his business or to pleasure walks. This arises chiefly from the fact, that by unconscious tacit agreement, as well as with outspoken conscious determination, the working-people's quarters are sharply separated from the sections of the city reserved for the middle-class. (p. 57)

The homes of Silver Hill were similarly set back from the main thoroughfares of Winston-Salem, and residents provided crucial labor for the city's economy. In this regard, the destruction of Silver Hill violates the logics of a capitalist system. However, the racialized nature of Winston-Salem's economic relations, as well as emphasis on land development (what Harvey [1985] refers to as "the second circuit of capital"), help illuminate the forces that shaped the fate of this neighborhood. Capital accumulation, in this sense, comes not only from the exploitation of labor but also the displacement of people from their land. As the concentration of wealth in Winston-Salem proceeded in the twentieth century, it relied upon not only the labor of tobacco, domestic, and other workers but also the capital flowing from the development of spatial inequality in housing and land use.

Marshal Berman (1983) uses examples of the embourgeoisement of Paris to illustrate the self-destructive nature of modernity. Specifically, he cites a Charles Baudelaire poem that suggests a mid-nineteenth-century prototype of gentrification, in which a "dazzling" new café on a new boulevard recently cut through working-class Paris is still surrounded by the rubble left behind from the former neighborhood's destruction. The "rubble" to be examined in the case of Silver Hill takes many forms yet still serves as evidence of a destructive displacement process.

Ruth Glass (1964) originally coined the term gentrification to describe how the working class are displaced by the bourgeoisie, who in turn change the character of those spaces. However, as Silver Hill exemplifies, this process does not proceed in a linear fashion. Residents resist displacement, grow their communities despite its threat, and even recreate the community in other spaces, such as reunions, storytelling, and other forms of commemoration. We look to Silver Hill as a prime example of how this process has played out, decades before we had the word "gentrification" to describe it.

First Traces of Silver Hill

The name Silver Hill first surfaced in a plat map recorded on September 19, 1894, showing 33 lots owned by William Edward Franklin ("W.E. Franklin Plat Filing" 1894). Franklin was a merchant, developer, and insurance agent who later became the treasurer and city clerk of Winston in the early 1900s. His parents were Stokes D. Franklin and Fetney Adams Franklin, who owned a farm in House Creek, Wake County, North Carolina, before coming to Forsyth County ("Franklin Family Researchers United" 2008). The map lays out two streets running north and south—Holiday Street to the west and Lincoln Avenue to the east. Cross Street bisects the neighborhood going east and west.

In 1886, a congregation of African Americans of the Primitive Baptist faith acquired land for a church just west of the lots that came to be known as Silver Hill ("Deed of Sale from Frank and Antoinette Brindle to Antiyork Primitive Baptist Church" 1886). The church was called by several different names but was most commonly known as "Antioch Primitive Baptist Church." The nearby West End Baptist Church (also an African American congregation) purchased three acres of land adjacent to the church for a cemetery in two separate transactions dated 1907 and 1908 ("Deed of sale from H.D. and Lillian Shutt to West End Baptist Church Trustees" 1907; "Deed of sale from H.D. and Lillian Shutt to West End Baptist Church Trustees" 1908). There were several African American families already in the area before it became known as Silver Hill. These included the Cain family, which was headed by Emaline and Richard "Dick" Cain. They purchased their property in 1881 for $15 ("Deed of Sale from Frank and Antionette Brindle to Dick Cain" 1881). They held this property at the eastern edge of Silver Hill until 1917, when they sold it for $2000 to real estate developer William L. Ferrell ("Deed of Sale from Dick and Emaline Cain to W.L. Ferrell" 1917). It would eventually become part of the new, upscale Buena Vista neighborhood. The expensive home that stands on the former Cain lot today was built in 1939, leaving no obvious trace of its connection to Silver Hill.

The first known newspaper mention of Silver Hill was in the *Western Sentinel* published on August 11, 1898 ("Around the Twin-City" 1898). It states that "An immense crowd attended the colored camp-meeting at Silver Hill, near Winston, Sunday." Camp meetings were religious events where worshippers congregated in rural areas for an extended period of time to live and pray together. They were particularly influential in the piedmont region of western North Carolina where Silver Hill lies (Lepley, 2006). The newspaper goes on to state that the crowd "came in from Reidsville and other places to attend a Primitive Baptist meeting" ("Around the Twin-City" 1898). This detail might help explain the appeal of the community to the McCullough family of Rockingham County (where Reidsville is located), as many of their children made Silver Hill their permanent home.

Others settling in the community included Ophelia Jane Scales. In 1899. Ms. Scales, at the approximate age of 18, was granted an acre of land in Silver Hill by the State of North Carolina ("Deed of Sale to Ophelia Scales" 1899). She posted 12 and a half cents to complete the transaction. Less than 3 years later, Ophelia Scales married (John) Henry Hunt. Reverend George Washington Holland, founder of Winston's (African American) First Baptist Church and a prominent member of the religious community, performed the ceremony ("Aphelia J. Scales" 1902).

Silver Hill Becomes Segregated

Silver Hill did not begin as an exclusively African American community. Census records from 1900 and 1910 indicate a mixed neighborhood, with several white residents more or less coexisting with African Americans. However, as Massey and Denton (1993) point out, many neighborhoods in the United States became more racially segregated with the growth of industrial cities in the early twentieth century. In some regards, Silver Hill fits this pattern, with most white residents moving out by 1920.

The exodus of whites from Silver Hill made the community a safer space for African American residents in some ways. Pleas Cline was one white resident that African American residents likely didn't mind leaving. MosaicNC describes Cline as "at various times, a laborer, carpenter, house painter, and machinist." He was frequently in trouble with the law for issues such as assault, attempted murder, public drunkenness, and the failure to quarantine while infected with smallpox (North Carolina Office of Archives and History, n.d.). On November 17, 1918, Cline left his Silver Hill home and went into Downtown Winston-Salem to join a violent mob of whites attempting to break a wrongfully accused African American man out of the city jail and lynch him. Cline allegedly entered the jail with the mob, and when asked to leave, he replied "You will have to put us out" ("Governor Asked to Call a Special Term of Surry Superiour Court" 1918). While the prisoner's life was spared, a riot spread throughout the city, leaving five people dead and dozens more injured (Clarey, 2016). Cline was sentenced to 14 months on a road crew, but

Governor Thomas W. Bickett pardoned him after serving 10 (North Carolina Office of Archives and History, n.d.). Along with the segregation ordinance of 1912, the riot of 1918 highlights the heightening racial tensions of the early twentieth century which led to the intensified segregation that continues to shape Winston-Salem today.

West Highlands and Buena Vista Surround

As Silver Hill became a segregated neighborhood of African American residents, it also became surrounded by wealthy white neighborhoods. Starting in the 1910s, decades after Silver Hill was established, developers of the West Highlands and Buena Vista neighborhoods built some of the city's most elite housing stock for executives of tobacco and other industries. As mentioned above, the Cain property became the site of one such house. After the Cains left the area, a peculiar section was added to a March 26, 1925, deed transfer of the property:

> This description also includes a 10 foot strip running along the South side of that part of said lot 17D sold to Linville K. Martin and shown on said map as an alley. To that that of the description this grantor only conveys all its right, title and interest in same, and does not covenant or warrant to defend the title as to that part of the property. ("Deed of Sale from W.L. Ferrell to Linville K. Martin" 1925)

A plat map of Buena Vista shows this alley leading into Silver Hill from Hawthorne Road along the edge of the former Cain property and the two properties adjacent to it. This alley served as an "old traveled way or farm road leading from what is now Hawthorne Road through Silver Hill" ("Winston Salem 1920–1929"). This had served residents of Silver Hill as the entrance to their community for several decades. However, the developers of Buena Vista claimed the road as part of lots 101, 102 (the former Cain property), and 17C, which were to become the property of wealthy white residents in the new neighborhood ("Standard Improvement Company Plat Filing" 1921). This left Silver Hill residents without a way in and out of their community, as the alley they had used was now located on private property.

Residents of Silver Hill fought back. They gathered petition signatures demanding the city build a road to get in and out of the neighborhood and presented their demand to the Winston-Salem Board of Aldermen. The Aldermen commissioned a report from the Public Works Committee, which in turn presented their findings to City Attorney Fred Parrish. On December 2, 1927, Parrish told the Board, "I feel that these colored people who built their homes on a well-defined cartway which led from Winston-Salem to a church and graveyard have been bottled up, but I do not think it is a fight of the city, as we have all of the streets and highway we can look after, without seeking others." The Board of Aldermen rejected their request while unanimously approving road construction for several other communities, including Buena Vista ("Winston-Salem 1920–1929," n.d.).

A public good (the alley) had been stolen from the neighborhood by private developers. The city chose not to intervene, despite the harm done to Silver Hill residents. Allowing a developer to cut off access to Silver Hill violated basic legal and economic principles. But the logic of racial capitalism helps explain this injustice. 1928 and 1930 maps of Winston-Salem show Holiday Street, Lincoln Avenue, and Cross Street in the shape of an "H," completely disconnected from the surrounding streets ("Map of the City of Winston-Salem" 1928; "N.C. Zoning Map" 1930). A 1951 aerial photograph of the neighborhood still showed a trace of the former path from Silver Hill across Horace Mann Avenue and into the backyard of a home that had built on Virginia Avenue in the intervening years ("Forsyth County Historic Resources Commission Celebrates Black History Month" 2022).

Despite the setback, residents of Silver Hill found new ways to get to and from their homes. As the years went by and development continued at a brisk pace, Silver Hill became connected to other roads in the surrounding area. Their efforts to resist the enclosure and persistence after losing their old entrance to the neighborhood speak to an incredible resilience forged by a small, close-knit community.

Love and Affection and One Dollar

After their marriage in 1902, Ophelia and Henry Hunt lived in Silver Hill for the rest of their lives ("Ophelia J. Hunt" 1944; "John Henry Hunt" 1948). They raised ten children and expanded their land ownership to three tracts, making them one of the most prominent families in the community. After a fire at the home in 1931 ("Fire breaks out in dwelling here" 1931b), the Hunts and their children rebuilt and continued to live in Silver Hill until the 1950s. News articles from the African American high society column in the *Winston-Salem Journal* in the 1930s and 1940s highlight their social status, as they entertained out of town guests, as well as hosting the Goodwill Industrial Club and the Nightingale Club ("Miss Hunt entertains" 1931a; "Special entertainment" 1933; "Visitor honored" 1937; "Club meet slated" 1941). At various times, public records list Mr. Hunt's employment as a worker in the R.J. Reynolds Tobacco Factory, a public works employee, and a gardener ("John Henry Hunt" 1917; "Hill's City Directory" 1940; "Walsh's Directory of the Cities of Winston and Salem, N.C. for 1902 and 1903" 1902). Ophelia taught French in the Winston-Salem schools and did domestic work (M. Hunt, personal communication February 9, 2022). A photograph shared by their great grandchildren shows Ophelia proudly seated in their garden with Henry standing next to her in a three-piece suit. Clearly from these historical traces, the Hunts were an upwardly mobile family. Ophelia passed away in 1944 and Henry died in 1948. They are both buried at the Silver Hill Cemetery.

By the time of Ms. Hunt's funeral in 1944, the white population surrounding Silver Hill had grown considerably and the African American population was starting to decline. However, two paragraphs devoted to her funeral in the *Winston-Salem Journal* described not only a prominent African American woman but also a community that came together for important moments in life and in death. The article identified "white citizens . . . who paid tribute to the life of the deceased" including Winston-Salem's superintendent of education, Professor J. W. Moore ("Hunt rites held Saturday" 1944). While that detail might grab the attention of some readers, the article also listed Robert Edwards and John Wilson among the pallbearers. Additionally, Ada Johnson and Angeline Hart served as two of the funeral's flower girls. These pallbearers and flower girls were all neighbors of Ms. Hunt's on Silver Hill's Wiley Avenue.

Silver Hill residents played a part in each other's lives. Several children from the McCollum family, whose parents Charles and Minerva McCollum were enslaved on a tobacco plantation in Rockingham County (C. Barber Johnson, personal communication January 17, 2022), settled in the community. On July 17, 1908, Eliza McCollum Neal purchased a lot in Silver Hill for $447 ("Deed of Sale from Henry and Lillian Shutt to Eliza Neal" 1908a). The next day on July 18, 1908, her sister Flora McCollum Johnson purchased the lot next door for $513 ("Deed of Sale from Henry and Lillian Shutt to Flora Johnson" 1908b). Other McCollum children and grandchildren would live in Silver Hill for decades to come.

Less than a year after purchasing it, Eliza Neal would sell her property to her daughters Nettie, Flora, and Margie Neal in consideration of "Love and affection and one dollar" ("Deed of Sale from Eliza Neal to Nellie, Flora and Margie Neal" 1909). The deed further describes how conveyance was "made to the said three daughters by Eliza Neal in consideration of their having helped her pay for said 3 room house and lot 93 ½ × 100 feet." However, the deed also made clear that "her son Jesse Neal did not assist in the payment for said house and lot." Flora Neal married and moved to Ohio ("Fourteenth Census of the United States" 1920). Margie died in 1917 at the age of 18 (Weller, 2009). Jessie died the following year (SleepingDog, 2009). The property would remain Nettie's until just before her death in 1947 ("Deed of Sale from Nettie Neal to Mabel and Prince Walker" 1946).

Similarly, in 1913, Flora McCollum Johnson sold her property to her daughters, Ada Sue and Flora Bell Johnson ("Deed of Sale from Flora McCollum Johnson to Flora Bell and Ada Johnson" 1913). Ada Sue Johnson Pinnix lived at the property for most of her life. She moved to live with her sons shortly before the City of Winston-Salem demolished it in 1976 ("Mrs. Ada Sue Johnson Pinnix" 1980; "Demolition Ordinance" 1973). Combined, these transactions stand out as remarkable intergenerational wealth transfers from African American women to their daughters in the midst of the Jim Crow era.

Other traces suggest a strongly interwoven community. Flora Johnson is listed as a witness on at least two Silver Hill marriages: her neighbors Frank Harrison and Eva Banner, as well as her sister Eliza's marriage to George McCauley in 1909 ("Frank Harrison," n.d.; "G.P. McCauley," n.d.). Lonon and Lessie Norwood, who procured two lots on the western end of Silver Hill, were able to parlay their investment into a larger farming property in the Old Richmond section of Forsyth County ("Deed of Sale from Jesse and Mae Mock to Lonon and Lessie Norwood" 1915). But they also sold one of their lots to a widow who was already living in the neighborhood, Lucy Harrison ("Deed of Sale from Lonon and Lessie Norwood to Lucy Harrison" 1926).

Lucy Harrison, in turn, sold the property to her daughter Cassie Allison, who owned it until the 1970s ("Deed of Sale from Frank and Lucy Harrison to Cassie Allison" 1929; "Deed of Sale from Cassie Allison to Russell R Flinchum" 1972). These transactions suggest a community that intended to stay firmly rooted on the land while supporting their children and neighbors.

A Gradual Gentrification

A zoning map from 1930, predating the notorious Home Owners' Loan Corporation (HOLC) redlining maps of the late 1930s, clearly demarcates Silver Hill as an A-2 residence district as compared to the A-1 district ratings given to the surrounding West Highlands and Buena Vista neighborhoods ("City of Winston-Salem, N.C. Zone Map" 1930). These designations had an effect similar to later HOLC maps, warning that investments would be risky in the Silver Hill area and steering capital away from the African American community (M. McCullough, personal communication, February 9, 2022).

City services came very slowly to Silver Hill. The neighborhood was annexed by the city in 1920 ("Supt. Latham's Annual Report on City Schools" 1920). But it did not receive the basic infrastructural investments afforded to its wealthy, white neighbors. In 1936, the city teamed with the state of North Carolina using federal Works Progress Administration (WPA) funds to finally construct a sewer and water system in Silver Hill ("City project gets approval" 1936). The undertaking was fraught with delays, including a zoning dispute between the city and wealthy industrialist P. Huber Hanes, Sr. that held up construction (Dinkins, 1937).

On Easter Monday in April of 1942, the Antioch Primitive Baptist Church was destroyed by a fire ("Other fires" 1942). Fire Chief M.G. Brown told the newspaper that the church was not believed to have much financial value. This dismissive attitude toward the loss of the community's foremost institution is contradicted by Chenita Barber Johnson, a Silver Hill descendant and historian of local African American life. She indicates that losing Antioch Primitive Baptist Church had a profoundly negative impact on the families who were connected with it (Personal communication, January 17, 2022). After their church was gone, West End Baptist Church (almost 2 miles away) became the religious home of many Silver Hill residents.

In 1948, the city upgraded the zoning of Silver Hill from A-2 to A-1 ("Rezoning" 1948). Whites began buying up property. Streets were still unpaved in Silver Hill, and the residents were still exclusively African American. But developers began building homes for white residents along the southern end of Silver Hill on Wiley Avenue and Carolina Circle. A 1952 city directory indicates that Silver Hill would now be renamed Wiley Avenue ("Hill's Winston-Salem City Directory" 1952). Three new homes were under construction on the portion of Wiley Avenue that approached Silver Hill from the southeast. Several more new homes for whites lined Carolina Circle, including five on the southern end of the Silver Hill Cemetery. In

1953, the city approved paving just that southeastern portion of Wiley Avenue ("Approved Paving of Nine Streets" 1953). But the Silver Hill portion of Wiley Avenue would remain unpaved for at least two more decades. (Photographs from *Winston-Salem Journal* articles in the 1970s show that portion of Wiley still unpaved.)

Slowly, the original Silver Hill enclave was in decline. In 1956, city directories began listing 433 Wiley Avenue, the former home of Ophelia and Henry Hunt, as vacant. A 1958 Sanborn map lists the house as a dilapidated structure. By the early 1960s, white families began moving into the last remaining section of Silver Hill. A decade later, only three African American families remained. By the late 1970s, William Blackburn was the only African American resident in the area.

(Mis-)Remembering Silver Hill

The descendants of the African American families of Silver Hill are now scattered across Winston-Salem and beyond. Yet, how we remember the lives of their ancestors and their neighborhood has profound implications for the study of community, gentrification, and displacement today. To better understand the process that subsumed and eradicated the neighborhood, one must critically examine the stories told about it and search for additional clues that might shed additional light.

What's in a Name?

The origin of the name Silver Hill is disputed. Multiple sources over the last half century have claimed that Silver Hill was so named because of a witch doctor who lived in the area and was paid in silver coins. Starting in 1970, several newspaper articles were written "in memory" of Silver Hill. The first article featured a claim from a man who was reported to have lived "in the area" for over 40 years. He indicated that his grandfather had told him Silver Hill got its name "because Negroes used to take silver change there to ward off witches they believed in" (Rochester, 1970). He added that everyone from those days was gone now, so the story could not be checked. Thus, it appears, a legend began. On July 4, 1976, the *Winston-Salem Journal* sourced a man living on Horace Mann Avenue, a street just beyond Silver Hill populated mainly by white residents, saying "It was a colored hill. You know how it got its name, don't you? Legend has it that there was an old black man back there who was a witch doctor, and for him to doctor folks, they had to give him silver—silver dollars. That's why it's called Silver Hill" (Loeb, 1976).

These claims have made their way into the official telling of the story of Silver Hill. The city of Winston-Salem repeats these claims, calling them "folklore" and "legend," on their Historical Marker Program website and in summaries of government meeting notes (Forsyth County Historic Resources Commission, 2018;

"Winston-Salem: 1920–1929," n.d.). Although it might be a compelling story of the neighborhood's past, it appears to be wholly concocted by nearby white residents and repeated by journalists and the city itself. And although people around the world have believed in various forms of witchcraft for centuries, there doesn't appear to be any other evidence that it was practiced in Silver Hill. Claims of witchcraft serve to "other" the former inhabitants of the community, depicting them as bizarre in comparison to their neighbors.

Occam's razor suggests that the etymology of the neighborhood's name was probably less complicated than the sensational stories first reported in the 1970s. It seems more likely that the community was dubbed Silver Hill by a developer the same way most subdivided communities are named: with the goal of enticing buyers. Mel White, the first director of African American programming at the nearby historic community of Old Salem and a respected local historian, believes the name was inspired by silver oak trees found in the vicinity (Personal communication, July 15, 2019). In fact, many early property deeds from the area mention oak trees as landmarks for the boundaries.

Tobacco Workers and Domestics?

Other accounts of Silver Hill have stated that the men in the neighborhood worked for R.J. Reynolds Tobacco Company and the women worked for white families in nearby wealthy areas (Forsyth County Historic Resources Commission, 2018). Indeed, many residents of Silver Hill did domestic and tobacco industry work. However, these were not the only occupations. Ophelia Hunt's great grandchildren indicated that she taught French for the public schools. Her husband did work at R.J. Reynolds, but was also listed as a public works employee, a gardener, and a general laborer at various times. Lonon Norwood was a successful farmer, due in large part to owning his own land. Others worked as carpenters, mechanics, cooks, chauffeurs, and car washers and at furniture and other non-tobacco factories (Hill's Winston-Salem City Directory," 1940, 1952). Even though Winston-Salem was driven by tobacco and wealthy whites hired many in the neighborhood as domestics, there was diversity in occupations, skills, and talents. Accounting for that variation further humanizes the people who lived there and the array of experiences they had.

Fragments: Material and Non-material

As in any historical research, what is found is only a fragment of what has been lost. The racist structure of US society makes locating these fragments more difficult, due to the denial of basic recognition that many African Americans suffered through. In its early years, many homes in Silver Hill lacked addresses and were not served with home delivery by the postal service. City directories often did not list Silver Hill as a community or did so with a lackluster accounting of who lived there and where. Newspapers gave little copy to the lives of Silver Hill residents. Mapmakers didn't bother to label the streets (which did have names since the 1894 platting). Even coroners might not have provided much detail on the causes of death listed.

Material evidence of Silver Hill is equally hard to come by. Two houses built in the 1920s remain, but they have been significantly altered since their construction. The cemetery was cleared of headstones in the 1980s. A lone fire hydrant sits in the field near the site of the old church. Other artifacts might be found outside the neighborhood. For example, Russell Flinchum, who grew up nearby on Virginia Road, has a Holiday Street sign from the 1970s hanging on the wall of his home in Raleigh, North Carolina (Personal communication, January 12, 2022). Undoubtedly, photographs like the one of Ophelia and Henry still exist, capturing the people and moments of Silver Hill. Chenita Barber Johnson shared two photos of descendants from the McCollum family gathering for a birthday celebration and another event in front of Eliza Neal's home. In the first photo, many are gathered for an outdoor event with elders seated around a table and younger family members standing behind them, some smiling and others looking serious. In the second photo, the family stands resolutely in front of their modest home with "Jocko," a small dog, placed at the center on a chair. These snapshots capture a thriving and beautiful community that cannot be gleaned from mere historical records.

Other fragments of memory shared through interviews provide more insight to the neighborhood. Chenita Barber Johnson recalls that the families would set their clocks by the sound of the clock tower at nearby Reynolds High School. Before the 1960s, Reynolds was an all-white school, meaning that children from Silver Hill would have to travel past it and across town to Atkins High School for their education (Personal communication, January 17, 2022). Librarian Fam Brownlee recalls seeing African American girls emerging from the woods surrounding Silver Hill on foot and walking past Reynolds High School as they traveled to schools for African Americans on the other side of town (Personal communication, June 27, 2019).

An Incomplete Telling

When the city of Winston-Salem erected a historical marker next to the Silver Hill cemetery in 2018, it marked another in a series of attempts to tell the story of the community. The commemoration of Silver Hill has been underway since at least the 1970s. But who decides the narrative of this community? And what does it mean when those telling it (including the authors of this chapter) have no direct connection to it? Approximately 40 years after the last African American resident from the original neighborhood left, the marker became a new trace left behind in the history of Silver Hill. Similar to other Winston-Salem neighborhoods, such as the African American West End (which was cleared for an expressway and a baseball stadium), the history of neighborhoods like Silver Hill seem to only be glorified after they've been destroyed. The same city that commemorated Silver Hill also refused to provide its residents access to their own community after private developers cut them off. Recently, Winston-Salem passed a resolution in favor of reparations, but has no concrete plans to pay those debts owed to local African Americans (Young, 2021). What are the descendants of Silver Hill owed?

Future Directions

Silver Hill was clearly a small, but impressive, neighborhood that was, over time, subsumed and eradicated by greedy developers and laissez faire local officials who did not provide material support to the community. Their history exemplifies gentrification before the word existed. It also highlights the racial capitalism that came to dominate Winston-Salem's social relations after Reconstruction (Korstad, 2003). Many African American residents of the community labored in ways that generated enormous amounts of wealth for the white capitalist class of Winston-Salem. Those capitalists, in turn, sought to expand their land and housing assets into the suburbs of Winston-Salem, which included the neighborhood of Silver Hill.

But can what took place in this unique pocket neighborhood be useful in understanding historical patterns of conflict and succession in other neighborhoods? How does the abuse and neglect like what Silver Hill experienced prime a neighborhood for gentrification? What clues of displacement can further be explored in Silver Hill and elsewhere? And how do we account for the parts of the story that cannot be recovered? A theory of spatial erasure might illuminate how this process unfolds, with a neighborhood's physical existence removed through gradual encroachment, which in turn leads to its removal from the collective memory of the broader community.

Counterfactuals must also be considered. Alternative outcomes to the struggles residents faced, such as earlier investments in public infrastructure, might have dramatically changed Silver Hill's long-term viability. Other events might have destroyed the community even sooner. For example, Silver Hill was one of nine sites considered for the city-county hospital that became Wake Forest Baptist Medical Center ("Commissioners, Aldermen will consider report" 1945).

Future research should seek to understand how gentrification has taken place in many different forms depending on the time period and circumstances of each community. It should further examine how those facing removal and erasure persist in surviving and communicating their stories. Above all, it should seek to understand how encroachments like these can stopped, and thriving communities of color can be preserved for generations to come. Uneven development and infrastructural neglect are racial and economic policies that continue to target African American communities for displacement and erasure, leaving behind traces and histories that must be better understood to create a more equitable future.

References

Berman, M. (1983). *All that is solid melts into air: The experience of modernity*. Verso.
Board of Aldermen. (1973, March 1). *Demolition ordinance*. City of Winston-Salem, North Carolina. Book 1170, Page 350.
Certificate of Death. (1944, May 6). *Ophelia J. Hunt*. Register of Deeds, Forsyth County, North Carolina. Page 7547.
Certificate of Death. (1948, March 6). *John Henry Hunt*. Register of Deeds, Forsyth County, North Carolina. Page 2716.
Certificate of Marriage between Ophelia J. Scales and John Henry Hunt, 22 January 1902, Forsyth County, North Carolina, Page 179. Register of Deeds, Forsyth County, North Carolina.
City of Winston-Salem City Zoning Commission. (1930). *City of Winston-Salem, N.C.* Zone Map.
City of Winston-Salem Department of Public Works. (1928). *Map of the City of Winston-Salem, North Carolina*.
City of Winston-Salem, NC – Government. 2022, February 15. *Forsyth County Historic Resources Commission Celebrates Black History Month. A historic marker installed in 2018 recalls the history of Silver Hill.* Facebook. https://tinyurl.com/4b799wxr
Clarey, B. (2016, September 14). *The Last Lynch Mob*. Triad City Beat. https://tinyurl.com/52p54jmc.
Department of Commerce – Bureau of the Census. (1920). *Fourteenth Census of the United States: 1920-Population*. Ancestry Library. Retrieved January 10, 2022 from https://tinyurl.com/ytd3vkrx
Dinkins, H. (1937, October 1). Zoning issue abated here by consent. *Winston-Salem Journal, 1*.
Engels, F. (1845). *The condition of the working class in England*. Otto Wigand.
Forsyth County Historic Resources Commission. (2018). *Silver Hill*. Retrieved from: https://www.cityofws.org/DocumentCenter/View/4025/49%2D%2D-Silver-Hill-PDF.
Franklin Family Researchers United Volume 60. (2008, February). http://freepages.rootsweb.com/~ffru/genealogy/Docs/FFRU_back/vol60.pdf
Glass, R. (1964). *London: Aspects of change*. MacGibbon & Kee.
Groeger, L. (2018, October 16). *Miseducation. ProPublica*. Retrieved February 15, 2022, from https://projects.propublica.org/miseducation/district/3701500
Harrison, F. (n.d.). *North Carolina, U.S., Marriage Records*. (1741–2011). Ancestry Library. https://tinyurl.com/566zxjp7
Harvey, D. (1985). *The urbanization of capital: Studies in the theory and history of capitalist urbanization*. Johns Hopkins University Press.
Herbin-Triant, E. A. (2017). Race and class friction in North Carolina neighborhoods: How campaigns for residential segregation law divided middling and elite Whites in Winston-Salem and North Carolina's countryside, 1912–1915. *Journal of Southern History, 83*(3), 531–572.
Hill Directory Company. (1940). *Hill's Winston-Salem City Directory*. Hill Directory Company. https://lib.digitalnc.org/record/25230?ln=en
Hill Directory Company. (1952). *Hill's Winston-Salem City Directory*. Hill Directory Company. https://lib.digitalnc.org/record/25215?ln=en
Korstad, R. R. (2003). *Civil rights unionism: Tobacco workers and the struggle for democracy in the mid-twentieth-century South*. UNC Press Books.
Lepley, L. S. (2006). *Camp meetings*. NCpedia. https://www.ncpedia.org/camp-meetings
Loeb, V. (1976, July 4). Silver Hill – A memory. *Winston-Salem Journal, B1*.
Massey, D. S., & Denton, N. A. (1993). *American apartheid: Segregation and the making of the underclass*. Harvard University Press.
Mayfield, A. A. (1941, February 4). Activities of colored people. *Winston-Salem (N.C.) Journal, 5*.
McCauley, G. P. (n.d.). *North Carolina, U.S., Marriage Records*. (1741–2011). Ancestry Library. https://tinyurl.com/2p8vtyft

North Carolina Office of Archives and History. (n.d.). *Pleas David Cline*. MOSAICNC. https://mosaicnc.org/index.php/name/1389
Register of Deeds. (1881, September 19). *Deed of Sale from Frank Brindle and Antionette Brindle to Dick Cain*. Register of Deeds, Forsyth County, North Carolina. Deed Book 151, page 154.
Register of Deeds. (1886, August 26). *Deed of Sale from Franklin Brindle and Antionette Brindle to The Antiyork Primitive Baptist Church*. Register of Deeds, Forsyth County, North Carolina. Deed Book 30, page 383.
Register of Deeds. (1894, September 14). *W.E. Franklin Plat Filing*. Register of Deeds, Forsyth County, North Carolina. Plat Book 8, page 57.
Register of Deeds. (1899, April 3). *Deed of Sale to Ophelia Scales*. Register of Deeds, Forsyth County, North Carolina. Deed Book 189, page 357.
Register of Deeds. (1907, January 8). *Deed of Sale from Henry D. Shutt and Lillian Shutt to Trustees of West End Baptist Church*. Register of Deeds, Forsyth County, North Carolina. Deed Book 84, page 108.
Register of Deeds. (1908, May 28). *Deed of Sale from Henry D. Shutt and Lillian Shutt to Trustees of West End Baptist Church*. Register of Deeds, Forsyth County, North Carolina. Deed Book 92, page 147.
Register of Deeds. (1908a, July 17). *Deed of Sale from Henry D. Shutt and Lillian Shutt to Eliza Neal*. Register of Deeds, Forsyth County, North Carolina. Deed Book 92, page 255.
Register of Deeds. (1908b, July 18). *Deed of Sale from Henry D. Shutt and Lillian Shutt to Flora Johnson*. Register of Deeds, Forsyth County, North Carolina. Deed Book 92, page 254.
Register of Deeds. (1909, March 10). *Deed of Sale from Eliza Neal to Nellie Neal, Flora Neal and Margie Neal*. Register of Deeds, Forsyth County, North Carolina. Deed Book 92, page 255.
Register of Deeds. (1913, July 13). *Deed of Sale from Flora McCollum Johnson to Flora Bell Johnson and Ada Johnson*. Register of Deeds, Forsyth County, North Carolina. Deed Book 151, page 154.
Register of Deeds. (1915, May 18). *Deed of Sale from Jesse and Mae Mock to Lonon and Lessie Norwood*. Register of Deeds, Forsyth County, North Carolina. Deed Book 143, page 260.
Register of Deeds. (1917, May 11). *Deed of Sale from Dick Cain and Emaline Cain to W.L. Ferrell*. Register of Deeds, Forsyth County, North Carolina. Deed Book 151, page 151.
Register of Deeds. (1921). *Standard improvement company plat filing*. Register of Deeds, Forsyth County, North Carolina.
Register of Deeds. (1925, March 26). *Deed of Sale from W.L. Ferrell to Linville K. Martin*. Register of Deeds, Forsyth County, North Carolina. Deed Book 242, page 25.
Register of Deeds. (1926, December 31). *Deed of Sale from Lonon and Lessie Norwood to Lucy Harrison*. Register of Deeds, Forsyth County, North Carolina. Deed Book 270, page 274.
Register of Deeds. (1929, July 29). *Deed of Sale from Frank and Lucy Harrison to Cassie Allison*. Register of Deeds, Forsyth County, North Carolina. Deed Book 315, page 300.
Register of Deeds. (1946, November 15). *Deed of Sale from Nettie Neal to Mabel and Prince Walker*. Register of Deeds, Forsyth County, North Carolina. Deed Book 558, page 373.
Register of Deeds. (1972, August 18). *Deed of Sale from Cassie Allison to Russell R Flinchum*. Register of Deeds, Forsyth County, North Carolina. Book 1037, page 485.
Rochester, B. (1970, November 22). Ever heard of Silver Hill? *Winston-Salem Journal, A14*.
SleepingDog. (2009, August 2009). *Jessie Neal. Find a Grave*. https://www.findagrave.com/memorial/40467219/jessie-neal.
The Chronicle. (1980, March 8). Mrs. Ada Sue Johnson Pinnix. *The Chronicle, 15*.
The Twin-City Sentinel. (1920, August 5). Supt. Latham's Annual Report on City Schools. *The Twin-City Sentinel, 8*.
Walsh's Directory Co. (1902). *Walsh's Directory of the Cities of Winston and Salem, N.C. for 1902 and 1903*. Walsh's Directory Co. https://lib.digitalnc.org/record/25196?ln=en
Weller, Rev. Dr. N. (2009, August 18). *Maggie Neal. Find a Grave*. https://www.findagrave.com/memorial/40838709/maggie-neal.
Western Sentinel. (1898, August 11). *Around the Twin-City*.

Winston-Salem Journal. (1918, November 22). Governor asked to call a special term of Surry Superiour court for hearing cases from Forsyth county. *Winston-Salem Journal, 1*, 10.
Winston-Salem Journal. (1931a, April 20). Miss Hunt Entertains. *Winston-Salem Journal, 10.*
Winston-Salem Journal. (1931b, September 25). Fire breaks out in dwelling here. *Winston-Salem Journal, 11.*
Winston-Salem Journal. (1933, October 4). Special Entertainment. *Winston-Salem Journal, 2.*
Winston-Salem Journal. (1936, September 15). City Project Gets Approval. *Winston-Salem Journal, 2.*
Winston-Salem Journal. (1937, June 26). Visitor Honored. *Winston-Salem Journal, 2.*
Winston-Salem Journal. (1942, April 7). Other Fires. *Winston-Salem Journal, 4.*
Winston-Salem Journal. (1944, May 2). Hunt Rites Held Sunday. *Winston-Salem Journal, 11.*
Winston-Salem Journal. (1945, December 29). Commissioners, Aldermen Will Consider Report. *Winston-Salem Journal, 1.*
Winston-Salem Journal. (1948, October 12). Rezoning. *Winston-Salem Journal, 5.*
Winston-Salem Journal. (1953, August 8). Approved Paving of Nine Streets. *Winston-Salem Journal, 4.*
Winston-Salem: 1920–1929. (n.d.). Retrieved from https://www.cityofws.org/DocumentCenter/View/2713/Winston-Salem-1920-to-1929-PDF
WWI Draft Registration Card. (1917–1918). *John Henry Hunt.* Ancestry Library. https://tinyurl.com/yckht6w5
Young, W. (2021, April 19). Winston-Salem City Council apologizes for slavery and discrimination against Black people. It also calls for a study of reparations. *Winston-Salem Journal.* https://tinyurl.com/4cb4yxb3

Daniel J. Rose is an Assistant Professor of Sociology in the Department of Behavioral Sciences at Winston-Salem State University. His primary research interests revolve around housing and health in urban communities. He is a mixed-methods sociologist, using ethnography, statistics, mapping, and archival research to better understand social issues. He does work on inequalities pertaining to aging, social class, race, and gender, as well as studying sociological pedagogy. Dr. Rose is also a community organizer. His work with Housing Justice Now, a grassroots group in Winston-Salem, NC, is directly aimed at combatting evictions, slumlords, and gentrification. He is a native of Detroit, Michigan, and earned his bachelor's in sociology from the University of Florida before earning his doctorate in sociology from the University of Michigan-Ann Arbor.

Thomas P. Flynn is the Assistant Director of Archives and Special Collections and library subject liaison at Winston-Salem State University. He earned his BA in History from Dickinson College, PA, and his MS in Information Studies with a concentration in Archives and Records Management from the University at Albany, NY. Thomas has experience working in county, state, religious, and academic archives. He is an active member of the Society of North Carolina Archivists, the Society of American Archivists, and the American Library Association. Thomas served on the SAA-ACRL/RBMS Joint Task Force on Public Services Metrics from 2014 until approval and publication in 2017.

Chapter 6
What Do Museum Visitors Leave Behind? The New Experience and the New Visitor in the Twenty-First Century

Aluminé A. Rosso

Visiting a Museum in the Twenty-First Century

Visiting modern art museums in the twenty-first century is not only about coming into contact with artworks but also about living an interactive and relational[1] experience typical of contemporary art which, after being incorporated into modern collections, has spread to the institutions themselves. All kinds of visual and technical resources are implemented to propose new ways of contact with the artworks, but above all with the museums: mobile applications, podcasts, hashtags, YouTube channels, live broadcasts with experts, numerous contents on social media, VIP artwork lists, photo booths, virtual reality, and the list goes on.

At the same time, museums regularly reorganize and expand not only the exhibition rooms but also the spaces surrounding them: merchandising stands at the exit of exhibitions, cafés, restaurants, children's rooms, boutiques, gardens, and all sorts of devices contributing to promoting this new museum experience on both the façades of buildings and wherever possible[2] in the public space.

This highlights the expansion of the physical and virtual boundaries of the museum: extension and renovation of buildings, multiplication of cultural and consumer activities, and increasing production of pedagogical and entertainment content on an increasing number of digital platforms. The expansion of the museum

[1]The notion of experientiality is a concept that appears recurrently in texts that discuss the emergence or characteristics of contemporary art, for example, the works of Nicolas Bourriaud (2002), Leo Steinberg (2004), Terry Smith (2012), Andrea Giunta (2014), Jean-Luc Nancy (2014), Boris Groys (2016), Alison Green (2018), and Nathalie Heinich (2018) and the articles published by the e-Fluxus journal in its edition entitled What is contemporary art? (2010).

[2]This observation is valid for any genre of art museums; however, we are particularly interested in the modern art museum.

A. A. Rosso (✉)
IIAEC, Buenos Aires, Argentina

F. Comunello et al. (eds.), *What People Leave Behind*, Frontiers in Sociology and Social Research 7, https://doi.org/10.1007/978-3-031-11756-5_6

and its audiences has allowed new modes of consumption of the museum experience.

This panorama leads to reflect on the nature of the museum visit in the twenty-first century. Even if inhabiting the space is different from interacting with the virtual platforms of the institutions, it is worth asking how these experiences coexist? In the case of the in-person visit, has the expansion of the surrounding spaces modified how the museum is visited? Can spaces dedicated to consumption, socialization, or entertainment be more important than the contact with the artworks, and could the visit end there, even before entering the exhibition room? Or can the visit *exist* without even entering or approaching the building? Do interactive contents (e.g., virtual tours or live videos) imply some kind of visit to the museum? Is it possible to have a *bond* with the museum without ever entering it?

To understand some aspects of the modern art museum visit in the twenty-first century, the spaces around the exhibition room have been studied, as these are the focus of many debates[3] on the type of experiences offered by museums today. To this end, 14 modern art museums in the Americas and Europe were analyzed. This chapter focuses on four of them, Malba (Buenos Aires), Moma (New York), Tate Modern (London), and the Centre Pompidou (Paris), and draws its conclusions from a semiotic-ethnographic analysis of museums carried out between 2017 and 2019, which is part of an ongoing research project. During that period, façades, esplanades, and entrance halls have been studied as *intermediary discourse* (Traversa, 2017).

The research was based on the hypothetical function of these *intermediary spaces*: concretizing the passage from the virtual experience of potential visitors to the material experience and, in turn, ensuring the transposition of the visitors' corporal traces to the virtual ones.

These *intermediary spaces* configure an *experiential promise* to visitors as they anticipate, comment on, organize, suggest, or inform something about what the public will experience inside the buildings. They also establish a certain kind of *visiting contract*. Both these functions feed back into each other and work together in the creation of the twenty-first-century museum experience materialized in a new visitor, the *frontalier*, who, in his or her spatial trajectories, highlights the importance of the *museum's boundaries* which are increasingly more difficult to identify.

[3] Some essential work on this issue: Smith, T. (2009). *What is contemporary art?* García Canclini, N. (2010). ¿Los arquitectos y el espectáculo les hacen mal a los museos? *El museo en escena. Política y cultura en América Latina*. Bishop, C. (2013). Radical museology. Preciado, P (2017). El museo apagado: pornografía, arquitectura, neoliberalismo y museos.

The Twenty-First Century: The Reign of the Visitor?

The research carried out in 1983 at the Centre Pompidou in Paris has been a precedent and methodological guide for this work. The French institution commissioned the semiologists Levasseur and Veron (1983) to study the bonds it maintained with its visitors. The authors define exhibitions as mass media, but with a specificity: their dominant order is metonymic. This means that the discourse is supported by the visitor's body, which functions as a space of resonance for all the indexes of the discourse that define the subject's contact with the spatio-temporal materiality of that discourse. Thus, the museum territory is constituted as a network of redirections in space, temporalized by the signifying body of the subject at the moment of appropriation (Levasseur and Veron, 1983).

In this way, the visitor's behavior expresses the gap between the *production* and the *recognition* (Verón, 1998) of the museum discourse that must be considered as the result of a negotiation that can only be understood as the complex articulation between the properties of the proposed discourse and the subject's appropriation strategies (Levasseur and Veron, 1983).

Based on these observations, a typology of museum visitors was made, metaphorically including *ants*, *butterflies*, *lobsters*, and *fish*. These categories show the strategies chosen by visitors to go through an exhibition—more or less ordered, more or less free, and more or less directed—and reveal the *bond* that these people establish with the Centre Pompidou. *Ants* and *butterflies* are interested in the thematic and pedagogical aspects of the visit, sustaining the classic museum imaginary: calm, contemplation, and silence. These visitors have been called, respectively, the *spectator-body* and the *book-body* as their visit strategies are structured by the exhibition design, the former to a greater extent than the latter (Verón, 2013).

The *fishes* regularly visit the institution and possess a global discourse on the cultural space, and frequent it as if it were part of their lifestyle, they pass through to have a look. The *fishes* are *passing-bodies*, accustomed to contact with the museum. The *lobsters* share certain characteristics with the *fishes*, but they are bodies with *pseudopods*. They also pass by from time to time and have a general idea of the institution, but for them, *Beaubourg's* (as Parisians call the Centre Pompidou) proposals are characterized by their *sophisticated, but not very solemn, themes*, which allow the absorption of the cultural product by a purely personal experience, which in this case defines the pleasure of the visit (Verón, 2013).

In considering the museum as a mass media (Verón, 1985), this research transposes the notion of the *reading contract* coined by Verón (1985) to refer to the bond that a medium establishes with its readers, which is revealed after an enunciative analysis. The bond between museum institutions and those who frequent them will therefore be a visiting contract.

Analyzing this *contract*, according to Verón (1985), is not a matter of analyzing the contents of the media (or of the museum's programming) but the regularities of its enunciative strategies and the positions it occupies in the relationship with its reader (its visitor), whether symmetrical or asymmetrical, distant, or complicit.

It is a matter of distinguishing, in the functioning of any discourse, two levels: the level of the enunciated and the level of the enunciation (*énoncé/énonciation*). The level of the enunciated is that of what is said (in a rough approximation, the level of the enunciated corresponds to the order of content); the level of enunciation concerns the modalities of saying. Through the functioning of enunciation, a discourse constructs a certain image of the speaker (the enunciator), a certain image of the receiver (the addressee), and, consequently, a link between these two *places* (Verón, 1985).

In the case of the museum, as a media of a metonymic order, the *reading contract* (or *bond* with its visitors) needs, to be established, connecting instances before entering the exhibition room: advertising, social media content, art reviews, and the experiential promise configured by the intermediary discourses-spaces. It is in these intermediary spaces where *some kind of bond* is established or reinforced but also where the museum *visit* could very well end.

The notion of *intermediary discourses* developed by Oscar Traversa (2017) designates a discursive subcategory that acts as an instance of connection between those who produce a good and those who yearn for it. Although he has been studying the functioning of this category in relation to the *radio effects* (Verón, 2014) produced by the cinematographic device, these intermediary discursivities can be considered as operating similarly when linking the instances of *production* and *reception* of a museum experience.

Traversa (2017) argues that the industrial nature of cinema requires it to be consumed to *exist* and therefore needs connecting instances that link two disjunct instances: film producers and potential spectators. Among them, we find commercial publicity, criticism, advertisements, and posters. The same can be said of the museum[4] experience: the museum needs its visitors to *exist*, and, like the cinema, it needs connecting instances, in particular, an architectural program[5] capable of luring potential visitors.

Oscar Traversa (2017) characterizes intermediary discursivity as a relationship between three machines: the *textual machine*, that is, the set of films—or the programming of a museum—offered to the public; the *spectatorial machine*, the complex that articulates our desire with the presumed satisfiers; and, finally, the machine that links the two.

From this perspective, any museum program can be understood as the first machine. The second machine consists of the connections between the visitors' experiences with other museum programs in general and with those previously carried out by that museum in particular. The third machine will link the two others:

[4]Numerous debates from 1980 to the present have highlighted the link between museums and cultural industries, tourism, and other economic sectors. See, for example, Mairesse, F. (2012). La logique de la gestion muséale: un système hybride. *Musées en mutation. Un espace à revisiter*, pp.159–172.

[5]We consider that the architecture of any building, whatever its function, can be considered an *intermediary discourse* (Traversa, 2017), even more so in those linked to cultural events.

the architecture, specifically, the façade, the esplanade, and the entrance hall. They will, together, configure a promise about what will be experienced in the building.

Traversa also explained that these intermediary discursivities are deployed based on plural enunciative strategies organized around three major units: *what is being talked about*; *the attribution of values*; and *an assumption about effects*. The three units play with the past experiences of the potential visitor and are articulated at the level of erudition (Traversa, 2017). In our case:

(a) What is being talked about? A museum of modern art.
(b) To what value is attributed? The experience inside a modern museum.
(c) What supposed effect it will produce? Entertainment, family bonding, team building, apprehension of knowledge, enjoyment, discussion of art, etc.

To arrive at this description, two fundamental concepts developed by Oscar Steimberg (2013) have been applied to the museum: the *genre* and the *style*. Genre and style are understood as two opposing and complementary sets of discursive organization, whose first member can be understood as a *mold* and the second as a way of *filling it*. Steimberg has proposed three dimensions to analyze genres and styles: the rhetorical, the thematic, and the enunciative dimension (2013).

According to these terms, the esplanade, the façade, and the entrance hall should be analyzed as *molds*, and how museums present their programming would be their *spaces of differentiation* that consolidate or reinforce a certain bond with visitors.

The observations collected during the field study have evidenced that in the twenty-first century, the modern museum presents a new institutional style—or epochal style, in Steimberg's terms (2013)—that involves not only the organization of exhibitions and cultural activities but also a new multidisciplinary experience happening inside its building and, fundamentally, in its margins.

According to this new institutional style[6], the exhibition of modern and contemporary art must achieve a balance between chronology and thematization, between the critical and pedagogical perspective, and between the re-reading of the history of twentieth-century art and the playful proposal and, above all, provide the visitor with various things to do.

From Experiential Promises to the Visiting Contract

The central role of *intermediary discourses-spaces* is grounded in their capacity to offer an *experiential promise* to visitors and, at the same time, to participate in the configuration of the *visiting contracts*, i.e., the *bonds* of the visitors with the institutions. These two instances represent the two poles of a scale of the visitor's

[6]See Rosso, A. (2019) El museo como marca: MALBA, museo del siglo XXI in *Los modos de la narración: medios, instituciones y empresas*. EditUCES. Retrieved April 14, 2022, from http://dspace.uces.edu.ar:8180/xmlui/handle/123456789/4768.

contact with the museum, containing the two pairs' *novelty/recurrence* and *differences/regularities*. The less familiar the visitors are with the museum, the more novel they would perceive the museum's program and the more different from their consumption habits they would perceive this experience (the novelty-differences pole). Conversely, the public which is more familiar with the institution would recognize recurrences in the museum's proposals and would perceive the visit as forming part of their lifestyle (the recurrence-regularities pole). The *experiential promise* operates at the *novelty-difference* pole, while the *visiting contract* operates at the *recurrence-regularities* pole.

Oscar Traversa (2017) explained that the industrial nature of cinema establishes certain modes of *discursive circulation* turning it into a triadic entity with a particular and, at first sight, contradictory objective: to carry a novel *difference* that must be stable enough for the public to accept and "enjoy." Thus, the film works at the same time as "a *film-text* which is shown as a spectacle and shows differences, as a *non-filmic film* which is integrated as a double-announcer of those differences with different processes (the critique or the street poster) and, finally, as the one that embodies the role of transit and economic product, the *film-merchandise*" (p. 116).

By applying this logic to it, the museum visit can be understood (a) as a cultural experience that periodically shows *differences*, (b) as an experiential promise that operates as a double-announcer of these *differences*, and (c) as a consumable experience that involves specific modes of access.

This *experiential promise* must be configured by the intermediary discourses of the museums in connection with and in consideration of the expectations of visitors and the social representations of the modern art museum visit in the twenty-first century (which have been presented at the beginning of this chapter).

Conversely, visiting contracts require stability and recurrence to be sustained over time. These contracts go beyond the differences presented in the programs and are built on the reiteration of certain modes of visit and the recognition of the discursive operations recurrently staged in the museum space. This is why different visiting contracts may be defined by their positions concerning the duos: interest in the general experience/interest in a particular experience (that is to say, the whole museum experience/a particular program or part of it), everydayness-exceptionality, guidance-freedom, and learning-entertainment[7]. These duos are materialized in different spatial discourses-trajectories and different enunciative strategies.

The promise and the contract are thus understood as complementary opposites based on which the bonds between museums and their visitors take shape. These two instances can be graphed in the museum territory in the following way (Fig. 6.1):

The beginning of the museum experience would be located on the pavement in front of the institution, the first physical space where the passer-by may already initiate its link with it. This first step toward the construction of the *visiting contract* corresponds to the *experiential promise* that, configured by the intermediary discourses, emerges at the moment of crossing this parcel of museum's territory and

[7] Depending on the museum program, the two terms of this last duo are not necessarily opposed.

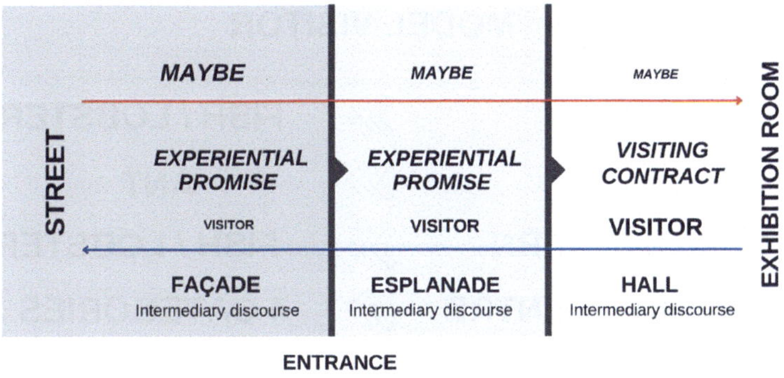

Fig. 6.1 The passage from the experiential promise to the contract of the visit represented in the museum territory

entering the esplanade of the building. In this graph, the *potential bonding* with the museum is illustrated (metaphorically) with a *maybe* decreasing gradually in size along the way to the exhibition room.

The passage from the second step (the esplanade) to the third step (the entrance hall) will depend on the enunciative strategies applied in the architectural discourses of this area and its capacity to convey the *experiential promise*: Does the building invite me to enter? Does it invite me to do so today, tomorrow, or during the weekend? Can I simply stay there? Can I simply contemplate or interact with the artworks located in the public space?

The last two questions also apply to the next stage, which is, logically, the entrance of the museum. At this point, the size of the maybe diminishes, but at the same time, the operations of the *intermediary discourses* must be even more effective to delimit the reading contract and to identify its strengths and weaknesses, its areas of ambiguity, and its eventual inconsistencies (Verón, 1985). It is precisely at this step that the institution proposes the *contracts* to the visitors and that the bonds may start to consolidate.

This progression is crucial since through these *intermediary spaces* the promise becomes the experience (regardless of whether or not the visitor continues to the exhibition rooms). The services, activities, and leisure spaces offered in the margins of the museum could, we assume, consolidate *bonds* as strongly or more strongly than the exhibition rooms[8].

Identifying these promises and contracts requires analyzing the *instances of production* and *reception* (*recognition*) of institutional discourse (Verón, 1985). This analysis includes the observation of the functioning of the selected architectural spaces, including all types of devices located therein (posters, counters, screens, display cases, benches, chairs, flyers, staff organization, security devices, entrance processes, etc.) and an ethnographic work focused on the trajectories, routes, and

[8]Our current fieldwork, using the categories of visitors proposed by Eliseo Verón (1985), aims at revealing the existence of such bonds.

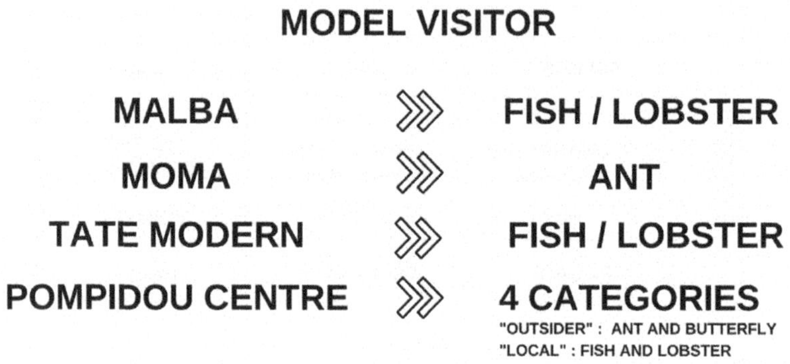

Fig. 6.2 Model visitor

actions enabled or prohibited by these spatial configurations, without neglecting the temporal factor. The performances of the people who inhabited these spaces have been observed and categorized as different types of visiting contracts.

This leads to the conclusion that each museum discourse has its types of experiential promises and visit contracts based on its institutional styles and its notions of museum, visitors, and art history. However, they all coincide in the following:

(a) The proposal of an interdisciplinary promise that includes artworks, sociability, consumption, and enjoyment.
(b) Sociability takes place beyond the physical territory of the museum and includes sharing the experience in other discursive scenarios, social media, for example.
(c) The configuration of a particular visitor: the *frontalier*.

Art, Eat, Shop: Case Study

The museum visit in the twenty-first century is characterized by its particular *time-space dynamism* underlying the manners in which its *intermediary discourses-spaces* anticipate everything that can (and cannot) be done inside the building. In the terms proposed by Eliseo Verón (2013), the modalities of enunciation built by each of Centre Pompidou, Malba, Moma, and Tate Modern configure its model visitor (Fig. 6.2):

The Malba's experiential promise is sustained by the idea of the museum as a space for entertainment, learning, enjoyment, and sociability. Its model visitor is similar to Verón's *fishes* and *lobsters* (1985) with whom the museum establishes two types of experiences: the complete and the concrete.

First, the *Malba experience* (complete experience) addresses a new visitor fish (Verón, 2013) who passes through, but also poses. The bond established with these visitors is based on the socialization enabled by the independence of the intermediary spaces of the building: the cafeteria, the boutique, the cinema, the park, and the esplanade that possess sufficient autonomy to be inhabited without even approaching the exhibition rooms. In the *Malba experience*, the contact with artworks is present as part of a multidisciplinary proposal and must involve *doing something* with the museum. That something must be socialized both in the physical space and in the social media (as indicated by the hashtags on the walls of the museum and in the spaces especially conceived for this purpose). The aim is to offer an attractive cultural experience for a specific social class: the Argentinian[9] middle class.

On the other hand, the *concrete experience* leans toward the pedagogical and specialist function of the museum. The contract that is established with the visitor is equivalent to the *lobsters* who only take what interests them. These visitors, for example, access the free space destined for contemporary art, even if it is uncomfortably located behind the boutique (and not always available). The spatial trajectories enabled by the museum acknowledge its existence, but they are opaque and not obvious to everyone. They undoubtedly have a bond with the museum, since this type of appropriation of its space reveals a certain familiarity with institutional life, but the trajectories of these *lobsters* show that they avoid the spaces of socialization and *everydayness* of the museum. The museum experience is based exclusively on the artistic proposal.

In the case of Moma, the intermediary discourses (of its old building) evidence an *experiential promise* based on the assumption that being an art museum implies teaching about, supervising, and protecting the artworks exhibited. The institution assumes that it must guide the visit, establish user manuals, and impose rules that cannot be modified. For this reason, the tours are designed so that order, the protection of the most valuable artworks of modern art in the world, and *good habits* prevail. Their model visitors are the *ants*.

Santos Zunzunegui (2003) questions the inclusion of this institution in the category of *the modern museum* given that nothing in its building comes close to abandoning hierarchy or rigid itineraries, nor does it bet on the retinal experience, nor does it trust that the visitor is capable of dispensing with mediations. Therefore, visitors pass through, follow the instructions, and learn.

Moma also offers its visitors a variety of services such as restaurants, cafés, bookshops, and shops but the order must prevail and these facilities, unlike the rest of our corpus, are reserved for those users who have paid the entrance fee. To preserve institutional norms, the Moma Design Store has positioned itself as a brand and is located outside the museum. Moma also recognizes itself as a brand and as a must-see place for tourists with cultural aspirations or interests.

The Centre Pompidou sets up an *experiential promise* based on the museum as a pedagogical and critical agent and as an educator of citizens, which in turn involves representing the culture of the country. The architectural discourse builds the four model visitors proposed by Verón (2013) which we have grouped into two types of

---

[9]Rosso, A. (2020). #ArteContemporáneo: La arquitectura del museo de arte moderno como discursividad intermediaria. Un análisis de la promesa experiencial configurada por los edificios de Centro Pompidou, Malba, Moma y Tate Modern. *Cuadernos Del Centro De Estudios De Diseño Y Comunicación*, (119), 133–150. https://doi.org/10.18682/cdc.vi119.4297

contracts. On the one hand, the *outsider* visitor would include *ants* and *butterflies* who are offered a unique experience in an iconic building located in the center of Paris. Here, the term *outsider* refers to familiarity with the institution and the frequency with which it is visited: exceptional, unusual, almost alien. This experience implies effort: understanding how the building works, where the entrances are, what to find on each floor, and where and how to find information (including understanding the French language)—in short, understanding its bureaucracy.

On the other hand, there are the *locals* or *everyday visitors* who are a mixture of *fishes* and *lobsters*, to whom the institution speaks in a complicit manner and even insists that they be part of the membership program and attend more frequently. They are invited to take ownership of the building, debate, have a coffee, visit the bookshop and the boutique, join the library, live unique experiences in contact with art and artists, and come back. For them, the visit is offered in a more pleasant, more accessible, practical, familiar, dynamic way and involves less effort: no queues, no tickets. These visitors do not come to the Centre Pompidou; they are part of *Beaubourg*. They pass through and reaffirm their belonging, while the *foreign* visitor passes through and learns or completes the checklist (as Moma, it is a must-see place for a particular type of tourist even if both remain less visited than their city's main museum, the Metropolitan Museum, and the *Musée du Louvre*, respectively).

Finally, the visitor of Tate Modern passes through but also *enjoys it*. Its *experiential promise* is based on the idea of the museum as an open and interactive space where to learn while enjoying. Conscious of the impressive size of its building, the institution offers keys to visitors to organize their routes, but, once these keys have been given, it frees them and lets them be. It is a museum that trusts in people's ability to find their way and choose what they want to do. For this reason, Tate Modern establishes its *visiting contract* with *fishes* and *lobsters*, whether those are coming to live the complete or specific experience.

Tate Modern invites the public to spend a large part of the day there, offering everything they need to stay within its boundaries. There are facilities dedicated to eating, resting, reading, shopping, photographing, playing, and learning inside and outside the building. The museum encourages the visitor to come frequently, whether alone, with friends, with a partner, or with the family, as it offers different experiences for everyone. It even highlights (on the walls or flyers) its free access to the collection and the freedom to return whenever possible.

Although each museum's experience has its particularities, the contemporary visit is a matter of activity and no longer of contemplation. So much so that each category of the Veronian bestiary has to do with a *passing* and a *doing*. In the four cases, the visitors (Fig. 6.3):

In this way, the museum proposal implies *being* in the museum and *doing* something *within* and *with it*. Institutions work toward making the visit more and more recurrent and offer not only exhibitions but also services, products, and the possibility of designing and sharing a customized experience. Hence, the importance acquired by memberships that grant discounts in shops and cafés, exclusive events. Most importantly, they ensure their members access to the exhibitions without waiting or queuing, thus guaranteeing a faster visit and the possibility of spending

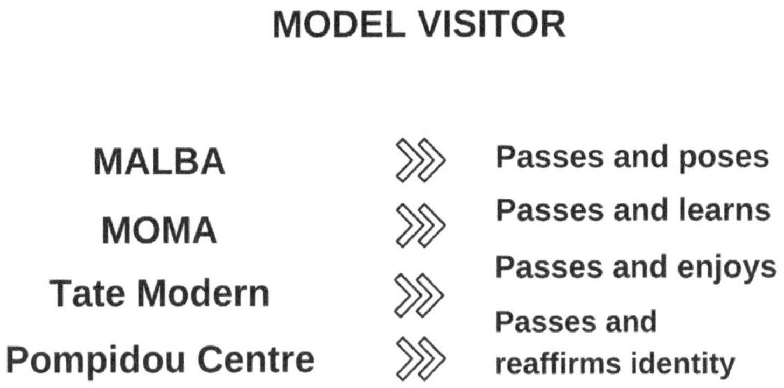

Fig. 6.3 Model visitor's action

some time in the margins of the museum where the promise of enjoyment, encounter, conversation, sociability, and doing something is fulfilled.

The Frontier Visitor: Amplitude and Speed

This *frontalier* visitor emerges from the enunciative recurrences that highlight the habitability and importance of the spaces adjacent to the exhibition room. In this way, the *frontalier* underlines the experientiality of the museum visit. The category arises both from the proposal of the architectural discourse and from the observation of the visitor performance in the museum space.

According to the spatial trajectories observed, these visitors share the features of the *lobsters* (Verón, 2013) and apply their strategies to the whole museum, taking only what they are interested in. They *resemantize* the museum's functions: it is a boutique, a café, a place to meet with others, a refuge from the heat or cold, a library, a bookshop, and a background for some pictures.

The *frontalier* establishes a different bond with the institution, emphasizing the sovereignty of the visitor who makes use of the museum facilities in his or her own way, establishing spatial hierarchies based on the time he or she allocates to each space. This *signifying body* materializes two fundamental concepts for the contemporary modern art museum visit: *amplitude* and *speed.*

Amplitude is an attribute of the buildings, their offerings of activities, and their audiences, while speed marks the contrasting paces of the trajectories inside the exhibition rooms and their surrounding spaces. The two concepts allow us to underline the existence of a reiterated *experiential promise* that requires much more than contemplating artworks.

The *amplitude* is observed not only in the scale of the buildings but also in the habitable intermediary spaces and in the possibilities for the visitor to appropriate them. It can also be seen in the programming and the size of the collections since it seems necessary for each museum to expand its collection with a certain frequency.

Amplitude is also accentuated, fundamentally, in the destination of the intermediary discourses (Traversa, 2017) capable of configuring experiential promises that appeal to different types of audiences, from children to the elderly. How? Museums redesign the esplanades, entrance halls, and façades to expose a large panorama of *things to do*.

The contrast in the *speed* of the routes through the museum spaces highlights the tension between two museum experiences: the traditional one and the one of the twenty-first century. The former could be described as one whose assumption about effects (Traversa, 2017) would include contact with the artworks and the apprehension of knowledge, whereas the latter's assumption about effects would be living an enjoyable multidisciplinary experience in connection with art.

In this sense, the *acceleration* within the exhibition rooms (already mentioned by Huyssen in 1994) contrasts with a *deceleration* of the time visitors spend at the edges of the museum. The entrance halls gain a place as exhibitors of services that host their visitors with care and invite them to enjoy themselves. The latest refurbishment of Malba and the new entrance hall of Moma as well as the Tate Modern's turbine hall and its large side vitrine exemplify this trend. The same is true of the aisles of the Centre Pompidou. Even their esplanades and parks, where some artworks or activities are located, invite one to spend time there, thus keeping the public longer in the museum territory.

Of course, the visitor's sovereignty lies in the freedom to spend time within the boundaries of the museum, as no such possibility would seem to be available within the exhibition rooms. While the exhibitions are the space of institutional and curatorial discourse, the boundaries of the museum belong to and are conceived for the visitors. The counterparty to the extension of the boundaries of the museum is the perceived narrowing and streamlining of the spaces dedicated to exposing art. The exhibitions are reached by escalators and the visit is paced. Shops, cafés, parks, and terraces are reached by foot, without haste nor pressure, and are advertised as part of the museum experience.

#TheMuseumExperience

A visit to a museum in the twenty-first century must include a nice café and a gourmet restaurant, a terrace with a magnificent view of the city or the open air, designer boutiques where you can buy exclusive products both for the home and for children, bookshops where you can find publications on current art, but also diaries, notebooks, and all kinds of merchandise, not forgetting that all the exhibitions must have beautiful catalogs. Who hasn't experienced a slight frustration when faced with a modest gift shop in a museum?

As Claire Bishop (2018) has pointed out, what some museums would seem to understand by contemporaneity is a good institutional image that positions them and links them with "the new, the cool, the photogenic, the well-designed, the economically successful" (p. 19).

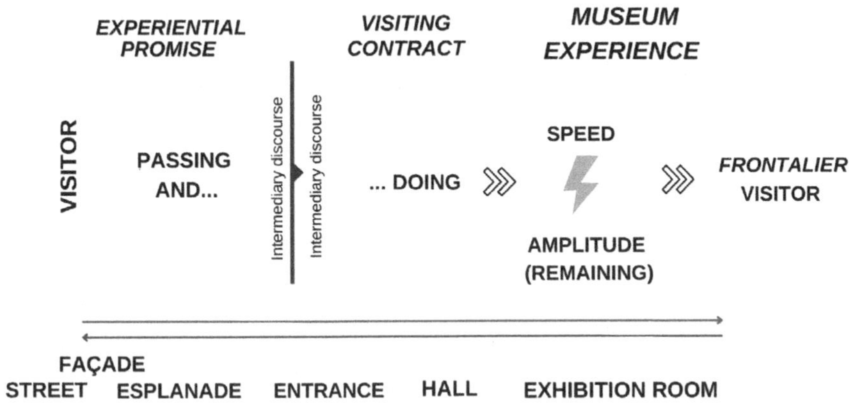

Fig. 6.4 Museum experience

The museum public of the twenty-first century is made up of active subjects who need to do things, more and more things. *Intermediary discourses* (Traversa, 2017) have highlighted a thematic recurrence linked to utilitarian notions and the controversial social function of art: to teach, to raise awareness, and, above all, to entertain . . . a notion that implies the mobilization of the subject, the enjoyment promoted by consumption at the edges of the exhibition experience (Fig. 6.4).

The end of the tour of the exhibition room is extended metaphorically: the visit does not end without shopping for a souvenir in the boutique, enjoying the café, taking a selfie in front of an artwork, or a panoramic view because our visit to the museum only *exists* if we follow the museum's advice by sharing our photos on social media. The spatial design, the photo booths, and the interactive artworks in the entrance halls or on the esplanades seem to indicate that, in the twenty-first century, a museum that does not successfully encourage visitors to take pictures will surely be empty.

Consumption is not limited to its most immediate action, i.e., shopping. The recurring hashtag present in the galleries, but also certain spaces in the hall and the visual materials, highlights the museum's need to expand its borders to offer its visitors a customizable experience, to allow them to be creators of new images, and to participate in the promotion of the museum experience. In this way, we answer the initial questions: the intermediary spaces of the museum contribute to the consolidation of this new type of visit.

This had already been anticipated by the most visited museum in the world:[10] the Louvre is the paradigmatic example of an institution exploiting its intermediary spaces. Its famous pyramid is only the visible surface of a museum that has extended its borders to the underground platforms, bus stations, and car parks. The

[10] Sharpe, E., da Silva, J., Bin V., Irwin, E. & Thill, V. (31 March 2020). Art's Most Popular: here are 2019's most visited shows and museums *The Art New Paper* https://www.theartnewspaper.com/2020/03/31/arts-most-popular-here-are-2019s-most-visited-shows-and-museums.

transformations undergone in the museum during the late 1980s, which opened to the public in 1993, reorganized the entrance hall as well as an underground area including boutiques and services functions that are completely independent of the visit but constantly remind people that they are under the civilizing mantle of the Louvre Museum.

Even the once controversial—and now iconic—glass structure operates as an experience in itself: a nice picture in front of it seems to have the same value on social media as a photo with its greatest masterpieces. This is what the number of tourists observed taking selfies in front of the Louvre pyramids during the period of closure of the museum in 2020 suggests.

The selfies, not only in front of a painting but also in the most emblematic spaces of the museum, become almost mandatory *proof* that one has been there. The building becomes the scenography of an experience. The modern art museum has already understood these changes, and the adoption of strategies to exploit and extend the time of the visit at its edges seems to be its new paradigm.

#IWantToGoToMuseum

> Acceleration has also affected the speed of the bodies passing in front of the exhibited objects. The disciplining of the bodies in the shows in the interest of the growth visitor statistics works with such subtle pedagogical tools as the walkman tour. For those who refuse to be put into a state of active slumber by the walkman, the museum applies the most brutal tactics of overcrowding which in turn results in the invisibility of what one has come to see: this new invisibility of art as the latest form of the sublime. And further: just as in our metropolitan centers the flaneur, an outsider already in Baudelaire's time, has been replaced by the marathon runner, the only place where the flaneur still had a hiding-out, namely the museum, is increasingly turned into an analogue to Fifth Avenue at rush hour—at a somewhat slower place, to be sure, but who would want to bet on the unlikelihood of a further speed-up? Perhaps we should expect the museum marathon to be the cultural innovation of the impending fin-de-siècle. (Huyssen, 1994)

When Andreas Huyssen (1994) proposed the term *acceleration* to describe museum visits, he warned that he was tempted to enter the polemics against the reconciliation between *the masses and the muses*. Such polemics, he clarified, lead "straight back to a nostalgia for the old museum, as the place of serious contemplation and earnest pedagogy, the leisure of the flaneur and the arrogance of the *connaisseur*" (p. 24) and do not explain the popularity of the museum and the desire to visit exhibitions and to live cultural events and experiences, which is common to all social classes and cultural groups. After all, as the author has said, the desire exists and should not be rejected no matter how much the culture industry may stimulate, tempt, seduce, manipulate, and exploit.

The interest in analyzing the physical and virtual footprints of visitors in the museum's intermediary spaces comes precisely from the need to understand this desire as a symptom of cultural change. The existence of the *frontalier* visitor highlights the place that these cultural institutions occupy in the lives of citizens.

Choosing to have a picnic in the park of Tate Modern, meet with friends to listen to music on the esplanade of the Pompidou Centre, or set up a rendezvous at the Malba café instead of heading to another park, square, or café is surely a symptom to pay attention to.

What motivates the appropriation by visitors of the *boundaries* of the museum? Are visitors expressing their desire to spend more time in the museum territory? Or is the desire to maintain the old image of the museum as the ancient guardian of high culture still present and, in reaction, pushing the masses out of the exhibition halls?

Studying the existence of the *frontalier* visitor would allow a better understanding of the motivations and needs of museum publics to conceive complex museum experiences capable of responding to their expectations, taking advantage of contemporary communications trends, and achieving academic excellence in exhibition design. This seems to be what museum visitors demand in the twenty-first century.

References

Huyssen, A. (1994). *Twilight memories: Marking time in a culture of amnesia* (pp. 13–35). https://doi.org/10.4324/9780203610213

Levasseur, M., & Veron, E. (1983). Ethnographie d'une exposition. Retrieved June 18, 2022, https://halshs.archives-ouvertes.fr/halshs-01484185/document

Steimberg, O. (2013). *Semióticas. La semiótica de los géneros, de los estilos, de la transposición.* Eterna Cadencia.

Traversa, O. (2017). La "discursividad intermediaria" del cine, revisitada. *Rutas de la lingüística en la Argentina, II*, 111–123.

Verón, E. (1985). El análisis del contrato de lectura, un nuevo método para los estudios de posicionamiento de los soportes de los media. *Les medias: experiences, recherches actuelles, aplications.* IREP. Retrieved April 19, 2022, from https://semioticaderedes-carlon.com/wp-content/uploads/2018/04/veron-analisis_del_contrato_de_lectura.pdf

Verón, E. (1998). *La semiosis social: Fragmentos de una teoría de la discursividad.* Editorial Gedisa.

Verón, E. (2014). Mediatization theory: A semio-antropological perspective. *Handbooks of Communications Science, Mediatization of Communication, 21*, 163–175.

Verón, E. (2013). *La semiosis social, 2: Ideas, momentos, interpretantes.* Paidós.

Zunzunegui, S. (2003). *Metamorfosis de la mirada.* Museo y semiótica. Cátedra.

Aluminé A. Rosso, Buenos Aires, Argentina: PhD student (ULiège). Master in Critique and Diffusion of Arts (UNA). Expert in Contemporary Art Curating (USAL). Bachelor of Science in Communication (UADE). Degree in Direction of Strategic Marketing (UADE)

Ms. Rosso is an active member of the Research and Experimentation Institute of Art and Criticism (IIEAC) since 2018. She studies the visitor experience in modern and contemporary art museums and the configuration of meaning in the exhibition space in Europe and America. She is currently professor of Arts and Media and Art and Market (USAL). Between 2017 and 2020, she was professor of Curatorial Projects III and Semiotics of the Arts (UNA), professor of Art History (UCES), and the coordinator of Institutional Communication in the Area of Criticism and Diffusion of Arts (UNA).

She lives in Paris, where she founded the Atelier-en-Valise, an art studio made for and by women, she works as a researcher and an indcpendent curator

Part II
Algorithms, Social Media, and Online Footprints

Chapter 7
Investigating Exhaust Data in Virtual Communities

Stefano Agostini, Giovanna Gianturco, and Peter Mechant

Introduction

In this chapter, we focus on how virtual communities (VCs) leave "traces" or "unintentional information" and study how they can affect VCs and their features. In doing so, we use qualitative data from a doctoral research project developed between Italy and Belgium. Firstly, in this introduction, we briefly describe how "traces" are considered. Secondly, we unpack the concepts "VC" and "sense of community." Thirdly, we explore the context in which VCs take place theoretically. Fourthly, we explain the methodology used and the case selection procedure. Then, we describe our results, and finally, the chapter ends with a discussion and a conclusion.

We consider the notion "traces" in Bloch's terms (1992: 51) and use the interpretation given by Ricoeur; traces are "documents in archives (which) for the most part come from witnesses in spite of themselves" (2009: 171); "The trace is thus the higher concept under whose aegis Bloch places testimony. It constitutes the operator par excellence of 'indirect' knowledge" (170). Information disseminated by social media users, considered as unconscious "tracks," can be used by others in different ways than the original intent, thus acquiring a different meaning.

In this chapter, our first research question polls for the features of information that are left unintentionally by the users of virtual communities (RQ1). Our second research question focuses on the role that such unintentional information has in

S. Agostini (✉) · G. Gianturco
Department of Communication and Social Research, Sapienza – University of Rome, Rome, Italy
e-mail: info@stefanoagostini.com; giovanna.gianturco@uniroma1.it

P. Mechant
Department of Communication Sciences, Ghent University, Ghent, Belgium
e-mail: peter.mechant@ugent.be

F. Comunello et al. (eds.), *What People Leave Behind*, Frontiers in Sociology and Social Research 7, https://doi.org/10.1007/978-3-031-11756-5_7

virtual communities (RQ2) or, in other words, on how users of VCs appropriate and apply these traces in different ways than originally intended.

Literature Review

Castells describes contemporary society as a social and economic network structure. Being the first one using networks as the basic category of the capitalist system analysis (Anttiroiko, 2015: 16), the contribution of Castells to social theory is undoubtedly important. Nevertheless, his concept of network could be criticized as it works on a high level of abstraction (Anttiroiko, 2015: 9) to a point that it could be considered as a metaphor rather than an analytical concept (15). On the other hand, Castells' view on society, based mainly on post-Marxism and in small part on Marxism, is very wide and comprehensive (Webster, 2006: 107–108). In addition, working on the macro level allows him to describe every tendency of the informational society in late modernity into a whole theory of contemporary society (Anttiroiko, 2015b: 9). Diving more into his theorization, according to Castells, this entire network structure is connected by ICT and shaped by *pervasiveness* (of effects of new technologies), *networking logic* (which is in any system or set of relationships using the ICT), *flexibility* (of processes, organizations, and institutions), *convergence* (of technologies into a highly integrated system), and the *information* as its raw material (2010: 69–71). He defines network as a set of interconnected points at which a curve intersects itself (501) and in its theorization a new social morphology takes place, affecting operation and outcomes basically concerning everything (processes of production, experience, power, and culture) (500). Networks, of course, also existed in past societies (Castells, 2010: 500), "but recent technological developments in communication have afforded their emergence as a dominant form of social organization" (Wellman, 2001b: 228). The terms information society and knowledge society, according to Castells, are poorly chosen because all societies in history have been about information and knowledge (2010: 21). "To be sure, knowledge and information are critical elements in all modes of development (...). However, what is specific to the informational mode of development is the action of knowledge upon knowledge itself as the main source of productivity" (2010: 17).

For this reason, Castell uses the concept "informational society," in which *quantity* (the volume, the size, and the speed) and *quality* of the transactions performed are different because the economy itself changed into "informational." Thus, information is merged with the material support of the product (Castells, 2010: 221), and companies become "network enterprises" (176–178); even states become "network states" (Carnoy & Castells, 2001). In order to support this global network system, and especially this new form of capitalism, time and space "have" to be fragmented and compressed; more specifically, time becomes "timeless" and space just "flows." Physical contiguity is then outdated by flows (of capital, information, and technology), and time is remodeled so that its sequential order can be contorted

Table 7.1 Differences between surveillance and interveillance

	Surveillance	Interveillance
Driving force	Check of users and fields	Identity evolution
Mode of practice	Standardized actions	Daily patterns
Power relation	Hierarchical, official	Multi-level, unofficial
Direction of flows	Essentially one way, vertical	Essentially two way, horizontal

Source: see Jansson (2015: 85)

to the point that linearity can be broken into simultaneity (Van Dijk, 1999: 131) or with random discontinuity in the sequence (Castells, 2010: 494), thus becoming "timeless" (491). Within informational capitalism, some dimensions of human life are connected, while others are excluded (Castells, 2010: xxxix), which is the manifestation of contradictions between space of flows and space of places. From network society (NS), Castells moves on to the mobile network society, which is just its enhancement driven by new wireless communication technologies (Castells et al., 2009: 6). In the NS, communication shifts to a new form named "mass self-communication": it is self-generated in content, self-directed in emission, and self-selected in reception by many who communicate with many. At the same time, it is mass communication because it reaches a potentially global audience through P2P networks and Internet connections (Castells, 2009: 70). This new platform of communication, now prevalent (Castells, 2012: 248), is mainly based on horizontal networks of communication (Castells, 2007: 239), and around people's initiatives and interests, it frequently stands on means of interactive communication—nevertheless, it is not only limited to high-end technology (Castells, 2009: 69–70). By these new means of communication, forms of surveillance (vertical and horizontal) can take place and among users can be defined as an interpersonal process which seems to them the normalization of surveillance, consequently, part of the social media communication process (Vittadini, 2018: 91), which can be named "interveillance."

Thus, interveillance can be referred to the social processes related to mediated monitoring and control, including everyday check-ups and "(. . .) peer-to-peer monitoring, understood as the use of surveillance tools by individuals (. . .) to keep track of one another (. . .)" (Andrejevic, 2004: 488); hence, "(. . .) they are not systematic and hierarchical per se. Rather, they are driven by the fundamental social needs through which identities are (re) created and manifested and thus take on a relatively non-reflexive and volatile character" (Jansson, 2015: 85) (see Table 7.1).

The concept "networked individualism" developed by Barry Wellman is deeply connected with Castells' theorization and can be resumed as an "individualized relationship to society" (Castells, 2002: 128) of "sparsely-knit, linking individuals with little regard to space" (Wellman, 2001a: 10). In the first part of his career, Wellman described the transition "from group to glocalized relationships" (13), as from "little boxes" to "glocalized networks" and then to "networked individualism." Even the kind of ties evolved: from place-to-place to individualized person-to-person interactions (2001b: 238) and also to specialized role-to-role (244). Three revolutions took place, which Wellman named, respectively, the development of social networks, the rise of the Internet, and the mobile connectivity. These led the world to this "new social operating system" (Rainie & Wellman, 2012: 11–12) which today is the dominant form of sociability (Castells, 2002: 132).

Virtual Community

Virtual communities have existed since the 1980s (Fuchs, 2014: 5) and are thus no new object of study in sociology or communication sciences. Wellman (2004) discerns different phases in research on virtual communities: a first enthusiastic phase, a second phase with systematic documentation of users and uses, and a third phase in which there is a shift from documentation to analysis. The concepts "community" and "virtual" are the basic elements of the concept "VC." There is a lack of consensus regarding this concept. Contemporary sociologists represent it in different ways: as an *imagined community* (Anderson, 1983), a *pseudo-community* (Beniger, 1987), or a *symbolic construction* (Cohen, 1985). The "virtual" is conceptualized as something which exists without being there, therefore, without space-time coordinates (Van Dijk, 1999), as something which is "real" according to Castells ("real virtuality"): "All realities are communicated through symbols. And in human, interactive communication, regardless of the medium, all symbols are somewhat displaced in relation to their assigned semantic meaning. In a sense, all reality is virtually perceived" (Castells, 2010: 404). Many scholars refer to Rheingold's definition for "virtual community" as a social aggregation that emerges online when enough people carry on public discussions and with sufficient human feeling (2000: xx). In this chapter, we use an empirically grounded definition: a virtual community is an aggregate of individuals and/or business partners that interact on a shared (or complementary) interest realized at least partially in a digital common space and that is supported and/or mediated by the Internet (see Agostini & Mechant, 2019).

VCs are often inscribed into Web 2.0 (Bennato, 2012: 57–60) and social media. The latter can be considered as all media as they are social artifacts and transmit human knowledge, or those media which support the reciprocal process of communication among humans, or those media which support collaboration or cooperative work, or those media which enable people to experience feelings of belonging or friendship by a regular communication process (Fuchs, 2014: 4–6). Regarding the latter, we can refer specifically to the sense of virtual community (Blanchard & Markus, 2002) or, in general, to the sense of community.

Sense of Community

Sense of community (SOC) is defined by McMillan and Chavis as a feeling of belonging that community members have and at the same time as a shared faith to be together (1986: 9). The authors divided the concept in four dimensions: membership, influence, integration and fulfillment of needs, and shared emotional connection (9).

The first dimension, "membership," presupposes there are *boundaries*, which is to say there are people who belong and people who do not (9); membership is a feeling that relates to the personal investment made by people who want to be part of the group, as well as to a common symbol system (10).

The second dimension, "influence," is considered as a bidirectional concept (11) and is related to cohesiveness, because "Influence of a member on the community and influence of the community on a member operate concurrently (. . .)" (12).

The third dimension, "integration and fulfillment of needs," can be interpreted, according to McMillan and Chavis, as reinforcement (12).

The fourth dimension, "shared emotional connection," is based on shared history and relates to identification with other members. Also, the quality of the interaction in shared events and the investment of each member is key in this context (13).

Case Selection

Porter's typology was used for the case selection of virtual communities studied in this chapter. Porter's categorization is exhaustive and applicable on an empirical level, although some adjustments are needed (see Agostini & Mechant, 2019). On a theoretical level, our focus was aimed at a "social," a "professional," a "non-profit," and a "commercial" VC (the "government" VC was not chosen because they were not widespread at that time). On an empirical level, we used specific selection criteria: VCs were mainly selected from VCs with members located in Rome and from VCs with a minimum level of significant interactions present (in terms of frequency and consistency) and a lifetime of at least 2 years.

Based on Patton's distinction on the role of the researcher (between complete immersion in the setting as a full participant and complete separation from the setting as a spectator) (Patton, 2002: 265), we chose the latter. For the "non-profit" and "commercial" VCs, online and offline observations were conducted. Due to the closed, non-accessible online environment for the "professional" and "social" VCs, only offline observations were made for these cases.

The first-level categorization element of Porter's typology (member-initiated or organization-sponsored VC) was hard to apply "in the field." More specifically, "member-initiated" or "organization-sponsored" VCs often did not match with the second-level categorization. Consequently, we chose the latter to drive the case selection. This second-level categorization element, relationship orientation, describes the type of relationship fostered among members of a VC. Thus, the selected cases were "GSCAI" as "social" (members have a hobby in common), "Diarioclown" as "professional" (members work together), "AZALEA" as "non-profit" (members support a non-profit organization), and "F & G" as "commercial" (members are students of a dancing school).

Methodology

Using offline ethnography, we collected qualitative face-to-face interviews with members of the four selected VCs in order to understand users' meanings and scopes (Caliandro, 2018: 5). Also, netnography was used (when possible) mainly for background research.

We selected four case studies from two different online platforms. On "Yahoo! Groups," we studied a "social" and "professional" VC, while on "Facebook," we studied a "non-profit" and "commercial" VC. Using a cross-sectional analysis, we explore and describe the role of unintentional information in VCs, especially regarding the SOC.

The main features of the four VCs that were studied are summarized in Table 7.2.

The VC "GSCAI" comprises a speleological group located in Rome. This VC was selected as the case study for a social VC because the relationship fostered among the members is based on a hobby. The group undertakes activities (explorations, visits) that require planning (equipment, travel, etc.). To manage such activities, they have set up an online group called "GSCAI" on "Yahoo! Groups." Expert members who are "retired" from group activities keep in touch exclusively with other members via the VC, read the online messages, and sometimes give suggestions (so-called sleepers). In January 2012, the group split due to a rotation in the management team, which led to an online and then an offline confrontation.

"Diarioclown" (professional VC) is a group created by therapists located in Rome working as "clown therapists." In their online group, "Diarioclown," they

Table 7.2 Virtual communities investigated

	GSCAI social (A)	Diarioclown professional (B)	AZALEA non-profit (C)	F & G commercial (D)
Established	Over 4 years	Over 4 years	4 years	Over 4 years
Platform	Yahoo! Groups	Yahoo! Groups	Facebook	Facebook
Open/closed	Closed	Closed	Open	Open
Members	49	11	>2000	>600
Respondents	10	10	12	12
Male	8	6	0	7
Female	2	4	12	5
Average age (y.o.)	37,6	35,7	37,1	41,9

Source: see Agostini and Mechant (2019)

communicate only "professional" messages such as the weekly shifts division and daily reports (which is an important element in order to keep the team job running properly). In January 2012, this group was also separated, and subsequently, four members decided to move to another workplace. Discontent was manifested online by not writing reports.

The VC "AZALEA" is a non-profit association located in Rome that supports a cat center where abandoned cats are hosted, fed, and cured. They use various social network sites (SNSs), but most of their activity is targeted at their Facebook fan page. This is mainly used in order to find adopters—for their abandoned cats—and to make follow-up checks on the "adoptions" already made, periodically asking adopters to share pictures of the adopted cat and replying to their questions in case of need.

The VC "F & G" is formed around a Latin American dance school in Rome. "F & G" also organizes events—not always related to dancing and music. "F & G" has a Facebook fan page in order to communicate information about its activities (e.g., changes in lesson schedules, special events, etc.).

Porter's typology (Porter, 2004) used for the case selection takes into account five attributes of virtual communities: *purpose* (content of interaction), *place* (extent of technology mediation of interaction), *platform* (design of interaction, synchronous, asynchronous communication, or both), *population* (pattern of interaction), and *profit model* (return on interaction). The cases selected incorporate the four attributes described as well as the minimum set of conditions required to label a cyber-place as a virtual settlement (Jones, 1997), so they can be considered VCs.

We collected 49 in-depth semi-structured qualitative interviews with an average length of 90 min. We conducted interviews until data "saturation" was reached. Respondents were divided in three subgroups: beginner users, less than 1 year of membership; average users, from 1 to 2 years of membership; and expert users, from 2 to 4 years of membership (see Agostini & Mechant 2015). We applied a deductive coding methodology on the transcripts of the interviews. Deductive coding encompasses three coding phases (Miles & Huberman, 1994). In the first phase, descriptive codes are assigned to text snippets based on predefined areas of interest, whether factual, thematic, or theoretical in nature (Lewins & Silver, 2007: 86). Focusing on the four dimensions of SOC, codes were assigned when VC's members described how they used the VC or how they experienced feelings of influence. Next, interpretative coding was done, digging deeper into the meaning of the descriptive codes. By using an exploratory-descriptive logic moving toward analytical generalization (Yin, 2003: 37), parallels, differences, and oppositions between the descriptive and interpretative codes were then examined, and pattern codes were assigned. Finally, thematic analysis was done.

Research has shown that elements of SOC can be found in specific VCs, such as feelings of membership (Nonnecke et al., 2004: 6), emotional contagion (Barsade, 2002) and the impact offline activities have on the influence over the members (Koh & Kim, 2001: 3), integration of members (Casaló et al., 2013), and emotional connection (Brook & Oliver, 2002).

Results

Dimensions of SOC in the Cases Selected

Each VC was created to support a specific topic or domain: a business ("commercial"), a cat center ("non-profit"), a speleological group ("social"), and a team of therapists ("professional"). We noted that traces left behind by users within the common shared space had a positive impact on the SOC of the groups investigated. In one case only, namely, "F & G commercial," there was a rather weak link with "emotional connection" because the platform structure and the communication flow within this VC seemed to give members an emotional connection which was not so deep (see Table 7.3). Results show that exhaust data within VCs can increase the manifestation of discontent ("social" and "professional" VCs) as well as increase quarrels because of the reduced non-verbal cues in CMC ("social" VC). These "side effects" were experienced as less important than positive ones on SOC: without the presence of a virtual space, the majority of the users would be lost within the "social" VC (only few join the offline activities from time to time), and the "professional" VC would be very hard to coordinate.

Subdimensions of SOC

Table 7.4 summarizes an evaluation of the subdimensions by the members of the selected cases. In a "professional" VC, feelings of influence are mostly expressed as a form of support and lesser forms of discontent, while in a "social" one, feelings of influence take the form of wellbeing and real quarrels. With regard to the integration and fulfillment of needs, we noticed that, while in the non-profit there is emotional support, this is manifested in the commercial VC through reinforcement. With reference to the single VCs, examining them *vertically* allows one to better understand how SOC is developed by exhaust data.

Table 7.3 Exhaust data and SOC

	GSCAI social	Diarioclown professional	AZALEA non-profit	F & G commercial
Feelings of membership	+	+	+	+
Feelings of influence	+	+	+	+
Integration and fulfillment of needs	+	+	+	+
Shared emotional connection	+	+	+	±

Table 7.4 Exhaust data and SOC—subdimensions

	GSCAI social (A)	Diarioclown professional (B)	AZALEA non-profit (C)	F & G commercial (D)
Feelings of membership				
Joining the group more easily	+	+	+	+
Feelings of influence				
Quarrels	+	±		
Wellbeing	+		+	+
Support		+		
Integration and fulfillment of needs				
Inspiring to participate in the activities	+			
Emotional support			+	
Reinforce		+		+
Shared emotional connection				
Emotional connection		±	+	
Shared history	+	+		±

Social VC (A)

In the "social" VC, beginners were able to get to know the social network of the group (sociogram) by reading the archived content shared within the VC (who is friend of whom, parties, subgroups, etc.) making conversations easier because the dialogues could be adjusted to the speaker (membership):

> I take the information (by the VC) about the group, history, bonds that were there before me, also because I can figure it out there (within the VC) then in case I ask for someone (laugh). Otherwise the group would be those 15 people I meet at the explorations (. . .). (A2F)

In GSCAI, a "simple" account cancellation, due to the change of the management team, erased the "supposed" non-active users from the mailing list. This caused harsh criticism and offline action by these so-called sleepers (influence). Those ex-members, who were very experienced, did not pay the annual fee and did not take part in the offline activities for a long time. They were supposed to be mostly inactive. However, while more active members were writing about their explorations leaving "traces behind," these sleepers were reading all of these updates and felt like part of the group, sometimes even replying and giving suggestions on how to proceed with certain explorations. Although their time with the group "passed by," they continued to perceive themselves as part of the group, thanks to the VC, similar to members who couldn't take part in the activities every time:

> Some people felt kicked out just because they weren't on the list. (. . .) They said it on the day of the assembly (. . .) they got angry about it (laughs) "I was there because I liked to read, even the squabbles" (. . .) "it's normal, but I liked being there" (. . .) none of the old people had told us . . . (. . .) we thought that it was now a dead email, it was there, they didn't write (. . .). But some actually read (laughs). (A4M)

Reading about the goals achieved by the group shared within the VC gives "sleepers" and the other members a sense of wellbeing (influence):

> (. . .) there are people online who make a weekly reporting of . . . what happened on Thursday night or Sunday, or the exploration report, so the whole group is always made aware (. . .) it is beautiful (. . .) being a group activity it is nice to know what the group does (. . .) I was happy that they managed to open it (the well), I can't wait to go and see what's down there (laughs). (A2F)

The online platform supporting the VC enables members to keep track of their (speleology) activities and, therefore, of the history of the group (emotional connection). Before it was done in a book but now it is done online. Reading the coordination messages inspires users to join the explorations (integration): "(. . .) Just, someone replies (within the VC) and says: 'Well done, great job', or says 'Ah, interesting, next time keep me in mind for these activities, I want to participate too'" (A1M).

> This is . . . another benefit of the mailing list. Because it allows those who, for work or family reasons, cannot join, still allow them to be satellite to this (. . .) and not to stray too far because otherwise their ties are broken. Instead, in this way the activity is alive. (. . .) a maintenance of ties. Because it is strengthened, those who have not come for 20 years say: "Hey! I want to come back." (A8M)

Despite the physical distance, a member who moved away from the city kept in contact with the group and its activities using the VC: "It was a way to continue seeing and hearing what those in the group were doing (. . .)" (A3M).

Professional VC (B)

Similar to the "social" VC are the "traces left behind" in the "professional" VC useful for beginners in order to join the group more easily (membership):

> That is, just to join the group, because (. . .) in my opinion, there is not yet such a consolidated group (. . .) because after a month, two months (. . .) in my opinion it is almost impossible (. . .) . . . and therefore (the VC is) also to, to share, therefore to get to know and to let others get to know me. (. . .) to join the group (. . .). (B5F)

Even experts find useful information about their co-workers, thanks to the written reports, making things easier when they join the group (membership): "(. . .) maybe the clown therapists who are a little more shy (. . .) however, from the emotional point of view they write a lot, so . . . (. . .) you get an idea about, about the clown therapist in front of you, about your companions (. . .)" (B6M).

Reports also provide information that helps to better understand group dynamics (membership):

> Well . . . now . . . you know, you can see that there's something wrong and that doesn't work. And yes, yes . . . (. . .) from reports (. . .) between the lines I can also understand other things (. . .) and I say to myself: "Ah! Look at him who is ruffling that one because it is convenient to take him to his side". You know what I'm saying? (B9M)

These reports heavily influence the working life of the team members because the shifts are detailed online (coordination) and above all they inform their colleagues about what has happened with specific patients, so that the other therapists—who alternate—are able to continue from where the previous pair left off. "In short, information is fundamental for us" (B8F).

Reports can make the group stronger (integration):

> (. . .) in the case of a child who has passed away, in short, there is a bit of a consolation, as we say, from the others. And to think that you are not alone in short, because it is as if it were a weight that you carry on your shoulders and is shared with everyone. (B3M)

This is confirmed by an expert, because, when reports are missing as a sign of discontent, or are done in a hurry without attention to details, the group cohesion is damaged, as it is hard for them to cooperate without reports: "Later I saw that the clown diary practically no longer existed. There were no longer reports, no one wrote the report anymore (. . .) So . . . it was just the . . . just like the desert at that time (smiles)" (B10F).

Reports also keep track of the history of the group, which has emotional elements due to the nature of the job (emotional connection):

> So every clown therapist in the end, we say, about the performance in the hospital should be, a daily (smiles) update for the other clown therapists, but also to elaborate what he experienced during the day (. . .) to elaborate them personally, because in any case it is important not to keep them inside, right? (. . .) Because (. . .) sooner or later you burst. And so this is important (. . .) to share them with the group (. . .) because perhaps reading what the other has experienced, you . . . relive it (. . .). We work on emotions so it is important that we also work on our emotions. (B5F)

Non-profit VC (C)

The "non-profit" VC was set up in order to check the cats' entrusted conditions and help cat custodians in case they need information. Sharing messages gives wellbeing to many users (influence), as the majority are not custodians but just supporters of the association and this happens especially for beginners. The messages shared in the VC involve also non-recipients, so when a user is helped by the association's members or by a supporter, other users also receive help (influence) indirectly:

> (. . .) reading this news, these tips also affect my behavior with my cat. I say to myself "Aaah see? They say that this brand of crunchies might not be good then, let's see if there's another one", I mean (. . .) I trust the group so if there is any advice maybe I try to follow it. (C8F)

Generally, through the exchange of "service messages" to the association or to a specific user, a sort of relationship is created, although it could not be defined as a real friendship. This process takes place explicitly when, during the offline events of the organization, they address each other by their Facebook nickname and not by their real name (membership):

> (. . .) you already have a bond with those people due to the fact that you have a cat. (. . .) It is a bond that is (. . .) I do not know how to explain, it is like if they were non-elective affinities but almost. (C1F)

Providing news about their cat by using a "service message," for instance, updating the health situation of their pet, results in many users asking for updates in the following days. The Facebook page of this VC collects the history of fostered cats and the users involved (emotional connection). Furthermore, this includes reactions from other readers, which are expressed in solidarity actions or comforting messages as emotional support (integration):

> (. . .) when there was (. . .) that lady's cat who was dying, there must have been like a hundred comments, a lot, because then they asked how she was, all the updates . . . (. . .). You don't feel alone, you know there are people like you. (C5F)

Commercial VC (D)

The "commercial" VC uses the Internet in order to manage its activities. Messages shared within the web space of the group mean for some "being active" on Facebook. For others, these messages symbolize being part of a community (membership) even when they are not able to take part in the real-life activities. Messages provide opportunities to know if there are new people involved in the group and to get to know them (online or offline). This is particularly true for beginners. They can deepen their knowledge in a "discreet" and comfortable manner, especially the more timid new members, and increase their involvement and participation in the activities:

> In short, it is also a way to socialize a little more (. . .) there are also other people you don't know that maybe if you write, I don't know . . . a comment, something, maybe they'll answer as well (. . .) (smiling) it's also a way, you know (. . .) to socialize, to get to know (. . .). (D4F)

The page on Facebook is thus not only the page itself; it has a deeper meaning for the users because it connects all of them (membership) and reinforces the group (integration):

> For me, being part of this online group means being part of a group of people who have an interest in salsa (. . .) I believe that most of the people who are interested in that page and write on that page have my same interest, in the sense of the interest of talking each other, being in contact with a group of people that you feel good with and with whom, beyond the dancing through this page, let's say, stay in touch. (D12M)

Reading the messages shared within the VC gives a sense of wellbeing to the users (influence): "(. . .) let's say when you see the photos, posts etc. . . . there is a moment of, a moment of leisure . . . a moment of relaxation, so to speak (. . .)" (D1M). The VC represents a sort of history of the group (emotional connection): "(. . .) maybe there are, often they are all comments like this, playful . . . laughing, joking, right? (. . .) I see that maybe in the photos that are shared, which are many, the parties rather than etc. . . ." (D1M).

Within the membership and integration dimensions of SOC, we found interveillance among the members, who looked each other over to better introduce themselves or see what is going on in the group: "(. . .) as I told you I read them and I can only see what is missing, that is, I notice how the group is not working well (. . .)" (B9M); "(. . .) surely through Facebook you have the possibility to know a little bit about people's lives and therefore maybe it happens that you go and see some photos (. . .)" (D3F).

Discussion and Conclusion

In this chapter, we showed how exhaust data can manifest itself in VCs and what effect it can have on users of VCs. More specifically, unintentional information left by users of VCs (RQ1) can be described as routine messages related to group coordination and management. Moreover, such unintentional information can play different roles in VCs (RQ2): exhaust data can definitely increment community building for professionals (see also Figenschou & Fredheim, 2020), non-profit (see Gruss et al., 2019; Sun & Asencio, 2019), commercial (see also Al-Kandari et al., 2019; Gruss et al., 2020), and social (see also Gnach, 2017; Allen et al., 2016) also by letting beginners join the group more easily by adjusting their communication (see Papacharissi, 2010) or by increasing sense of belonging as well as strengthening the group (Bock et al., 2015); they can also give wellbeing to users. Nevertheless, they can increase quarrels and increment the manifestation of discontent. Our results also demonstrate the usefulness of a qualitative approach in studying exhaust data: using software to extract and process (meta) data from VCs would, for example, not have identified so-called sleepers in the VCs.

Furthermore, we found a specific kind of surveillance based on the "digital footprints" users leave behind and which can be observed within the VCs selected (Vittadini, 2018: 91). According to Trottier, there is evidence of interpersonal surveillance on Facebook in two directions; Facebook users are the subject and the agent of surveillance (2012: 320) and it "(. . .) is framed not so much as a violation than a condition that users need to manage" (330).

Of course, this research is not exhaustive, and further study could have been made on different topics like domestication of technology, social capital, or identity. However, in order to improve the scope of this investigation, this could be done in the future.

References

Agostini, S., & Mechant, P. (2015). Virtual communities and feelings of influence: Four case studies. *International Journal of Electrical, Electronics and Data Communication (IJEEDC), 3*(5), 19–23.

Agostini, S., & Mechant, P. (2019). Towards a definition of virtual community. *Signo y Pensamiento, 38*(74). https://doi.org/10.11144/Javeriana.syp38-74.tdvc.
Al-Kandari, A. A., Gaither, T. K., Alfahad, M. M., Dashti, A. A., & Alsaber, A. R. (2019). An Arab perspective on social media: How banks in Kuwait use instagram for public relations. *Public Relations Review, 45*(3), 101774. https://doi.org/10.1016/j.pubrev.2019.04.007
Allen, C., Vassilev, I., Kennedy, A., & Rogers, A. (2016). Long-term condition self-management support in online communities: A meta-synthesis of qualitative papers. *Journal of Medical Internet Research, 18*(3), e5260. https://doi.org/10.2196/jmir.5260
Anderson, B. (1983). *Imagined communities: Reflections on the origin and spread of nationalism*. Verso.
Andrejevic, M. (2004). The work of watching one another: Lateral surveillance, risk, and governance. *Surveillance and Society, 2*(4), 479–497. https://doi.org/10.24908/ss.v2i4.3359
Anttiroiko, A. V. (2015). *Networks in Manuel Castells' theory of the network society*. MPRA Paper 65617. https://mpra.ub.uni-muenchen.de/65617/1/MPRA_paper_65617.pdf
Anttiroiko, A. V. (2015b). Castells' network concept and its connections to social, economic and political network analyses. *Journal of Social Structure, 16*(1), 1–18. https://doi.org/10.21307/joss-2019-021
Barsade, S. G. (2002). The ripple effect: Emotional contagion and its influence on group behavior. *Administrative Science Quarterly, 47*(4), 644–675. https://doi.org/10.2307/3094912
Beniger, J. R. (1987). Personalization of mass media and the growth of pseudo-community. *Communication Research, 14*(3), 352–371. https://doi.org/10.1177/009365087014003005
Bennato, D. (2012). *Sociologia dei media digitali: relazioni sociali e processi comunicativi del web partecipativo*. Laterza.
Blanchard, A. L., & Markus, M. L. (2002). Sense of virtual community-maintaining the experience of belonging. In *Proceedings of the 35th Annual Hawaii International Conference on System Sciences* (pp. 3566–3575). doi:https://doi.org/10.1109/HICSS.2002.994449).
Bloch, M. (1992). *The historian's craft*. Manchester University Press.
Bock, G. W., Ahuja, M. K., Suh, A., & Yap, L. X. (2015). Sustainability of a virtual community: Integrating individual and structural dynamics. *Journal of the Association for Information Systems, 16*(6), 418–447. https://doi.org/10.17705/1jais.00400
Brook, C., & Oliver, R. (2002). Supporting the development of learning communities in online settings. In *Proceedings of the ED-MEDIA 2002 World Conference on Educational Multimedia, Hypermedia & Telecommunications*. http://files.eric.ed.gov/fulltext/ED476977.pdf
Caliandro, A. (2018). Digital methods for ethnography: Analytical concepts for ethnographers exploring social media environments. *Journal of Contemporary Ethnography, 47*(5), 551–578. https://doi.org/10.1177/0891241617702960
Carnoy, M., & Castells, M. (2001). Globalization, the knowledge society, and the Network State: Poulantzas at the millennium. *Global Networks, 1*(1), 1–18. https://doi.org/10.1111/1471-0374.00002
Casaló, L. V., Flavián, C., & Guinalíu, M. (2013). New members' integration: Key factor of success in online travel communities. *Journal of Business Research, 66*(6), 706–710. https://doi.org/10.1016/j.jbusres.2011.09.007
Castells, M. (2002). *The Internet galaxy: Reflections on the Internet, business, and society*. Oxford University Press.
Castells, M. (2007). Communication, power and counter-power in the network society. *International Journal of Communication, 1*(1), 238–266. https://ijoc.org/index.php/ijoc/article/view/46
Castells, M. (2009). *Communication power*. Oxford University Press.
Castells, M. (2010). *The rise of the network society* (Vol. 1, 2nd ed.). Wiley-Blackwell.
Castells, M. (2012). *Networks of outrage and hope: Social movements in the Internet age*. Polity Press.
Castells, M., Fernandez-Ardevol, M., Qiu, J. L., & Sey, A. (2009). *Mobile communication and society: A global perspective*. MIT Press.
Cohen, A. P. (1985). *The symbolic construction of community*. Routledge.

Figenschou, T. U., & Fredheim, N. A. (2020). Interest groups on social media: Four forms of networked advocacy. *Journal of Public Affairs, 20*(2), Article e2012. https://doi.org/10.1002/pa.2012

Fuchs, C. (2014). *Social media: a critical introduction*. Sage.

Gnach, A. (2017). Social media and community building. In C. Cotter & D. Perrin (Eds.), *The Routledge handbook of language and media* (pp. 191–207). Routledge.

Gruss, R., Abrahams, A., Song, Y., Berry, D., & Al-Daihani, S. M. (2019). Community building as an effective user engagement strategy: A case study in academic libraries. *Journal of the Association for Information Science and Technology, 71*(2), 208–220. https://doi.org/10.1002/asi.24218

Gruss, R., Kim, E., & Abrahams, A. (2020). Engaging restaurant customers on Facebook: The power of belongingness appeals on social media. *Journal of Hospitality and Tourism Research, 44*(2), 201–228. https://doi.org/10.1177/1096348019892071

Jansson, A. (2015). Interveillance: A new culture of recognition and mediatization. *Media and Communication, 3*(3), 81–90. https://doi.org/10.17645/mac.v3i3.305

Jones, Q. (1997). Virtual-communities, virtual settlements & cyber-archaeology: A theoretical outline. *Journal of Computer-Mediated Communication, 3*(3). https://doi.org/10.1111/j.1083-6101.1997.tb00075.x

Koh, J., & Kim, Y. G. (2001). Sense of virtual community: Determinants and the moderating role of the virtual community origin. *Proceedings of the ICIS, 2001*, 47. https://aisel.aisnet.org/icis2001/47

Lewins, A., & Silver, C. (2007). *Using software in qualitative research*. Sage.

McMillan, D. W., & Chavis, D. M. (1986). Sense of community: A definition and theory. *Journal of Community Psychology, 14*(1), 6–23. https://doi.org/10.1002/1520-6629(198601)14:1%3C6::AID-JCOP2290140103%3E3.0.CO;2-I

Miles, M. B., & Huberman, A. M. (1994). *Qualitative data analysis: An expanded sourcebook*. Sage.

Nonnecke, B., Preece, J., & Andrews, D. (2004). What lurkers and posters think of each other. In *Proceedings of the 37th Annual Hawaii International Conference on System Sciences.* doi: https://doi.org/10.1109/HICSS.2004.1265462.

Papacharissi, Z. (2010). A networked self. In Z. Papacharissi (Ed.), *A networked self: Identity, community, and culture on social network sites* (pp. 304–318). Routledge.

Patton, M. Q. (2002). *Qualitative research and evaluation methods: Integrating theory and practice*. Sage.

Porter, C. E. (2004). A typology of virtual communities: A multi-disciplinary foundation for future research. *Journal of Computer-Mediated Communication, 10*(1). https://doi.org/10.1111/j.1083-6101.2004.tb00228.x

Rainie, H., & Wellman, B. (2012). *Networked: The new social operating system*. MIT Press.

Rheingold, H. (2000). *The virtual community: Homesteading on the electronic frontier*. MIT Press.

Ricoeur, P. (2009). *Memory, history, forgetting*. University of Chicago Press.

Sun, R., & Asencio, H. D. (2019). Using social media to increase nonprofit organizational capacity. *International Journal of Public Administration, 42*(5), 392–404. https://doi.org/10.1080/01900692.2018.1465955

Trottier, D. (2012). Interpersonal surveillance on social media. *Canadian Journal of Communication, 37*(2), 319–332. https://doi.org/10.22230/cjc.2012v37n2a2536

Van Dijk, J. A. (1999). The one-dimensional network society of Manuel Castells. *New Media and Society, 1*(1), 127–138. https://doi.org/10.1177/1461444899001001015

Vittadini, N. (2018). *Social media studies. I social media alla soglia della maturità: storia, teorie e temi*. FrancoAngeli.

Webster, F. (2006). *Theories of the information society*. Routledge.

Wellman, B. (2001a). Little boxes, glocalization, and networked individualism. In M. Tanabe, P. van den Besselaar & T. Ishida (Eds.), *Lecture notes in computer science: Vol. 2362. Digital cities II: Computational and sociological approaches* (pp. 10–25). doi:https://doi.org/10.1007/3-540-45636-8_2.
Wellman, B. (2001b). Physical place and cyberplace: The rise of personalized networking. *International Journal of Urban and Regional Research, 25*(2), 227–252. https://doi.org/10.1111/1468-2427.00309
Wellman, B. (2004). The three ages of internet studies: ten, five and zero years ago. *New Media & Society, 6*(1), 123–129. https://doi.org/10.1177/1461444804040633
Yin, R. K. (2003). *Case study research. Design and methods* (3rd ed.). Sage.

Stefano Agostini holds a PhD in Communication Sciences ("UGent"—University of Ghent) and in Theory and Social Research ("Sapienza"—University of Rome). His research focuses on social media studies, preferably investigated by a qualitative approach. He also did research about non-profit organizations and genre studies.

Giovanna Gianturco, PhD, Full Professor of Sociology at Department of Communication and Social Research. Professor of Qualitative Methods and Sociology at Sapienza University of Rome, Faculty of Politic Sciences, Sociology and Communication

Scientific Topics

Research and teaching focus on some sociological themes (social change, migration, sport, family, and education) and on the research's methodology, with particular reference to the use of the qualitative approach. Such experience is documented from publications, researches, and conferences (national and international) shares as chairman or speaker from 1993, as well as from the didactic (national and international) activity from 1997.

Peter Mechant holds a PhD in Communication Sciences from Ghent University (2012) which focused on interactivity in a Web 2.0 context and posited a conceptual framework to explore how software enables and constrains agency and engagement.

Until mid-2005, Peter worked as an ICT project coordinator for an e-business firm. He studied several scripting and programming languages during and after this period. After joining MICT, Peter has been mainly working on a variety of research projects related to e-gov (open and linked data), smart cities, social software, and online communities.

As senior researcher, he is involved in managing projects and project proposals on a European, national, as well as regional level, and he helps expanding and enhancing MICT's offering toward the scientific research community. Peter currently works as a doctoral assistant at the Department of Communication Studies where he is, among others, lecturer-in-charge for the course Encyclopedia of Communication Sciences and promotor of bachelor and master theses.

Chapter 8
Retracing Algorithms: How Digital Social Research Methods Can Track Algorithmic Functioning

Biagio Aragona and Francesco Amato

Introduction

The expanding use of algorithms in society has called for the emergence of "critical algorithm studies" (Seaver, 2013; Gillespie, 2014). In this chapter, we present four cases of how digital traces may be used for studying algorithms and testing their quality in terms of data, models, and outcomes. We employ digital unobtrusive methods, such as search as research and Application Programming Interfaces (APIs).

The contextual use of algorithms that support decision-making processes is an increasingly frequent phenomenon within social organizations (Nakamura, 2013; Grosser, 2014; Aragona & De Rosa, 2018). Studies that analyze the contextual nature of algorithms have unfolded in several fields, spanning from media studies to chemistry and from social sciences to humanities. These critical algorithm studies pay particular attention to the social and political consequences of outputs, for example, the algorithmic circulation of content influences cultural consumption (Beer, 2013), how the massive use of algorithms affects markets and finance (Mackenzie, 2019), or how algorithms can reinforce inequalities and embed cultural bias (Lupton, 2015; Noble, 2018; Espeland & Yung, 2019; Airoldi, 2020; Aragona, 2020). Over the past 5 years, substantial literature has developed on the subject (Beer, 2013; Pasquale, 2015; O'Neil, 2016; Bucher, 2018; Eubanks, 2018). The critical study of algorithms is a process by which the social sciences can make an important contribution (Koene et al., 2019).

This chapter focuses on the methods of social research that can be employed for auditing algorithms to gain a greater understanding of algorithmic functioning (Amaturo & Aragona, 2021).

B. Aragona (✉) · F. Amato
Department of Social Science, University of Naples Federico II, Naples, Italy
e-mail: aragona@unina.it; francesco.amato2@unina.it

F. Comunello et al. (eds.), *What People Leave Behind*, Frontiers in Sociology and Social Research 7, https://doi.org/10.1007/978-3-031-11756-5_8

Different social science methods can be used for the critical study of algorithms. These can be classified through two basic elements: the level of obtrusiveness and whether they require access to the algorithm assemblage. Here, the main focus is on the use of two digitally unobtrusive methods. The first is the search as research, which uses the queries that users make on search engines for research objectives (Salganik, 2019). The second unobtrusive method relies on the Application Programming Interfaces (APIs). Through four examples, it is shown how digital traces could be effectively used for auditing algorithms (Aragona, 2021).

The first example is taken from the Noble's academic research (2018), run between 2009 and 2015, that investigated the relationship between search engines and racism particularly focusing on gender. Noble notes that algorithms are not neutral, but rather can be influenced by the biases of those who produced them. Noble employed different combinations of keywords related to gender and race on Google search engine to estimate discrimination biases. The second example is based on the "Happy white woman" case on Google Images. The third example is by *Algorithm Watch* (Kayser-Bril, 2020) and shows how the algorithm used by Google Vision Cloud API, an automatic image classification service, produced different results based on the color of the skin of individuals. The last example is a quasi-experiment created by Barsan (2021) of *Wunderman Thompson*, who tested different image classification services (Google, IBM, and Microsoft) for gender bias.

All the four pieces of research highlights how digital traces may be analyzed with different digital research methods for the study of algorithms.

In the next section, we present the rationale of critical algorithm studies by explaining why they should become privileged objects of social research. In Sect. "Methods for Researching Algorithms," we outline the methods for researching algorithms through digital traces. The final section illustrates the four examples and the main results. Some final remarks and the limits of our work are drawn in the conclusions.

Critical Algorithm Studies

With the rapid intensification of the datafication process, which is concerned especially with bureaucracies, governments, and policies, the need for a critical study on algorithms has arisen (Espeland & Stevens, 1998; Visentin, 2018). In response to this, various scholars from different research fields have begun to focus on the nature of algorithms more generally (Geiger, 2014; Montfort et al., 2012), on the effects they produce in specific sectors of society (Amoore, 2006; Pasquale, 2015), or, even more specifically, on the code construction procedures (Gillespie, 2014; Seaver, 2013).

Several authors overcame the technical vision, in favor of a more complex approach that recognizes the crucial role that algorithms play in traditional social, political, and economic institutions, for example, to prevent and combat crime in the context of predictive policing or to support choices regarding hiring and firing in the workplace and, more generally, their influence on social reality (O'Neil, 2016; Boyd & Crawford, 2012; Nakamura, 2013; Grosser, 2014; Tufekci, 2015). Recent literature is cohesive in the identification of algorithms as socio-technical constructs, considered as the result of the combination of social and technical knowledge (Aragona & Felaco, 2018). In the context of "critical algorithm studies," there is widespread agreement in considering the algorithm as a more complex set of steps defined to produce specific results in which social and material practices that have their own cultural, historical, and institutional nature are intertwined (Montfort et al., 2012; Takhteyev, 2012; Napoli, 2013; Dourish, 2016; Aragona & De Rosa, 2017). The objectivity, impartiality, and consequent claim of reliability of algorithms are contested, underlining that the same codes are not mere abstractions but also have a social and political value (Porter, 1995; Gillespie, 2014). This socio-technical production implies a socio-cultural influence that—deeply stratified at the various levels of the development of the algorithmic formulation—emerges during the implementation of the algorithm. As a result, algorithms cannot be defined as neutral constructs. The technical implementation of the code is influenced by the *milieu* of the producer and is imbued with its personal evaluations (Simondon, 2017).

At the same time, the algorithms could have unexpected effects and automatically disadvantage and discriminate against different social and demographic groups. Eubanks (2018), for example, notices that in the United States, bad designed algorithms, uncorrected indexes, and poor computer systems are denying many requests for health, food, or economic aid. The redlining of beneficiaries through algorithms, which was supported by neoliberal logic as an antidote to inefficiency and waste, has in some cases impacted heavily on the lives of the poorest citizens and socially excluded, especially African Americans. Another famous case that shows the opacity of algorithms is the Correctional Offender Management Profiling for Alternative Sanctions (COMPAS). This is an algorithmic decision tool employed by US courts in many states to estimate the recidivism of the defendants The fairness of this tool has been questioned, because it may exacerbate inequalities. Black defendants were almost twice as likely as whites to be labelled a higher risk of recidivism but not actually re-offend, whereas white defendants were much more likely than blacks to be labelled lower risk but went on to commit other crimes. Different false-positive rates suggested racial bias.

Both cases show that one of the main problems that specifically concerns algorithms is the lack of transparency and accountability. Often, they are defined as codes, whose attribution of accountabilities remains opaque and ends up weighing on the overall system of those who produced it. Digital traces may allow us to investigate the fairness of the algorithms and to make them accountable.

Methods for Researching Algorithms

The critical study of algorithms makes use of both technical and social research methods.

The methods for studying algorithms are distinguished on two dichotomies. The first distinction is whether the methods are used in an analogue or digital environment. This choice is a critical step for the researcher to achieve his goals. If the primary objective is to study the assemblage, it might be possible to conduct a participatory observation using ethnography. Otherwise, on the other hand, if the goal is to investigate the algorithm's outputs based on certain inputs, the use of the digital context would be an adequate choice.

The second dichotomy sees obtrusive methods contrasted with unobtrusive ones. For example, the discrete deconstruction of algorithms via document analysis or code testing may provide insight into how an algorithm works, but provide little understanding of the algorithm's designers' intent. The danger is that the researcher may interpret the data using a self-referential method based on ideas that solely correspond to its normative, cognitive, and emotional foundations. Interviews with designers and programmers, as well as the ethnography of a coding team, are examples of obtrusive research within the algorithm assemblage (Aragona & Felaco, 2019). The interviewees are asked how they defined the objectives and turned them into code in terms of languages and technologies, practices, influences, and limits (Diakopoulos, 2016).

A method that could be used for the study of black-boxed algorithms is the walkthrough. The walkthrough method is an unobtrusive method that allows the researcher to interact with the user interface of an algorithm when it cannot use the APIs. This research method allows us to understand the technological mechanisms and the cultural references that underlie its functioning. The researcher, through its application, can approach the algorithm by experiencing the effects as perceived by the users. The walkthrough method involves the production of documentation, such as the field notes. Through this method, it is possible to develop further research focused on the user and his relationship with the algorithm. Experiments and quasi-experiments are further methods for studying algorithms. Through the use of experiments, it is possible to investigate the risks of algorithms in automating inequalities. However, an experimental design must satisfy several conditions. Sampling and assignment of units to groups is probabilistic. Furthermore, there is a control group that does not receive the treatment. Also, the treatment needs to be measured. The experiments can be conducted in both analogue and digital contexts and allow the researcher to study characteristics of the algorithms such as fairness and transparency.

Two methods are presented below, both of which are digital and unobtrusive and make use of digital traces.

The first method is the search as research, where the researcher makes use of the search engines of the digital platform as a tool for gathering data. By querying the search engine, it is possible to investigate the answers that the algorithm provides to the researcher's requests. This method allows the researcher to investigate the social impact of algorithms when their assemblage is black boxed (Pasquale, 2015). In many cases, the use of this technique is necessary, since the product and its code have very high levels of opacity, effectively making the entire algorithmic assemblage unintelligible.

The second method is the Application Programming Interfaces, which are a set of functions and procedures that allow us to interact with the algorithm being studied. Products and services that offer this possibility are certainly at a different level of opacity compared to black boxes, but at the same time, they place constraints on the methods and purposes of use that can be obtained through the use of these tools. It is important to note that the APIs are not provided for research purposes only. Their origin is to be found in the value production and datafication that lead digital companies to provide third-party manufacturers with the tools to integrate these services into their applications. In some cases, such as that of Twitter, the use of APIs for research purposes is highly regulated. Through the use of APIs, it is possible to obtain some of the information that the algorithm processes, and therefore, the researcher approaches how the data is collected and constructed by the algorithm. The APIs are designed primarily as a tool to be granted to third-party producers with a view to integration between platforms. This possible use of APIs allows the creation of new products that can process data and information through the recombination of multiple services, opening the doors to unconventional uses or not implemented by those who produced the algorithm in the first place.

Digital Traces and Algorithm Studies

A first example of the use of digital traces for researching algorithms is the one offered by Noble's research work described thoroughly in her book, *Algorithms of Oppression*. The scholar was able to highlight how, between 2009 and 2015, the Google Search algorithm perpetrated gender and racial discrimination. Noble interrogated the Google search engine to reconstruct how its algorithm interpreted certain keywords. Her research interest, also driven by a feminist perspective, led her to investigate the representation of the female gender in the search engine and more specifically the condition of black women. Starting from these premises, Noble questioned the search engine in various ways regarding the representation of women and men and then, again, between white women and black women. By querying the search engine, Noble analyzed the results proposed by Google's autocompletion function, noting how the proposals suggested by the algorithm were discriminatory. It is in this context that the scholar develops the formulation that gives her study its title. The use of the self-completion proposed by Google search engine is only one of the techniques used by Noble. She spent a significant amount of time analyzing the results pages and related content, noting how the portrayal of black women was always associated with erotic behaviors. White men and women, on the other hand, had very different outcomes. The search was not limited to the search engine's suggested web results and web pages but also included other observations made on the images. Noble continued her investigation using the image search. It is precisely from this in-depth analysis that the researcher obtained further results which highlighted the serious discrimination implemented by the search engine.

Fig. 8.1 Anonymised screenshot of Google search results images of "Happy black woman." Obtained on 02/23/22

Noble notes that there is almost a monopoly in the search engine sector that, together with the presence of advertising systems and services that underlie private interests, there has been strong support for sponsoring the content of white people. Research carried out on paid advertising was an additional element in highlighting discrimination against black women. At this point, Noble argues that the combination of these factors can lead to a culture of racism. The growth of search engines, as tools increasingly used, would represent the main point in the spread of these biases. Specifically, she points out how the errors and discrimination carried out by algorithms have concrete consequences on people's lives, directing toward the need to define their responsibilities. The results of her research have greatly contributed to contest algorithmic neutrality. Following Noble's research work, Google has repeatedly changed the Google search algorithm.

The second example that shows how biases may be incorporated in algorithms is the "Happy white woman" case. As Noble's research, also this algorithm bias was identified by using the search as research. Some early references about this case started in January 2021, but as of February 2022, it does not appear to have undergone significant changes. We carried out two searches on the Google Images search engine with the keywords "Happy black woman" and "Happy white woman." The results obtained by looking for the "Happy black women" are mainly photos and stock images, which represent black women intent on smiling and apparently happy. The images obtained from this search then appear to be in line with content that presumably would have been expected from the query entered. On the contrary, the results for "Happy white woman" show some particular images and do not feature many stock images or photos of smiling women. Rather, in most of the photos on the first page of the results, the "Happy white woman" is always along with a black man. Although it is not the aim of this chapter to develop a content analysis on the results of these searches, it is clear that the Google algorithm presents some problems in this specific query (Figs. 8.1 and 8.2).

A third recent experiment was carried out by Kayser-Bril of the non-governmental organization (NGO) *AlgorithmWatch*, engaged in monitoring

Fig. 8.2 Anonymised screenshot of Google search results images of "Happy white woman." Obtained on 02/23/22

and analyzing the impact of automated decision systems on society, which has produced evidence regarding the discriminatory criticalities present in Google Cloud Vision API. Cloud Vision is a Google service that allows developers to analyze image content through the use of ever-evolving machine learning models (Kelleher, 2019). This description indicates that Google is providing a business-to-business service that is not intended for non-commercial use. These Cloud Vision APIs, according to Google, would be able to detect the content of an image with extreme precision. When the APIs' functionalities are examined in detail, it becomes clear how they can detect labels, explicit contents, places, reference points, faces, and image attributes. Kayser-Bril submitted two similar images to Vision API, representing a hand holding a laser thermometer, with the difference that one hand was white-skinned and one black-skinned. The result proposed by Vision API has not been the same for the two images. The algorithm determined that the object in the white hand was a "monocular," while it mistook the same object for a gun when it was detected in the black hand. The cause of this error is inherent in the machine learning techniques and models used to train the Cloud Vision algorithm. In this regard, Kayser-Bril concludes that probably more images of black people in violent contexts were provided to the algorithm than those of white people. As a result of this type of learning process, black people may be associated more frequently with the concept of violence. From this experiment, it is clear how, even in the absence of human manipulation, given by the socio-technical nature of the algorithms, through an uncontrolled learning process, the algorithmic constructs can develop the same bias that concerns individuals (Konrad & Böhle, 2019). Individuals may suffer severe consequences as a result of such biases. In contexts where algorithmic tracking associates facial detection with that of weapons, serious discrimination can arise for citizens if these algorithms present similar biases. The police forces, but especially the airport ones, often equipped with cutting-edge technologies to prevent threats, use predictive algorithms which, through the use of algorithms trained through specific models, can provide important support in the prevention of crimes (Uchida, 2014; Dieterich et al., 2016; Ferguson, 2017). If the algorithms were to present such biases, how would it be possible to still consider them as reliable sources for the security of citizenship? Critical studies on algorithms through digital traces allow in these circumstances to investigate the algorithmic construct and provide clear evidence of the social impact that the algorithm has on society. On April 6, 2020, Google implemented the changes suggested by Kayser-Bril, correctly detecting the laser thermometers without being influenced by the user's skin color.

A final example of how using traces for studying algorithms is a quasi-experiment that revealed sexist bias was conducted by Barsan (2021), director of data science at Wunderman Thompson, a marketing firm. Barsan was developing a tool that would allow authorities to connect to thousands of street cameras and determine the percentage of pedestrians wearing masks at any given time. As in the previous case study, the image recognition software APIs offered by Google Vision Cloud, IBM Watson, and Microsoft Computer Vision were also used in this research. These software were intended to enhance the mask detection tool developed by Wunderman Thompson. However, these reports showed gender bias when tested on self-portraits of people wearing partial face masks. This was found directly by Barsan when she uploaded a photo of herself wearing a mask to test the accuracy of the Vision Cloud APIs. The analysis resulted in ten labels, two of which are of particular interest: the first, 94.51% "Duct tape," and the second, 73.92% "Mask." Although most of the labels were adherent to the image inserted by Barsan, the presence of the "duct tape" with a confidence level associated with 94.51% was surprising. Based on these results, Barsan wondered why Vision Cloud identified the mask with the duct tape with so much association and continued her investigation. Two more tests were conducted after the first. Firstly, she wore a ruby red mask and then a blue surgical mask. The confidence levels for "duct tape" decreased in these cases, but they were still 87% and 66%, respectively. Surprisingly, the keyword "mask" from the labels, which was applied to 74% in the first example, was not applied at all in this case. This evidence led Barsan to conduct the quasi-experiment. Her hypothesis was to see if Cloud Vision API could classify differently men and women who were wearing masks. To achieve this, her team formed 2 groups of 265 images each, one with images of men and the other with those of women. The final corpora contained two groups of images, respectively, of men and women, in different contexts, dressed in different ways, and with various types of masks. As for the male group, Vision Cloud correctly identified 36% of personal protective equipment (PPE), while 27% of cases identified an association with facial hair and, finally, 15% as duct tape. For the female group, on the other hand, the PPE was associated only 19% of the time, while for 28%, it was identified as duct tape. In the case of women, the association with facial hair was detected at 8%. From these data, it emerges that as regards women, duct tape was associated almost twice as often as men. This quasi-experiment conducted by Barsan produced results similar to what Kayser-Bril noted the previous year. Again, Cloud Vision's machine learning algorithm may have been trained with inadequate data and which, as a result, produced this bias. Moreover, even before the arrival of the SARS-CoV-2

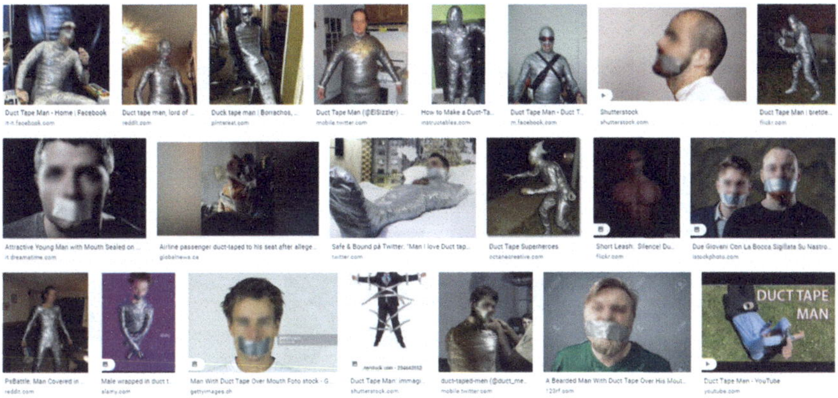

Fig. 8.3 Anonymised screenshot of Google search results images of "Duct tape man." Obtained on 02/23/22

pandemic, generic masks and PPE were tools widely used in healthcare facilities and laboratories.

Barsan and her team ran the same experiment on the image recognition services of IBM Watson Visual Recognition and Microsoft Azure Cognitive Services Computer Vision. In the case of IMB Watson, the labels "Restraint chains" and "gag" were returned with the same value, indicating that they were present in 10% of men's images and 23% of women's. The mask, on the other hand, was detected 12% for men and only 5% for women. The average confidence value for the gag label was around 0.79 for women, while it was 0.75 for men. This indicates how, unlike Google's algorithm, IBM's was found to be less partial. With Microsoft Azure, no gender bias was detected, but the algorithm correctly classified the masks only 9% for men and 5% for women. The biggest associations were with the "fashion accessories" label with 40% for women and 13% for men.

Through these experiments and the results obtained, Barsan reports that such evidence is not the result of bad intentions. Rather, they serve as a reminder that prejudices and stereotypes can exist in learning models. This is one of the ways that social biases are replicated in software. Figures 8.3 and 8.4 show the results of our search on the Google Images search engine using, respectively, the keywords "Duct tape man" and "Duct tape woman." This research was performed during the month of February 2022. The results show that even using different services, the bias of the Google search engine's algorithm is still present.

However, if Barsan hadn't conducted these tests, it's unlikely that the algorithms' hidden bias would have been discovered, and a tool to detect how many people on the streets wear masks would have been developed with the help of these algorithms. Testing the tools on digital traces such as images was a valuable research strategy to control the biases and reliability of the Vision API system.

Fig. 8.4 Anonymised screenshot of Google search results images of "Duct tape woman." Obtained on 02/23/22

Conclusions

The examples shown here are all primarily linked to Google services, but similar problems can be retraced in any algorithmic assemblage. They all served us to observe how digital traces can represent valuable data for finding evidence on the functioning of algorithms and increasing transparency and accountability. Interacting with the black boxes implies the need to consider the levels of opacity that separate the researcher from the algorithm. As Noble has effectively shown, through the search as research method, it is still possible to trace how algorithms work. In addition, the last two examples clearly shown how, through the APIs, it is possible to identify the presence of racial and gender discrimination. In a digital society where the presence of algorithms is at all levels of society, the need for critical studies on algorithms becomes a fundamental requirement to which the social sciences can and should make their contribution. As emerged from the examples, the issues that an unregulated use of algorithms can raise concern typical biases and controversies investigated by social research. The use of digital traces can provide valuable evidence on the social impact that algorithms have on society, something that the technical sciences alone cannot address.

References

Airoldi, M. (2020). Lo spettro dell'algoritmo e le scienze sociali. Prospettive critiche su macchine intelligenti e automazione delle disuguaglianze. *Polis, 35*(1), 111–128.

Amaturo, E., & Aragona, B. (2021). Critical optimism: A methodological posture to shape the future of digital social research. *Italian Sociological Review, 11*.

Amoore, L. (2006). Biometric borders: Governing mobilities in the war on terror. *Political Geography, 25*, 336–351.

Aragona, B. (2020). Sistemi di decisione algoritmica e disuguaglianze sociali: le evidenze della ricerca, il ruolo della politica. *La Rivista delle Politiche Sociali, 2*(20), 213–226.
Aragona, B. (2021). *Algorithm audit: Why, what, and how?* (1st ed.). Routledge.
Aragona, B., & De Rosa, R. (2017). Unpacking big data in education. A research framework. *Statistics, Politics and Policy, 8*(2), 123–137.
Aragona, B., & De Rosa, R. (2018). Policy making at the time of big data: Datascape, datasphere, data culture. *Sociologia Italiana, 11*, 173–187.
Aragona, B., & Felaco, C. (2018). La costruzione socio-tecnica degli algoritmi. Una ricerca nelle infrastrutture dati. *The Lab's Quarterly, 20*(4), 97–115.
Aragona, B., & Felaco, C. (2019). Big data from below. Researching data assemblages. *Tecnoscienza: Italian Journal of Science & Technology Studies, 10*(1), 51–70.
Barsan, I. (2021). *Quantifying the accuracy of vision/facial recognition on identifying PPE masks*. Retrieved February 20, 2022, from https://www.wundermanthompson.com/insight/ai-and-gender-bias
Beer, D. (2013). *Popular culture and new media: The politics of circulation*. Palgrave Macmillan.
Boyd, D., & Crawford, K. (2012). Critical questions for big data: Provocations for a cultural, technological, and scholarly phenomenon. *Information, Communication & Society, 15*(5), 662–679.
Bucher, T. (2018). *If .... then: Algorithmic power and politics*. Oxford University Press.
Diakopoulos, N. (2016). Accountability in algorithmic decision making. *Communications of the ACM, 59*(2), 56–62.
Dieterich, W., Mendoza, C., & Brennan, T. (2016). *COMPAS risk scales: Demonstrating accuracy equity and predictive parity*. Northpoint.
Dourish, P. (2016). Algorithms and their others: Algorithmic culture in context. *Big Data & Society, 3*(2), 1–11.
Espeland, W. N., & Stevens, M. L. (1998). Commensuration as a social process. *Annual Review of Sociology, 24*(1), 313–343.
Espeland, W. N., & Yung, W. (2019). Ethical dimensions of quantification. *Social Science Information, 58*(2), 238–260.
Eubanks, V. (2018). *Automating inequality: How high-tech tools profile, police, and punish the poor*. St. Martin's Press.
Ferguson, A. G. (2017). *The rise of big data policing: Surveillance, race, and the future of law enforcement*. New York University Press.
Geiger, R. S. (2014). Bots, bespoke, code and the materiality of software platforms. *Information, Communication & Society, 17*(3), 342–356.
Gillespie, T. (2014). The relevance of algorithms. In T. Gillespie, P. Boczkowski, & K. A. Foot (Eds.), *Media technologies: Essays on communication, materiality, and society* (pp. 167–194). MIT Press.
Grosser, B. (2014). What do metrics want? How quantification prescribes social interaction on Facebook. *Computational Culture, 1*(4).
Kayser-Bril, N. (2020). *Google apologizes after its vision AI produced racist results*, Algorithm Watch. Retrieved February 20, 2022, from https://algorithmwatch.org/en/google-vision-racism/
Kelleher, J. D. (2019). *Deep learning*. MIT Press.
Koene, A., Clifton, C., Hatada, Y., Webb, H., & Richardson, R. (2019). *A governance framework for algorithmic accountability and transparency*. European Union.
Konrad, K., & Böhle, K. (2019). Socio-technical futures and the governance of innovation processes—An introduction to the special issue. *Futures, 109*, 101–107.
Lupton, D. (2015). *Digital sociology*. Routledge.
MacKenzie, D. (2019). How algorithms interact: Goffman's "interaction order" in automated trading. *Theory, Culture & Society, 36*(2), 39–59.
Montfort, N., Baudoin, P., Bell, J., Bogost, I., Douglass, J., Marino, M. C., Mateas, M., Reas, C., Sample, M., & Vawter, N. (2012). *10 print chr$ (205.5 + rnd (1)): GOTO 10*. MIT Press.
Nakamura, L. (2013). The socio-algorithmics of race: Sorting it out in jihad worlds. In M. Shoshana & G. Kelly (Eds.), *The new media of surveillance* (pp. 159–162). Routledge.

Noble, S. (2018). *Algorithms of oppression: How search engines reinforce racism*. New York University Press.
Napoli, P. M. (2013). *The algorithm as institution: Toward a theoretical framework for automated media production and consumption*. Fordham University Schools of Business Research Paper.
O'Neil, C. (2016). *Weapons of math destruction: How big data increases inequality and threatens democracy*. Crown Random House.
Pasquale, F. (2015). *The black box society: The secret algorithms that control money and information*. Harvard University Press.
Porter, T. M. (1995). *Trust in numbers: The pursuit of objectivity in science and public life*. Princeton University Press.
Salganik, M. J. (2019). *Bit by bit: Social research in the digital age*. Princeton University Press.
Seaver, N. (2013). Knowing algorithms. *Media in Transition, 8*, 1–12.
Simondon, G. (2017). *On the mode of existence of technical objects*. Univocal Publishing.
Takhteyev, Y. (2012). *Coding places: Software practice in a South American City*. MIT Press.
Tufekci, Z. (2015). Algorithmic harms beyond Facebook and Google: Emergent challenges of computational agency. *Colorado Technology Law Journal, 13*(2), 203.
Uchida, C. (2014). Predictive policing. In G. Bruinsma & D. Weisburd (Eds.), *Encyclopedia of criminology and criminal justice* (pp. 3871–3880). Springer.
Visentin, C. (2018). Il potere razionale degli algoritmi tra burocrazie e nuovi idealtipi. *The Lab's Quarterly, 20*(3), 47–72.

Biagio Aragona is Associate Professor of Sociology at the University of Naples "Federico II," where he teaches Social Research Methods and Digital Methods and Big Data. He is managing editor of the AIS Journal of Sociology—Sociologia Italiana and board member of the Italian Sociological Association (AIS). His research activity has always been dedicated to the use of secondary data for the analysis of inequalities and, more recently, to the social challenges risen by the increasing use of big data and algorithms in policy making. He has extensively published on these subjects.

Francesco Amato, Ph.D. student in Social Sciences and Statistics at the University of Naples "Federico II." His research project intends to produce evidence regarding the intentional and unintended social impacts of algorithms, through the use of social research techniques. He has a master's degree in digital sociology and web analysis with a thesis in digital law developed through empirical research on cookies and the processing of personal data. His research doctorate was funded by the PON Research and Innovation plan in the field of innovative research doctorates relating to innovation issues.

Chapter 9
Visible and Invisible Traces: Managing the Self on Social Media Platforms

Gaia Casagrande

Introduction

When we talk about *traces* in digital environments, we mean all the information that we leave online which profiles our activities, tastes, and preferences. These can be conveyed directly or indirectly and can refer to actions that we decide to perform online or even the responses to such actions.

The most classic example of traces that we experience when we access any web page concerns the accepting of *cookies*—strings of text that are used to report and store server-side the information we are going to produce on that website. The cookies keep track of the information we enter online. Two more classic examples of traces are our browsing history, which records our navigation paths, and web mapping services like Google Maps. Even activities, such as uploading a new profile photo, sharing a funny piece of content, or a conversation with a friend, are pieces of information that say something about us, which become *traces that we leave behind* in the social media digital environment.

This work aims to question the traces we leave on social media platforms, either intentionally or unintentionally, and, especially, those we *do not* want to leave. These traces describe us, providing clues about us that are accessible to third parties, precisely because of the "public" dimension of these platforms: they portray us and, in turn, influence the idea that we have of ourselves. For this reason, this chapter focuses on the traces that we voluntarily leave behind on social media platforms, dictated by the selection of what we want to show and what we want to hide and how these affect our perception of ourselves.

Firstly, this research topic will be addressed by framing the concept of *social media platforms* and investigating via what processes the activities we perform in

G. Casagrande (✉)
Department of Social and Political Sciences, University of Milan, Milan, Italy
e-mail: gaia.casagrande@unimi.it

F. Comunello et al. (eds.), *What People Leave Behind*, Frontiers in Sociology and Social Research 7, https://doi.org/10.1007/978-3-031-11756-5_9

these digital environments are translated into data—which are then collected and organized.

Consequently, the focus will shift to how the data that we enter into these platforms profile us, thus offering a description of ourselves that is the result of a dynamic relationship between the user and the platform. This process influences the perception we have of ourselves, of our image mediated by the platform, and induces us to manage those pieces of information.

Thereafter, these theoretical premises will be discussed and compared with the empirical data which emerged from 20 qualitative interviews conducted with 20 young journalists who are accustomed to mediating their public image online. The interviews were conducted for the research of my doctoral dissertation, from which part of this chapter is taken (Casagrande, 2021).

The findings suggest that both the intentional and the unintentional traces we leave online contribute to the profiling of our public image. They tell something about ourselves, and by managing these traces, we also manage the image we want to portray. Moreover, the decision of what to share and make visible, and what to keep private, is the consequence of a personal interpretation of the algorithm, as a result of the dynamic between data, users, and platforms. Therefore, not only the data we input but also those we receive as outputs shape not only our public image but also the perception we have of ourselves.

Social Media Platforms: How Do They Collect and Organize Our Data?

Social Media Platforms and Online Traces

The analysis proposed in this chapter starts from the digital environments of social media platforms, in which we leave traces of ourselves, directly or indirectly, voluntarily or involuntarily. Primarily, it is useful to clarify what a "digital platform" is.

For van Dijck, Poell, and de Waal, "an online 'platform' is a programmable digital architecture designed to organize interactions between users—not only end users but also corporate entities and public bodies. It is geared towards the systematic collection, algorithmic processing, circulation, and monetization of user data" (van Dijck et al., 2018 p. 4). Thus, the main characteristic of digital platforms is "to host and organize user content for public circulation, without having produced or commissioned it" (Gillespie, 2017 p. 1). Furthermore, the techno-commercial nature of social media brings out the communicative trend of the personalization of contents (Poell & van Dijck, 2015). This is determined by the platforms' algorithms which, by including or excluding certain signals, decide what can be "considered 'relevant' or 'trending'" (Ibid. p. 530). Indeed, through the specific affordances, social media enables users to make their connections as "personal" as possible, i.e., they encourage the tendency toward personalization.

From this perspective, the symbolic significance of the platforms' design choices and affordances is well explained by Facebook's "Like" button. Initially enabled only for content sharing, the "Like" button changed its function and meaning in 2011, when it was transformed into a content approval and rating index. Gerltiz and Helmond argue that the "Like" button enables data flows, turning user engagement into numbers. This has further consequences such as enabling device tracking and creating an infrastructure in which social interaction, as well as users' emotions and affections, is immediately transformed into data (Gerlitz & Helmond, 2013). These *social buttons* are present in many platforms and serve to recommend posts and pages. At the basis of the principle of recommendation or ranking, there is the possibility of creating a comparison: the recommendation or ranking vote is, in fact, visible both to the user affected by the evaluation and to the others, in order to establish some comparisons.

In short, the design choices as well as the algorithms underlying social media platforms modulate our social interactions, simultaneously transforming the information, or traces, we leave behind whenever we access or use these platforms into codified data.

Datafication, Big Social Data, and Self-Tracking

The process by which any object or phenomenon can be translated into data is described as *datafication* (Mayer-Schönberger & Cukier, 2013). Indeed, this process is about making any phenomenon or object quantifiable, so that it can be measured through shared parameters, cataloged, analyzed, and predicted.

Potentially everything can be translated into data; even intangible aspects such as emotions, experiences, and relationships can undergo this process. In social media platforms, every comment, word, recorded image, and emotion is part of an information flow that starts from the users, as an expression of sociality, and is converted into data.

Mark Coté (2014) identifies as *Big Social Data* all the information which comes from the mediated practices of our daily lives. To access any social media platform, we must generate *social data*, for instance, when we create our profile, and this is a structurally unavoidable requirement. Big Social Data, then, are generated as symbolic, affective, or informational contents and are the "result of spontaneous, contingent and free-form communicative sociality" (Ibid. p. 129). They materialize our daily symbolic practices, deployed in sociality and relationality.

This process, according to Cheney-Lippold (2017), also impacts our identity, since the data used to categorize users do not directly describe the users themselves, but rather standardized subjects according to the rules of the platforms. It is precisely from the act of sorting, categorizing, and evaluating that a user moves from being a person to being a "profile."

As academic Frank Pasquale pointed out, we live in the *black box society* (Pasquale, 2015), in which anyone can be labeled based on the information entered and then collected by, usually, companies or special analytics firms. Then, these companies can, for example, assign a score to each profile and decide how to rate a user. Therefore, a person may be marked as "unreliable" or "dangerous" in the database, without even being aware of it. However, the meaning of such labels, as "unreliable" or "dangerous," is not agreed upon, but attributed by the author of the algorithm.

Given this logic, characteristics related to our identity also undergo the same process. Aspects such as gender or age, for example, will not be consequent to the actual representation of the self, but to consumer choices: a subject will be identified as a woman or a man, young or old if the information entered identifies them as such. Consequently, our online identities are the result of a constant reshaping between the information we enter into the system and how it is interpreted by algorithms in an ever dynamic composition of our digital selves (Cheney-Lippold, 2017).

To better explain the circular dynamic involving data, users, and platforms, Deborah Lupton (2016) analyzes *self*-tracking practices and the digital devices that enable them such as apps that monitor weight control or evaluate a sports performance. Lupton states that through these apps, people who practice *self*-tracking can monitor themselves and, as a result, know themselves through data. Indeed, the information collected creates patterns and associations that can be identified and understood by the users. They recognize their own behaviors and can make changes in their lifestyles, for example, by deciding which food to buy for their diet or which route to take on their morning run. Consequently, *self*-knowledge and *self*-management pass through *self*-monitoring, mediated by the digital technologies.

In the process of intersection and interrelationship between data and users, people can get involved and respond emotionally to the outputs generated through *self*-tracking technologies. Such emotional responses are triggered especially when relationality is involved, and this is particularly true in the case of social media platforms, where it is impossible for users not to make a comparison between their own performances and those of others.

The practice of *self-tracking* (Lupton, 2016) causes users to be personally responsible for their own *self*-management and, consequently, also for all the invisible ensuing repercussions. For example, when the app compares daily miles traveled with those of another user, someone may respond to this information by deciding they want to "perform" better.

In social media platforms, among the various objects and phenomenon that can be datafied, there are also traces that are not immediately tangible such as our emotions and feelings and symbolic elements that animate our daily social and relational practices. We have just seen how this dynamic produces outputs that can easily manifest themselves even outside the online dimension and that, in turn, induces an activity or reaction in users.

Digital Selves and Digital Data: How Do We Manage Our Visible and Invisible Traces?

There is therefore a significant correlation between the data we enter online and the perception of our own identity, here understood as the result of the interpenetration between online and offline (Floridi, 2015).

For Goffman, "the self emerges from a social situation" (Goffman, 2009 p. XVI) and serves as an "indispensable code for conferring meaning on all social activities and for providing a basis for organizing them" (Ibid. p. XVIII). Individuals convey their identities both voluntarily, often verbally, and indirectly, via involuntary behaviors.

In this sense, social media platforms represent the ideal stage for *self*-presentation, for the interaction of public and private life, and for the negotiation of individual and collective identities (Papacharissi, 2011). This is partly due to the specific functions of the platforms, which allow users to manage aspects of their identity, at times strategically. In fact, through their architecture and design, these environments enable the creation of profiles, networks of contacts, and expressive and communicative capabilities. The affordances of social media platforms allow the representation of multiple online identities, in relation to different situational contexts, creating a new, mediated, perception of the self.

Identity and Visible Traces, Direct and Indirect

Nancy K. Baym (2010) emphasizes the presence of multiple representations of self in online environments, each of them authentic and genuine yet distinct. Both online and offline, these identities are often the result of a negotiation of what a person wants or can show, wants or can hide, wants or can communicate.

She argues that online we have several functions and tools at our disposal to trace our personal and social identity. Falling into the first case are the most well-known operations, which we could describe as *voluntary actions*, such as the identification through one's name or nickname; images, photos and video, or also avatar customization; the technical skills needed to costume and manage personal sites, or blogs; as well as more sophisticated functions on social network sites, which also provide information about our capabilities; finally, many social media platforms require—sometimes compulsorily—the compilation of certain categories of data, from biographical or demographic ones to more generic categories such as those related to cultural identification, like musical preferences or favorite books and TV shows.

All this information can be described as *traces* that, regardless of privacy settings, we can define as equally *visible to the user, to their contacts, and "to the platform,"* as data that will be recorded. These pieces of information are obtained *directly*, often through compilation operations.

Moreover, Baym explains that the quantity and type of our contacts also provide insights of users' identities and, when connections are made visible and traceable, become very useful in determining social reputation. Also, social status and political affiliations can be easily guessed by third parties through our social connections (Ibid. p. 112), even if this is sensitive information that people may not necessarily want to circulate.

Other sensitive data related to users' identities may be, for example, those related to gender, social class, and nationality. In addition, information can transpire from our language. Do we communicate in a formal or colloquial manner? Do we use foreign languages or dialects? Do we use interjections or quotations? Does our language indicate our age cohort or nationality? Again, preferences or dislikes could be indicators of users' class, socioeconomic level, and education.

In all these cases, the traces we leave of ourselves on the various platforms are *visible* because, for example, if we comment on a piece of content, we are revealing a language style that characterizes us. At the same time, these traces are also *indirect*, since they are not information explicitly requested by the platform. All the data we enter into social media provide traces, *direct or indirect*, which shape the various representations of ourselves.

For van Dijck (2013), users have learned to manage this information strategically, for example, by showing different sides of themselves in different platforms—in other words, *staging different identities*. Thus, a person can show a more playful and flirty side on Instagram while conveying an exclusively professional profile on LinkedIn, etc. However, in doing so, users are incentivized by the design and affordances of each platforms.

Context Collapse and Imagined Audience

The way we present ourselves changes according to the personal and public network, the context, and the environment. Therefore, even the practices related to *self-promotion* will have different characteristics depending on the social platform, the affordances it implies, the type of contacts in the network, and so on.

Moreover, in the digital environment of social media platforms, the traditional distinctions imposed by space and time are blurring, affecting what we imagine our target audience to be.

In this regard, Marwick and Boyd (2011) define as *imagined audience* the specific audience to which users *think* they are directing their content, even if on social media platforms *anyone* can potentially enjoy a piece of content. Indeed, users tend to "imagine" their audience based on clues, or traces, that they perceive within the digital environment. Therefore, when users present themselves on social media, they relate to an *imagined audience*, which does not necessarily reflect a real one.

This happens because social media "flattens multiple audiences into one—a phenomenon known as *context collapse*" (Ibid. p. 122). Users find themselves having to "manage" this type of audience that, due to the coexistence of various planes that we previously imagined as separate, brings out tensions between public and private aspects, between frontstage and backstage, thus shaping the identity and content conveyed by the user.

However, this dynamic also brings out the need to balance the desire of sharing the performance of the self with the necessity for privacy and to protect some sensitive or personal data from the risk of public dissemination.

Management of Personal Online Traces

Users are able to implement forms of control in managing their online identity. These actions are identified by Duffy and Chan (2019) with the concept of *imagined surveillance*, indicating the kind of responses consequent to both the scrutiny and the interaction with an "imagined audience (Litt, 2012; Litt & Hargittai, 2016) and the imagined affordances of individual platforms (Nagy & Neff, 2015)" (Ibid. p. 121). Indeed, with the term of *imagined surveillance*, these scholars identify those response mechanisms that users enact through social media as attempts in finding a balance between the tendency to visibility incentivized by platforms and the need to protect personal information.

In social media platforms, therefore, people modulate their activity according to the *imagined audience*, calibrating content, activities, and functions. In doing so, *surveillance practices* are put in place with respect to audiences, for example, through privacy settings; content, through self-surveillance or platform-specific presentations; and connections, which may point to one's identity, using pseudonyms or multiple pseudonyms (Ibid.).

According to Duffy and Chan, users have internalized an approach to a *surveillance culture* (Lyon, 2018; Zuboff, 2019) that leads to these acts of ubiquitous monitoring. In the qualitative study conducted by the two academics, it emerges that most respondents claim that ""you never know who is looking" at your social media profile(s)" (Duffy & Chan, 2019 p. 132), and consequently, preventive measures are put in place, such as the self-monitoring of their activities, which also includes the elimination of contents or materials as forms of *self*-surveillance, or the settings for the use of privacy, which refer to the technological possibilities of the platforms. Duffy and Chan argue that these activities cannot be understood as separate from each other, but rather as one.

Therefore, users manage representations of themselves online, both by strategically using the affordances of the platforms and, at the same time, by *self*-regulating and *self*-monitoring in order to protect their private and sensitive data.

On Self-Branding and Online Traces

The branding of the self for economic and career purposes (*self*-branding) is one of the main activities in which users must manage all the data that identifies and represents themselves. The online *self*-branding is declined in communicative practices that have the purpose of enhancing the reputation of the user, creating a professional, uniform, and credible public image. Underlying online *self*-branding is the idea that *visibility* is something to be strategically managed, because it implies as much the manifestation of one person's social situation as its economic value (Gandini, 2016; Draper, 2019). Therefore, these communicative acts are linked to the manifestation of a social identity, precisely because they are aimed to *build* a public self, and they can be directed and exhibited, but can also be subtle and implicit.

In this sense, the work of Brems et al. (2017) provides an interesting contribution, analyzing how journalists create their own brand on Twitter and certifying how *self*-branding activities expressed in an overly direct and assertive way can become counterproductive. The journalists they interviewed negatively evaluated activities that are too *self*-referred or too openly devoted to promoting their own content. In fact, they prefer a subtle and moderate approach, for example, by discussion with other users, expressing their opinions, and interacting with colleagues via private messaging.

This particular approach on *self*-branding is categorized by scholars as *implicit*, as opposed to more explicit forms of *self*-branding (Molyneux, 2014), which are flawed in conveying *authenticity* toward their audience. Among the forms of *implicit self-branding*, there are, for example, sharing a personal experience or a persona image rather than communicating strictly professional content, commenting and reacting to other users' content, and interacting through private messaging. All these activities create information that users leave in the digital environment: *traces* that describe them, *visible but indirect*.

Journalists are an effective professional target to investigate when exploring *self*-branding practices on social media. On the one hand, journalism has undergone processes of radical transformation precisely because of the innovations introduced by digital media and especially by social networks and mobile devices (Anderson et al., 2012; Bell et al., 2017). On the other hand, news and media professionals often have a need to publicly interact and, consequently, become able to manage the communication trends incentivized by these technologies in order to enlarge and reach their audience. Unavoidably, this implies embracing the trend toward personalization, as previously described by van Dijck.

Methodological Note

The aim of this chapter is to offer an insight into the traces we leave on online platforms, especially focusing on describing *both visible and invisible traces*, and the resulting implications on the perception we have of ourselves.

In this regard, the theoretical premises previously outlined have been supplemented by the empirical data obtained from 20 in-depth interviews, conducted with 20 young journalists at the beginning of their careers. The interviews were conducted between 2019 and 2020, with young professionals who represent the Millennial generation who grew up with digital technologies and social networks, in the shadow of the economic crisis of 2008 (Dimock, 2019). The participants, aged between 23 and 35, work in journalism in a variety of sectors—from cultural to political journalism, from foreign affairs to crime or local news—and with different contractual modalities, freelance, permanent, and fixed-term contracts.

This chapter focuses on the *intangible and invisible elements* that form part of the flux of data at the basis of the structure of social media platforms. As discussed previously, these invisible elements—or invisible *traces*—simultaneously provide indications about the public image of users while also affecting their perception of themselves.

Therefore, the analysis was carried out through a qualitative and hermeneutic-discursive approach, which better responded to the need to *qualify* the experiences of the participants, which can be complex and difficult to standardize. This approach, in fact, prioritizes *questioning* in order to be able to engage with the personal experiences of the subjects, accessing their worldview and the meanings of certain situations, actions, attitudes, and feelings, as well as the vision of themselves (Blumer, 1969). Among the various techniques used, the non-standardized and semi-structured interview is preferable, as it allows participants to deepen their point of view and provide details about their experiences, thoughts, and feelings (Pitrone, 1984; Losito, 2004; Gobo, 2011; Gobo & Mauceri, 2013).

As the questionnaire touched on personal topics, it was conducted by face-to-face interviews. All the participants were identified by using a non-probabilistic sample, *snowball sampling*, and all the information obtained from the questionnaires was anonymized.

Finally, the data collected from the interviews was processed via thematic analysis, following a survey strategy inspired by grounded theory (Strauss & Corbin, 1990), which is used to explore social processes not yet fully defined and, consequently, to propose new theoretical frameworks. The analysis, therefore, moves from the empirical material of the interviews by creating codes identified from the most recurrent keywords for each thematic area and then gives rise to new conceptual categories.

Tracking the Traces

Social Media and Self-Branding

From the data collected through the interviews, it emerges that for most participants, the use of social media platforms is professionally necessary, for *self*-branding purposes and as tools for keeping up to date, finding breaking news, and identifying and getting in touch with useful contacts.

The participants also demonstrated familiarity with the promotional strategies to be conveyed through their profiles or pages. These strategies vary, ranging from the simple scheduling of content sharing—i.e., on which days and at what time to post certain content—to more sophisticated monitoring and publishing techniques, sometimes using dedicated apps and software, or paid sponsorships. These activities are diversified for each social media platform, paying particular attention to make the most of the specific affordances.

In using these promotional strategies, the interviewees operate a conscious monitoring of their activities, thus putting in place a form of *self*-monitoring of their performance, as described by Deborah Lupton.

Self-Tracking and the Algorithmic Imaginary

As briefly described earlier, the movement between data, users, and platforms can induce forms of emotional responses in the users, even despite the stated familiarity with the use of communication strategies, and an approach geared toward the constant monitoring of data.

For example, one participant reported feeling directly responsible if their post receives fewer interactions than expected. In fact, even if that is a platform-mediated response, they addressed it to personal characteristics that their audience may "dislike" or to their personal failure in their ability to master "the algorithm" in order to engage with the audience.

This aspect was also confirmed in other interviews and indicates how users enact a sort of *interpretation of the algorithm* that gives reasons for both the activities performed and the outputs obtained. The interpretation of the algorithm confirms what Taina Bucher called with *algorithmic imaginary*, that is, how users "imagine, perceive and experience" (Bucher, 2017 p. 31) the way the algorithm works and react accordingly. Experiencing the algorithm through imagined processes produces real and concrete effects (Ibid.).

Therefore, it is not unusual to try to understand the logic underlying the platforms, while not actually knowing their mechanisms, but proceeding by intuition or by "rules" dictated by common sense. Thus, the interpretation of the algorithm induces the users to read the data input and output in a certain way, which is useful in justifying the promotional choices to be made, but, also, in trying to give an explanation when these choices are not particularly efficient. However, from a different perspective, the outcomes seem to fall in the personal sphere, as if the failure of a certain goal, like trying to reach more people, was to be attributed to an individual failure.

The concrete effects of the algorithm's interpretation manifest not only in the form of actions but also in the form of feelings and emotions. In this sense, *self-monitoring* activities related to the user's (online) performance are strictly linked to how users perceive or, indeed, *imagine* the platform to work. In short, when users try to keep *track of the traces* that concern them online, these can produce outputs that involve strictly personal aspects and encourage different types of reactions, *visible*—for example, when a user purchases a content sponsorship service—and *invisible*, for instance, when a user feels at fault.

Indirect Traces, Invisible Traces

I mentioned previously how users implement self-promotion practices that do not necessarily have to be direct and explicit but which, while remaining *visible*, are designed to convey communicative messages *indirectly*.

Among these, reporting the geographic location emerged frequently among interviewees. This can be done, for example, by creating an explicit post indicating that the person is or is about to go to a specific place, by posting unequivocal photos, or by using specific platform features such as registration or tagging. Sharing the geo-localization is useful for publicly communicating the physical presence in a particular place, in order to meet old and new contacts. Therefore, by publicly reporting their location, users leave visible traces on their profiles or pages, which have also an indirect communicative function. At the same time, the geo-location indirectly provides insights about users, for example, if they go to a certain place, such as a restaurant, and how often; if they travel more willingly within their country or if they prefer experiences abroad; if they frequently visit a certain city; and so on.

Another example of *visible but indirect traces* that users learn to manage on social media platforms concerns the selection of personal contacts. In fact, interviews have shown that managing the audience is part of *indirect* self-promotion activities. This can take various forms such as eliminating the connection with all those people who are no longer considered in line with the user's social media profiles, carefully selecting the people who can comment and interact with the published contents, or directing specific updates to a particular audience, for instance, tailoring the professional contents having already in mind a particular group of professionals.

Regarding the management of personal and professional contacts for promotional purposes, two interview respondents declared an interesting additional strategy. They stated that they purposely avoid communicating news, or any work update before the due date, for the fear that some colleague might steal their idea and in order to be among the first to deal with a specific topic. In such cases, it emerges that even the act of *not* posting and the act of *not* communicating are part of the user online relationships' management.

As stated by many scholars (Donath & Boyd, 2004; Walther et al., 2008; Baym, 2010), online relationships can provide information about us and determine our social status. The contacts we have on social media platforms and the people we interact with are traces, visible but indirect, that can tell something about us. Therefore, selecting contacts means managing the information about us, both *indirectly but visibly*, the contacts with whom we interact, and *indirectly and invisibly*, since even the contacts with whom we *do not* interact are instrumental in building a personal image.

Managing the Self Online Through Invisible Traces

The creation and management of the personal image is fundamental from the perspective of *self*-branding and can have an impact, direct or indirect, even on the perception of oneself.

For many of the interview participants, professional identity and personal identity overlap, especially online. In fact, in the logic of *self*-branding, a piece of work published on a rather anonymous social media profile might have less possibility of circulation and engagement compared to those who, instead, convey their content through better defined and recognizable profiles.

Several interviewees declared that they had made, either consciously, drastically, or more gradually, a change of image on their social media profiles in parallel with the progression and development of their careers. This "restyling" manifests in various forms such as changing personal information, like the profile photo and name or nickname, or paying greater attention to personal details. This kind of information can be labelled as *visible traces* on personal profiles, entered *directly and voluntarily*, in order to convey a certain public image.

However, the personal image can also be built as *a negative*, not only by deciding to select the content to be shared but also by selecting the "rhythm" and therefore sparing the posting so as not to overload potential readers and, at the same time, demonstrating to have a *quality* profile.

From the interviews with the target group, in fact, it emerged that they pay attention not only to what—and how much—to share but also to other kinds of activities, such as *minimizing* and measuring the interactions, deciding *not* to use the sharing (or *social)* buttons and carefully selecting the targeted audience. All these activities serve to build the desired public image, and therefore they too can be categorized as information that profiles the user—*traces*, in this case, *indirect and invisible*.

Conclusions

In this chapter, I have briefly explored some of the different types of traces that might profile us on social media platforms, traces that tell something about our (online) persona. There are *visible and direct traces*, usually the result of an explicit request to fill in, such as a request to create a social media profile: a photo or an image that describes us and details about tastes and preferences.

Some elements can be *visible*, but are the result of an *indirect* action, such as the amount and type of our contacts or the type of language we use.

There are also *visible traces that encompass both categories*, such as sharing geographical location. Sharing a location can be both a direct action that the user performs in order to report where they are and can also have the indirect function of being a communicative tool for the people who are in that place—instead of informing them directly, for example, through private messaging.

Finally, also *non-actions* can provide information about the user. *Not* over-producing and over-sharing contents, *measuring* reactions and comments to the content of other users, and *selecting* the audience and the type of interaction with that audience: on social media, all these activities are used to shape the image, both public and private, of users. Therefore, on social media platforms, *both direct and indirect visible traces, as well as invisible ones*, contribute to shape a certain public image of the self.

The construction and management of this image is also the result of the *interpretation of the algorithm*, on the basis of which users make promotional activities using different strategies that differ according to the platform used and its relative functions. This phenomenon underlines the affective dimension in the user-platform dynamic since it overlaps, often through imaginative processes, personal aspects and technological functions. Many interview participants stated that they set their activities depending on *how they imagine the algorithm to work*. This interpretation process, in turn, may refer the platform's outputs, for example, a post that received just few interactions, to personal aspects, like the idea of not being "smart" enough with the readers. The interpretation of the algorithm also highlights how the dynamic intersection between data, platforms, and users can lead to emotional responses.

In the previous pages, I briefly described how, through the process of *datafication*, almost every object and phenomenon can be translated into data, including those derived from the mediated practices of everyday life. Even if these data circulate autonomously, out of the control of the users, subjects tend to feel equally responsible for the outputs that emerge from the dialectic dynamic between users and data. Indeed, every *trace* we enter into the digital environment of social media platforms, whether direct or indirect, visible or invisible, provides information about us.

Clearly, these findings are limited to narrow research data and do not claim to be generally applicable. Nevertheless, they provide food for thought to be explored more fully in future research, especially regarding the relationship between digital environments, identity, and the practice of *self*-monitoring and *self*-management.

References

Anderson, C. W., Bell, E., & Shirky, C. (2012). *Post industrial journalism: Adapting to the present*. https://academiccommons.columbia.edu/doi/10.7916/D8N01JS7

Baym, N. K. (2010). *Personal connections in the digital age*. Polity Press.

Bell, E., Owen, T., Brown, P., Hauka C., & Rashidian N. (2017). *The Platform Press. How Silicon Valley reengineered journalism*. https://academiccommons.columbia.edu/doi/10.7916/D8R216ZZ

Blumer, H. (1969). *Symbolic interactionism: Perspective and method*. Prentice-Hall.

Brems, C., Temmerman, M., Graham, T., & Broersma, M. (2017). Personal branding on Twitter: How employed and freelance journalists stage themselves on social media. *Digital Journalism, 5*(4), 443–459. https://doi.org/10.1080/21670811.2016.1176534

Bucher, T. (2017). The algorithmic imaginary: Exploring the ordinary affects of Facebook algorithms. *Information, Communication & Society, 20*(1), 30–44. https://doi.org/10.1080/1369118X.2016.1154086

Casagrande, G. (2021). *Il lavoro relazionale in negativo. Auto-promozione e connessioni affettive sui social media*. Doctoral thesis, Sapienza University of Rome. https://iris.uniroma1.it/handle/11573/1607684

Cheney-Lippold, J. (2017). *We are data. Algorithms and the making of our digital selves*. New York University Press.

Coté, M. (2014). Data motility: The materiality of big social data. *Cultural Studies Review, 20*(1), 121–149.

Dimock, M. (2019). *Defining generations: Where Millennials end and Generation Z begins*. Pew Research Center. https://www.pewresearch.org/fact-tank/2019/01/17/where-millennials-end-and-generation-z-begins/

Donath, J., & Boyd, D. (2004). Public displays of connection. *BT Technology Journal, 22*(4), 71–82. https://doi.org/10.1023/B:BTTJ.0000047585.06264.cc

Draper, N. A. (2019). *The identity trade. Selling privacy and reputation online*. New York University Press.

Duffy, B. E., & Chan, N. K. (2019). "You never really know who's looking": Imagined surveillance across social media platforms. *New Media and Society, 21*(1), 119–138. https://doi.org/10.1177/1461444818791318

Floridi, L. (2015). *The online manifesto. Being human in a hyperconnected era*. Springer. https://www.springer.com/gp/book/9783319040929

Gandini, A. (2016). Digital work: Self-branding and social capital in the freelance knowledge economy. *Marketing Theory, 16*(1), 123–141. https://doi.org/10.1177/1470593115607942

Gerlitz, C., & Helmond, A. (2013). The like economy: Social buttons and the data-intensive web. *New Media and Society, 15*(8), 1348–1365.

Gillespie, T. (2017). Governance of and by platforms. In J. Burgess, A. Marwick, & T. Poell (Eds.), *The SAGE handbook of social media*. Sage. https://culturedigitally.org/wp-content/uploads/2016/06/Gillespie-Governance-ofby-Platforms-PREPRINT.pdf

Gobo, G. (2011). Back to likert. Towards the conversational survey. In M. Williams & W. P. Vogt (Eds.), *The Sage handbook of innovation in social research methods* (pp. 228–248). Sage.

Gobo, G., & Mauceri, S. (2013). *Collecting survey data*. Sage.

Goffman, E. (2009). *La vita quotidiana come rappresentazione*. Il Mulino.

Litt, E. (2012). Knock, knock. Who's there? The imagined audience. *Journal of Broadcasting & Electronic Media, 56*(3), 330–345. https://doi.org/10.1080/08838151.2012.705195

Litt, E., & Hargittai, E. (2016). The imagined audience on social network sites. *Social Media + Society, 2*(1), 1–12. https://doi.org/10.1177/2056305116633482

Losito, G. (2004). *L'intervista nella ricerca sociale*. Laterza.

Lupton, D. (2016). *The quantified self. A sociology of self tracking*. Polity Press.

Lyon, D. (2018). *The culture of surveillance: Watching as a way of life*. Polity Press.

Marwick, A. E., & Boyd, D. (2011). I tweet honestly, I tweet passionately: Twitter users, context collapse, and the imagined audience. *New Media and Society, 13*(1), 114–133. https://doi.org/10.1177/1461444810365313

Mayer-Schönberger, V., & Cukier, K. (2013). *Big data: A revolution that will transform how we live, work, and think*. Houghton Mifflin Harcourt.

Molyneux, L. (2014). What journalists retweet: Opinion, humor, and brand development on Twitter. *Journalism*, 1–16. https://doi.org/10.1177/1464884914550135

Nagy, P., & Neff, G. (2015). Imagined affordance: Reconstructing a keyword for communication theory. *Social Media + Society, 1*(2), 1–9. https://doi.org/10.1177/2056305115603385

Papacharissi, Z. (2011). *The networked self. Identity, community, and culture on social network sites*. Routledge.

Pasquale, F. (2015). *Black box society: The secret algorithms that control money and information*. Harvard University Press.

Pitrone, M. C. (1984). *Il sondaggio*. Franco Angeli Editore.

Poell, T., & van Dijck, J. (2015). Social media and activist communication. In C. Atton (Ed.), *The Routledge companion to alternative and community media* (pp. 527–537). Routledge.

Strauss, A., & Corbin, J. (1990). *Basics of qualitative research: Grounded theory procedures and techniques*. Sage.

van Dijck, J. (2013). 'You have one identity': Performing the self on Facebook and LinkedIn. *Media, Culture and Society, 35*(2), 199–215. https://doi.org/10.1177/0163443712468605

van Dijck, J., Poell, T., & de Waal, M. (2018). *The platform society. Public values in a connective world*. Oxford University Press.

Walther, J. B., Van Der Heide, B., Kim, S. Y., & Westerman, D. (2008). The role of friends' appearance and behavior on evaluations of individuals on Facebook: Are we known by the company we keep? *Human Communication Research, 34*, 28–49. https://doi.org/10.1111/j.1468-2958.2007.00312.x

Zuboff, S. (2019). *The age of surveillance capitalism: The fight for a human future at the new frontier of power*. Public Affairs.

Gaia Casagrande obtained her Ph.D. in 2021 at the Department of Communication and Social Research, Sapienza University of Rome. In her doctoral thesis, she analyzed self-branding practices and explored the concept of relational labor on social media platforms.

Her research interests mainly concern the impact of new technologies in society. In particular, she is interested in platform studies, critical media and internet studies, social movements and media activism, drone studies, and ICT4D.

Previously, she was Visiting Ph.D. Researcher and GTA at the Department of Digital Humanities, King's College London, where she taught seminars on digital communities and subcultures.

Currently, she is postdoctoral researcher at the University of Milan, working at the ERC-funded project "Craft work: Understanding the relationship between identity and work in the context of the future of work."

Chapter 10
Performative Intermediaries Versus Digital Regulation. A Multidisciplinary Analysis of the Power of Algorithms

Emma Garzonio

Introduction

Recent years have witnessed an increasing amount of research and interest in the complex matter of digital platforms, which has been examined from diverse and multiple academic perspectives. The phenomenon of platformisation, defined as the penetration of infrastructures, economic processes and governmental frameworks of digital platforms in different economic sectors and spheres of existence, as well as the reorganisation of cultural practices and imaginations around these platforms (Poell et al., 2019), still represents a complex and deeply investigated subject, with visible repercussions on many aspects of public and private life. A concrete example is the widespread diffusion of globally operating platform businesses—from Facebook to Google, to Amazon, etc.—that are becoming increasingly central to public and private life, transforming key economic sectors and spheres of life.

Following the evolution and the increasing significance of platforms and digital intermediaries, institutions have been focusing their attention and their policymaking more and more on the issue of data and digital transition, which requires digital governance to adapt to each country's regulatory culture and capacity, as well as understanding that these structures will continue to change over time (OECD, 2019:147). In this context, at least 73 countries worldwide have adopted a digital strategy or plan (ITU, 2020:3), while another recent trend is for countries to adopt strategies tailored to specific technologies or issues, such as automation, robotics, 5G, artificial intelligence (AI) and the Internet of Things (IoT). At the EU level, the latest Proposal of Regulation (EC)2020/825 on a Single Market for Digital Services (Digital Services Act, DSA) represents the culmination of a long-standing regulatory

E. Garzonio (✉)
Department of Communication and Social Research, Sapienza – University of Rome, Rome, Italy
e-mail: emma.garzonio@uniroma1.it

F. Comunello et al. (eds.), *What People Leave Behind*, Frontiers in Sociology and Social Research 7, https://doi.org/10.1007/978-3-031-11756-5_10

process that, over the years, has touched on numerous issues related to digital regulation. Particular attention has been paid to the implications for democratic stability caused by the extensive power of digital platforms and intermediaries: in the document published in 2020 by the European Commission's Joint Research Centre, "Technology and Democracy: understanding the influence of online technologies on political behaviour and decision-making", causal connections are established between how platforms work and how fundamental rights online are impacted. The research highlights how automated newsfeeds and recommendation systems are designed to maximise the attention and engagement of users by satisfying their alleged preferences, which may mean giving relevance to polarising and misleading content.

All these subjects—data-driven performances, data-agile economies and services, content's ranking and recommendation systems—are linked by a common component: algorithms. Understanding algorithms, their role and functions in our digital world, the possible repercussions of their being more and more at the centre of the co-production of meaning in our society, is a key challenge of our times. The algorithmic power is transversal to many areas of life, and a single lens cannot magnify all of its complexity: a multidisciplinary approach can fruitfully help understand this all-encompassing phenomenon.

On the one hand, we need to understand the meaning of the "power of algorithms": how does it concretely work, how it is related to platform performance and what are the possible implications, especially in terms of real interference with human knowledge and perception of reality. On the other hand, we will be examining the "counteractions" set out in the European regulation: how it has been developing over time and how algorithms have become increasingly central to the debate, subsequently highlighting the importance of *algorithmic transparency* and accountability. We will be looking at how lawmaking—in particular the European legal framework for AI—is trying to intercept that same algorithmic power and establish new benchmarks for transparency. In conclusion, we will assess how the most recent regulation proposal addresses the matter and what are the criticalities that might occur.

Performative Intermediaries and Their Political Power

As individuals, we are deeply immersed in a "datafied reality", and we constantly interact with and through data-driven intermediaries, the vital functions of which depend on the capacity of algorithmic components to aggregate and elaborate users' digital traces and to transform them into means of production, both of meaning and profit. Simple actions like looking for services through a search engine, shopping online, chatting with friends and so on, all implicate a high degree of interaction with algorithmic media (Deuze, 2012). Through the processes of selecting, ranking and suggesting contents—information, services, products, friends—algorithms show the capacity to build and shape our digital reality based on our previous activities and choices within the digital space.

On these premises is built the conception of digital platforms as *performative intermediaries* (Bucher, 2018:1) that is, types of media relying on predictive analytics, whose nature is inherently algorithmic and that don't just represent our many worlds but actively participate in shaping them. When we define platforms as "inherently algorithmic", we are pointing at some patterns, relations and processes that the structure of platforms intrinsically activate. For instance, let's consider users' registration when first accessing a platform: a definition of one's identity according to fixed, measurable, comparable standards. This definitory process needs to provide information that is compatible with the algorithmic logic driving the system, that is, to provide comparable and compatible data for the algorithm to process. To be "algorithm-ready", data need to be encoded according to schemes and a fixed set of standards, to be categorised. *Categorisation* is a powerful semantic and political process: how categories are defined, what belongs in each one of them and who decides how to implement these categories in practice are all powerful assertions about how things are and are supposed to be (Bowker & Star, 2000; Gillespie, 2014).

Information needs to fall within a database, which is much more than a simple "collection of data": it is an ordered space, a structured repository that streamlines management and updating of data according to fixed criteria, without which complex searches would be impossible. As Tarleton Gillespie puts it, "algorithms are inert, meaningless machines until paired with databases upon which to function" and "before results can be algorithmically provided, information must be collected, and sometimes excluded or demoted" (Gillespie, 2014:169). There's a precise political valence—intending "politics" as ways of world-making—in what the author defines as *patterns of inclusion*: the subsequent phases of data collection, readying and exclusion of "less relevant" information all imply upstream decisions about which pieces of information will be indexed in the first place and which will be excepted. Since the main characteristic of algorithms is to be functionally automatic, namely, to be activated and prompted without any regular human intervention or oversight (Winner, 1978), this means that the information included in the database must be rendered into data, formalised so that algorithms can act on it automatically. To the purpose of database design and management, categorisation represents a critical process. Categories draw demarcations, help establish and confirm standards and imply by nature the exclusion of certain items, while "algorithms can be touted as automatic, the patterns of inclusion are the ones that predetermine what will or will not appear among their results" (Gillespie, 2014:173).

As information technology has converged with the nature and production of scientific knowledge, we assist the social and political process of creating an explicit, indexical memory of what is known, the making of "memory infrastructures". In Geoffrey Bowker's words, today we "database the world" in a way that excludes certain spaces, entities and times: "the archive, by remembering all and only a certain set of facts/discoveries/observations, consistently and actively engages in the forgetting of other sets (...) The archive's jussive force, then, operates through being invisibly exclusionary" (Bowker, 2006:12–14).

I'll allow myself just a brief digression on the theme of archives since the matter is too vast to be addressed here and that would fall beyond the scope of this contribution. At the same time, this reflection is nonetheless essential to understand the in-built partiality of the indexing process and the power of database infrastructural invisibility deployed on, or against, certain sets of items and subjects. I will borrow the concept of the *silence of the archive* (Hartman, 2008:3–4) from the historiographical reconstruction outlined by Saidiya Hartman in her essay "Venus in Two Acts". The theme of her study is very far from what we are dealing with—her potent dissertation addresses the scarcity of African narratives of captivity and enslavement opposed to the abundance of direct testimonies of colonial ferocity. However, her concept powerfully represents the exclusionary forces mentioned also by Bowker: sometimes histories are destroyed, aren't collected or aren't even told—in all the cases, in our collective history something extremely significant gets lost.

Jacques Derrida reminds us of the etymology of the word "archive", the ancient Greek *arkheion*: literally "the house of whom command". In ancient Greece, the citizens who held and signified political power (the archons) "were considered to possess the right to make or represent the law. (…) it is at their home (…) that official documents are filed" (Derrida & Prenowitz, 1995:9–10). From the beginning of history, adding or excluding something from the archive has been an essentially political action, determined by the archivist and by the political context in which he lives. At times, information and proof have not been entrusted to the archive because they are not considered important enough to be preserved; at others, acts of intentional destruction have prevented the collection of those pieces of history in the archive and, as a consequence, have inhibited human awareness: "the complete archive is a myth, it is only theoretically possible. Maybe it is in some recess of Jorge Luis Borges' Library of Babel, buried under the detailed story of the future" (Machado, 2020:12). The "digital version" of the concept of the silence of the archive depicts a situation where "some information initially collected is subsequently removed before an algorithm ever gets to it" (Gillespie, 2014:172).

On the one hand, we have large-scale information services, providers and indexes that are not comprehensive by nature, since they act as *censors* as well. For instance, YouTube algorithms bring down the rankings of certain videos, so they do not become "most watched" nor do they get suggested on the customised home page of new users (Gillespie, 2010). Twitter, at the same time, does not censor profanity from public tweets, but its algorithms remove them from the evaluation of "trending terms/hashtag" (Gillespie, 2012). On the other, we must acknowledge that the digitalisation of all information and the acceptance of computational tools as our primary means of expression lead to specific implications, especially when we use algorithms—as above, automated tools that don't need human oversight—to select what is "most relevant" from a corpus of data composed of traces of our activities, likings, languages.

Algorithms, Relevance and Influence on Perception

By definition, algorithms are encoded procedures for transforming input data into the desired output, based on specified calculations. These calculations have never been simple, but today we are facing an unprecedented expansion and growth in their complexity, as billions of people daily use the services provided by algorithmic media. The algorithmic components lying behind automated newsfeeds, sharing platforms or search engines, scrape and select contents and information—according to predetermined criteria of *relevance*—and build up a custom configuration of each individual's digital reality, which can influence our perception of the world not only within but also outside the digital environment. Just think of all the pieces of information we searched for but were eventually lost because they were ranked low on our Google results: at the end of the day, a complex, automatic, profit-driven mechanism drew a line between what we could easily find and access and what was to remain silent. Again, this represents an exercise of power, both in terms of *control* over the availability and concrete accessibility of knowledge and in terms of *influence* on the meaning we subsequently construct over that same knowledge.

The criteria by which algorithms determine what is relevant, how those criteria are obscured from us and how they endorse political choices about the portion of knowledge that results in being appropriate and legitimate all fall within the process that Gillespie defines *evaluation of relevance* (2014:168). When users perform activities that depend on automated systems, they are running a query. In computer science, this means to search a database to extract or update data that meet a certain criteria, specified in the query and based on variables and values in the source data. The search algorithm then examines a vast amount of signals to retrieve cases that match the specified criteria. Through these signals, the algorithm approximates "relevance", and that is the most concerning aspect: "relevant" in fact is a fluid term, loaded with connotations of value and attributes that depend on the subjectivity of who's performing that specific query. "Relevant" is not quantifiable nor measurable, and it's a concept at the other extreme of objectivity. In Gillespie's words, since "there is no independent metric for what *actually* are the most relevant search results for any given query, engineers must decide what results look "right" (...) treating quick clicks and no follow-up searches as an approximation, not of relevance exactly, but of *satisfaction*" (Gillespie, 2014:178, italics added). We are not getting what could be important for us but what is going to satisfy us based on our collected, layered digital traces: this is a relevant way in which our perception of the world is influenced by heteronomous criteria, implemented by algorithmic components.

As we pointed out above, the algorithm is a set of coded instructions to be followed to perform a given task; in the digital context, they are set to select and make visible "in a meaningful way" portions of the endless amount of data produced and available on the web. Therefore, *classifying*, *ranking* and *recommending* (or, on the contrary, reducing visibility) are the elemental activities that sustain algorithmic functioning and performance: the question that arises is then who or what has the power to establish the conditions for what can be seen and known (Bucher, 2018:3).

It is not possible to interrogate the underlying criteria of algorithms: in nearly all cases, the evaluative assumptions that algorithms are potentially requested to make remain hidden, in accordance with the precise wishes of platform owners. Being unambiguous or accurate about the working of algorithms would likely allow competitors to replicate and improve that service—a potential commercial suicide. The opacity of the underlying criteria in algorithmic performance means that how those criteria are measured, weighed against one another, incorporated with other criteria—it all remains unstated: this leaves algorithms open to the suspicion of their inclination to the provider's commercial or political benefit (Gillespie, 2014:177).

We know, more or less, that Facebook uses a machine learning-based algorithm to give users a more personalised newsfeed, which relies on constantly increasing categories and subcategories of *affinity* (how close the relationship is between the user and the content/source) and multiple *weight* levels (the type of action that was taken by the user on the content). When Facebook attempts to measure the strength of a relationship between users, that measurement is not only based on personal interactions, but global interactions on the platform can outweigh them if the signal is strong enough. This means that if Facebook shows an update to a given amount of users and only a few of them interact with it, "we may not show it in your newsfeed. But if a lot of people are interacting with it, we might decide to show it to you, too" (McGee, 2013). This practice is what Bucher defines *guilt by association* (2018:12), an advertising technique used in the case of users who are not particularly active or engaged in the platform. Since they don't provide enough personal information and data on which the algorithm can build their newsfeed—that is, the portion of reality they perceive on that platform—these pieces of information are inferred by the users' friends: advertisement and contents are then targeted and customised on the base of the friends' online behaviour. That is, our activity online plays a crucial role not only in determining the content we will ourselves see on our preferred platforms but also in determining what *other* people will see on theirs.

Another interesting and concrete sample of the reality-shaping power of algorithms brought by the author is *computable friendship*, a model example of how algorithms actively intercept human behaviours (Garzonio, 2021). On social media platforms, friendship is put at the centre of the business model, "because better-connected users tend to increase their use of the social networking system (...) [bringing a] corresponding increase in advertising opportunities" (Schultz et al., 2014). Online friendship becomes subjected to mechanisms that privilege quantification and automation: the algorithm "measures social impact, reputation and influence through the creation of composite numbers that function as *score*" (Gerlitz & Lury, 2014:175), which is typically used to feed rankings and enhance predictions on users' behaviour. In this way, this computational and computable friendship is nothing more than an equation geared toward maximising engagement with the platform (Bucher, 2018:11), ultimately serving revenue purposes. The "drive toward more"—more friends, connections, likes, interactions—is materialised by the pervasive enumeration of everything on the user interface, pushed by algorithmic rankings and scores and compelling people to reimagine friendship as a quantitative space (Grosser, 2014).

We have so far observed several declinations of algorithmic influence on "world-making", intended here as the capacity to impact on people awareness through relevance evaluation and on people's online behaviour through different patterns of predictive analysis. To conclude, I'd like to bring another example of algorithmic active influence on perception, with its worrying implications in terms of polarisation: *echo chambers*. The relation between algorithms and echo chambers is clarified, among the others, in an interesting comparative study on four different social media platforms (Quattrociocchi et al., 2021) which displays that feed algorithms—the ones that select what we visualise compared to the entire content offer of our social network, based on similarities and interactions—play a fairly important role in polarisation dynamics. This is because, despite the unprecedented potential of social media platforms in terms of free expression and exchange of public information, these same platforms are articulated on self-regulatory mechanisms pushing customised content, tailored to users' interests, tastes and beliefs. The portion of reality that we are driven to see confirms our previous ideas and nourishes ideological polarisation (Van Alstyne & Brynjolfsson, 2005). Echo chambers are attributable to the existence of structures of exclusion, which *actively* obstruct the flow and consumption of information and prevent large groups of social media users from acquiring awareness of certain types of data and contents (Nguyen, 2018).

The human tendency to aggregate with people with the same attitudes and interests, when we shift to the online world, is widely encouraged and directed by automated components filtering for us contents we are most likely to engage with. This implies that the inputs provided by users—I like it, I buy it, I interact with it—and the patterns that emerge from them are transformed into means of *data-driven* content production. What we see on platforms, the world that is built online before our eyes, is the result of what we have previously done and chosen on these same platforms. Our inclinations and preferences will be accommodated and we will be exposed to content we enjoy and believe in, which don't question our opinions and don't require to enlarge our views: in a world of minimised effort, this sounds more than reassuring.

AI, Algorithms and Transparency: The European Agenda

In the European context, the current definition of AI can be retrieved in the Communication of the European Commission "Artificial Intelligence for Europe", COM(2018)237 of April 25th, 2018:

> Artificial intelligence (AI) refers to systems that display intelligent behaviour by analysing their environment and taking actions—with *some degree of autonomy*—to achieve specific goals. AI-based systems can be purely *software-based*, acting in the virtual world (e.g. voice assistants, image analysis software, search engines, speech and face recognition systems) or AI can be embedded in hardware devices (e.g. advanced robots, autonomous cars, drones or Internet of Things applications). (...) Many AI technologies *require data to improve their performance*.

Predictive algorithms fall within this domain: they are software-based automated systems that learn from the surrounding environment, improving their performance as they process more and more data. Targeted ads, suggestions and content pushed by algorithms on e-commerce or social media platforms, for instance, are the result of machine learning procedures, made possible by the automated processing of data and traces provided—consciously or not—by the users.

The communication was preceded by a study on the protection of human rights in the field of automated data processing techniques, published in March 2018 by the Council of Europe, in which clear requirements for algorithmic transparency were already enucleated. The document denounced the increasing opacity of algorithms, which stems not from technological needs, but precise entrepreneurial choices, and highlights the negative impact of this lack of transparency on the exercise of various important rights and freedoms enshrined in the European Chart of Human Rights. The potentiality of introducing by legislative means certain minimum standards of technical *accountability and transparency* for algorithms was already envisaged in the CoE document, which also proposed mediation between the entrepreneurial need to protect intellectual property in the creation of algorithms and the public need for transparency (Allegri, 2020:57). In fact, "the provision of entire algorithms or the underlying software code to the public is an unlikely solution in this context, as private companies regard their algorithm as key proprietary software that is protected. However, there may be a possibility of demanding that key subsets of information about the algorithms be provided to the public (. . .)" (CoE, 2018:38).

Following this study, "The European Ethical Charter on the use of Artificial Intelligence in judicial systems and their environment" was adopted in December 2018 by the European Commission for the Efficiency of Justice (CEPEJ). The fourth principle proposed in the Charter replicates the need to balance between intellectual property and the need for *transparency* (access to the design process), *impartiality* (absence of bias), *fairness* and intellectual integrity (prioritising the interests of justice) when tools are used that may have legal consequences or may significantly affect people's lives. This last aspect specifically refers to the ingrained habit by companies and governments of relying upon algorithms to make decisions on very delicate aspects of human livelihood—from loan approvals to recruiting, legal sentencing and college admissions.

In the context of weighing of interests, a more viable alternative to complete technical transparency is to explain the data processing system and to describe how results are produced "in clear and familiar language, by communicating, for example, the nature of the services offered [and] the tools that have been developed" (CEPEJ, 2018:11). Moreover, independent authorities or experts could be tasked with certifying and auditing processing methods or providing advice beforehand, while public authorities could grant certifications to be regularly reviewed. We have here two core elements which will also be retrieved in the Digital Services Act: the objective of *public accessibility* to data processing methods through comprehensible explanations and the possibility of *external audits* by groups of experts or independent authorities, to certify the completeness and reliability of such explanations.

The "Ethics Guidelines for Trustworthy AI" published by a High-Level Expert Group on AI set up by the European Commission in April 2019 further specifies the concept of technological transparency. It provides AI systems to be *auditable*, *comprehensible* and *intelligible* by human beings at varying levels of understanding and expertise: "business model transparency means that human beings are knowingly informed of the intention of developers and technology implementers of AI systems" (AI HLEG, 2019:18). Another important transparency requirement that AI systems should meet is related to *traceability*: AI systems should indeed document both the decisions they make and the whole process that yielded the decisions. While traceability is not (always) able to tell us why a certain decision was reached, it can tell us how it came about, enabling reasoning as to why an AI decision was erroneous. Traceability is thus a facilitator for auditability: whenever an AI system has a significant impact on people's lives, laypersons should be able to understand the causality of the algorithmic decision-making process and how it is implemented by organisations that deploy the AI system.

Dealing with the interpretations and decisions made by learning algorithms, a known issue is the difficulty to provide clear reasons for the results delivered, because the training process implies setting the network parameters to numerical values that are difficult to correlate with the results. For a system to be trustworthy, it is necessary to be able to understand why it had a given behaviour and why it has provided a given interpretation: a whole field of research, explainable AI (xAI), as we will see shortly, is trying to address this issue.

Concluding this overview on the challenges of algorithmic accountability, it seems appropriate to address some critical issues that the approaches so far presented might raise, especially when dealing with technical transparency. As we have commented thus far, the line proposed in the various guidelines is to compromise between private interests and public disclosure. Enlarging the focus to binding norms, Regulation (EU)2016/679—General Data Protection Regulation (GDPR)—somehow reflects this approach, and it also offers a tool, indicating in its Recital 63 that a data subject should have the right of access to his or her collected personal data and "to know and obtain communication in particular with regard to (...) the logic involved in any automatic personal data processing". The recital specifies that this right should not adversely affect the already mentioned trade secrets, intellectual property and the copyright protecting the software, but it also states that "the result of those considerations should not be a refusal to provide all information to the data subject". In other words, while trade secrets cannot be extended as to refuse to disclose any information on automated data processing, the same right to disclosure still cannot reach the source code but only the features and the specific logic of the employed algorithms. In this difficult balancing, wide discretion is assigned to the Independent National Authorities and the extension of the right to access the algorithmic logic remains variable, "it shortens or lengthens according to the recipient of the explanation. If the information is addressed to the data subject, the communication will extend to the logic of the algorithm functioning, but without reaching the source code (...) if the conflict of rights arises in the court, the judge will have the authority to open the source code and conduct the judicial review over it" (De Minico, 2021:30).

Despite offering a key for a correct interpretation—that the trade secret cannot be an alibi to refuse any information to the data subject or the judge—what's written in the Regulation still clashes with the fact that technical transparency is not attainable in most cases of algorithms managed by for-profit companies. Some scholars have also suggested that revealing in case of conflict the source code to regulators or auditors merely shifts the "burden of belief" from the algorithm itself to the regulators (Hosanagar & Jair, 2018). In addition, technical transparency makes algorithms vulnerable to gaming, but the biggest problem is that source code in modern AI, after all, is less relevant compared with other factors in algorithmic functioning—which is to say, some of today's best-performing algorithms are often the most opaque. Specifically, machine learning algorithms logic is mostly built on training data and is rarely reflected in its source code: high transparency might involve having to untangle countless amounts of data and then still only being able to guess at what lessons the algorithm has learned from it (*idem*). Focusing on the sole disclosure of source code appears to be an important criticality.

An achievable declination of transparency could be the one carried on by xAI: to provide basic insights on the factors driving algorithmic decisions. This approach to transparency carries with it the theme of the *right to explanation*, not explicitly mentioned in GDPR articles but outlined in Recital 71. The fact that this requirement is defined in a nonbinding part of the regulation has created another scholarly debate on the very existence of this right (Wachte et al., 2017; Kaminski, 2019), nevertheless dismissing the right to explanation because of the nature of recitals "would be too formalistic, and less attentive to the Court of Justice case law which regularly uses recitals as an interpretative aid" (De Minico, 2021:31). The GDPR thus establishes that users be able to demand the data behind the algorithmic decisions made for them, including in recommendation systems, credit and insurance risk systems, targeted advertising and social media platforms. XAI systems help combine this right with the technical challenges associated with transparency because they analyse the various inputs used by the algorithm, measure the impact of each input individually and in groups and finally report the set of inputs that had the biggest impact on the final decision. This kind of analysis could help programmers get around the *black box* problem—that is, they don't always know what is motivating the decisions of their machine learning algorithms—while identifying relationships between inputs and outcomes and spotting possible biases (Hosanagar & Jair, 2018).

The European Legal Framework for AI and the New DSA

The digital transition is one of the key priorities established by the European Commission under the presidency of Ursula von der Leyen. In her political guidelines for the period 2019–2024 period, the President announced that the Commission would put forward legislation for a coordinated European approach on the human and ethical implications of AI. Following that announcement, on 19 February 2020, the Commission published the "White Paper on AI: a European approach to excellence and trust". The Conclusions of the Council of the European Union, on 21 October 2020 ("The Charter of Fundamental Rights in the context of Artificial Intelligence and Digital Change") further called for addressing the opacity, complexity and bias a certain degree of unpredictability and partially autonomous behaviour of certain AI systems, to ensure their compatibility with fundamental rights and to facilitate the enforcement of legal rules.

The European Parliament has also undertaken a considerable amount of work in the area of AI, adopting various resolutions related to AI in October 2020, including on ethics, liability and copyright. In 2021, these were followed by resolutions on AI in criminal matters and in education, culture and the audiovisual sector. The Resolution EP A9-0186/2020 "on a Framework of Ethical Aspects of Artificial Intelligence, Robotics and Related Technologies" specifically recommends the Commission to propose legislative measures to harness the opportunities and benefits of AI while ensuring the protection of ethical principles; it also includes a text of the legislative proposal for a regulation on ethical principles. Moreover, it establishes the need for any AI (including software, algorithms and data used or produced by such technologies) to comply with Union law and respect human dignity and other fundamental rights set out in the Charter (Article 5), and it outlines the ethical characteristics and of "human-centric and human-made artificial intelligence" (Article 7). These principles have been taken into account by the subsequent "Proposal for a regulation laying down harmonised rules on AI" of April 2021 (Artificial Intelligence Act, COM(2021)206), which composes the current European legal framework concerning AI in conjunction with the aforementioned Framework Resolution, the GDPR and the Proposal of regulation (EC)2020/825 or Digital Services Act (DSA), all representing the foundations of the "regulatory work in progress".

The GDPR, in particular, has been scrupulous in placing narrow limits to the use of algorithms: its Article 22 defines the minimum standard which cannot be downgraded by Member States and specifies that the data subject shall have the right not to be subject to a decision based solely on automated processing; joined with Articles 13 and 14, it recognises the core right to be immediately informed about "the existence of automated decision-making". Nevertheless, this provision sets out just a mere declaration of the right without specifying its content, and, more in general, the GDPR seems not so prescriptive as it should be; in some of its parts, the text does not excel in clarity, again leaving too much room to Member States' discretionary power (De Minico, 2021:28).

In principle, the regulation provides that private codes of conduct are subordinate to the European regulation in progress, in line with the co-regulation model, "characterized by a hierarchical distribution of the normative power between public and private sources" (De Minico, 2021:20). However, both the EP Framework and the DSA refrain from laying down the basic rules to which the private soft law has to conform: EU norms just deal with the distribution of competencies among subjects, but they abstain from establishing the constituent elements of illegal conduct. In other terms, they are stating who is entitled to issue the rules but not how these rules should manage conduct, and this translates into delegating the task to private self-regulation. This criticality can be traced back to "an old vice affecting the European legislation, namely not taking a well-defined and courageous position (...) [concerning the] co-regulation regime" (ibidem).

The DSA represents so far the last stage of this "regulatory journey", proposed in December 2020 by the European Commission to upgrade the rules governing digital services. The reform of the European digital space is contained in two legislative initiatives, the DSA and the Digital Markets Act (DMA). Both are based on a comprehensive set of new rules for all digital services that connect consumers to goods, services or content operating in the EU: intermediary services offering network infrastructure (e.g. Internet access providers, domain name registrars), hosting services (cloud, web hosting) and online platforms of different nature.

The DSA establishes binding EU-wide obligations to tackle specific concerns raised by the accelerating digitalisation and consolidation of online platforms as systemic intermediaries, and it identifies different categories of systemic risk (Recital 58 and Article 26) connected to very large platforms (reaching more than 10% of the EU's population, 45 million users). Among the obligations, a new oversight structure to which big platforms are subjected is established: platform representatives are obliged to provide qualified researchers access to data, to allow transparency monitoring. These data will include information on the accuracy and functioning of algorithmic content moderation (Article 13), recommendation (Article 29) and advertising systems (Articles 24 and 30). Moreover, European Commission representatives, auditors and experts can carry out on-site inspections and require access to the platform's algorithms and database (Articles 28 and 57).

Regarding the processes interested by algorithms, in particular the issue of recommender systems that prevent users from finding and interacting with online information, the general principle of transparency is outlined in Article 12. It's the users' right to be adequately informed on any restrictions that providers of intermediary services impose in relation to the use of their service: that information "shall be set out in clear and unambiguous language and shall be publicly available in an easily accessible format". Users should also understand how the content presented to them is filtered, and they should be offered alternative options that are not based on profiling.

On paper, the DSA would constitute a major qualitative step forward on the issue of large platforms accountability and algorithmic transparency, setting a new benchmark for the regulation of digital services. This higher purpose, nevertheless, clashes with some of the criticalities we have identified. In particular, the tendency to leave space for self-regulation by private subjects can be spotted as a potential weakness. This "kind of blank endorsement from heteronomy to autonomy" (De Minico, 2021:21) can be detected for instance with the issue of unfair and misleading information. The DSA does not specify when "news has to be removed because they stop being a lawful exercise of a fundamental right and become an illegal act (...) Hence, the norm in blank about misleading information opens the way for self-regulation codes or, more precisely, for private platforms to mark the borderline between right and wrong" (ibidem). The subjects that should be regulated are the same that will assess whether the content they're sharing is misleading or not, within a "vicious cycle" that witnesses private platforms establishing their codes of conduct and being at the same time the only judge to decide upon them. Consequently, the co-regulation model fails to be factually implemented, while the way norms are framed "appears not far from giving rise to an anarchic soft law", in contrast with the expected and desirable combination between heteronomous sources and private acts.

Conclusions

To identify the meeting point between the power of performative intermediaries and digital regulation, we started our analysis with the definition of "algorithmic power", and the investigation of the influence algorithms can display over human knowledge, perception and behaviour. We have reviewed approaches, ideas and contributions from very different fields of research, keeping in mind the multidisciplinary attitude proven to be the most useful for the understanding of complex and transversal phenomena. Enucleating and analysing algorithmic characteristics and influence—the "political power" of algorithms—helped us defining what are the most complex problems to be solved and the most obscure points of their underlying workings.

It's exactly at these problems and opacities that digital regulation should aim. We have reconstructed, then, both the European agenda built along the years to create ethical guidelines for AI and the legal framework for this same issue, trying to define its strengths and potential weaknesses. The most evident criticalities encountered are related to the lack of prescriptive intention of the regulation, which still leaves much space both to Member States' discretionary powers, as in the GDPR, and to private self-regulation, in the case of DSA. In addition, a major definitory clearness could avoid the "blank endorsement" that ultimately leads to private subjects' autonomy in establishing their own rules to follow.

The subject of algorithms thus represents a concrete case study to test two regulatory alternatives, self-regulation alone or in conjunction with binding regulation. Having analysed the contributions on the theme of exclusionary powers and patterns of inclusion, we can fairly assess that algorithms and performative intermediaries are not neutral elements, but they replicate biases and discriminations already existing in the offline world, and on top of that, they have the power to silence voices, to inhibit awareness and to influence our perception. The discriminations one could quite easily detect in reality don't appear as such if they're kept hidden. This is why algorithms should be kept under policymakers' control and why a binding regulation, although held to a minimum standard, could be able to design algorithms consistent with European Constitutional values, respectful of fundamental rights and acquiescent to the democratic institutional framework.

References

AI HLEG. (2019). *Ethics guidelines for trustworthy AI*. Retrieved April 6, 2022, from https://www.aepd.es/sites/default/files/2019-12/ai-ethics-guidelines.pdf

Allegri, M. R. (2020). *Oltre la par condicio. Comunicazione politico-elettorale nei social media, fra diritto e autodisciplina*. Franco Angeli.

Bowker, G. C. (2006). *Memory practices in the sciences*. MIT Press.

Bowker, G. C., & Star, S. L. (2000). *Sorting things out: Classification and its consequences*. MIT Press.

Bucher, T. (2018). *If. . .then. Algorithmic power and politics*. University Press.

CEPEJ. (2018). *European ethical charter on the use of artificial intelligence in judicial systems and their environment*. Retrieved April 6, 2022, from https://rm.coe.int/ethical-charter-en-for-publication-4-december-2018/16808f699c

Council of Europe. (2018). *Algorithms and human rights. Study on the human rights dimensions of automated data processing techniques and possible regulatory implications*. Retrieved April 6, 2022, from https://rm.coe.int/algorithms-and-human-rights-en-rev/16807956b5

Council of the European Union (2020). Presidency conclusions – The charter of fundamental rights in the context of artificial intelligence and digital change. Retrieved April 6, 2022, from https://www.consilium.europa.eu/media/46496/st11481-en20.pdf

De Minico, G. (2021). Fundamental rights. European digital regulation and algorithmic challenge. *MediaLaws. Rivista di diritto dei media*, (1) Retrieved April 11, 2021, from https://www.medialaws.eu/wp-content/uploads/2021/04/RDM-1-21-De-Minico.pdf

Derrida, J., & Prenowitz, E. (1995). Archive fever: A Freudian impression. *Diacritics, 25*(2), 9–63. https://doi.org/10.2307/465144

Deuze, M. (2012). *Media life*. Polity.

European Commission COM(2018)237. Artificial intelligence for Europe, April 25, 2018. Retrieved April 6, 2022, from https://ec.europa.eu/transparency/documents-register/detail?ref=COM(2018)237&lang=en

European Commission COM(2020)65. White paper on artificial intelligence – A European approach to excellence and trust, February 19, 2020. Retrieved April 6, 2022, from https://ec.europa.eu/info/sites/default/files/commission-white-paper-artificial-intelligence-feb2020_en.pdf

European Commission COM(2020)825. Proposal for a regulation of the European Parliament and of the Council on a single market for digital services (Digital Services Act), December 15, 2020. Retrieved April 6, 2022, from https://eur-lex.europa.eu/legal-content/en/TXT/?uri=COM%3A2020%3A825%3AFIN

European Commission COM(2021)206. Proposal for a regulation of the European Parliament and of the Council laying down harmonised rules on AI (Artificial Intelligence Act) of April 21, 2021. Retrieved April 6, 2022, from https://eur-lex.europa.eu/legal-content/EN/TXT/?uri=CELEX%3A52021PC0206

European Parliament resolution EP(A9-0186/2020) with recommendations to the commission on a framework of ethical aspects of artificial intelligence, robotics and related technologies of 20 October 2020. Retrieved April 6, 2022, from https://www.europarl.europa.eu/doceo/document/TA-9-2020-0275_EN.html#title1

Garzonio, E. (2021). L'algoritmo trasparente: obiettivi ed implicazioni della riforma dello Spazio digitale europeo. *Rivista Italiana Di Informatica E Diritto, 3*(2), 25–32. https://doi.org/10.32091/RIID0037

Gerlitz, C., & Lury, C. (2014). Social media and self-evaluating assemblages: On numbers, orderings and value. *Distinktion: Scandinavian Journal of Social Theory, 15*(2), 174–188.

Gillespie, T. (2010). The politics of 'platforms'. *New Media & Society, 12*(3), 347–364. https://doi.org/10.1177/1461444809342738

Gillespie, T. (2012). Can an algorithm be wrong? *Limn, 2*. Retrieved February 15, 2022 from https://escholarship.org/uc/item/0jk9k4hj

Gillespie, T. (2014). The relevance of algorithms. In T. Gillespie, P. Boczkowski, & K. Foot (Eds.), *Media technologies: Essays on communication, materiality, and society* (pp. 167–194). MIT Press.

Grosser, B. (2014). What do metrics want? How quantification prescribes social interaction on Facebook. *Computational Culture*, (4). Retrieved July 16, 2022 from http://computationalculture.net/what-dometrics-want/

Hartman, S. (2008). Venus in two acts. *Small Axe by Duke University Press, 12*(2), 1–14.

Hosanagar, K., & Jair, V. (2018). We need transparency in algorithms, but too much can backfire. *Harvard Business Review*. Retrieved February 15, 2022 from https://hbr.org/2018/07/we-need-transparency-in-algorithms-but-too-much-can-backfire

ITU. (2020). *Digital regulation handbook*. International Telecommunication Union and the World Bank.

JRC Science for Policy Report. (2020). *Technology and democracy understanding the influence of online technologies on political behaviour and decision-making*. Publications Office of the European Union. https://data.europa.eu/doi/10.2760/593478

Kaminski, M. E. (2019). The right to explanation, explained. *Berkeley Tech L.J., 34*, 189ss.

Maria Machado, C. (2020). *In the dream house*. Codice edizioni. Monica Capuani trans. Original work published 2019.

McGee, M. (2013). *EdgeRank is dead: Facebook's news feed algorithm now has close to 100K weight factors*. MarTech. https://martech.org/edgerank-is-dead-facebooks-news-feed-algorithm-now-has-close-to-100k-weight-factors/

Nguyen, C. T. (2018). *Echo chambers and epistemic bubbles*. University Press.

OECD. (2019). *Going digital: Shaping policies, improving lives*. OECD Publishing. https://doi.org/10.1787/9789264312012-en

Poell, T., Nieborg, D., & van Dijck, J. (2019). Platformisation. *Internet Policy Review, 8*(4). https://doi.org/10.14763/2019.4.1425

Quattrociocchi, W., Cinelli, M., De Francisci Morales, G., Galeazzi, A., & Starnini, M. (2021). The echo chamber effect on social media. *Proceedings of the National Academy of Sciences Mar, 118*(9). https://doi.org/10.1073/pnas.2023301118

Regulation (EU)2016/679 of the European Parliament and of the Council of 27 April 2016 on the protection of natural persons with regard to the processing of personal data and on the free movement of such data (General Data Protection Regulation). Retrieved April 6, 2022, from https://eur-lex.europa.eu/legal-content/EN/TXT/PDF/?uri=CELEX:32016R0679&from=EN

Schultz, A. P., Piepgrass, B., Weng, C. C., Ferrante, D., Verma, D., Martinazzi, P., Alison, T., & Mao, Z. (2014). *U.S. patent no. 20140114774 A1 ("Methods and systems for determining use and content of pymk based on value model")*. U.S. Patent and Trademark Office.

Van Alstyne, M. V., & Brynjolfsson, E. (2005). Global village or cyber-balkans? Modeling and measuring the integration of electronic communities. *Management Science, 51*(6), 851–868. https://doi.org/10.1287/MNSC.1050.0363

Wachte, S., Mittelstadt, B., & Floridi, L. (2017). Why a right to explanation of automated decision-making does not exist in the general data protection regulation. *Int'l Data Privacy L., 7*(2), 76ss.

Winner, L. (1978). *Autonomous technology: Technics-out-of-control as a theme in political thought*. MIT Press.

Emma Garzonio graduated in 2018 from La Sapienza University of Rome, Department of Communication and Social Research (CoRis) discussing her Master's Degree thesis on "Migratory flows and EU policies. The juridical perspective on the Eurosceptic phenomenon".

She is currently a PhD candidate enrolled in the last year of the doctoral course in Communication and Media studies at the same Department. Her research has maintained the focus on EU governance and regulatory framework, specialising in media regulation, data protection and digital political communication at the EU level.

She is a member of the Research unit EuPoliS, "Transnational political participation, representation and sovereignty in the European project", at the CoRis Department and participated in many international media and electoral monitoring projects, such as the European Elections Monitoring Center (EEMC) project in 2019 and the Global Media Monitoring Project (GMMP) in 2020.

Her published works discuss ISP and SNS liability for automated data processing (2019, "Media Laws. Rivista di diritto dei media" and 2020, "Contemporary approaches in social science researches"), AI and disinformation (2020, "Comunicazionepuntodoc"), social media and new styles of political communication (2021, "Saperi, conoscenze ed esperienze in formazione"); and European regulatory framework and algorithms (2021, "Rivista Italiana di informatica e diritto").

Part III
Traces and Political Sphere: Capitalism, Surveillance, Personal Rights, and Moral Concerns

Chapter 11
Surveilling the Surveillants: From Relational Surveillance to WikiLeaks

Andrea Borghini, Vincenzo Scalia, and Daniela Tafani

The Assange Affair amid Biography and History

Can the historical-biographical story of Julian Assange and his "creature" WikiLeaks be interpreted in a Historical Sociology key?

In other words, drawing on the systems of thought of authors such as Charles Wright Mills and Norbert Elias, among the best known, is it possible that the biography of the Australian journalist helps to illuminate his (and our) historical time and, vice versa, that historical time helps to place his biography and his courageous journalistic campaigns more precisely?

This is what we will try to highlight in these initial few pages, using a tradition of studies that finds reference figures in the authors mentioned, as in others—here I am thinking in particular of Pierre Bourdieu, who has also become an author of today's sociological canon.

The usefulness of this approach should be immediately clarified. It is found above all in its ability to integrate with the other contributions that make up the mosaic of this essay. In this way it centres on the two concepts of relationality—declined in terms of relational surveillance (Scalia, Section "Surveillance, Counter-Surveillance, Counter-Power. Are Assange and WikiLeaks a Counter-Power Agency?")—and the

---

Sections "The Assange Affair Amid Biography and History" and "Brilliant Historical Evidence" are by Andrea Borghini; Sects. "Surveillance, Counter-Surveillance, Counter-Power. Are Assange and WikiLeaks a Counter-Power Agency?" and "Conclusions" by Vincenzo Scalia; Sect. "On Assange's Enlightenment Principles" by Daniela Tafani.

A. Borghini (✉) · D. Tafani
University of Pisa, Pisa, Italy
e-mail: andrea.borghini@unipi.it; daniela.tafani@unipi.it

V. Scalia
University of Florence, Florence, Italy
e-mail: vincenzo.scalia@unifi.it

F. Comunello et al. (eds.), *What People Leave Behind*, Frontiers in Sociology and Social Research 7, https://doi.org/10.1007/978-3-031-11756-5_11

story of Assange, who, in his journalistic and professional action, was to strongly refer to the values dear to the Enlightenment (Tafani, Section "On Assange's Enlightenment Principles").

Thanks to this multi-perspective reading, it is possible not only to reconstruct Assange's story in the least obvious and rhetorical terms but also to restore the human, painful and even violent complexity of the journalist's existence, a collective affair, which affects us all, because it deals with the foundations of our democracies and reflects the times in which we live.

A final remark: what we are going to do briefly here is clearly not a mere erudite or rhetorical exercise, because, as some of the narrative evidence to which we shall refer teaches us, this reconstructive method provides us with the vividness of the existence—with its disappointments, baseness and nobilities—of the historical individuals in question, as well as the time through which they passed. And it makes these biographies in some ways a "living social life" (Petrillo & Tarantino, 2015) which lends further dignity to the classic scientific essay.

Brilliant Historical Evidence

In order to give substance to the experiment, it is necessary to identify the precedents that encourage this interpretation.

We will briefly refer to some of the felicitous sociological insights of Norbert Elias, particularly in his essay on Mozart, and, secondly, to the critique of classical biographies made by an author like Pierre Bourdieu.

Mozart: Portrait of a Genius (Elias, 1993) is a case study in which the German sociologist, based on his critique of the *homo clausus* of the classical sociological tradition and his theory of figurations, frames Mozart's personal destiny as a biographical trajectory influenced and dependent on the social situation of the times. According to Elias, reconstructing Mozart's life does not mean elaborating a simple and linear historical narrative but, rather, opting for a theoretical model based on the reconstruction of the social constraints that social actors are subjected to, of those configurations "which a person [...] has formed through his interdependence with other social figures of his time" (Elias, 1993: 14).

In the discussion on Mozart and his life, genius is not separated from man but is brought back into the social categories of the times. As has been written, "Elias reconstructs Mozart's life as a biographical event with unique traits—his capacity for sublimation—universally human traits—the need for love, for recognition—and historical and social traits that need to be reconstructed—his being part of a bourgeois stratum that began to claim its right to autonomy and professional freedom" (Tabboni, 1993: 99).

In our opinion, scrolling through the pages of Elias' text and putting it in parallel with Assange's biographical and journalistic story—here we refer to Stefania Maurizi's reconstruction (2021)—some analogies can immediately be made. For instance, the following definition of Mozart seems to us to fit perfectly with

Assange's biographical trajectory: "not the least of the reasons for Mozart's tragedy was the fact that he tried, both personally and in his work, to break through the barriers of the social power structure by his own individual efforts, [. . .] and that he did so in a phase of social development when the traditional power structure was virtually intact" (Elias, 1993: 15). In the same way, Assange and his creation, WikiLeaks, have set themselves the objective of unmasking the "secret" power that which rhetorically sets out to safeguard our democracies but, in reality, ends up controlling them and undermining their principles. An ethical and human mission, as defined by Assange in Maurizi's report: "You only live once and so we have a duty to make good use of the time we have and to devote it to doing something meaningful and satisfying. This is something that I consider meaningful and satisfying. It's my nature: I like to create large-scale systems; I like to help vulnerable people and I like to tear bastards apart. And so, it's a job that makes me feel good" (Maurizi, 2021: 56).

Just as Mozart "was putting his life, his whole social existence, at stake" (Elias, 1993: 29) to fight traditional power, so Assange, by attacking the power of the CIA, the NSA and the US government, condemned himself to an existence first as a persecuted person and then as a prisoner awaiting extradition. Another brief remark concerning Mozart's social existence in comparison with his time could be taken as a corollary to be explored further. Elias, at one point, makes Mozart's life more intelligible by considering it "as a micro-process within the central transformation period of this macro-process", despite being aware that the Viennese musician made his existential choices too early, "at a time when the development of society made it possible, but was not yet ready to accept it institutionally" (Elias, 1993: 43). The analogy here lies in the fact that free citizens, journalists who in the past have performed similar feats to Assange's, e.g. Daniel Ellsberg or Glenn Greenwald, or simple people with a love for democracy and a belief in the necessity that this form of government must be safeguarded from the arrogance of power, like Manning and Snowden, constitute an avant-garde that tries to awaken the conscience of public opinion, opposing power and challenging institutions but who are (for now) subjected to deprivation of liberty and persecution because those same institutions do not yet seem ready for this historical turning point.

In short, the Mozart-Assange parallelism does not seem daring because, beyond the different historical and temporal contexts, there are constants—the biographical event generated by social ties established with the institutions of the time or the struggle against power—that reveal the need to interpret biography and history as two poles in close dialectic with each other.

On a similar level, Pierre Bourdieu reiterates his opposition to the genre of life stories or classical biographies in several publications.

For instance, in *Sketch for a Self-Analysis* which, paradigmatically, bears the warning *in exergo* "this is not an autobiography", he first of all emphasises, referring to himself, how "to understand [a person] is first to understand the field with which and against which one has been formed" (Bourdieu, 2008: 4). In other words, in order to reconstruct the genesis and choices of a historical individual, it is necessary to position them in the social space that generated them and the change of which they, in turn, promote. In *The Biographical Illusion*, he emphasises that an individual's biography can be traced back to a series of passages that have to take account of the social space that changes like the life trajectory itself: "a series of successively occupied positions by the same agent (or the same group) in a space which itself is constantly evolving and which is subject to incessant transformations. [...] The biographical events are defined as just so many investments and moves in social space, or more precisely, in the different successive states of the distribution structure of the different types of capital which are in play in the field considered" (Bourdieu, 2017: 215).

Bourdieu lashes out against classical biographies which constitute, in a small way, a reproduction of a kind of philosophy of history and therefore invites—as he does in *Sketch for a Self-Analysis*—in reconstructing the existence of individual X, to start not from the first years of life but from the socio-historical context in which said life was formed and against which it was formed (the field).

Furthermore, a condition of conflict with respect to the field of formation can also generate, according to Bourdieu, a system of dispositions, in other words a habitus, a split, that is, a "coincidence of contraries", for example, "between high academic consecration and low social origin" (Bourdieu, 2008: 100).

Also in this case, we can highlight several stimulating analogies between Bourdieu's way of reconstructing biography and Assange's existential story.

Again drawing on Maurizi's text, we learn of a complex personality "the logical intelligence and inquisitive mind, the originality of behaviours that from the outside may seem bizarre, [...] the interest in intellectual work carried out with an intensity and almost an obsession, that are to the detriment of human interaction" (Maurizi, 2021: 73), as well as of an unconventional childhood, reminiscent of the notion of the field "with which and against which one is made". Born to parents who later separated, "he grew up with his mother [...]. Art and theatre were his mother's main interests and she brought him up moving from one town to another. This nomadic life led him to attend dozens of different schools, some of them for only 1 day. This need to travel would remain one of his characteristics, together with his being a child of the network, not geolocated: someone who looked at the world in its globality. It is no coincidence that he created the stateless journalistic organisation WikiLeaks" (Maurizi, 2021: 73).

And Maurizi goes on to say that this supports our interpretation: "You can tell a lot about a person by meeting or interacting, even from a distance, with his parents. And when I was to later talk or exchange correspondence with [them], I could see that Julian Assange had his father's logical thinking and his mother's anti-authoritarianism and independence. Concerned that her son's intelligence and character would be torn to shreds in the state school system, Christine had encouraged a libertarian and critical education. It was books and his Commodore 64 computer that fired Assange's mind, not traditional education" (Maurizi, 2021: 74).

If we look further into the cultural context in which he had grown up, we find the Cypherpunks, visionaries and libertarians who help to make him a "politically anti-war, libertarian, convinced of the individual's right to protect himself from surveillance and total state control, but not one in favour of the unregulated market"

(Maurizi, 2021: 76). From such a formulation emerged a spirit, once again, willing to challenge power, "the courage to reveal very risky documents, challenging institutions which, legally and even extra-legally, intimidated even the most prosperous media outlets with important power relationships" (Maurizi, 2021: 25).

Finally, there are additional elements that can be interpreted at the intersection of Bourdieu's and Elias's perspectives, which we merely mention here. For instance, the indomitable spirit that has characterised and continues to characterise Assange's professional action is recalled by Elias when the latter says in relation to Mozart: "to understand a person, one needs to know the primordial wishes he or she longs to fulfil" (Elias, 1993: 7).

As for the revolutionary nature of Assange's positions, we could say, together with Maurizi, that it coincides with the means used, namely, "exploiting the power of the network and encryption to obtain and 'leak' confidential documents of great public interest. Just as the traditional media receive information from strangers who send letters or parcels of documents to their editorial offices, Assange and his organisation received hot files sent electronically to their online platform from anonymous sources. The protection of those sharing sensitive documentation was ensured by advanced technological solutions, such as encryption, and other ingenious techniques" (Maurizi, 2021: 20).

In drawing the lines of our observations, it emerges how the interpretative key suggested by classic authors such as Elias and Bourdieu helps to illuminate our times and authorises us to develop a reconstruction, through a relational approach, of Assange's historical trajectory. In his case, we are not dealing with a genius who lived before the age of genius, as Elias claims about Mozart—although many of the Australian journalist's personality traits could make him resemble a genius—but with a figure whose journalistic passion and conflict with power make him a (still unfortunately) lonely hero who casts a sinister shadow over our democracies. As Maurizi suggests, "the objective of the military and intelligence complex of the United States and its allies is to destroy WikiLeaks, to do away with a journalistic organisation that, for the first time in history, has created a deep and persistent crack in that secret power, which has always been accountable to no one and uses state secrecy not to protect the security of citizens, but to ensure impunity and conceal incompetence and corruption" (Maurizi, 2021: 286).

Surveillance, Counter-Surveillance, Counter-Power: Are Assange and WikiLeaks a Counter-Power Agency?

The practices enacted by Julian Assange and WikiLeaks can be defined as *counter-surveillance*, or an opposition not only to the existing power relations but also to the practices of control that are implemented both by political actors, such as the state, and by economic actors, such as contractors, private companies and the IT majors through the manipulation of Big Data (Lyon, 2019). Assange, with the help of

Edward Snowden and Chelsea Manning, enacted a counter-manipulation, as he accessed the Big Data provided by the governments and made them public so that public opinion would become aware of state crimes.

In order to discuss the nature of counter-surveillance, it is necessary to analyse the concept of *surveillance* in depth. The term surveillance refers to all those activities aimed both at preventing and repressing any formal or informal breach of the rules that keep the social fabric together. The activity of watching the way the members of a society behave allows those actors vested with formal and legitimised power to intervene to repress the risk of anomic drifts (Durkheim, 2000). Surveillance is strongly related to power relations, as the dominating social groups, or the *insiders*, make and enforce the rules against the marginal social groups, or outsiders (Becker, 1963). Surveillance can thus be defined as an activity aimed at reproducing the existing force relations and the uneven power distribution within the social spectrum.

There are two different kinds of surveillance one can perceive: the first is *formal*, that is, all those activities of control that are carried out by the state through its apparatuses by relying on legal entitlements (Weber, 1971): police, magistrates and the army are the agencies entitled to wield formal social control, to deploy a surveillance one can define as *vertical*, due to being wielded from the top, i.e. state power, to the bottom, i.e. society. Vertical surveillance requires a high degree of obedience, both to the rules and their enforcers. Whereas it is possible for the members of society to change those who make the rules, so as to eventually indirectly change the rules, it is not possible to dodge the respect of formal rules, the violation of which entails sanctions, from fining to imprisonment. Other authors depict a wider spectrum of formal surveillance, by using the concept of *social control* (Cohen, 1985). This concept also encompasses those agencies whose aims are ostensibly those of support and care, as in the case of a welfare state. Also here we find relations of subjugation and domination, as individuals are required to adhere to the dominating system of values and aims.

Another form of surveillance is the *informal* one, that is, surveillance wielded by the group of peers, neighbours, family, religious groups and work colleagues or the social capital that individuals are embedded in (Coleman, 1988). This is a *horizontal* kind of surveillance that usually requires a cognitive adherence of individuals to the rules underpinning inter-individual interaction, although also in this case it is possible to formally abide by the rules while enacting a secret deviance. Michel Foucault (1976) defines both horizontal and vertical surveillance as *disciplinary powers*, as they draw on social relations to produce a web of domination that is deployed across society. The aim of disciplinary power is that of producing docile bodies that comply with the discipline required by industrial society. On the trail of Foucault's reflections, Deleuze (1999) defines contemporary society as a *society of control*, mostly relying on a web of mutual surveillance to make sure that individuals comply with rules and expectations that are moulded and conveyed through the media. In Deleuze's view, society has assimilated control to the point of letting technology catalyse surveillance and report what happens to the agencies in charge of social control.

Deleuze's view leaves little room for resistance to surveillance, making it impossible to understand what Assange and his WikiLeaks network have done. To this end, it is important to explore in depth the work of David Lyon (2007, 2009, 2016, 2019) who develops the concept of *relational surveillance*. It is a brand new kind of surveillance we are dealing with: it is not vertical, as the state performs it through the subcontract mechanism, with private actors performing the duty of surveillance on its behalf. It is not even a horizontal kind of surveillance as it does not rely on social capital. Relational surveillance draws on the fluidity and anonymity provided by the web, which enables the garnering of as much personal data as possible concerning the private identity and the most hidden aspect of both collective and individual identities and merging them into Big Data. The next step is that of Mega Data, or the totality of Big Data which is used for both public and private purposes. Government subcontractors, in addition to feeding the governments they work for with the information needed, also sell the Mega Data they own to the major economic groups, so that they can use the material for their commercial purposes. At the end of the day, relational surveillance turns out to be a pillar of surveillance capitalism as depicted by some authors (Zuboff, 2019). It is two-tier surveillance that individuals are subjected to: the first is *political* surveillance, i.e. the control on the web of their political opinions, lifestyles and cultural orientation. This kind of surveillance is mostly discriminatory, as it is usually aimed at a specific target such as radical political activists, minorities or groups considered "at risk", such as the Muslims after 9/11 (www.aclu.org). The Patriot Act, enforced under the Bush administration after the terrorist attacks that shook the world, allows both the police and intelligence to put under surveillance both the web and the telephones of individuals who are suspected of belonging to those social groups thought to be siding with terrorists. Despite the protests of human rights organisations, the American government has carried on with this policy, resulting in the unjust surveillance and arrest of hundreds of people just for being Muslims, including the detention in such inhuman places as Guantanamo. The other surveillance is the *economic* one. Economic majors use the data they buy from subcontractors to draft their database of potential customers who are classified according to class, ethnicity, sex education and the record of their surfing in the web. We are evidently dealing with an overt violation of individual privacy, as well as a classification and labelling of individuals without their consent. It is, however, a contradictory process, as Big Data are provided by the web surfers themselves: when they buy an airway ticket or visit the internet page of their favourite singer. Likewise, when they give their data to government agencies, for instance, by booking their anti-COVID vaccination, they willingly provide a great deal of sensitive data about themselves. Their date of birth, credit card number and place of residence are submitted spontaneously. On the other hand, web surfers ignore the use made of their data beyond the use they deem necessary. There is no awareness of who collects Big Data, if and how they are processed and, finally, how they are commercialised. As a result, there is a pervasive control underlying an apparent freedom of surfing the web, not only in the domain of consumption and lifestyles but also in the political context.

However, it is the relational quality of this new surveillance that provides new potentialities to fight and counterbalance the control and subjugation attempts that surveillance capitalism conveys. Both on a micro and on a macro level, it is possible to enact and develop a plurality of strategies of *counter-surveillance*, or those practices that both individuals and groups implement to protect their liberties by *controlling the controller.* On a *micro* level, counter-surveillance is a widespread practice that all of us are involved in on a daily basis. To check a Facebook page or a university site in order to gather information about someone we know is an act of counter-surveillance, as it enables us to know many things we need about a person: residence, the place where they are at a certain time, lifestyle, political ideas, sexual orientation and so on. All this information is provided spontaneously by the users, who often neglect the issue of privacy and security. In any case, they make it possible for anyone with a basic knowledge of IT to easily acquire an amount of information about as many people as possible. On a *macro* level, it is necessary to possess more sophisticated skills, such as the use of more advanced search engines (like Tor) or the know-how to hack and crack the websites of governmental agencies and corporations. Another requirement is that of a network, both among hackers and crackers and those who work within the surveillance network who can leak classified news. The case of Julian Assange and WikiLeaks matches all these requirements. Firstly, because of the use of Tor, which allows for developing an underground connection between the sources and the members of WikiLeaks. Secondly, Assange and his group possess those skills that enable them to hack the IT systems containing the information to be made public. Finally, the cases of Chelsea Manning and Edward Snowden demonstrate the importance of a network of infiltrates inside the surveillance apparatus, as Manning was a soldier and Edward Snowden worked for Booz Allen Hamilton, one of the subcontractors spying the public on behalf of the American government. It was thanks to this articulated organisation that WikiLeaks was able to get hold of the news about state crimes and circulate them among the public. In other words, Assange and his partners exploited the potentialities of relational surveillance at its best.

As watchful and disrespectful of civil liberties as surveillance can be, its contradictions allow those who are surveyed the possibility of resisting and counteracting such surveillance, both by creating an alternative network to that of the dominating political and economic power and by using the information acquired through this network to reveal the abuses committed by the dominating rulers to the public, thus enforcing a real democracy. Some authors (De Lagasnerie, 2020) have argued that the activism of WikiLeaks proves that the only possibility of resisting power, nowadays, lies in the deployment of a strategy based on underground resistance. As surveillance is very invasive, activists have to carry out their sabotaging of power by keeping and developing secret identities and activities. We believe this is not the case of WikiLeaks for two reasons: firstly, because Assange and all his partners have always made public what they were doing and why. In the second case, because their activity consists precisely of revealing to the public what the power conceals, thus reaffirming the value of public discourse against the *arcana imperii*, or the idea that the security of a state relies on the performing of secret activities by those vested with power. Norberto Bobbio (1987: 81) argued that the security of power relies on the insecurity of citizens.

Assange and WikiLeaks have endorsed Bobbio's theorisation by overthrowing it: the more power is insecure, the more citizens feel secure. Tony Blair's lies about the Gulf War, Guantanamo, Abu Ghraib and the bombing of Iraq and Afghanistan, as well as the news about financial and environmental crimes leaked by WikiLeaks, reveal the real aspects of power and, at the same time, show its weak spots, by empowering the public with the resource of information. Moreover, WikiLeaks and Assange suggest making a fluid, democratic, open use of the web, unlike some other attempts, such as the Rousseau platform adopted by the Italian populist five Star Movement (Stockman & Scalia, 2020), for using the web to produce a plebiscitarian form of politics. The American government considers Assange, Manning and Snowden as criminals because they revealed state secrets in violation of the web. While we appreciate that Julian and his partners might not have respected the law completely, they did not behave any differently from those governments that had been spying on private individuals and sold information to private operators without obtaining consent. Finally, the real crimes, as many human rights organisations and civil society groups have pointed out, are those committed in Guantanamo, in Abu Ghraib and in the rendition protests. Such crimes need someone to push the boundaries of legality to reinforce civil liberties and democracy. Julian Assange and WikiLeaks are the ones who have done this.

On Assange's Enlightenment Principles

A defining characteristic of democratic political systems is publicity. Publicity is understood here as the opposite of secrecy and concerns every activity of those in power. Popular sovereignty requires, if not the direct exercise of power by the people, at least that this exercise be open to public scrutiny and control (Bobbio, 1987: 81).

Thus, the term "publicity" can be understood in this first sense as transparency of democratic political and government action, as opposed to the opacity and secrecy of despotic regimes. In addition, it can be also taken to mean freedom of the press (or, more broadly, freedom of expression) as opposed to prior restraint and subsequent sanctioning of authors. Historically, from the very beginning of the French Revolution, both meanings were condensed into the motto "publicity is the safeguard of the people". At the end of 1789, this motto quickly became very popular and could be found in newspapers as a quotation in *exergo*. It was also visible on those who distributed them, namely, on the bronze medal worn by the *colporteurs* (authorised paper sellers), surrounding the image of a wide-open eye—symbol of democratic vigilance—from which rays of light emanated (Plenel, 2020).

Julian Assange explicitly embraces the Enlightenment defences of freedom of expression and the press (quoting John Milton's *Areopagitica*, Thomas Paine and John Wilkes) and cites the French Revolution as an example of the "fight against oppressive regimes" which "begins, and will end, always, with the fight for information and communication", i.e. as one of the "revolutions of the people sharing ideas and information using the technology available to them and expressing themselves in the public space". Consequently, any debate on the activity of WikiLeaks should also address the question of the validity of the underlying Enlightenment principles on which, as Assange emphasises, many modern states are founded (Assange, 2011).

This paragraph traces the Enlightenment sources of three of Assange's theses: the connection between the duty to improve knowledge and the right to communicate, publicity as a test to reveal injustice and the understanding of freedom of the press—by virtue of its automatically subversive nature, in despotic regimes—with an antitotalitarian device.

In Enlightenment thought, the thesis of the collective nature of rational activity is a recurring argument in defence of freedom of expression and the press. From Tindal (1698: 293 ff.) to Gaetano Filangieri (1785: 149 ff.), Immanuel Kant (1786: 144) and Maximilien Robespierre (1791: 161 ff.), the thesis is constantly reiterated that the right to communicate is based on the very right to think, confront and correct one another, thus contributing to the public good of society: rational activity is a public process, the very essence of which is constitutively dialogic (Tafani, 2021). The same thesis is formulated by Assange regarding the "right to communicate knowledge", which he claims is the right to know and the right to speak "taken together" (Assange, 2011):

> We as human beings shepherd and create our intellectual history as a civilization. And it is that intellectual history on the shelf that we can pull off the shelf to do stuff, and to avoid doing the dumb things again [. . .]. There are several different processes that are creating that record, and other processes where people are trying to destroy bits of that record, and others that are trying to prevent people from putting things into that record in the first place. We all live off that intellectual record. So what we want to do is get as much into the record, prevent as much as possible being deleted from the record, and then make the record as searchable as possible. (Assange, 2014: 124)

It is worth noting, with regard to the last lines of the quote above, that for Assange—as already for Kant—what is right in theory must also apply in practice (Kant, 1793) and hence "if we recognise that somebody possesses a right, we must also recognise our own responsibility to protect that right" and to act accordingly (Assange, 2011).

Assange's campaign to achieve "transparency for the powerful" ("what I opposed, and continue to oppose, is the use of secrecy by institutions to protect themselves against the truth of the evil they have done")—always accompanied by the fight to protect "privacy for the weak"[1] (Assange, 2011)—has its immediate precedents in the cypherpunk ethic (Anderson, 2021) but also echoes analogous

[1] We cannot dwell here on the anarchic root of the nexus between Assange's claim of "privacy for the weak" and his reliance on the laws of physics (through cryptography) rather than on the laws of men (through, e.g. democratic controls). On the question of the role of public policies and the state in decentralisation processes, see Morozov (2022).

Enlightenment battles. From Tindal (1698: 309, 319) to Wilkes (1762: 1), Kant and French revolutionaries, the demand for transparency was always garnered from the thesis that secrecy is suspect, since rulers who fear the light invariably have something to hide (Tafani, 2021).

As is well-known, the requirement of publicity is for Kant constitutive of the concept of law itself ("all actions affecting the rights of other human beings are wrong if their maxim is not compatible with their being made public"), and justice can only be thought of as *publicly knowable*, as opposed to the "deceitfulness of a politics that flees the light" (Kant, 1795: 381, 386). The negative version of Kant's test of publicity—which allows the unjust character of a maxim to be recognised through the general opposition it would arouse if it were known—is revived by Assange[2] (Nida-Rümelin, 2010):

> why do powerful organizations engage in secrecy? Well, usually it's because if the plans that they have are made public, the public would oppose them. (Assange, 2014: 134)

> Plans which assist authoritarian rule, once discovered, induce further resistance. Hence such schemes are concealed by successful authoritarian powers until resistance is futile or outweighed by the efficiencies of naked power. (Assange, 2006)

Conversely, transparency of the actions of the powerful and freedom of communication are capable, according to Assange, of preventing injustice and totalitarianism:

> It would mean the inability of neo-totalitarian states to arise in practice because of the free movement of information, the ability for people to speak to each other privately and conspire against such tendencies. (Assange et al., 2012: 158)

Assange shares the Enlightenment view that the right to freedom of communication is a sui generis right, guarding all others and protecting them from the abuses of the established power. It is a right that citizens hold within but also against the state and therefore at the same time, a fragile and very powerful right, frowned upon by governments because of its intrinsic connection with the right of resistance and its potentially subversive nature.

The subversive nature of the power represented by freedom of the press was underlined, among others by Junius (Wade, 1890: 102), Camille Desmoulins (1793 : 45), Jean-Louis De Lolme (1771 : 232 ff.) and Kant (1784 : 41) in a country ruled by a despotic government, the mere existence of freedom of the press would almost infallibly provoke a change in the form of government. This countervailing power was constantly assimilated to a judicial power, i.e. to the court of the people or of public opinion, capable of overseeing the correspondence between the general, sovereign will and the actions of the constituted powers.

This close conceptual link between freedom of the press, surveillance of constituted power and popular sovereignty entails, for those who wish to deny the first two,

---

[2]Kant also stated the following affirmative principle of public right (which is not adopted by Assange): "All maxims which *require* publicity if they are not to fail in their purpose, can be reconciled both with right and with politics" (1795: 386).

the burden of proving that they are not also denying the third and, therefore, democracy itself.

Conclusions

At the end of this long and multifaceted path, there are a few aspects of this discussion that need to be clarified. Assange's figure stands out as a sort of metaphor of modernity, in individual, sociopolitical and philosophical terms. Firstly, Assange echoes the Kantian caveat: "be bold enough to know", which is the individual initiative and risk that characterises modern people. His passion for freedom and his quest for the truth make him push the boundaries of embedded information, as well as of a society that, since 1989, has been imprisoned in the "end of history" thrall. His radical, but at the same time straightforward, choice sheds new light on the possibility of a different society, as he reveals the hidden side of power and the possibility of overturning the trend. Assange challenges the patterns of social control, insofar as he operates in the network of surveillance while filling the structural holes within it to initiate and develop a practice of radical liberation. Ancient Romans wondered who guarded the guards. Assange tell us we can be the guards both of ourselves and our surveillants, thus reducing, or even invalidating, any authoritarian temptations they may have. If power is a positive resource, the building of a relational web differing from the existing one is the necessary condition for a change of power purposes. Finally, Assange is modern insofar as he shows that all the emancipatory purposes of the Enlightenment-inspired political philosophy are far from being old fashioned. Publicity, transparency, individual and collective initiative for creating a shared truth, out of which we can build a freer, fairer and more equal society, start from our courage to know and to act. Let us hope the British Supreme Court will learn this lesson and free Julian.

References

Anderson, P. D. (2021). Privacy for the weak, transparency for the powerful: The cypherpunk ethics of Julian Assange. *Ethics and Information Technology, 23*, 295–308. https://doi.org/10.1007/s10676-020-09571-x

Assange, J. (2006, December 3). *Conspiracy as governance.* Retrieved January 13, 2022, from https://archive.fo/kr8Pr

Assange, J. (2011). *The unauthorized autobiography.* Canongate Books.

Assange, J., Appelbaum, J., Müller-Maguhn, A., & Zimmermann, J. (2012). *Cypherpunks. Freedom and the future of the internet.* OR Books.

Assange, J. (2014). *When Google met WikiLeaks.* OR Books.

Becker, H. (1963). *Outsiders.* Free Press.

Bobbio, N. (1987). *The future of democracy. A defence of the rules of the game*. University of Minnesota Press. Trans. R. Griffin, Original work published 1984. https://archive.org/details/futureofdemocrac00bobb

Bourdieu, P. (2017). The biographical illusion. In W. Hemecker, E. Saunders, & G. Schima (Eds.), *Biography in theory. Key texts with commentaries* (pp. 210–216). De Gruyter.

Bourdieu, P. (2008). *Sketch for a self-analysis*. University of Chicago Press. Trans. R. Nice, Original work published 2004.

Cohen, S. (1985). *Visions of social control*. Transaction.

Coleman, J. (1988). Social capital in the creation of human capital. *American Journal of Sociology, 94*, S95–S120. Supplement: Organizations and Institutions: Sociological and Economic Approaches to the Analysis of Social Structure. http://www.jstor.org/stable/2780243

Deleuze, G. (1999). *Apparati di cattura*. Castelvecchi.

De Lolme, J. L. (1771). *Constitution de l'Angleterre ou État du gouvernement anglais comparé avec la forme républicaine et avec les autres monarchies de l'Europe*. https://archive.org/details/constitutiondel02lolmgoog/page/n241/mode/2up

Desmoulins, C. (1793). *Le Vieux Cordelier*, 3. https://gallica.bnf.fr/ark:/12148/bpt6k1045474h/f21.item

De Lagasnerie, G. (2020). *L'Arte della Rivolta*. Stampa Alternativa.

Durkheim, E. (2000). *La Divisione del Lavoro Sociale*. Edizioni di Comunità.

Elias, N. (1993). *Mozart: Portrait of a genius*. Polity Press. Trans. E. Jephcott. https://archive.org/details/mozartportraitof0000elia/

Filangieri, G. (1785). La scienza della legislazione del Cavalieri Gaetano Filangieri. In *Della Libertà della Stampa* (pp. 145–157). Stamperia Raimondiana. Libro IV, Parte III, Capo LII. https://archive.org/details/bub_gb_WDpHhK_4JpUC/page/n161

Foucault, M. (1976). *Sorvegliare e Punire. Nascita della Prigione*. Einaudi.

Kant, I. (1784). Beantwortung der Frage: Was ist Aufklärung? In *Kant's gesammelte Schriften* (Vol. VIII, pp. 33–42). W. de Gruyter. In Preussische Akademie der Wissenschaften (ed.) (1900). https://korpora.zim.uni-duisburg-essen.de/kant/verzeichnisse-gesamt.html

Kant, I. (1786). Was heißt: Sich im Denken orientiren? In *Kant's gesammelte Schriften* (Vol. VIII, pp. 131–147).

Kant, I. (1793). Über den Gemeinspruch: Das mag in der Theorie richtig sein, taugt aber nicht für die Praxis. In *Kant's gesammelte Schriften* (Vol. VIII, pp. 273–313).

Kant, I. (1795). Zum ewigen Frieden. Ein philosophischer Entwurf von Immanuel Kant. In *Kant's gesammelte Schriften* (Vol. VIII, pp. 341–386).

Lyon, D. (2007). *Massima sicurezza*. Raffaello Cortina.

Lyon, D. (2009). *Oltre il Panopticon*. Raffaello Cortina.

Lyon, D. (2016). *Surveillance after snowden*. Wiley.

Lyon, D. (2019). *The culture of surveillance*. Polity.

Maurizi, S. (2021). *Il potere segreto*. Chiarelettere.

Morozov, E. (2022, January 8). *Francesca Bria on decentralisation, sovereignty, and Web3*. Retrieved January, 17, 2022, from https://the-crypto-syllabus.com/francesca-bria-on-decentralisation/

Nida-Rümelin, J. (2010, December 16). *Demokratie will Öffentlichkeit*. Die Zeit. https://www.zeit.de/2010/51/WikiLeaks

Petrillo, A., & Tarantino, C. (2015). Introduzione. In P. Bourdieu (Ed.), *La Miseria del Mondo*. Mimesis.

Plenel, E. (2020). *La sauvegarde du peuple. Presse, liberté et démocratie*, La Découverte. https://www.academia.edu/42807416/Edwy_Plenel_La_sauvegarde_du_peuple_Presse_libert%C3%A9_et_d%C3%A9mocratie

Robespierre, M. (1791). *Discours sur la liberté de la presse, prononcé à la Société des amis de la constitution, le 11 mai 1791*. Imprimerie Nationale. In Idem (1867). *Oeuvres*, recueillies et annotées par A. Vermorel. Paris: Achille Faure, pp. 161–182. https://numelyo.bm-lyon.fr/f_view/BML:BML_00GOO0100137001101984420/IMG00000177

Stockman, C., & Scalia, V. (2020). Democracy and the five stars movement. *European Politics and Society, 21*(5), 603–617.

Tabboni, S. (1993). *Norbert Elias. Un ritratto intellettuale*. Il Mulino.

Tafani, D. (2021). Il palladio dei diritti dei popoli. La libertà di stampa come contropotere in Kant e negli scritti rivoluzionari. *Bollettino telematico di filosofia politica*. https://doi.org/10.5281/zenodo.5806511

Tindal, M. (1698). *A letter to a member of parliament, shewing, that a restraint on the press is inconsistent with the Protestant religion, and dangerous to the liberties of the nation*. J. Darby. Reprinted as *Of the Liberty of the Press; in a letter to a member of Parliament*, in Idem (1709). *Four Discourses,* London, pp. 293–329. https://babel.hathitrust.org/cgi/pt?id=nnc1.cu56691041&view=1up&seq=303

Wade, J. (Ed.). (1890). *The letters of Junius* (Vol. 1). George Bell and Sons. https://archive.org/details/juniusincludingl01juniuoft/page/102

Weber, M. (1971). *Il Lavoro Intellettuale come Professione*. Einaudi.

Wilkes, J. (1762, June 5). *The North Briton*, 1. https://archive.org/details/northbriton00wilkgoog/page/n12/mode/2up

Zuboff, S. (2019). *The age of surveillance capitalism*. Public Affairs.

Andrea Borghini is Full Professor of Sociology at the Department of Political Sciences, University of Pisa (Italy), where he teaches also History of Sociology and Sociology of Deviance. He mainly investigates topics related to the political transformations of the Nation State, the sociology of Pierre Bourdieu, the public sociology, the historical sociology and the transformation of the social control. He is editor of the scientific journal "The Lab's Quarterly" and member of several Editorial Boards of sociological journals. He has been visiting professor in England and the USA in the last years, and he is author of many articles and books in different languages.

Among his recent works are *Science and Society in Karl Raimund Popper: Some Reflections Starting from Positivismusstreit*, (*Journal of Classical Sociology*, 2, 2015); *Exploring the Crisis: Theoretical Perspectives and Empirical Investigations* (Pisa, 2015); *The Role of the Nation State in the Global Age* (Brill, 2016); *The Relationship Between Globality and Stateness: Some Sociological Reflections* (Palgrave, 2018); *Carcere e disuguaglianze socio-economiche: una ricostruzione del dibattito sociologico* (Pisa, 2018); *Public Sociology and Southern European Societies: A Critical View* (Revista espanola de sociologia, 1, 2020); and Carcere e scienze sociali (ed. with G. Pastore), Maggioli, 2021.

Vincenzo Scalia is Associate Professor of Sociology of Deviance at the University of Florence. He was Reader in Criminology at the University of Winchester (UK) from 2015 to 2021. He has been active in the field of criminology for 25 years, since he collaborated on the Città Sicure project of the Emilia-Romagna Region. He mainly deals with prisons, organised crime and police brutalities. He has taught and carried out research in Italy (Bologna, Macerata, Padua, Palermo, Rome III), Mexico (Universidad Autonoma de Tlaxcala, UNAM) and Argentina (Universidad del Museo Social). His works are published in English, Spanish and Turkish. He is a member of the Editorial Board of both Italian and international criminology journals.

His recent works include *Crime, Networks and Power: The Structural Transformation of Sicilian Cosa Nostra* (Palgrave, 2016); *Deadly Dialogues: The Magherini Case and Police Brutalities in Italy* (Journal of Organizational Ethnography, 2021); and *The Stench of Canteen Culture: The Death of Federico Aldrovandi and the Italian Police Culture* (Social Justice Journal, 2021).

Daniela Tafani is a fixed-term researcher of Political Philosophy at the University of Pisa. She has been a research fellow at the University of Bologna. She has worked on Kantian moral philosophy, the philosophy of law in German idealism, the relationship between ethics and law in the twentieth century and contemporary libertarian paternalisms. Her current research interests include the ethics and politics of artificial intelligence and the neuroscience of moral judgment. Among her publications are *Virtù e felicità in Kant* (Leo S. Olschki 2006), *Distinguere uno Stato da una banda di ladri. Etica e diritto nel XX secolo* (Il Mulino 2011) and *Beiträge zur Rechtsphilosophie des deutschen Idealismus* (Lit Verlag 2014).

Chapter 12
When the Footprint Is a Carbon One: A Sustainable Paradigm for the Analysis of the Contemporary Society

Arianna Calderamo and Mariella Nocenzi

Introduction

The quick pace of the radical transformations required to face environmental problems challenges the social sciences' focus on the change, its factors and dimensions—economic, political, social, environmental—and on their running to deal with its interpretation (Delanty, 2020). Among all the other scientific targets, what is relevant seems to be the highlighting of the transformations that affect the social sciences principles, theories and methodologies themselves in order to better understand social change, especially its connection to the crisis—not only of the environment—and the development trade-offs.

The authors suppose that three key factors characterise social change and, at the same time, are constitutive elements for social sciences: time, space and relations (Nocenzi & Sannella, 2020). Sustainable change and the change towards sustainability, as research subjects, are based on the transformation of these concepts, and their adoption in social research outlines a real paradigm shift for the social sciences. Thanks to the pandemic experience, it is possible to make use of a pivot study for the application of the sustainability paradigm. It contemplates that the models of human actions are not sustainable to preserve the environment and society from their negative effects. The production and the consumption processes, the use of raw resources and waste management assume a different meaning as social processes and, with them, the meaning that the individuals assign them, and, at the end, the individual and collective behaviour itself (Jorgenson et al., 2019).

After a mature theoretical interpretation of environmental sociology about the interaction between humans and the environment, it seems the time for sociology is arriving for a revision of the basic concepts of the discipline to analyse society and

A. Calderamo · M. Nocenzi (✉)
Department of Communication and Social Research, Sapienza University of Rome, Rome, Italy
e-mail: arianna.calderamo@uniroma1.it; mariella.nocenzi@uniroma1.it

F. Comunello et al. (eds.), *What People Leave Behind*, Frontiers in Sociology and Social Research 7, https://doi.org/10.1007/978-3-031-11756-5_12

individuals as they appear, thanks to the crucial common awareness and scientific knowledge of the current cultural transformations (Gallino, 2016). Some aspects can be considered strategical: what the shared assumption of the carbon footprint reveals is, firstly, a limit of human action and, secondly, its outlines in terms of temporal, spatial and relational dimensions. The article aims at highlighting how social actions could be redefined starting from their consequences, represented by the carbon traces produced in particular and sustainable development in general.

From the New Meaning of a "Human" Footprint to New Perspectives for a Changing Social Theory of Sustainability

Over the last few decades, environmental issues have gradually permeated all social spheres with their relevance and urgency, manifesting themselves in their consequences and triggering a reflection on their causes that can no longer be postponed. Since these are mainly attributable to human action in a specific geological era, such as the present one, which is why we call it the Anthropocene (Crutzen, 2006), it is not surprising that the mark left by a body, which constitutes a clear indication of its passage, can only be increasingly evoked by that left by man on the ecosystem.

It is no coincidence that when the two scholars Wackernagel and Rees (1996) conducted their analysis of the consequences of the environmental crisis in the 1990s, they preferred to replace the measurement tool that was widespread at the time and based on the planet's ability to regenerate its resources—consumed by man—with a new one, namely, the units of carbon dioxide (CO_2) produced also by man. This allowed them to measure the gases emitted into the atmosphere and the primary cause of climate change, leading them to focus attention on the consequences of each individual action and no longer on the sum of collective actions acting on the planet's resources.

As many awareness-raising campaigns that followed the definition of this new indicator underlined, it would be possible for each individual to calculate his or her own personal trace left in the environment by estimating the emission of CO_2, to which everyone knew the deterioration of the environmental balance was linked.

The subjective dimension acquired by this indicator probably made the representation of human responsibility for the environmental crisis more effective than a norm or a scientific explanation but, above all, also the possibility of what it would be possible to do—or not do—thanks to daily micro-actions to try to reverse the course (Puech, 2019). Although there are now widespread smartphone apps that allow us to estimate this indicator while eating a plate of meat or more and more tickets of our travels indicate how much CO_2 our movement involves, the measurements are becoming increasingly complex, and the effectiveness of human action is limited. Carbon dioxide emissions come from the production and consumption processes of goods and services, affecting the whole chain of transformation and the use of each individual resource (Moore & Rees, 2013).

Despite the increasing visibility of the traces left on the planet with one's behaviour, many factors contribute to the repetition of those that leave the most unsustainable traces with respect to the use of resources: lower economic cost in the present, habits, traditions, poor knowledge of direct and indirect consequences and low level of trust in science, in its definition of consequences and in the preparation of these tools. In short, a mix of lack of knowledge, poor connection with institutions and the persistence of a past model of development are natural opposites to the evidence of a change in progress (Urry, 2009).

Compared to the past, however, there is now a more shared awareness that human action can affect physical and symbolic spaces even more extensively than those directly affected by an act performed and can have a temporal development no longer limited to its implementation. If we add to this the fact that the globalised and hyperconnected world makes the actions of each individual particularly integrated with those of the other (Giddens et al., 1999), we define the conditions for a redefinition of the constitutive principles of social life: space, time and relationships.

It can be agreed that the worsening of the problems of nature has accelerated the process of crisis of the previous model of social development, the so-called modernity model, on the basis of which the social sciences had precisely defined those constitutive quantities, giving priority to man and recognising his/her action as a capacity without limits, not even those placed in the coexistence of nature (Nocenzi, 2019). The downsising of man, of the potential of his/her actions and of his/her expectation of development today is witnessed not only by the irreversible trace (s)he has left on the planet but also by the comparison with other agent beings, non-humans, whose actions and connected space, time and relationships circumscribe even more those of humans: for instance, software, sensors, algorithms and cyborgs that are increasingly present in every human action and that populate relationships with humans, on par with them and even independently of humans themselves (Accoto, 2019).

In this specific context, that is, technological and cultural, political and economic, the change taking place cannot but appear radical because it transforms the constituent magnitudes of social life, as already mentioned, but also the identities of the social actors themselves and the purpose towards which social action, whether individual or collective, tends, in light of the traces it leaves behind.

The shift away from a previous model of development, the modern one, can be recognised by the elements described so far, relating to the increasingly intrinsic limitation of human actions and their changed spatial, temporal and relational conditions (Meadows et al., 1972; Turner, 2008). To have clear evidence of this, it is sufficient to refer to the definition of development coined as early as 1987 by the World Commission on Environment and Development set up by the United Nations and chaired by the Norwegian politician Gro Harlem Brundtland, which stressed that "development is sustainable when it meets the needs of the present without compromising the ability of future generations to meet their own needs" (United Nations, 1987). The objective towards which individual and collective social action tends, therefore, according to the alternative model of development that was being proposed, changes the very nature of social action:

- Its results extend through direct and indirect effects beyond the present, influencing, however, the same present in terms of its preconditions, expectations and realisation.
- The beneficiaries of the action are identified in those future generations that symbolically open up the potential involved to the whole of humanity, insisting, therefore, in a space coinciding with that of the entire planet.
- The object of the action oriented towards future generations on the planet is needs, the fundamental basis for building social relations and redefining them in their deepest meaning, i.e. that which sees their satisfaction in nature.

The revisiting of the constitutive principles of social action could not fail to prefigure a real paradigm shift for the social sciences, and among those that have attempted it, the one proposed by Dunlap (2008) with the manifest name of *new ecological paradigm* is of some interest. Starting from the four assumptions of (a) the nature of human beings, (b) the causes of human actions, (c) the context within which humans act and, indeed, (d) the limits on those actions, Dunlap recognises environmental crises as determinants of equally radical transformations in social action that go beyond the modern anthropocentric and exemptionalist models (Dunlap & Catton, 1980, 1994):

- The exceptional, but no longer dominant, capacities of human action referring to cultural, technological, economic production, etc. are part of a composite set of actions implemented also by other living species with which humans are interdependent in the global ecosystem.
- Human actions are not only characterised by social and cultural determinants but also by a complex set of causes and effects located within the natural system, not only social but such that unintended consequences of human actions can be identified.
- On the other hand, human action is limited by objective biophysical resources that are exhaustible and whose accessibility and usability cannot always be modified by human capabilities.
- The laws of nature cannot be abrogated by the potential of human action.

This is a new paradigm of analysis of human action and, more generally, of social life, which for many scholars has meant recognising the crisis of society itself in favour of a "more extensive and composite system", which some have called no longer society but *ecology* as a set of spatio-temporal constructs experienced by all sentient species (Latour, 1995; Serres, 2009). That this is also a challenge for science in general, and not only for social science, is evident in the very scope of the reformulation of basic cognitive categories.

Factors and Dimensions of Change: Development Trade-offs and Citizen Science

The change described so far, which focuses on the sustainability-oriented development model, seems to affect the very dynamics in which the change manifests itself. Indeed, it is no longer conceived as a linear development but as a contingent emergence or social becoming, that is, as a process of construction/destruction of cultures and societies by their members, under the conditions created by previous constructive and destructive efforts. The result of these efforts, the social world that emerges (or becomes), is not necessarily marked by progress; there is at most a possibility of progress (Beck, 1999, 2000). Societies are no longer reified systems but rather as fluid networks of interrelated actions, as sociocultural fields of various dimensions that contract and expand in terms of uncertainty (Bauman, 1999). The outcome depends entirely on human decisions and choices, and whether they are aware of it or not, individuals are confronted with a range of alternative options and choices (Bauman, 2000).

Although human actions seem to remain at the centre of the dynamics of change, it actually experiences for the first time since its "modern" definition (Eisenstadt, 1973) the relocation of its meaning to the realm of human actions: the set of transformations in the structure and organisation of a society in a given period of time (Tilly, 2004) measurable through the factors of rapidity, direction, flow, driving force and governability. Precisely through these identifying factors, it is possible to reduce the human dimension to one of the dimensions of change: more likely, it is the human dimension that is the most tangible for human knowledge, which, however, inevitably ends up absorbing all the other—interrelated—dimensions, for example, the ecological one. It's the case of the factor of the governability of change, according to which it can be managed by following rules that leave a certain margin for personal or collective initiative but which also occur spontaneously, not foreseen by man.

It is on this "ecological" meaning of change that the model of sustainable development insists, which sections "Social Change and Human Action: The Case Study of the Complex Construction of Environmental Policies" and "An Effective Environmental Policies Evaluation Model: The *Positive Thinking* Framework" will illustrate through a case study applied precisely to the construction of environmental policies and the evaluation of their results. To complete the description here by linking it also to human action and its traces—understood as the outcomes of the action carried out—it is possible to dwell on two aspects characterising change: trade-offs and the shared creation of knowledge.

Starting with the first element in order, it has already been pointed out that change does not necessarily follow improving trajectories. This acquisition, which seems to be consolidated in the history of human organisations, has actually seen change connoted as an ineluctable destiny or an error in the line of progress when it has brought negative transformations to social life. Thus, a partial meaning of change has in fact been recognised. Experts from different disciplines, for example, are aware of this, as they were brought together by the United Nations to agree on the objectives of change for a sustainable development model. First the Millennium Development Goals (MDGs) and then the 2030 Agenda Goals (SDGs) incorporate all the strands of change, even providing for development trade-offs. Although they are aimed at achieving sustainable development, the achievement of the latter is not the ultimate evolutionary stage but rather the result of the combination of several factors and outcomes that produce profitable synergies but also trade-offs that must be constructive. The realisation of one SDG can slow down the achievement of another, just as it can be independent of another—think, for example, the industrial innovation activities envisaged by SDG9 that can have deleterious effects on the survival of animal species, hindering the achievement of SDG15. This in itself constitutes a limit to human action to control its results and effects, which fits well with the conceptual framework of sustainability. It will be observed in the following paragraphs how theoretical models, such as *positive thinking* (Lo Presti & Stame, 2015), allow useful outcomes to be obtained from action more from successes than from failures, from which the causal dynamics are explained and not only the predetermined objectives and desired effects of the intervention itself (Stame, 2016) but a reversal of the understanding of change.

However, this reversal also requires the widest possible sharing of knowledge and expertise in order to be able to describe and analyse all possible actions. Models such as citizen science, for example, not surprisingly much discussed in the last decade, propose activities relating to scientific research to which non-experts, such as citizens, can also contribute (Bonney et al., 2016). These contributions take place in different collaborative processes from which possible problem-solving strategies or new projects are determined. In addition to providing an effective representation of the different potentials for change linked to human action, this collaborative model also offers evidence of how change itself is transforming, drawing a new relationship between science and society.

Social Change and Human Action: The Case Study of the Complex Construction of Environmental Policies

In recent years, the evidence (EEA, 2016) has led to the evolution of environmental public policies, with an increasing focus on behavioural and attitudinal changes in society, starting from the policy design stages. Today, environmental public policies can be regarded as one of the most important drivers of change, the cornerstones on which all efforts of the international community to address environmental issues rest. They are also the means to induce individuals towards a more responsible and concrete action as an active and conscious part of change.

Looking at individual behaviour, however, does not mean looking away from the systemic problems of human beings and their production patterns. It is very clear that it is not possible to solve the climate crisis or halt the loss of biodiversity simply by changing people's behaviour. Similarly, it is also correct to consider the systems and patterns underlying environmental problems as the resulting sum of several individual behaviours implemented by different groups of people. The social changes that have taken place over the last decade necessarily imply a rethinking of the impact on environmental issues that the change of an individual can have. The increasing availability and constant access to information related to environmental issues, advances in information and communication technologies and the intensification of action-oriented social networks around the world make it possible to consider citizens as infinite potential agents of change with respect to the current environmental situation (EEA, 2016). In this sense, rethinking the role and type of environmental communication carried out at the institutional level can also be a decisive and effective strategy in supporting the social transition needed for sustainable change. Better communication can help to make environmental policies more efficient by fostering their social acceptance. The integration of behavioural studies in the process of public policy design and implementation has shown that obtaining a higher level of engagement of people leads them more strongly to adopt truly sustainable behaviour and to support the policies adopted at the public level.

Similarly, a decisive focus on behaviour and attitudes in the field of systemic change-oriented environmental public policies could also be imagined. The individual's acceptance of the policy always plays a key role. As observed by Hirschman (1967), in the field of development cooperation projects, very often the difference between the failure and success of a project can be found in the project behaviour of the people involved in the front line of implementation. Attitudes, beliefs and actions of individuals interact with each other and define the mechanisms and structural characteristics that produce project results. This, in the field of environmental public policy, is a strategy that should be considered.

Most environmental policies require a behavioural change, very often a radical one, not only for individual citizens but also for those who occupy operational and decision-making positions within public administration structures and who, therefore, have a duty to implement the policy in question. A lack of acceptance of these roles within the public administration can be a crucial factor in determining a reduced structural effectiveness of public environmental policy. As an example, one could apply this reasoning to one of the best-known environmental public policies: the Green Public Procurement (GPP) system. GPP is one of the main tools through which the European Union is trying to contain the carbon footprint of the public administrations of the Member States and, consequently, of the private actors involved in the market of goods and services on which they rely. The criteria and standards introduced by GPP have, in some respects, led to changes in the way public procurement is managed by many public administration employees and managers. The degree to which these changes are integrated into existing management processes and, therefore, the degree of acceptance of the environmental policy by the employees and managers of the public administration as a whole can make a difference in terms of the overall effectiveness of the implemented policy and, therefore, the positive impact on the carbon footprint of the public administration.

An Effective Environmental Policies Evaluation Model: The *Positive Thinking* Framework

The relevance of environmental public policy and the ever-increasing urgency of fostering sustainable change make the use of evaluation theory and practice in environmental public policy imperative.

With regard to sustainable change and change towards sustainability, the evaluation of environmental policies makes it possible to investigate in detail the mode and nature of this "movement" in time and space. Unfortunately, it should be noted that Italy does not yet have a robust and extensive system for evaluating public policies. Moreover, the term "evaluation" is often used with a profoundly different and limited meaning from the one deepened in social science studies as a research methodology that adds a value judgment and as a democratic process of social learning (Stame, 2016).

To date, public policy evaluation has focused on the relationships between policy inputs and outputs, and on ex post, exclusively effectiveness evaluations conducted through mostly quantitative methods. But, as mentioned, sustainable change plays its game on people's behaviour and attitudes. These aspects, which are so crucial for social change, can hardly be grasped and analysed in the context of effectiveness evaluations that mainly focus on policies.

Examining environmental public policies both ex ante and *in itinere* in the evaluation process allows us to "get inside" the proposal, in both the design and implementation phases. The proposal is therefore to use evaluation approaches that can shed light both on the "black box" (Weiss, 1997) of the management and decision-making processes that determine the successes and/or failures of public policies and on the real social, economic and cultural impacts these policies have on the population, on those that are unexpected as well as expected. Therefore, an integration of current evaluation systems is envisaged, using the theoretical and applicative framework of *positive thinking* approaches (Lo Presti & Stame, 2015; Lo Presti, 2020), which share the idea that we learn more from successes than failures, as a proactive driver for action. Moreover, success adds information about the causes of events, while failure merely reproduces the initial lack of knowledge, highlighting obstacles to change (Hirschman, 1967; Tendler & Stame, 1992).

The approach is based on the analysis of available resources and strengths, directly observing what in the specific context is considered a positive outcome rather than the predetermined objectives and desired effects of the intervention itself (Stame, 2016; Lo Presti, 2016). Evaluation is understood in a positive sense as a valid tool for improving the effectiveness of environmental policy in order to add information about why and how change occurs, and not just its mere occurrence. This type of evaluation is not only concerned with what the public policy does but also with how all stakeholders, implementers and recipients respond. Thus, it is possible to investigate aspects that mediate between input and output, such as intermediate processes and psychological and organisational factors. A useful reflection is to observe the effects that arise from the policy beyond the expected and desirable direct results (Hirschman, 1967 in Stame, 2017). Thanks to its intrinsic democratic nature (Bezzi, 2016), the involvement of all policy actors allows this type of participatory evaluation to retain every nuance of the phenomenon studied in terms of knowledge and thus in empowerment capacity, whereby one only learns what increases one's ability to master a change, unleashing new and better ideas (Senge, 1990 in Stame, 2016).

A concrete example of a case study in which this methodological crisis is being tested is the creation of an evaluation model for Italian National Parks. SDG 15 "Life on Earth" of the 2030 Agenda aims to protect and restore terrestrial ecosystems and safeguard biodiversity. The rate of biodiversity loss is considered among the most serious threats to human well-being in the twenty-first century (Rockstrom et al., 2009; Cardinale et al., 2012). Robust scientific evidence confirms the substantial role of protected areas in national environmental public policies (Costanza et al., 1997; Hoffmann et al., 2018; da Silva et al., 2017). Among the most important challenges for protected areas are the search for efficient management close to the needs of populations and the ability to estimate and communicate the multiple effects of nature conservation (Lopoukhine et al., 2012). The overriding prerogative of national parks is nature conservation, which must nevertheless be able to consider the persistence and prosperity of the local communities living within them.

Protected areas are the expression of one of the most important national environmental public policies: the tool of evaluation appears decisive in deepening their strengths and weaknesses and in analysing the impacts they have on the territories in which they exist, with a view to improving them. However, it also represents a valuable opportunity to broaden the research and knowledge horizons of evaluation in an area that is still too little explored.

At the international level, the International Union for Conservation of Nature (IUCN) has established effectiveness evaluation as the main evaluation approach for protected areas, defining the IUCN-WCPA framework for management effectiveness evaluation (Hockings et al., 2000). This framework, later revised in 2006 (Hockings et al., 2006), still constitutes the basis for most of the methodologies and evaluation systems for protected areas applied worldwide, which are flexible and able to return homogeneous and standardised results, allowing them to be compared globally.

In Italy, the only experiment is MEVAP (Metodologia di Valutazione delle Aree Protette) (Marino, 2012). As a quantitative and structured methodology, MEVAP allows for a macro-level assessment of the management of protected areas to the extent that they achieve national and international nature conservation objectives, as well as a micro-level assessment of the management of protected areas at the local level. MEVAP makes it possible to assess the effectiveness of the protected area and to set standards by making reasonable and objective comparisons without, however, paying attention to the processes, mechanisms and causes that lead to certain results, failing to understand the process of why and how they occur. In this regard, there is an attempt to integrate the existing systems of effectiveness evaluation with the use of *positive thinking*, which are complementary evaluation approaches in providing a vision that is certainly more comprehensive than the current one. The importance of the human and social elements is such that recourse to an intellectual background of the human sciences in the evaluation of the Italian National Parks is more than necessary, following a largely interdisciplinary and not exclusively quantitative approach. Protected areas represent a real experience of sustainability capable of imagining new scenarios of coexistence between man and nature and innovative territorial development strategies. With Italy's immense natural heritage, it is important for there to be greater attention to the instrument of evaluation, which, however, goes beyond the idea of mere performance monitoring. The hope, as a courageous attempt, is to increase political, social and cultural attention to the issue of the environment, questioned by professionals with different and at the same time complementary points of view and preparation (Gallino, 1992).

The importance of the relationship between research in the natural sciences and research in the social sciences should be strongly emphasised, and this should be encouraged and supported. As many points of view as possible are needed when talking about the environment, ecology and nature conservation in the full and most recent holistic vision of sustainable development. Scientific and biological knowledge, which studies ecosystems and their functioning, must be easily integrated with social and economic knowledge, which is indispensable for the interpretation and implementation of development processes. Only through such an association will it really be possible to devise evaluative research designs capable of investigating sustainable development in a comprehensive and functional manner, especially on a local scale, whose aspects are so peculiar and difficult to transfer elsewhere.

The position that evaluation is gaining within the design and management of ecosystem conservation is an excellent signal for all environmental evaluations. Environmental policies need to be able to engage with the dynamics and processes of both natural and man-made ecosystems.

Some Concluding Remarks

Looking at the environmental crisis we are discussing from a conceptual and anthropological point of view, it is possible to say that it stems from a profound cognitive crisis in the construction of environmental policy linked to the existing fracture between the socio-human and natural sciences (Saragosa, 2005). It is absolutely necessary to rethink development in a version that is sustainable, shifting from a strictly environmentalist vision to an ecological vision (Gallino, 1992). The same is true for human action that promotes change. The models that organise all the structures of our existence must always represent starting points for reflection and never points of arrival: they must be confronted with reality, and they must be destroyed and reconstructed because they live in action and therefore in change and always in a given context that brings all the elements together. A social ecology capable of overcoming the dichotomy and antagonism between man and nature is required, since it is not suited to respond to the requirements of a global discipline, to the instances of the different territorial realities or, even less, to the elements capable of guaranteeing a future and the safeguarding of the natural heritage (Giacomini, 1980).

But what is even more relevant is that the expression "sustainable development" is increasingly a protagonist of the common language, as the signal of a deep change in sensitivity, of a more widespread and conscious ecological awareness, of a sustainable change. Understanding how sustainable development can be achieved in practice on the ground in every part of the world is a matter of fundamental importance. We have the technology and the know-how to be able to direct energies and ideas towards a concrete and possible transformation of our usual mental clothes. Sachs (2015) is convinced that through a great deal of effort in the study and design of sustainable business processes and new technologies, sustainable development is achievable and within our reach: an alternative to today's "business as usual"(BAU) scenarios must be found, because it is a truly viable, as well as necessary, path.

The role of research in this is absolutely crucial; there is an urgent need to understand the problems and find the best solutions as far as possible. In the current state of affairs, it is no longer the task solely of naturalists and biologists to deal with the "sciences of planet Earth", and, in an absolutely holistic and interdisciplinary vision, this definition must include all the disciplines useful and necessary to study the complex processes that enable life on the Earth ecosystem (Wilson, 2016).

The role of the social sciences in this research is far from secondary or marginal. On the contrary, it is now more crucial than ever to study the connections between societies and ecosystems from a social perspective too, with the aim of the continuing quest for a longed-for sustainable, equitable, just and inclusive development.

References

Accoto, C. (2019). *Il mondo dato. Cinque brevi lezioni di filosofia digitale*. Egea.

Bauman, Z. (1999). *La società dell'incertezza*. Il Mulino.

Bauman, Z. (2000). *La solitudine del cittadino globale*. Feltrinelli.

Beck, U. (1999). *Che cos'è la globalizzazione. Rischi e prospettive della società planetaria*. Carocci.

Beck, U. (2000). *La società del rischio. Verso una seconda modernità*. Carocci.

Bezzi, C. (2016, Maggio 3). *Perché la valutazione è migliore se è partecipata*. Retrieved Gennaio, 2021, from https://bezzicante.files.wordpress.com/2014/06/perchc3a9-la-valutazione-c3a8-migliore-se-c3a8-partecipata.pdf

Bonney, R., Cooper, C., & Ballard, H. (2016). The theory and practice of citizen science: Launching a new journal. *Citizen Science: Theory and Practice, 1*(1), 1–4.

Cardinale, J., Emmett Duffy, J., Gonzalez, A., Hooper, D., Perrings, C., Venail, P., Narwani, A., Mace, G., Tilman, D., Wardle, D., Kinzig, A., Daily, G., Loreau, M., Grace, J., Larigauderie, A., Srivastava, D., & Naeem, S. (2012). Biodiversity loss and its impact on humanity. *Nature, 486*(7401), 59–67. https://doi.org/10.1038/nature11148

Costanza, R., Groot, R., Farberk, S., Grass, M., Hannon, B., Limburg, K., Naeem, S., O'neill, R., Paruelo, J., Raskin, R., Sutton, P., & Belt, M. (1997). The value of the world's ecosystem services and natural capital. *Nature, 387*, 253–260. https://doi.org/10.1038/387253a0

Crutzen, P. J. (2006). The "Anthropocene". In E. Ehlers & T. Krafft (Eds.), *Earth system science in the Anthropocene*. Springer. https://doi.org/10.1007/3-540-26590-2_3

da Silva, M., Paviolo, A., Tambosi, L., & Pardini, R. (2017). Effectiveness of protected areas for biodiversity conservation: Mammal occupancy patterns in the Iguaçu National Park, Brazil. *Journal for Nature Conservation, 41*, 51–62. https://doi.org/10.1016/j.jnc.2017.11.001

Delanty, G. (2020). *Critical theory and social transformation: Crises of the present and future possibilities*. Routledge.

Dunlap, R. E. (2008). The new environmental paradigm scale: From marginality to worldwide use. *Journal of Environmental Education, 40*(1), 3–18.

Dunlap, R. E., & Catton, W. R. (1980). A new ecological paradigm for post-exuberant sociology. *American Behavioral Scientist, 24*(1), 15–47.

Dunlap, R. E., & Catton, W. R. (1994). Struggling with human exemptionalism: The rise, decline and revitalization of environmental sociology. *American Sociologist, 25*, 5–30. https://doi.org/10.1007/BF02691936

Eisenstadt, S. N. (1973). *Tradition, change, and modernity*. Krieger Publishing.

European Environment Agency. (2016). *Communication, environment and behaviour. A scoping study on the links between public communication, environment policy implementation and behavioural science*. Publications Office of the European Union.

Gallino, L. (1992). *L'incerta alleanza. Modelli di relazioni tra scienze umane e scienze della natura*. Einaudi.

Gallino, L. (2016). L'idea di flessibilità sostenibile. *Quaderni di Sociologia [Online]*, 70–71. http://journals.openedition.org/qds/783; https://doi.org/10.4000/qds.783

Giacomini, V. (1980). *Perché l'ecologia*. . .. Edizioni La Scuola.

Giddens, A., Beck, U., & Lash, S. (1999). *Modernizzazione riflessiva. Politica, tradizione ed estetica nell'ordine sociale della modernità*. Asterios.

Hirschman, A. O. (1967). *Development projects observed*. Brookings Institutions.

Hockings, M., Stolton, S., & Dudley, N. (2000). *Evaluating effectiveness: A framework for assessing the management of protected areas*. IUCN. https://doi.org/10.2305/IUCN.CH.2005.PAG.14.en

Hockings, M., Stolton, S., Leverington, F., Dudley, N., & Courrau, J. (2006). *Evaluating effectiveness: A framework for assessing management effectiveness of protected areas* (2nd ed.). IUCN. https://doi.org/10.2305/IUCN.CH.2005.PAG.14.en

Hofmann, S., Beierkuhnlein, C., Field, R., Provenzale, A., & Chiarucci, A. (2018). Uniqueness of protected areas for conservation strategies in the European Union. *Scientific Reports, 8*, 45–64. https://doi.org/10.1038/s41598-018-24390-3

Jorgenson, A. K., Fiske, S., Hubacek, K., Li, J., McGovern, T., Rick, T., Schor, J. B., Solecki, W., York, R., & Zycherman, A. (2019). Social science perspectives on drivers of and responses to global climate change. Wiley interdisciplinary reviews. *Climate Change, 10*(1), e554. https://doi.org/10.1002/wcc.554

Latour, B. (1995). Moderniser ou écologiser. A la recherche de la Septième Cité. *Écologie & politique : sciences, culture, société*. Le bord de l'eau éditions/Presses de Sciences Po/Syllepses/Ecopresse, 5–27.

Lopoukhine, N., Crawhall, N., Dudley, N., Figgis, P., Karibuhoye, C., Laffoley, D., Miranda, L. J., MacKinnon, K., & Sandwith, T. (2012). Protected areas: Providing natural solutions to 21st century challenges. *S.A.P.I.EN. S Surveys and Perspectives Integrating Environment and Society, 5.2*. http://journals.openedition.org/sapiens/1254

Lo Presti, V., & Stame, N. (2015). Positive thinking and learning from evaluation. In S. Bohni-Nielsen, R. Turksema, & P. van del Knaap (Eds.), *Success in evaluation: Focusing on the positives*. Transaction Publishers.

Lo Presti, V. (2020). L'uso dei positive thinking nella ricerca valutativa. Franco Angeli.

Lo Presti, V. (2016). Positive thinking e sviluppo locale: quali approcci per la promozione dell'innovazione. *Sociologia e Ricerca Sociale*, 138–155. https://doi.org/10.3280/SR2017-112007

Marino, D. (2012). *La valutazione di efficacia per le aree protette – Proposta di un modello di analisi (MEVAP) e manuale di applicazione*. Franco Angeli.
Meadows, D. H., Meadows, D. L., Randers, J., & Behrens, W. W. I. I. I. (1972). *The limits to growth*. Potomac Associate.
Moore, J., & Rees, W. E. (2013). Getting to one planet living. In *State of the world 2013 is sustainability still possible?* World Watch Institute.
Nocenzi, M. (2019). *Verso una società sostenibile. (Non)umani, reti, città e la sfida del cambiamento*. La Nuova Cultura.
Nocenzi, M., & Sannella, A. (Eds.). (2020). *Perspectives for a new social theory of the sustainability*. Springer.
Puech, M. (2019). Come rendere sostenibile l'Homo Sapiens Technologicus. In M. Nocenzi (Ed.), *Verso una società sostenibile. (Non)umani, reti, città e la sfida del cambiamento*. La Nuova Cultura.
Rockström, J., Steffen, W., Noone, K., Persson, Å., Chapin, F. S., III, Lambin, E. F., Lenton, T., Scheffer, M., Folke, C., Schellnhuber, H., Nykvist, B., de Wit, C., Hughes, T., van der Leeuw, S., Rodhe, H., Sörlin, S., Snyder, P., Costanza, R., Svedin, U., & Foley, J. (2009). A safe operating space for humanity. *Nature, 461*, 472–475. https://doi.org/10.1038/461472a
Sachs, J. D. (2015). *The age of sustainable development*. Columbia University Press.
Saragosa, C. (2005). *Insediamento umano, ecologia e sostenibilità*. Donzelli.
Senge, P. M. (1990). *La quinta disciplina. L'arte e la pratica dell'apprendimento organizzativo*. Editoriale Scientifica.
Serres, M. (2009). *Temps des crises*. Le Pommier.
Stame, N. (2017). *Some observation on Hirschman production line. In bias for hope*. Colorni-Hirschman.
Stame, N. (2016). *Valutazione Pluralista*. Franco Angeli.
Tendler, J., & Stame, N. (1992). *Progetti ed effetti*. Liguori.
Tilly, C. (2004). *Social movements, 1768–2004*. Paradigm Publishers.
Turner, G. M. (2008). A comparison of the limits to growth with 30 years of reality. *Global Environmental Change, 18*(3), 397–411.
United Nations. (1987). Report of the World Commission on environment and development: Our common future. .
Urry, J. (2009). Sociology and climate change. *The Sociological Review, 57*(2_suppl), 84–100. https://doi.org/10.1111/j.1467-954X.2010.01887.x
Wackernagel, M., & Rees, W. (1996). *Our ecological footprint: Reducing human impact on the Earth*. Society Publishers.
Weiss, C. H. (1997). *Theory-based evaluation: Past, present, and future*. New Directions for Evaluation.
Wilson, E. O. (2016). *Half-Earth, our planet's fight for life*. WW Norton.

Arianna Calderamo is a PhD candidate in Communication, Marketing and Social Research (curriculum in Methodology of Social Sciences), at the CoRiS Department of Communication and Social Research of the University of Rome La Sapienza. Her main research field is the evaluation of public environmental policies and projects related to nature conservation and sustainable local development in inland Italian areas. Research interest that she is pursuing also during the doctoral thesis which consists in the design and empirical experimentation of an evaluation model for the Italian National Parks. In 2020 she was the winner of the AIV Thesis Award of the Italian Evaluation Association from which some publications will derive:

2020. Sustainability and local development: the evaluation of the Rewilding Europe-Apennines program
2021. The integration of approaches in the evaluation of the Rewilding Europe-Apennines program
2021. Rewilding Europe-Apennines: the evaluation of a sustainable local development program.

Mariella Nocenzi PhD in "Sociology of culture and political processes", is Assistant editor of the *International Review of Sociology* (https://www.tandfonline.com/loi/cirs20) and member of the Editorial board of the *Rivista di studi sulla sostenibilità* (https://www.francoangeli.it/riviste/Sommario.aspx?IDRivista=168). She manages *Sostenibilia—International Observatory of social theory on the new technologies and the sustainability https://www.sostenibilia.net/* and the editorial series of the Observatory with the same name (https://www.nuovacultura.it/catalogo/scientific-areas/area-14-scienze-politiche-sociali/collane-14/collana-sostenibilia/). Professor of "Fundamentals of Social Sciences", "Social impact Assessment" and "Sustainability, Innovation and Gender Inclusion" at the Department of Communication and Social Research of the Sapienza University of Rome has also taught at the University of Florence and Verona. He was a member of the National executive of the Italian Association of Sociology (AIS) after having served as Secretary of the AIS Section "Sociological theories and social changes" (2007/2010 and 2010/2013). She edited several national and international publications, drawn from research on environmental issues, risk and social risk, security and safety in globalisation, Europe, young people, equal opportunities and gender policies. Among her recent publications are "Qualitative Analysis of Digital Technology Research and Practice in the Field of Social and Human Sciences" (with Beatrice Bonami and Brasilina Passarelli); Journal of E-Learning and Knowledge Society, Vol. 16, No. 03 (2020), pp. 50–59; and New Perspectives for a Social Theory of Sustainability, (with Alessandra Sannella), Springer, AG Switzerland, 2020

Chapter 13
Material Traces of a Cumbersome Past: The Case of Italian Colonial History

Giovanna Leone, Laurent Licata, Alessia Mastropietro, Stefano Migliorisi, and Isora Sessa

From Consensual Glorification to Amnesia or Social Conflict: The Changing Effects of Material Traces of Colonial Past

The physical contexts in which people live their daily lives are filled with traces from the past. A statue in a park, the name of a street, or an advertisement for a food product can all recall specific historical moments or periods. It is this everyday phenomenon that distinguishes the higher processes of human memory from the more basic associative processes that are shared by humans and animals alike. In a famous quote, Lev Simonovic Vygotsky described this unique feature as follows:

> The very essence of human memory is that human beings actively remember with the help of signs. (. . .) As one psychologist (Dewey) has said, the very essence of civilization consists in the fact that we deliberately build monuments so as not to forget. In the knotted handkerchief and the monument we see the most profound, most characteristic and most important feature which distinguishes human from animal memory (Vygotsky, 1978: 51).

The unique capacity of human memory being to guide its own recollections by means of signs, Vygotsky cited voluntary strategies based either on private choice (tying a knot in one's own handkerchief) or on the decision of a community (erecting a statue in a public garden in memory of an excellent citizen) as examples of such intermediations. However, the private strategy given as an example is intended for

G. Leone (✉) · S. Migliorisi · I. Sessa
Department of Communication and Social Research, Sapienza University of Rome, Rome, Italy
e-mail: giovanna.leone@uniroma1.it; stefano.migliorisi@uniroma1.it; isora.sessa@uniroma1.it

L. Licata
Center for Social and Cultural Psychology, Université libre de Bruxelles, Bruxelles, Belgium
e-mail: Laurent.Licata@ulb.be

A. Mastropietro
Department of Psychology, Sapienza – University of Rome, Rome, Italy
e-mail: alessia.mastropietro@uniroma1.it

F. Comunello et al. (eds.), *What People Leave Behind*, Frontiers in Sociology and Social Research 7, https://doi.org/10.1007/978-3-031-11756-5_13

short-term remembrance, whereas the public choice cited uses a kind of material intermediation designed to be durable, even beyond the life cycle of those who were contemporaries of the persons or events signified by the statue. If we consider the tools of memory intermediation not as a strategy of individual but as a community memory, this choice can be explained by the short duration of human life: the stones will be there long after the death of those who decided to use them to signal the duty of historical memory (Apfelbaum, 2010). However, in the long term, the material intermediation of selected elements of the community's past, which was perfectly clear at the time of the monument's creation, may become blurred and difficult to understand for those born after that time.

From this briefly sketched theoretical perspective, the aim of this chapter is to observe how a community constructs its own collective memory by using material memory intermediations. However, groups evolve as generations change. Moreover, different meanings of the same trace can emerge because over time the meaning of the social representations of the historical period symbolized by this material intermediation can shift. Consequently, traces of the past that were designed to maintain a consensual version of historical times across generations may instead become a source of social conflict.

In this chapter, we will address these theoretical questions by discussing a specific case, that of the *material traces of the colonial past* that still persist in the European environment today. Originally intended to glorify a past that, in the eyes of Europeans, appeared rich and benevolent toward more "primitive" societies, these traces have now become the object of intense controversy within the former colonizing countries. In the wake of the Black Lives Matter movement, European anti-racist movements have carried out symbolic actions challenging the colonial legacy of European societies in an unprecedented way, such as the toppling of the statue of former slaveholder Edward Colson in Bristol, UK, or the painting of statues of Belgian King Leopold II in red. Part of public opinion in national majorities reacted to these minorities by denouncing the "cancel culture" or the danger of "erasing" history.

Because of the massive censorship that still weighs on its colonial past (Del Boca, 2005), Italy represents an interesting case study. Indeed, colonial traces are present in many Italian places, in particular in the city of Rome, which the Fascist regime tried to redesign through numerous architectural interventions, to underline after the colonial invasions that the city was once more the capital of an empire as in the time of the ancient Romans. However, for many contemporary inhabitants of Rome and for most Italian citizens, the colonial traces seem less visible today than in other former European countries and metropoles.

Similar research on African and European respondents' reactions to the colonial legacy shows that younger generations in European countries where memories of the colonial past are less censored than in Italy seem increasingly aware of the moral errors of colonial paternalism and increasingly question the violent legacy of the colonial past (Licata et al., 2018). Therefore, even though the short-sighted cultural policies that manage the colonial legacy have meant that, for many Italians, the link with the colonial signifier is fading or even being lost (Palma, 2018), the time may have come for colonial traces to be detectable again, as signs that cannot be hidden and must be understood.

To explore such a theoretical interpretation of the current impact of past colonial traces in contemporary Italian society, this chapter describes the results of a first qualitative research, devoted to the reactions to the suggestion of a colonial meaning hidden in a seemingly unimportant object of everyday life, namely a candy still bearing on its wrapping the icon of a little African boy. However, before commenting on these data and their possible implications for the question of detectable contemporary impact in a specific European environment, some further theoretical points should be addressed.

Emotional Reactions to Historical Traces

A first intriguing aspect of the material intermediations leading to the recall of history is their capacity to induce a specific type of emotional reaction. A poetic description of such a phenomenon is offered by a famous episode from Book I (29–19 BC) of *the Aeneid* by the Roman poet Virgil. In his unfinished masterpiece, the poet describes how Aeneas—a refugee, driven by the loss of his beloved homeland Troy—finally reached the shores of Italy, where his descendants founded the Roman culture, born from the union of the lost Trojan culture and the Latin culture of the inhabitants of the new land. In the long wanderings through which Aeneas and his Trojan companions slowly fulfilled their destiny, they first arrived on the North African coast. There, while exploring the city of Carthage, Aeneas discovered in a richly decorated temple a mural depicting battles from the Trojan War and showing the deaths of his friends and countrymen. Aeneas was moved to tears and explained his reaction to the presiding friend by saying "*sunt lacrimae rerum, et mentem mortalia tangent.*" This classic quote is so difficult to translate because the Latin word "*res, rerum*" refers to both "material object" and "facts"—history being called "*res gestae.*" Virgil poetically used such indeterminacy to produce an implicative richness that made this phrase capable of leading to different meanings (Wharton, 2008). Among them, it could also imply that "there are tears in historical facts."

Today, scholars would define these reactions to historical memories as *group-based emotions*, to distinguish them from emotions triggered by events that solely involve personal goals. Moreover, when they burst their "*lacrimae rerum*" in the face of material intermediaries recalling past historical events, people are not only expressing their group-based emotions, but also a *moral evaluation* of their own group's past. Depending on the moral evaluation, group emotions can thus express different types of self-consciousness: either positive, involving a sense of pride, when traces of glorious episodes are shown, or negative, expressing emotions of embarrassment, shame, and guilt, when traces of less glorious pasts persist in the material environment (Iyer, Schmader, & Lickel, 2007).

More than defeats, which can also encompass glorious and heroic aspects, self-conscious negative emotions are linked to historical actions that may tarnish the overly idealized moral standard attributed to the group (Shepherd, Spears, & Manstead, 2013). It is therefore easy to understand why communities multiply memorial intermediations designed to produce positive emotions at the group level, while traces that recall immoral episodes from the group's past are avoided or self-censored (Bar-Tal, 2017).

However, judgments about the moral aspects of a group's history change both from one generation to the next and as more advanced moral standards shape social discourse. Thus, intermediations originally intended to recall what appeared to be a glorious and morally commendable past may, over time, remind citizens of a period that now seems shameful. However, such a profound change does not happen easily or quickly. Therefore, when the material traces refer to types of collective behavior that conform to moral norms that were once dominant but are now increasingly unacceptable to many, depending on the type of representation of history that the perceivers have, different reactions can be observed simultaneously, ranging from negative to positive collective emotions. Such a shift in reactions is more evident for the intermediation of institutional memory. However, a different and intriguing question is related to the question of whether everyday objects, which are meant to be quickly consumed and not intended to last, can also be the source of emotional reactions, and whether these reactions can change significantly in accordance with the new historical awareness of the cruelty of European colonialism.

The Colonial Legacy of the Ephemeral Traces of the Past

Like any historical period, the colonial era left not only institutional but also ephemeral traces. Representing colonial domination in material objects used for private consumption such as toys, advertising, food packaging, and gadgets, to name but a few examples among the multitude of material goods intended to embellish everyday life, these ephemeral traces shaped the mentality of ordinary Europeans in a way that corresponded to the important role that colonialism played in their societies at the time of their production. Abandoned by the tide of time, in some forgotten part of the home, these objects slowly lost their original communicative intent, becoming a nostalgic reminder of past family moments. Their status as unimportant objects, linked to personal and familiar life and therefore less conspicuous than the formal intermediaries of community memories glorifying colonial rule, such as statues or street and place dedications, made their racial implications more difficult to grasp. However, as a function of generational change and the emergence of a new sensitivity to racial injustice, these objects have recently begun to be seen not as an innocent legacy of the past, but as a troubling testament to the pervasiveness of colonial imagery in everyday routines of the past, such as buying food or choosing gifts for children (Forsdick, 2020).

In our research, we chose to address the issue of colonial traces left in ephemeral objects still available in European contexts, by observing the reactions of participants exposed to the advertisement of an Italian chocolate candy that is still frequently found today in some Italian cafés, internationally known under the Italian label of *caffé*. Recent historical contributions have convincingly investigated how the history of chocolate and coffee culture was used to intertwine the imaginary of three continents (Brazil, Ethiopia, and Italy) during the Fascist *ventennio* (1922–1945). According to researcher Diana Garvin (2021), coffee-centered narratives, describing the long journey from the bean in the field to the machine used in Italian coffee shops, were used to construct a colonial imagery based on all kinds of advertisements placed in this specific type of shop. In fact, alongside the growing success of their products, Italian *caffé* became key sites for the promotion of fascist imperial projects in East Africa—an architectural and artistic legacy that remains in place today. By unraveling the trade in coffee beans and human bodies between Italy, Brazil, and Ethiopia in the interwar period, and expanding our understanding of how food and agriculture were politicized during the Fascist period, this new type of historical and cultural studies has clarified the untold story of colonialism, also seen as the story of "caffeinated imperial aggression and resistance" (Garvin, 2021: 292).

It is interesting to note that traces of the politicization of food and agriculture during the Fascist period persist in the objects that can still be found in contemporary Italian cafés, whether they are old advertisements used to create a nostalgic scenario or images printed in the packages of sugar sachets made freely available to customers. Moreover, a similarity between the different colors of coffee preparations (latte, brown coffee, etc.) and the colors of human skin also remained as an intangible colonial trace, linking old marketing strategies with contemporary ways of speaking. A sentence by a black German activist quoted in an article significantly entitled "Chocolate advertising, consumption of race?" may illustrate how these links could be critically internalized.

> For brown skin, the German language only has terms borrowed from eating and drinking like 'chocolate brown' or 'coffee brown'. If someone tries to put me on a color scale, I could be classified as 'coffee brown'. Does that even exist? Oh sure, in people's perception there are any number of shades and corresponding labels. What you people have in common is the divergence from the generally unspoken norm – whiteness (Hackenesch, 2014: 97).

The following qualitative research aims to observe the reactions of white Italian participants to the packaging of a classic chocolate candy, which still shows the stereotypical face of an "African Moor" printed on the wrapper. This candy has already been selected by historical researchers as a relevant Italian example of European colonial ephemera (Hackenesch, 2014). Also, an image of the advertisement "L'una tira l'altra: Nougatine Unica" ("One thing leads to another: Nougatine Unica"), painted by Severo Sepo for Venchi chocolates (Turin, Italy, c. 1935, 30.5 cm × 61 cm. Archivio della Communicazione, Parma, Italy), showing the same wrapper still present in a contemporary Amazon link selling this candy online, was used by Garvin (2021: 304) as an example of his examination of racialized chocolate advertising. Building on these historical and cultural studies, the research discussed in this chapter aims to understand the extent to which the connections between chocolate advertising and racial categorizations might begin to be noticed by the white majority as well, in a society where socio-psychological research has shown that the historical faults of Italian colonialism are largely self-censored from the historical consciousness of many citizens (Leone, d'Ambrosio, Migliorisi, and Sessa 2018; Leone, Giner-Sorolla, D'Errico, Migliorisi, and Sessa 2018; Leone & Sarrica, 2014).

The Research

Participants and the Interview Process

Twenty-two people— 9 men and 13 women—participated in the study. Their ages ranged from 18 to 59 years, with a mean age of 37.9 years and a median age of 33.5 years.

A semi-structured interview was offered individually to each participant. Due to the COVID-19 pandemic, the interviews were conducted either face-to-face or online; in both cases, according to the Code of Ethics of the Italian Association of Psychologists (AIP),[1] participants were fully informed about the research and agreed to be recorded. The interview consisted of two parts: after asking for the participants' informed consent, in the first part the interviewer asked sociodemographic questions—such as age and occupation—and introduced the research and the chosen candy, showing a picture of the chocolate wrapper (Fig. 13.1).

The image, which remained available to the participant throughout the interview, is freely available at an Amazon web address, aimed at sending the product online.[2]

After this introduction, the interviewer asked the respondent a few questions about the chocolate, including his or her prior knowledge of it and his or her reactions to its package: "*Do you know this product?*"; "*What comes to your mind when you look at the image on the chocolate wrapper?*"; "*Looking at it more closely, what do you think it represents?*"

Following these initial questions, the interviewer introduced some aspects of chocolate packaging's history associated with Italian colonialism: "*I would like to tell you about the history of this confectionery. The packaging of this confectionery*

[1] http://www.aipass.org/node/11560

[2] https://www.amazon.it/Nougatine-Venchi-500-caramellate-cioccolato/dp/B07Y6BKNXD/ref=asc_df_B07Y6BKNXD/ ?tag=googshopit-21&linkCode=df0&hvadid=387657378711&hvpos=&hvnetw=g&hvrand=4269039819438657727&hvpone=&hvptwo=&hvqmt=&hvdev=c&hvdvcmdl=&hvlocint=&hvlocphy=1008736&hvtargid=pla-828318752530&psc=1&tag=&ref=&adgrpid=74424520450&hvpone=&hvptwo=&hvadid=387657378711&hvpos=&hvnetw=g&hvrand=4269039819438657727&hvqmt=&hvdev=c&hvdvcmdl=&hvlocint=&hvlocphy=1008736&hvtargid=pla-828318752530

Fig. 13.1 Image of the chocolate wrapper shown to respondents

represents a child of African origin. This is a possible reminder of the children belonging to the Italian colonies conquered during the colonization campaign launched by the Fascist regime. During the Fascist regime, this image was intended to convey to the Italian consumer the idea of a product made with raw materials from the colonies, in order to reinforce the propaganda ideal of colonization as an affirmation of Italian power." This revelation led to the second part of the interview, which included questions aimed at assessing the possible change in the interviewee's reactions and emotions toward the candy as a result of the new clues provided by the history of the packaging: "*What do you think of this image after learning more about its history?*"; "*What do you think of this candy now?*"; "*Could you have imagined that this candy could be associated with such a historical period?*"; "*Do you think that there are other products on the food market associated with this same period?*"; "*What do you think about the fact that this product is still being advertised using this image?*"

Results

Based on the median age (33.5 years) of the participants, the sample was divided into two groups—the younger and the older, both consisting of 11 respondents. Reactions to the image of the candy were therefore explored before and after allusions associating the packaging with Italian colonial history (as part of comparisons) and observing differences between younger and older respondents. Controlling for prior knowledge of the product, only one of the 11 younger participants and five of the older ones were already familiar with it.

First Reactions to the Image of Chocolate

In the first part of the interview, when the respondent has already seen the image but has not yet heard about its possible associations with the colonial era, interesting differences appear between the two age groups. In response to the question, "*What is the first thing that comes to mind when you look at this picture?*" the younger participants paid attention to the taste and packaging of the chocolate, quickly linking them to Africa and black people, as follows:

> *Hazelnut, caramel, Africa.*

> Erm... so, first I think of the logo drawn on the packaging, which seems to me to be an indigenous figure, reminding me, I suppose, of a particular chocolate.... And then, if I have to look at the chocolate, I think more of something crunchy, tasty. I don't know why it reminds me of caramel.

The responses of older respondents, on the other hand, are mainly experiential, consisting of memories of the taste of chocolate and the emotions provoked by it, related to their childhood and youth memories:

> Well, ... I remembered the taste of the chocolate and the crunchy interior and then I liked it as it was made, beyond the classic candies, which were rolled here and there, this one instead was rolled only on the top. It's not the classic candy that opens by pulling on the two pigtails.

Ideas on Chocolate Packaging

Furthermore, in answering questions that explored the interviewees' ideas arising spontaneously from the image ("*What comes to your mind when you look at the image on the chocolate wrapper?*"; "*Looking at it more closely, what do you think it represents?*"), the issue of the link with Africa emerges again among the young participants. Indeed, they read the image as a representation of the country where the raw materials (i.e., chocolate) come from, as in the exempla:

> *Africa comes to mind. Maybe a bit of a stereotypical image.*

> Well, maybe a... a call to... umm... a reference to... Maybe this wrapper represents, I don't know, chocolate and so, in fact, a reference to the land in which this chocolate is produced.

At the same time, even before hearing the researcher's directions, some among the young participants spontaneously recognized the link between the image of the wrapper, the color of the chocolate, and the color of their skin, for example:

> Then, if I pause to think, I just say: a person of color, then, chocolate color, you can say, right? chocolate color... But, of course, then, you have to think for a moment because if, well, there is an association exclusively with the fact that a person of color... I mean, anyway, I don't think white chocolate has a white person's face on it, so...

A kind of racist aspect transmitted by the image, associated with a moral perplexity, thus seems to emerge among the young participants. This awareness does not emerge among older participants, who instead pay more attention to the exotic origin of chocolate. Interestingly, these older respondents see instead a link with the country of origin of the raw materials which is associated not only with Africa but also with Brazil, through a spontaneous connection between the image of the candy and coffee:

> It looks like coffee, I would say. Um, if I were to look at the... uhm... the drawing, the one he wants to represent, with the figure I see, gives me the image, it seems to me.... It gives me an image a little bit Brazilian, a little bit exotic, and so it would make me think, if I dwell on, on the image of a chocolate coffee...
>
> I can think of coffee, a coffee bean.
>
> *Brazil. A Brazilian.*

The theoretical hypothesis of a perceived triangle linking Italian coffee to Africa and Brazil (Garvin, 2021) thus seems to be confirmed by these free associations of older respondents. Only one of the older participants' responses fully captures the colonial significance of the packaging image, in the very first stage of the interview, by stating:

> It gives me a bit of an idea of those Mamies... those ladies who used to guard the colonial houses.

With regard to the emotions spontaneously evoked in the first part of the interview, most participants, when looking at the image on the chocolate wrapper, said they had positive feelings, associated with joy, lightness, cheerfulness, positivity, and sympathy. Some participants attributed these positive emotional reactions to the smiling expression on the wrapper. Only two participants deviated somewhat from this general positive response.

The first case is that of a 26-year-old participant, who identified the image as an African woman, but immediately spoke of his "displeasure" at seeing it, as it seemed to border on racism:

> To me, it seems to represent an African woman, a bit stereotypical, ironically represented, even a bit like a caricature.... In fact, I've never really looked at it that closely. To be honest, it's a bit off-putting, because it associates a sweet product like that with an image, it might not be an African woman. It seems to me that you associate skin color with chocolate color, which almost has a slight tinge of racism, perhaps.

In contrast, a 55-year-old man said that the image's reference to the land where the chocolate is produced, and more generally its link to the extraction of raw materials in third-world countries, was for him a source of uniquely positive feeling: "*Definitely well-being for people who usually suffer a lot.*" This older interviewee grasped the almost generous aspect of helping people who are usually in conditions of suffering, without saying anything more about the exploitation of raw materials from disadvantaged countries.

Ideas Coming to Participants' Minds After the Researcher's Indications

Following the researcher's suggested cues, which associated the image on the chocolate wrapper with the Italian colonial period, a difference emerged between younger and older participants. Here, the citing of examples is enriched by the age of the respondents, since, according to the theoretical frame briefly described above, the division of the sample according to their median age affects participants' responses. Specifically, younger participants seemed to be more influenced by the unexpected associations with the Italian colonial period and showed strong reactions to this new interpretation of the hidden meaning in the commercial image.

Below are some examples:

> Uhm... well let's say that... (unintelligible) from what you've told me, let's say... that things are changing a bit... and that this same child seems to me perhaps a potentially let's say... exploited person, subjected perhaps to some... not really commendable treatment by the... precisely the fascist regime towards the African colonies..... I don't associate it with positive feelings anymore, but with more negative feelings, let's say. (Man, 22 y.o.)

> Sadness because I'm against those ideals anyway, so... I'm sorry that this kind of advertising is used for a confectionery product. (Woman, 27 y.o.)

> Well, oh my God, that's a bit scary. In the sense that it's contrary to what I thought... I had interpreted it as, what a beautiful thing, we are putting an African product into our food culture, but in this way it means you are emphasizing white supremacy, it seems like a bit of a sad situation. (Woman, 27 y.o.)

On the contrary, older participants reported being less impressed by the new suggestions they received on the image printed in the package, as in the following quotes:

> But, beyond the story, I see this face, I thought it was a lady, this little black boy very nice, very endearing.... (I see) Nothing different from before. (Woman, 54 y.o.)

> In a way, all the chocolate we eat comes from exploitation in Africa and South America, so when you come to chocolate, there is an exploitation side behind it.... I'm not surprised. (Man, 37 y.o.)

> I'm not very impressed with this story because for me, my end goal is to enjoy a taste... if I have to make a choice towards this product, I expect to find the taste I like... honestly it (the new information) brings me an emotion yes, but not a major emotion. For me, it's sort of a speech of relative importance... I honestly don't care about it. If I focus on this product, the fact that I know the story you told me doesn't change my choice. If I choose it, basically because I liked it... It doesn't involve me much, if I may say so, knowing that it was made in

a particular environment, at a particular time, perhaps taking advantage of a situation, of certain particular moments... no, it really doesn't move me. (Man, 58 y.o.)

Finally, a small number of respondents, regardless of age, wanted to emphasize that they retained a positive view of the sweet even after receiving information about its possible links with a colonial meaning, as in the following example:

I think it is still a very good product; however, I think there must be a reason behind the fact that the image has not been changed. Honestly, (...) neither my view of the candy nor my view of the candy company has changed that much. (Man, 26 y.o.)

Despite these reactions minimizing the consequences of the information provided by the researcher, after hearing the allusions linking the image of the package to Italian colonial history, the young participants reported a change in their self-reported emotions, with reference to emotions such as regret, sadness, surprise, disgust, shame, anger, or anxiety.

An important set of concluding remarks refers to the participants' critical assessment of the marketing choice to retain the old colonial image and their willingness to buy the product anyway, or to avoid buying it. On this crucial point, a wide range of reactions was collected, again with interesting differences between the two age groups:

The image definitely needs to be replaced, because even though it's something that belonged to the past, in the end it's a theme that's always present... it's too important for the product, the image is the first... the first look you get at a product, and if it makes you think of bad things, you don't want to buy it... because it doesn't affect a person physically but psychologically yes. If a person has... an African background or whatever, background... or (if) they're people who have suffered these abuses in the past, it doesn't seem right to make them, so to speak, to make them see these things again. (Woman, 27 y.o.)

Among the older respondents, other reactions were evident:

Probably over time, the image has lost the value it had in the beginning and nobody, not even the current producers, knows what the purpose of the image was anymore. (Woman, 54 y.o.)

In addition, among the older participants, someone cited the positive value of tradition, strictly related to nostalgic feelings (Kessous, 2015):

Keeping a brand, an image that is the same as it was several decades ago makes me curious. It's a marketing choice, which I may or may not agree with, but... it's nice. It takes you back in time and gives you that fun feeling of when you were a carefree boy or received an award; in short, it's a nice thing to remember... Standing still in a certain position means courage to me, so it means .... courage, so it means trust from the manufacturing company, saying: 'no, it's my product, I'm still advertising like this because it's a winning product. (Man, 51 y.o.)

On the contrary, some of the younger members of the group were adamant that they would never buy racialized food:

... I'm against racism, so if you look at it from a fundamental point of view, this product is also an emblem of a justification of racial supremacy, so I would keep it away. (Woman, 27 y.o.)

Finally, many participants suggested that this product continues to be distributed and purchased, despite the image on the packaging, because of a lack of knowledge of the story behind the image:

> Well, it's completely... I don't know... many... a lot of people maybe, not knowing the context, might have the first reaction that I had... but if a lot of people could know the origin of the logo and... contextualize it historically, maybe they wouldn't... I don't know how tempted they would be to buy it, knowing the original reference it's from, that's all. (Man, 22 y.o.)

Discussion

The manipulation implemented in the qualitative research discussed in this chapter, where a colonial meaning of a candy wrapper still depicting the face of a small African boy was suggested to the participants after collecting their initial reactions, was intended to simulate these processes of social influence by which minority groups now bring to the fore some of the material traces of colonialism that remain unnoticed in the background of European environments. As for the consequences of the actions of these minorities, whereby previously ignored colonial traces trigger reactions among members of the national majority, sculpting or transforming social representations of colonialism, the unveiling of a possible colonial meaning hidden in the wrapping of a sweet also allowed the participants—especially the younger ones—to take a deeper look at this ephemeral object.

It can be noticed that young participants showed a stronger reaction to the association of the candy image with Italian colonial history. More than the older respondents, they expressed negative moral emotions and many of them were puzzled by the marketing decision to keep the same image until now. While acknowledging that today the meaning of the image is probably not the same because only a few consumers know what is behind it, the younger participants nevertheless stated that this lack of perception does not justify keeping the image of the African boy on the packaging. For the group of participants older than the median age, on the other hand, the responses in the second part of the interview were much less harsh and critical. None of them wanted to shun the product completely and, above all, none of them made it clear that they would not buy it again. When asked about the emotions they felt toward the product after having grasped a possible association with the colonial era, they never managed to express them explicitly. In addition to the vague responses, the declaration of nostalgic reminders associated with the declared image by some older respondents seemed to reinforce the marketing strategy of predicting more sweet than bitter reactions to this "traditional" choice (Kessous, 2015).

In sum, two different types of reactions, observed among older and younger respondents, seem to both confirm but also challenge the findings of a large study conducted on collectibles such as porcelain figurines, enamel plates, and "nostalgic" tin cans, all of which depict stereotypical colonial images of African Moors:

"The collection of artefacts depicting indigenous cultures of former European colonies as well as images of racialized individuals as cultural commodities serve as vehicles for constructing white Western identities. Juxtaposed with a racialized other, in this case the black servant or slave, Western identities have taken on the position of the normalized subject who, by virtue of being positioned as the norm, loses his or her equally racialized status. As a result, race becomes something that exclusively concerns people of color, but is in fact held by white people" (Cserno, 2008: 69–101; 81).

While this racialization of food that made certain products successful is still detectable among our research participants, confirming the link between white respondents' nostalgia and the reassuring associations of racialized advertising (Hackenesch, 2014), the taste of these nostalgic reminders seems to change from sweet to bitter when younger generations come to discuss this issue in the civic forum.

Conclusions

In this chapter, we have addressed the theoretical question of conflicting moral reactions to traces of the community's past by discussing a specific case concerning the ephemeral traces of colonialism left in everyday consumer objects. We focus on one such material artifact, still present in many nostalgic settings in European spaces, related to food advertisements recalling past colonial domination. While chocolate and coffee advertisements often refer to colonial exchanges in many European countries (Hackenesch, 2014), they are particularly significant in the Italian context, where coffee is not only a food consumer product, but also a symbol of Italian culture (Garvin, 2021). In order to understand the consequences of awareness of the colonial meaning of such ephemeral objects, the results of a qualitative research were discussed, comparing the reactions of Italian respondents of different generations to the unveiling of a possible colonial reference hidden in the packaging of a candy still showing the image of the African boy. Although still at a preliminary stage, these data seem to suggest that generational turnover can change the reaction to these nostalgic objects, from the sweet taste of familiar memories to the bitter recognition of the violent past enacted by one's own group. Understanding and confronting these reactions will help us to build a more welcoming place for young Europeans and young foreigners who choose to live in our cities.

References

Apfelbaum, E. (2010). Halbwachs and the social properties of memory. In S. Radstone & B. Schwarz (Eds.), *Memory: Histories, theories, debates* (pp. 77–92). Fordham University Press.

Bar-Tal, D. (2017). Self-censorship as a socio-political-psychological phenomenon: Conception and research. *Advances in Political Psychology, 38*, 37–65. https://doi.org/10.1111/pops.12391

Cataldo, V., Schettino, L., Savy, R., Poggi, I., Origlia, A., Ansani, A., Sessa, I., & Chiera, A. (2020). Phonetic and functional features of pauses, and concurrent gestures, in tourist guides' speech. In D. Piccardi, F. Ardolino, & S. Calamai (Eds.), *Gli archivi sonori al crocevia tra scienze fonetiche, informatica umanistica e patrimonio digitale* (pp. 205–231). Studi AISV. https://doi.org/10.17469/O2106AISV000013

Cserno, I. (2008). Pancakes, chocolate, and the trap of eternal servitude: A reading of race in the United States and Germany. In L. Lewis & G. Griffith (Eds.), *Color, hair, and bone: Race in the twenty-first century* (pp. 69–101). Bucknell University Press.

Del Boca, A. (2005). *Italiani, brava gente? Un mito duro a morire (Italians, good fellows? A myth that dies hard)*. Neri Pozza Editore.

Forsdick, C. (2020). Ephemera and the dynamics of colonial memory. In B. Sèbe & M. G. Stanard (Eds.), *Decolonising Europe? Popular responses to the end of empire*. Routledge.

Garvin, D. (2021). The Italian coffee triangle: From Brazilian colonos to Ethiopian colonialisti. *Modern Italy, 26*(3), 291–312. https://doi.org/10.1017/mit.2021.26

Hackenesch, S. (2014). Advertising chocolate, consuming race? On the peculiar relationship of chocolate advertising, German colonialism, and blackness. *Food and History, 12*(1), 97–112. https://doi.org/10.1484/J.FOOD.5.105144

Iyer, A., Schmader, T., & Lickel, B. (2007). Why individuals protest the perceived transgressions of their country: The role of anger, shame, and guilt. *Personality and Social Psychology Bulletin, 33*(4), 572–587. https://doi.org/10.1177/0146167206297402

Kessous, A. (2015). Nostalgia and brands: A sweet rather than a bitter cultural evocation of the past. *Journal of Marketing Management, 31*(17–18), 1899–1923. https://doi.org/10.1080/0267257X.2015.1088889

Leone, G., d'Ambrosio, M., Migliorisi, S., & Sessa, I. (2018). Facing the unknown crimes of older generations: Emotional and cognitive reactions of young Italian students reading an historical text on the colonial invasion of Ethiopia. *International Journal of Intercultural Relations, 62*, 55–67. https://doi.org/10.1016/j.ijintrel.2017.06.007

Leone, G., Giner-Sorolla, R., D'Errico, F., Migliorisi, S., & Sessa, I. (2018). It's time to be ashamed! Reactions to the breaking of a long-lasting self-censorship on ingroup war crimes. *Testing, Psychometrics, Methodology in Applied Psychology, 25*, 519–535. https://doi.org/10.4473/TPM25.4.4

Leone, G., Migliorisi, S., & Sessa, I. (2016). Detecting social signals of honesty and fear of appearing deceitful: A methodological proposal. In *Cognitive Infocommunications (CogInfoCom), 2016 7th IEEE International Conference on Cognitive Infocommunications* (pp. 289–294). IEEE.

Leone, G., & Sarrica, M. (2014). Making room for negative emotions about the national past: An explorative study of effects of parrhesia on Italian colonial crimes. *International Journal of Intercultural Relations, 43*, 126–138. https://doi.org/10.1016/j.ijintrel.2014.08.008

Licata, L., Khan, S. S., Lastrego, S., Cabecinhas, R., Valentim, J. P., & Liu, J. H. (2018). Social representations of colonialism in Africa and in Europe: Structure and relevance for contemporary intergroup relations. *International Journal of Intercultural Relations, 62*, 68–79. https://doi.org/10.1016/j.ijintrel.2017.05.004

Mastropietro, A., & Leone, G. (2021). Helping my Romani pupils also when they do not need it. A research on teachers' Benevolent overhelping. In *Proceedings of the 2nd International Conference of the Journal Scuola Democratica "Reinventing Education," VOL. 2, Learning with New Technologies, Equality and Inclusion* (pp. 787–795). Associazione "Per Scuola Democratica".

Origlia, A., Savy, R., Cataldo, V., Schettino, L., Ansani, A., Sessa, I., Chiera, A., & Poggi, I. (2019). Human, all too human: Towards a disfluent virtual tourist guide. In *Adjunct publication of the 27th Conference on User Modeling, Adaptation and Personalization* (pp. 393–399). ACM.

Palma, S. (2018). Colonial archives, memory and political culture in Italy. *Rassegna di Studi Etiopici, 2*, 23–40.
Sessa, I., D'Errico, F., Poggi, I., & Leone, G. (2020). Attachment styles and communication of displeasing truths. *Frontiers in Psychology, 11*, 1065.
Shepherd, L., Spears, R., & Manstead, A. S. R. (2013). 'This will bring shame on our nation': The role of anticipated group-based emotions on collective action. *Journal of Experimental Social Psychology, 49*(1), 42–57. https://doi.org/10.1016/j.jesp.2012.07.011
Vygotsky, L. S. (1978). *Mind in society: The development of higher psychological processes*. Harvard University Press.
Wharton, D. (2008). Sunt lacrimae rerum: An exploration in meaning. *Classical Journal, 103*(3), 259–279.

Giovanna Leone, Psychologist (Sapienza University of Rome, 1977, *cum laude*) and Psychotherapist. Full Professor of Social Psychology at the Sapienza University of Rome, where she teaches social and communication psychology and political psychology. Previously (1980–1994) she was a clinical psychologist and psychotherapist at the Santo Spirito Hospital in Rome. Later (1994–2005), Researcher and Associate Professor at the Aldo Moro University of Bari. Full member of several national and international academic associations, including AIP (Italian Association of Psychology), EASP (European Association of Social Psychology), and International Society of Political Psychology (ISPP). Member of the Board of the *Italian Journal of Community Psychology* (Giornale Italiano di Psicologia di comunità). Review Editor on the Editorial Board of Personality and Social Psychology (specialty section of *Frontiers in Psychology*). Associate Editor of the *Journal of Social and Political Psychology*. Italian member of the MC of COST European action IS1205 "Social psychological dynamics of historical representations in the enlarged European Union" (Chair Prof. Laurent Licata). Coordinator of the Ethics Committee that, on behalf of the AIP (Italian Psychology Association), revised the Code of Ethics currently used by the association. She wrote more than 150 scientific works. Her research mainly refers to the following thematic issues: social and collective aspects of autobiographical memories; historical narratives of past violence and reconciliation between groups; multimodal analysis of political communication; and ambivalent effects of intergroup help toward socially stigmatized recipients.

Laurent Licata, PhD in Psychology, Université Libre de Bruxelles (ULB), 2001; MSc in Social Psychology, London School of Economics and Political Science, 1994; and License in Psychological Sciences, ULB, 1992. Full Professor of Social Psychology and Vice-rector for the academic policy and career management, in charge of the diversity and gender policies of ULB. Chair of COST Action IS1205 "Social Psychological Dynamics of Historical Representations in the Enlarged European Union," 2012–2016. He wrote more than 150 works, mainly referred to the following research interests: collective memory; social identity; intergroup relations; group-based emotions; intercultural relations

Alessia Mastropietro, Psychologist (Sapienza University of Rome, 2014). Ph.D. Student in Psychology and Cognitive Sciences (Tutor, Prof. Giovanna Leone) at Department of Psychology, Sapienza University of Rome. 2020: Expert on the subject "Social Psychology of Communication" and "Political Psychology," Sapienza University of Rome Department of Communication and Social Research (CORIS). 2017: Collaboration assignment within the project "Immigrant children in primary schools in Rome," Sapienza University of Rome Department of Communication and Social Research (CORIS). 2016: Collaboration assignment within the project "Between fears and hopes. Analysis of the media communication on the economic situation in times of crisis, Sapienza University of Rome Department of Communication and Social Research" (CORIS). Research interests: helping relations and over-helping; historical narratives of in-group violence; emotional expressions in political communication.

Other scientific works: Mastropietro and Leone (2021)

Stefano Migliorisi, Psychologist (PhDPsy, 2019) and Psychoterapist (2020). 2015: Collaboration assignment in the study area of Social Psychology and Information Technology awarded by the Department of Computer Science, Sapienza University of Rome. 2017: Collaboration assignment for the project "Immigrant children in primary schools in Rome" awarded by the Department of Communication and Social Research (CORIS), Sapienza University of Rome. 2020: Winner of an annual research grant entitled "Facing the social denial of climate change: a study of Greta Thunberg's communication methods" conferred by the Department of Communication and Social Research (CORIS), Sapienza University of Rome. Research topics: Multimodal analysis of communication; intergenerational narratives of violence and reconciliation between groups; ambivalent effects of intergroup helping in intercultural societies; emotional effects of climate change.

Other scientific works: Leone, d'Ambrosio, Migliorisi, and Sessa (2018), Leone, Giner-Sorolla, D'Errico, Migliorisi, and Sessa (2018), Leone, Migliorisi, and Sessa (2016).

Isora Sessa, Psychologist (Sapienza University of Rome, 2013, *cum laude*) and Psychotherapist. Ph.D. (Sapienza University of Rome, Psychology and Cognitive Sciences, 2020), doctoral dissertation "Adult attachment styles and communicative strategies for conveying difficult truths" (Tutor, Prof. Francesca D'Errico).

Other scientific works: Sessa, D'Errico, Poggi, and Leone (2020), Cataldo et al. (2020), Origlia et al. (2019), Leone, d'Ambrosio, et al. (2018), Leone, Giner-Sorolla, et al. (2018)

Chapter 14
Video Surveillance and Public Space: Surveillance Society Vs. Security State

Tatiana Lysova

Introduction

Surveillance and surveillance practices are not a new phenomenon in urban spaces. Among the traditional forms of surveillance are face-to-face surveillance, i.e., the physical presence of an observer and observed in the same space and time and paper files usually produced by bureaucracies. However, since the second half of the twentieth century, various technologies and their development have been adopted into surveillance practices, gradually driving out the traditional ones (Marx, 1998). The main distinctive feature of these technologies, including video surveillance, from the traditional forms of surveillance, is their ubiquity and systematic nature (Dandeker, 1990).

The number of installed video surveillance cameras in public urban spaces has been growing in most countries globally since the end of the twentieth century (Phillips, 1999; Welsh, Farrington, & Taheri, 2015). In the 1980–1990s, the authorities justified the installation of closed-circuit televisions (CCTVs) by claiming that they would reduce not only crime rates but the fear of crime as well (Bannister, Fyfe, & Kearns, 1998). In particular, it was expected that a visible presence of a video camera would deter a criminal from breaking the law, as they would rationally estimate a probability of being caught and punished, which is higher than the benefits of committing a crime (Ratcliffe & Groff, 2019). At the same time, law-abiding citizens would feel more secure in the presence of CCTVs. In turn, this feeling of security would stimulate a higher usage of public spaces and economic activity (Cerezo, 2013).

So, the rationalization for the introduction of public video surveillance systems had a double logic: on the one hand, it should have deterred a rational criminal, and,

T. Lysova (✉)
University of Milano-Bicocca, Milan, Italy
e-mail: t.lysova@campus.unimib.it

F. Comunello et al. (eds.), *What People Leave Behind*, Frontiers in Sociology and Social Research 7, https://doi.org/10.1007/978-3-031-11756-5_14

on the other hand, it was supposed to improve the quality of life of citizens. However, later empirical studies demonstrate that the impact of video surveillance cameras on crime rates and the perception of insecurity is disputable, relatively low (if detected), and highly context-dependent (Piza, Welsh, Farrington, & Thomas, 2019; Welsh & Farrington, 2009).

In the academic literature, two main approaches have been formed to comprehend video surveillance in urban public spaces: surveillance society and security state. Both theoretical approaches are based on Foucault's works. The former is grounded on the concepts of discipline and disciplinary power as presented by Foucault in *Discipline and Punish* (1995). The notion of the apparatus of security (Foucault, 2009) inspired the theorization of the security state. The theoretical approaches have a lot in common; however, they rarely communicate (Bigo, 2006). Simultaneously, as some research shows, such a dialogue could be very productive to deepen understanding of the phenomenon of video surveillance in urban spaces. In particular, one of the recent research projects demonstrates that surveillance technologies can enact several modes of governmentality within one city as their operationalization is context-dependent (Kitchin, Coletta, & McArdle, 2017).

The chapter follows the development of Foucault's thoughts. Therefore, it first describes Foucault's idea of disciplinary power (Foucault, 1995) and the theorization of the surveillance society inspired by it. Later in his life, Foucault (2009) presented the notion of apparatus of security that is discussed in the following section of this chapter, along with the theory of the security state. In particular, the two sections briefly overview Foucault's thought and its further developments, focusing on the role of video surveillance as a technology of data collection and its implementation in urban spaces. The chapter concludes with a brief discussion of the main similarities and disparities between the theories. Lastly, it suggests some considerations of a possibility to combine the theoretical approaches for conducting empirical research.

Video Surveillance in a Surveillance Society

Foucault's notions of discipline and disciplinary power induced the theorization of a surveillance society (Lyon, 2011). Foucault considered discipline to be a spatial technology of power that exercises control over individuals and their bodies by generating knowledge about them (Foucault, 1997). The concept of a norm is crucial for understanding disciplinary power as the discipline aims at instilling norms that are dominating in a society. The disciplinary power is exercised by surveying individual bodies and normalization of their behavior, that is, modifying the behavior to conform to the existing norms. So, disciplinary power draws on the pre-established normative model (Foucault, 2007). Technologies of surveillance and inspection are vital for organizing individual bodies into "a field of visibility" and tailoring their functionality.

In *Discipline and Punish* (1995), Foucault illustrates the disciplinary potential of surveillance on an example of a perfect prison, the panopticon, developed by Jeremy

Bentham. This prison should be ring-shaped so that all the cells are visible from the center of the building. In the center of the panopticon, a guard tower is located with an unseen observer who can observe the inmates, notice if their behavior deviates from the established norms, and introduce the punishment for it. So, at any given moment, the inmates of the panopticon are uncertain whether the guard is watching them or not. Eventually, the inmates become convinced that they are constantly watched over, and since then, the prison can work effectively even without the physical presence of the guard in the tower. Foucault refers to this process as the internalization of the knowledge of being constantly observed. In turn, this knowledge transforms the inmates as they start behaving in a normalized way like "docile bodies," even without any concrete evidence that there is actual surveillance. In such a way, the main aim of the panopticon—"a prison without wardens"—is achieved.

According to this framework, reality consists of a multiplicity of activities, bodies, individuals, objects, etc. Disciplinary power is exercised in such a reality through individualization techniques (Foucault, 1995). Thus, it is capable of normalizing individuals by disaggregating a multiplicity of an individual into constituent components. Surveillance is used for collecting information on individual bodies, which is then analyzed. Based on this analysis, punishment may be implemented if a deviation from the norm is detected. Following the logic of the exercise of disciplinary power, it is possible to say that it is centralized and concentrated as it requires a centralized aggregation of data for further analysis.

However, disciplinary power is not exercised only over subjects from outside (for instance, by a sovereign or a surveyor) but also from inside subjects. Thus, Foucault states that discipline creates subjectivity as an individual "is subjected to the field of visibility, and who knows it, assumes responsibility for the constraints of power; [...] he inscribes in himself the power relation in which he simultaneously plays both roles; he becomes the principle of his own subjection" (Foucault, 1995: 202–203).

The ideal of disciplinary power is an entirely transparent social and physical space that could create complicit individuals. At the same time, agency (sovereign) and agents (guards) exercising power can preserve their invisibility and anonymity (Forrester, 2014). Ideally, such social space should exist in an enclosed and fixed physical space designed to allow the individualization and disaggregation of multiplicities of observed bodies (Foucault, 1995). Besides, the organization of the physical space should correspond to a pre-established normative model and serve the aim of normalization (Foucault, 1995). Therefore, there is a rationality behind such spatial organization, including the economic one, as it implies individualization and self-discipline.

Based on these Foucauldian ideas, Deleuze (1992) proposes a theory of control society. According to Deleuze, modern society is characterized by expanding discipline from physically enclosed spaces (prisons, factories, schools, etc.) to whole societies (Deleuze, 1992). Under this framework, a state aims at managing and controlling its population. Technologies capable of collecting and accumulating data on the population underlie the mode of governmentality in the control society because they allow for extending and deepening surveillance (Deleuze, 1992). In particular, they can collect and accumulate data by tracking movement, transactions, and other routine actions determined by technologies. So, surveillance technologies are distributed across society and omnipresent. Besides, the ongoing technological development allows them to transcend borders (Hagmann, 2017); therefore, the control society is not territorially limited anymore.

Another direction in which Foucault's ideas have been further developed and transformed is the surveillance society theory. G.T. Marx (1985), inspired by G. Orwell's novel *1984*, coined the term "surveillance society." Such a society is based on technologies, their constant development, and ever-increasing adaptation. Thus, surveillance builds not only upon surveillance practices but also upon devices, technologies (Haggerty & Ericson, 2000). In particular, technologies serve daily collection, storing, retrieving, and processing of information on individuals (Lyon, 1994).

So, one of the underlying assumptions of a surveillance society is that technological development and its adaptation result in an increased amount of gathered information on the members of this society. In such a way, technologies eliminate "the inability to retrieve, aggregate, analyze vast amounts of data" (Marx, 1985: 26). Such inability was a mechanism of social control as bureaucracies were limited in their data aggregation and analysis capacity.

Due to technological development, the efficacy of surveillance systems in data collection, systematization, and individualization increases. For example, modern technologies have a growing ability to communicate and merge, which results in an increase in the extent and depth of surveillance (Gray, 2002). Thus, merging databases of biometric ID and CCTV systems with facial recognition can facilitate the systematization of the collected data and allow identifying a person within several seconds. Additionally, due to the spread of technologies, participation in modern (at least Western) society implies leaving electronic footprints during routine activities (paying with a bank card, using social networks, going outside and being caught by a CCTV, etc.) (Lace, 2005). So, surveillance becomes more profound, and individuals are subject to it on an ever-increasing scale.

Another outcome of the development of surveillance technologies is that they are rendered less apparent, visible to the subjects of surveillance (Lyon, 2001). This low visibility of surveillance instruments signifies a critical departure from the Foucauldian description of disciplinary power and its mechanisms. In particular, Foucault suggests that individuals should be aware that they are subjected to constant surveillance and monitoring. Quite contrary to it, as surveillance becomes subtler, individuals are less aware of being subjected to surveillance and its scope (Wood & Webster, 2009). Therefore, the major part of such interactions with surveillance is unnoticed and considered normal. For this reason, some authors suggest that it is not entirely correct to consider video cameras in public spaces as a modern embodiment of the panopticon. Instead, CCTV signage takes the role of instilling discipline as, according to the legislation of many countries, it should be highly visible and remind people that they are in a zone under surveillance (Lippert, 2009).

D. Lyon, who is among the founders of surveillance society theory, considers video surveillance to be one of the modes of disciplinary power. In particular, within this approach, CCTV is regarded as a context for collecting, storing, and structuring information on individual members of society (Lyon, 2007; Wood & Webster, 2009). An observer could detect and punish those who show deviance from "normal" behavior based on the collected information. Hence, within this framework, it is expected that individuals will internalize the knowledge of being watched over and will start behaving in compliance with rules, that is, in a normalized way (Ericson & Haggerty, 1997; Graham & Wood, 2003). Therefore, video surveillance aims to anticipate and pre-manage risks that could arise within society by imposing disciplinary power.

Video surveillance also takes the asymmetry between an observer and observed after the Foucauldian description of disciplinary power (Lippert, 2009). In the panopticon, the inmates cannot reconstruct the guard's personal or social identity since they are invisible, hidden from the inmates. The operation of CCTV implies almost the same discrepancy. Video surveillance is "placeless and faceless," as it is nearly impossible to verify the presence and character of an observer because CCTV does not require an observer to be physically present in a place of observation (Koskela, 2002).

Given the asymmetry between a surveyor and surveyed, increasingly low visibility of video surveillance cameras, and its decentralization, in many countries, the legislation obliges private or public bodies to inform through appropriate signs that it is they who operate CCTVs in a public space. However, this information is frequently limited in the content as it allows reconstructing where the observer works and maybe their position in the organization, but any further particulars about the observer's personality are not publicly available. So, the amount of information provided is insufficient for rendering an "unobservable observer" into an observable one to potential subjects of surveillance (Goold, 2002). Simultaneously, workers of CCTV control rooms can access such information about those under surveillance as their sex, age, social status, ethnicity, frequented places, time patterns of being in some locations, and so on. They can reconstruct it by observing the behaviors and appearances of the individuals caught by the gaze of video surveillance (Lippert, 2009).

Due to this transformative power of video surveillance and the asymmetry between a surveyor and surveyed, a surveillance society can be considered a constant threat to privacy and liberty. In particular, just like G.T. Marx, Garfinkel (2000) also appeals to the novel *1984* and the image of Big Brother as an extreme example of a surveillance society. At the same time, contrarily to it, CCTV can be considered an instrument of providing better public services, in particular, enhanced security, including the national one, and improved fight against crime and terrorism (Garfinkel, 2000).

Therefore, there is a dichotomy between providing better services, which comprises security provision, and privacy invasion in implementing surveillance technologies. So, data collection technologies (CCTV, ID cards, mobile phones, etc.) represent in the terminology proposed by Taylor, Lips, and Organ (2008) "information capture" for both enhanced and better services and increased surveillance over people. These two sides of surveillance are interlinked and interdependent, therefore, they happen simultaneously, and there is no choice between a safe, efficient society and a surveillance society.

The spread of surveillance technologies also affects the design of public spaces as they should meet requirements of "omnipresent visibility" (Lyon, 2011) and risk anticipation (Koskela, 2002). Therefore, they should be transparent. In turn, this transparency could facilitate the collection of more data on people in such spaces.

The incorporation of video surveillance in urban planning might aim to increase surveillance over specific groups of population (Fussey & Coaffe, 2012). In particular, areas with a higher concentration of people showing deviant behavior can be under heightened scrutiny as the local government would like to instill discipline there. At the same time, as Lyon (2011) points out, disciplinary spaces emphasize and might even provoke disorder, misbehavior, and signs of physical disturbances (pollution, abandonment, etc.). It happens because such individuals start to perceive their bodies as being constantly subjected to surveillance and, consequently, they feel the need to "produce selves for the observer" (Lyon, 2011: 6).

Citizens have a rightful expectation of privacy in the public spaces; however, video surveillance revokes this liberty as it allows a surveyor to scrutinize one's behavior and patterns of everyday routine (von Hirsch, 2000). As a consequence, video surveillance could lead to the erosion of privacy. Thus, it can be used to track an individual for the purposes of security provision (someone shows deviant, suspicious, "abnormal" behavior, seems somehow different) and for the abuse of power (increased surveillance of someone who is known to CCTV operatives) (Smith, 2012; Webster, 2009). Therefore, the challenge is to prevent surveillance tools from evolving into more significant threats to the urban fabric than the ones they are utilized to solve (Gray, 2002).

Curry (1997) claims that individuals should be able to decide what pieces of information about themselves they want to make public and what they want to keep to themselves. Video surveillance deprives them of this control and an opportunity to adjust or change their social identity that they believe to be best in a given context. Once it is recorded on the footage, it stays fixed. Moreover, there is an inequality in surveillance: based on their observable behavior, people are differentiated not by who they are but by whom they are perceived to be. As the spaces of surveillance expand and private spaces shrink in cities, urban inhabitants exercise less and less control over the data collected about them (Gray, 2002).

Despite increasing levels of surveillance, a surveillance society approach considers this exposure to surveillance to be usually benign. Relative anonymity is preserved due to "informatization" (Frissen, 1989): each individual's data is relatively insignificant by itself, and personal details are not utilized in any meaningful way. So, collected information is analyzed in a generalized or aggregated way.

Video Surveillance in a Security State

The theorization of the security state is based on Foucault's notions of governmentality, security, and security apparatus. According to Foucault, governmentality is a power modality with "the population as its target, political economy as its major form of knowledge and apparatuses of security as its essential technical instrument" (Foucault, 2009: 143). So, governmentality comprises the logic, rationality, and techniques that make populations governable and enable government and other agencies to enact governance (Foucault, 1991). As logic, rationality, and techniques of governance change over time to correspond to the current needs and aims of government, the nature of governmentality evolves with time. Additionally, different power actors can simultaneously implement diverse or intersecting modes of governmentality. In turn, it contributes to the fluidity of governmentality.

Therefore, Foucault suggests examining reality as molded in a relativistic way within this framework. Constituent components of reality are constantly coordinated and adjusted in dependence on each other, and through it, the process of normalization happens. Consequently, security considers reality being plural and relative, and it does not have an "ideal" reality it should aspire to accomplish. Quite the opposite, the goals and circumstances of reality undergo a continuous change accounting for shifts in circumstances and contexts of the regulation (in particular, calculation of costs of interventions, availability of control techniques, public opinion, and others). Therefore, the improvement and optimization of the interplay of the components of reality is constant.

The apparatus of security starts normalization by disaggregating the reality on components. Then it identifies what normality is and, finally, it seeks to improve the interplay of the components of reality (Foucault, 2009). Just like reality, the process of normalization is also flexible as it depends on and accounts for reality and changes there. Therefore, one of the main problems of normalization is to identify the best ways to regulate such reality within a "multivalent and transformable framework" (Foucault, 2009: 35).

The proper work of the security apparatus requires disciplinary and juridico-legal techniques as they help identify conditions and boundaries within which the components or reality could be optimized. In particular, the former serves for enforcing control over individual bodies through surveillance over them, classification of their mental structures, pathologies, and so on (Foucault, 2009). In turn, the legal system is needed to establish and further sustain a force and strength relationship in society (Foucault, Simon, & Elden, 2017).

Security functions in a specific space called "milieu" in which a series of uncertain elements and events take place and which combines already existing givens (rivers, hills, etc.) and artificial ones (constructed by people) (Foucault, 2009). Hence, a milieu is "a medium of an action and an element in which it circulates" (Foucault, 2009: 36). The milieu is designed to regulate, optimize, and manage circulations of the population "in the very broad sense of movement, exchange, and contact, as a form of a dispersion, and also as a form of distribution" (Foucault, 2009: 92). The spatial design accounts for the flexible nature of reality because its basic principle is multidimensionality and the interplay of these dimensions.

A population, defined as a variety of individuals who are biologically bound to spaces of their inhabitation, exists in a milieu. The security apparatus serves to plan and organize a milieu and, consequently, exercise power over and govern the population. In particular, power structures actions that could have been different if the power had not been exercised (Foucault, 1991).

Given that governmentality seeks to rationalize every practice, the government's main aim is to calculate risks arising within a population and choose measures for tackling and preventing them. At the same time, the political economy should be applied; therefore, benefits from the realization of preventive measures should exceed their costs. So, the security apparatus plays a crucial role in managing the population in modern states (Foucault, 2009).

Proponents of the security state develop the ideas of security, the apparatus of security, and governmentality. A security state considers a society to be in a "permanent state of emergency" or a "generalized state of exception" as it is engaged in a self-declared war against an invisible, permanent, and general threat—crime, terrorism, etc. (Agamben, 2017; Bigo, 2006). Although the state of emergency is usually limited in time, space, and object, a permanent and invisible threat removes these limitations. This theoretical approach considers a sovereign as the one who decides about the introduction of the state of emergency and who has the legitimate power to name the public enemy.

Being in a state of emergency makes it possible, under special circumstances, to act beyond the rule of law and justify the illiberal practices and violation of civil rights. The exploitation of security discourse, conjuring images of exceptional violence or threat, gives precedence to the speed and efficiency in identifying a (potential) criminal at the expense of liberal rights (Bigo, 2006). Simultaneously, a government can still adopt a liberal discourse appealing to the privatization of security, making security not a public good anymore but a private commodity (Loader, 1999). The privatization of surveillance is essential to rationalize the expenditures for the security provision. Therefore, video surveillance is not only increasingly ubiquitous but also privatized (Braithwaite, 2000). Besides, authorities stimulate inter-agency cooperation between state, private, and non-governmental bodies and exchange information between them (Crawford & Evans, 2017). For instance, private security organizations can hand in their videotapes if the police require them for crime investigation.

Among the drawbacks of the privatization of security is that the multiplicity of actors hinders creating a reliable data protection system. It happens because controls vary and might have different logic for different actors exercising surveillance; therefore, they might not be equal and target the same people in the same way (Zedner, 2003). Furthermore, despite the privatization of security, the penal state has not diminished, but on the contrary, expanded even more (Braithwaite, 2000). States introduced more strict and repressive penal codes, more stringent regulatory legislation, and provisions for licensing, inspection, and audit (Zedner, 2003).

The security state relies on the governmentality of unease. Practices of exceptionalism, profiling, and containing "others" characterize the governmentality of unease (Bigo, 2006; O'Malley, 2004). Therefore, a security state protects one part of the population from another. Monahan (2010) suggests that surveillance produces and sustains social inequalities in the security state because surveillance technologies are inherently biased and not neutral. Firstly, implemented through surveillance, social categorization facilitates the identification of one's place in society and does not allow people to deviate from their category. Secondly, people are exposed to surveillance based on their social category. For instance, according to Monahan, marginalized people could be surveyed to a greater extent than other social groups. Besides, the process of surveillance affixes categories of risky, dangerous, or untrustworthy to these marginalized groups and, consequently, it contributes to the sustenance of the discrimination.

With time, the "state of exception" and governmentality of unease become unremarkable, mundane, and not even challenged (Agamben, 2005). Normalized populations silently consent to surveillance as it symbolizes protection from danger, "others" (Bigo, 2006). This positive attitude toward surveillance generates a lack of opposition to the implementation of video surveillance. On the contrary, the population might require it or ask for its enhancement (Bigo, 2006).

Following Foucault's assumption about the lack of an "ideal" secure reality, authors suggest that, given the flexible and evolving nature of (potential) risks and threats, the pursuit of security is endless, and an absolute security state is practically unachievable (Freedman, 1992). Besides, security is not an objective state; instead, it is constructed continuously by an interplay of social and political processes (Williams, 2003). Powerful "securitizing actors" (for instance, policymakers, the media, big private corporations, and non-governmental organizations) play a significant role in constructing the notion of security (Taureck, 2006).

Under this framework, crime is considered rational and motivated by utility maximization (Clarke, 1995; Felson, 2002; Garland, 2001). Furthermore, it concerns the evolution of new forms of crime as criminals might be interested in developing crime activities only if they assume that their benefits would exceed the probability of being caught. Therefore, the main tools to tackle criminal activity are a statistical calculation of its probability and preventive interventions to reduce an opportunity for crime (situational crime prevention, risk assessment, monitoring, and surveillance) (O'Malley, 2004).

Video surveillance is among the tools facilitating the statistical calculation and prevention of dangerous situations as it allows observing, collecting, and analyzing patterns of behavior. Therefore, it is a proactive tool for tracing deviations from a normal behavior through analyzing observable characteristics caught on a record and their correlations (Zedner, 2003). In turn, it contributes to the governmentality of unease by facilitating the practices of exception of those who show deviance.

The way of tackling risks in a security state facilitates the proliferation of surveillance technologies. Expanding control and monitoring is possible due to technological advancements and their growing ability to transcend distance, physical barriers, and time. In a security state, bureaucracies have a deterministic belief that technologies and, especially, their capacity to trace people's movements, recognize behavioral patterns, etc., can fix any political or security problem. Such technological determinism encourages technological adaptation as reflected in public policy and its further implementation (Bigo, 2006; Douglas & Wildavsky, 1983).

Therefore, authorities encourage and invest in technological development, especially in those allowing an increasing exchange of information that is collected and stored through different technologies. For instance, the information exchange between electronic ID systems and records of CCTV with facial recognition allows a surveyor to identify quickly those who are captured by video surveillance cameras. Authorities' interest can be attributed to their expectation of high returns from these investments; therefore, they consider them profitable from an economic point of view (Bigo, 2006).

According to Garland (2001), urban fortification and intensified surveillance in private and public urban areas result from increased awareness of risk and governmentality of unease. This logic of dealing with threats affects how public spaces are designed. As Sorkin puts it: "if every person is under suspicion and every place is vulnerable, the only solution is to put everyone under surveillance and fortify every place" (Sorkin, 2008: viii). The possibility of a threat becomes an obligatory part of urban planning (Sorkin, 2008).

In addition, practices of exceptionalism penetrate urban design through gated communities and homogeneous gentrification that could result in radical segregation because any deviance can be banned from the gated territory (Sorkin, 2008). In turn, this urban design transforms people's perception of others and trains citizens to be wary of others and anything different or suspicious.

This securitization and fortification of cities simultaneously threaten and encourage "the right to the city" (Lefebvre, 1996). On the one hand, situational crime prevention measures and increasing surveillance practices threaten social and political dynamism and civil disobedience, which are considered deviations from norms. On the other hand, the presence of, for instance, physical vehicle barriers and video surveillance can encourage more pedestrians to be present in the streets and more people to use public spaces (Simpson, Jensen, & Anders, 2017).

In a security society, the population is accustomed to accepting that the pursuit of security takes precedence over other public goods and services in particular situations (e.g., airport security checks, border checkpoints) (Zedner, 2003). This normalization of security precedence leads to a spillover of different security measures from "high-risk" situations and zones (airports, national borders) to everyday life (public transport, theaters, cinemas, city squares, etc.). In this expansion of security, video surveillance observes behavior and creates predetermined criminal profiles by collecting data. Simultaneously, CCTV is used as an instrument of management not only real but also perceived risks and threats.

Also, if previously some surveillance and biometric techniques (fingerprints and other biometric data collection) were applied to criminals only, since the beginning of the twentieth century, their application has expanded to all citizens and started to penetrate everyday life (Agamben, 2017). The whole population is put under surveillance, but those who show deviant, suspicious behavior require more intense and further surveillance, which can be realized not only through CCTV but also through checking the information in other databases. Any deviation from current norms is possible to detect due to constant social ordering, and measures should be undertaken to "alienate" deviant individuals from the population (Feeley & Simon, 1992; Goold, 2002; Zedner, 2003). Besides, with time, the biometric techniques are considered banal and go unnoticed that nobody from the population challenges its legitimacy and questions their efficiency in preventing risks (Bigo, 2006).

Discussion and Conclusions

This chapter has reviewed the key aspects of surveillance society and security space theories. More specifically, it focused on video surveillance, which facilitates data collection on members of society, and its implementation in urban spaces. As it follows from the previous sections, both theoretical approaches are deeply grounded in Foucault's ideas. While the theory of surveillance society is primarily based on the concept of discipline, the approach of a security state draws on Foucault's notion of apparatus of security and governmentality.

The theories have some points of coincidence and disparity. For instance, the extent and depth of surveillance are considered similarly. Thus, the proponents of both approaches suggest that surveillance technologies are the basis of exercising control in societies as they allow the collection, storage, and analysis of a vast amount of information. Furthermore, technological development could lead to deeper surveillance over members of societies by generating more knowledge about them. Therefore, the authorities usually facilitate it.

Simultaneously, the conceptualization of control is different. The surveillance society approach considers discipline as the only power and control modality; the security society theory offers a more complex understanding of control through governmentality and the functioning of the apparatus of security. Additionally, in a surveillance society, control aims to normalize all the members of the society and prevent deviance and security provision. Therefore, there is a dichotomy between, on the one hand, expanding control and surveillance and, on the other hand, provision of better services, which also entail security. In a security state, control extends as a state engages in a self-declared and constant war against crime and terrorism. Therefore, the state seeks to protect one part of its population from another, "dangerous" one. Such a battle against an invisible and permanent enemy allows for the expansion of control and surveillance as a mean of security provision.

Both approaches account for the invasion of one's privacy due to increasing surveillance. Furthermore, the surveillance society and security state members are ready to sacrifice a part of their rights (in this case, a right to anonymity in public spaces) in exchange for security. At the same time, if the surveillance society approach suggests relative anonymity of "ordinary" citizens, the security society framework supposes that their further social ordering is needed. It also happens because video surveillance helps detect behavioral patterns that are then scrutinized by those in power to calculate risks or benefits.

The theories also differ in their understanding of those who can exercise surveillance. Thus, the disciples of a surveillance society suggest concentration and centralization of power, while the proponents of a security state allow for the privatization of security. Privatization also has implications for privacy concerns as there is a multitude of actors who can implement surveillance.

Within both approaches, the surveillance technologies are considered to serve the prevention of risks that could arise within societies, although the mechanisms of prevention are different. Thus, the surveillance society framework suggests that the knowledge of being watched over is internalized, and gradually the potential for deviance is eliminated. In contrast, the theory of the security state emphasizes the role of governmentality in prevention: calculation of possible crimes or deviations and their prevention.

Additionally, the theoretical approaches also perceive the presence of video surveillance in urban spaces differently. Thus, surveillance society theory highlights that urban design should account for increasing surveillance and provision of security; therefore, it should be highly visible and transparent. In contrast, the proponents of a security state suggest that the design of urban spaces should account for the declaration of war against crime and, consequently, be fortified against any possible threat.

Therefore, this brief discussion shows that the theories have some similarities and disparities. However, applying only one theoretical approach to conducting an empirical study and analyzing its results might lead to an insufficient understanding of the complexity of society. Thus, Borch (2015) suggests that applying surveillance society theory might lead to a tendency of finding traces of disciplinary power everywhere which might not account for some other processes evolving in society.

The empirical research indicates that there might be different logics of security provision and implementation of surveillance in contrasting contexts (for instance, affluent and marginal neighborhoods) within one city (Stefanizzi & Verdolini, 2018; Valente & Crescenzi Lanna, 2019). As to video surveillance, the research, conducted by Monahan (2010), indicates that the logic of surveying marginalized and wealthy areas of the same city could be different. If in the former, video surveillance is used for instilling discipline (surveillance society), in the latter, it serves for security as a tool for profiling and excepting those showing deviance (security state).

Therefore, drawing on the two theoretical approaches might enrich and inform the interpretation of the empirical findings, which, in turn, contributes to our understanding of society. Future research might investigate how these two logics of implementation of surveillance and security provision might coexist within one society, what are the implications of their coexistence, and what factors contribute to the dominance of one of the approaches in a given context.

References

Agamben, G. (2005). The state of exception. In A. Norris & G. Agamben (Eds.), *Politics, metaphysics, and death* (pp. 284–298). Duke University Press.

Agamben, G. (2017). For a theory of destituent power. Public lecture in Athens, November 16, 2013. In D. Simpson, V. Jensen, & A. Rubing (Eds.), *The city between freedom and security. Contested public spaces in the 21st century* (pp. 34–54). Birkhäuser Verlag GmbH.

Bannister, J., Fyfe, N., & Kearns, A. (1998). Closed circuit television and the city. In C. Norris, J. Moran, & G. Armstrong (Eds.), *Surveillance, closed circuit television, and social control* (pp. 21–40). Ashgate.

Bigo, D. (2006). Security, exception, ban and surveillance. In D. Lyon (Ed.), *Theorizing surveillance: The panopticon and beyond* (pp. 46–68). Taylor & Francis. https://doi.org/10.4324/9781843926818

Borch, C. (2015). *Foucault, crime and power. Problematisation of crime in the twentieth century*. Routledge.

Braithwaite, J. (2000). The new regulatory state and the transformation of criminology. In D. Garland & R. Sparks (Eds.), *Criminology and social theory* (pp. 47–69). Oxford University Press.

Cerezo, A. (2013). CCTV and crime displacement: A quasi-experimental evaluation. *European Journal of Criminology, 10*(2), 222–236. https://doi.org/10.1177/1477370812468379

Clarke, R. V. (1995). Situational crime prevention. *Crime and Justice: A Review of Research, 19*, 91–150.

Crawford, A., & Evans, K. (2017). Crime prevention and community safety. In A. Leibling, S. Maruna, & L. McAra (Eds.), *The Oxford handbook of criminology* (pp. 797–824). Oxford University Press.

Curry, M. R. (1997). The digital individual and the private realm. *Annals of the Association of American Geographers, 87*(4), 681–699.

Dandeker, C. (1990). *Surveillance, power and modernity: Bureaucracy and discipline from 1700 to the present day*. St. Martin's Press.

Deleuze, G. (1992). Postscript on the societies of control. *October, 59*, 3–7.

Douglas, M., & Wildavsky, A. (1983). *Risk and culture: An essay on the selection of technological and environmental dangers*. University of California Press.

Ericson, R. V., & Haggerty, K. D. (1997). *Policing the risk society*. University of Toronto.

Feeley, M. M., & Simon, J. (1992). The new penology: Notes of the emerging strategy of corrections and its implications. *Criminology, 30*(4), 449–474.

Felson, M. (2002). *Crime and everyday life* (3rd ed.). Sage.

Forrester, J. (2014). Foucault's face: The personal is the theoretical. In J. D. Faubion (Ed.), *Foucault now. Current perspectives in Foucault studies* (pp. 113–130). Polity Press.

Foucault, M. (1991). Governmentality. In G. Burchell, C. Gordon, & P. Miller (Eds.), *The Foucault effect: Studies in governmentality with two lectures by and interview with Michel Foucault* (pp. 87–104). The University of Chicago Press.

Foucault, M. (1995). *Discipline and punish: The birth of the prison* (2nd ed.). Vintage Books.

Foucault, M. (1997). *Ethics, subjectivity and truth: The essential works of Michele Foucault 1954–1984, volume I*. The New Press.

Foucault, M. (2007). Spaces of security: The example of the town. Lecture of 11th January 1978. *Political Geography, 26*(1), 48–56. https://doi.org/10.1016/j.polgeo.2006.08.004

Foucault, M. (2009). *Security, territory, population. Lectures at the College de France, 1977–78*. Palgrave Macmillan.

Foucault, M., Simon, J., & Elden, S. (2017). Danger, crime and rights: A conversation between Michel Foucault and Jonathan Simon. *Theory, Culture and Society, 34*(1), 3–27. https://doi.org/10.1177/0263276416640070

Freedman, L. (1992). The concept of security. In M. Hawkesworth & M. Kogan (Eds.), *Encyclopedia of government and politics, volume II* (pp. 730–741). Routledge.
Frissen, P. H. A. (1989). The cultural impact of informatization in public administration. *International Review of Administrative Sciences, 55*(4), 569–586.
Fussey, P., & Coaffe, J. (2012). Urban spaces of surveillance. In K. Ball, K. D. Haggerty, & D. Lyon (Eds.), *Routledge handbook of surveillance studies* (pp. 201–208). Routledge.
Garfinkel, S. (2000). *Database nation: The death of privacy in the 21st century*. O'Reilly.
Garland, D. (2001). *The culture of control*. Oxford University Press.
Goold, B. J. (2002). Privacy rights and public spaces: CCTV and the problem of the "unobservable observer". *Criminal Justice Ethics, 21*(1), 21–27.
Graham, S., & Wood, D. (2003). Digitizing surveillance: Categorization, space, inequality. *Critical Social Policy, 23*(2), 227–248.
Gray, M. (2002). Urban surveillance and panopticism: Will we recognize the facial recognition society? *Surveillance & Society, 1*(3), 314–330.
Haggerty, K. D., & Ericson, R. V. (2000). The surveillant assemblage. *British Journal of Sociology, 51*(4), 605–622. https://doi.org/10.1080/00071310020015280
Hagmann, J. (2017). Security in the society of control: The politics and practices of securing urban spaces. *International Political Sociology, 11*(4), 418–438. https://doi.org/10.1093/ips/olx020
von Hirsch, A. (2000). The ethics of public television surveillance. In A. von Hirsch, D. Garland, & A. Wakefield (Eds.), *Ethical and social perspectives on situational crime prevention* (pp. 59–76). Hart Publishing.
Kitchin, R., Coletta, C., & McArdle, G. (2017). *Urban informatics, governmentality and the logics of urban control*. The Programmable City Working Paper 25. Preprint retrieved April 19, 2022, from https://osf.io/preprints/socarxiv/27hz8/
Koskela, H. (2002). Video surveillance, gender, and the safety of public urban apace: "Peeping Tom" goes high tech? *Urban Geography, 23*(3), 257–278. https://doi.org/10.2747/0272-3638.23.3.257
Lace, S. (2005). Introduction. In S. Lace (Ed.), *The glass consumer: Life in a surveillance society* (pp. 1–16). National Consumer Council.
Lefebvre, H. (1996). *Writings on the cities*. Wiley.
Lippert, R. (2009). Signs of the surveillant assemblage: Privacy regulation, urban CCTV, and governmentality. *Social and Legal Studies, 18*(4), 505–522. https://doi.org/10.1177/0964663909345096
Loader, I. (1999). Consumer culture and the commodification of policing and security. *Sociology, 33*(2), 373–392.
Lyon, D. (1994). *The electronic eye: The rise of the surveillance society*. University of Minnesota Press.
Lyon, D. (2001). *Surveillance society: Monitoring everyday life*. Open University Press.
Lyon, D. (2007). *Surveillance studies: An overview*. Polity Press.
Lyon, D. (2011). The search for surveillance theories. In D. Lyon (Ed.), *Theorizing surveillance: The panopticon and beyond* (pp. 3–20). Routledge.
Marx, G. T. (1985, June). The surveillance society: The threat of 1984-style techniques. *The Futurist*, 21–26.
Marx, G. T. (1998). Ethics for the new surveillance. *Information Society, 14*(3), 171–185. https://doi.org/10.1080/019722498128809
Monahan, T. (2010). *Surveillance in the time of insecurity*. Rutgers University Press.
O'Malley, P. (2004). The uncertain promise of risk. *The Australian and New Zealand Journal of Criminology, 37*(3), 323–343.
Phillips, C. (1999). A review of CCTV evaluations: Crime reduction effects and attitudes towards its use. *Crime Prevention Studies, 10*, 123–155.

Piza, E. L., Welsh, B. C., Farrington, D. P., & Thomas, A. L. (2019). CCTV surveillance for crime prevention: A 40-year systematic review with meta-analysis. *Criminology and Public Policy, 18*(1), 135–159. https://doi.org/10.1111/1745-9133.12419

Ratcliffe, J. H., & Groff, E. R. (2019). A longitudinal quasi-experimental study of violence and disorder impacts of urban CCTV camera clusters. *Criminal Justice Review, 44*(2), 148–164. https://doi.org/10.1177/0734016818811917

Simpson, D., Jensen, V., & Anders, R. (2017). Introduction: On urban indefensibility: Friction lines in the production of the open city. In D. Simpson, V. Jensen, & A. Rubing (Eds.), *The city between freedom and security. Contested public spaces in the 21st century* (pp. 11–14). Birkhäuser Verlag GmbH.

Smith, G. J. D. (2012). Surveillance work(ers). In K. Ball, K. D. Haggerty, & D. Lyon (Eds.), *Routledge handbook of surveillance studies* (pp. 107–116). Routledge.

Sorkin, M. (2008). Introduction: The fear factor. In M. Sorkin (Ed.), *Indefensible space: The architecture of the National Insecurity State* (pp. vii–xvii). Routledge.

Stefanizzi, S., & Verdolini, V. (2018). Bordered communities: The perception of insecurity in five European cities. *Quality and Quantity, 53*(3), 1165–1186. https://doi.org/10.1007/s11135-018-0810-x

Taureck, R. (2006). Securitization theory and securitization studies. *Journal of International Relations and Development, 9*(1), 53–61. https://doi.org/10.1057/palgrave.jird.1800072

Taylor, J. A., Lips, M., & Organ, J. (2008). Identification practices in government: Citizen surveillance and the quest for public service improvement. *Identity in the Information Society, 1*, 135–154. https://doi.org/10.1007/s12394-009-0007-5

Valente, R., & Crescenzi Lanna, L. (2019). Cross-cultural nuances of the sources and consequences of subjective feelings of unsafety: A qualitative analysis in four cities. *International Journal of Comparative Sociology, 60*(5), 1–18. https://doi.org/10.1177/0020715219879190

Webster, W. (2009). CCTV policy in the UK: Reconsidering the evidence base. *Surveillance and Society, 6*(1), 10–22.

Welsh, B. C., & Farrington, D. P. (2009). Public area CCTV and crime prevention: An updated systematic review and meta-analysis. *Justice Quarterly, 26*(4), 716–745. https://doi.org/10.1080/07418820802506206

Welsh, B. C., Farrington, D. P., & Taheri, S. A. (2015). Effectiveness and social costs of public area surveillance for crime prevention. *Annual Review of Law and Social Science, 11*(1), 111–130. https://doi.org/10.1146/annurev-lawsocsci-120814-121649

Williams, M. C. (2003). Words, images, enemies: Securitization and international politics. *International Studies Quarterly, 47*(4), 511–531.

Wood, D. M., & Webster, C. W. R. (2009). Living in surveillance societies: The normalisation of surveillance in Europe and the threat of Britain's bad example. *Journal of Contemporary European Research, 5*(2), 259–273.

Zedner, L. (2003). Too much security? *International Journal of the Sociology of Law, 31*(3), 155–184. https://doi.org/10.1016/j.ijsl.2003.09.002

Tatiana Lysova is a PhD student in the Analysis of Social and Economic Processes at the University of Milan-Bicocca. Her current work focuses on video surveillance and its impact on subjective urban insecurity in the European context (Hungary and Italy). Before her PhD, she worked as a sociologist in a leading independent Russian research company, "Levada-Center," studying the living standards of the Russian population. During her work, she published several papers investigating the entrepreneurial potential and attitudes toward digital technologies in Russia.

Chapter 15
The Right to be Forgotten in the Digital Age

Maria Romana Allegri

Introduction

The idea behind the right to be forgotten (RTBF) is to provide individuals with a correct and updated representation of their personal identity by obtaining the erasure (or at least the so-called de-referencing) of their past "digital traces" left online. In fact, the Internet is not designed to forget, but to store our "digital footprints" almost permanently, even in cases when they may harm our dignity and reputation. A key role to this respect is played by search engines, engaged in facilitating the retrieval of information that would not be so easily discoverable otherwise.

Starting from this premise, this chapter first tries to define the nature of the RTBF as part of the right of personality, related to concepts such as dignity, reputation, privacy, and protection of the person's moral and legal integrity. Indeed, the term "right to be forgotten" may be perceived as ambiguous and misleading, comprising various components, and referring to different situations that sometimes overlap and can be confused with one another. Moreover, it seems to be significantly determined by "external" elements, such as the passage of time, the public interest for the information, and the role played by the data subject in society.

The Court of Justice of the European Union's (CJEU) landmark decision *Google Spain* contributed to shaping the RTBF at EU level, thus "creating" a new right not enshrined in the Data Protection Directive 95/46/EC, namely the right to obtain from search engines the interruption of the links between personal name and information previously published online. The second part of this chapter is dedicated to analyzing the reasons for which the CJEU's ruling raised doubts, concerns, and criticisms, especially from American commentators in detail. Unfortunately, interpretative

M. R. Allegri (✉)
Department of Communication and Social Research, Sapienza – University of Rome, Rome, Italy
e-mail: mromana.allegri@uniroma1.it

F. Comunello et al. (eds.), *What People Leave Behind*, Frontiers in Sociology and Social Research 7, https://doi.org/10.1007/978-3-031-11756-5_15

uncertainties have not been cleared out by the European Regulation in force since May 2018 (GDPR), where the RTBF seems to be conceived as a mere extension of the right to erasure (Article 17).

Since neither the CJEU nor the General Data Protection Regulation (GDPR) has defined precise criteria for the practical implementation of the RTBF, one may turn to the European Court of Human Rights (ECtHR) case law in an effort to shape the contours of the right in question. In the third part of this chapter, some relevant decisions of the ECtHR are examined, outlining that the positions of the two European courts are not easily reconcilable with each other, where the ECtHR is inclined to consider the seriousness of the harm caused to the individual by the information published online, while the CJEU is rather indifferent to the damage suffered by the data subject, revolving its reasoning around the legitimacy of the data processing.

The final part of this chapter briefly examines a recent decision of the Italian Court of Cassation, which has many features in common with the ECtHR's *M. L. and W. W. v. Germany*. However, the reasoning of the ECtHR does not seem to have influenced the Italian Court, which has come to opposite conclusions, marking a difference between the right to report and the right to carry out historical re-enactment of past events: in this last case the individual's right to anonymization was considered to prevail over the public interest in being informed.

Should Our "Digital Past" Be Forgotten?

In the digital age, data collection and automated memorization have become pervasive and can keep affecting one's life for a long time: "A past mistake, an involuntary negligence, a sudden emotional manifestation may unexpectedly surface long after someone and others have already forgotten about them, thus continuing to spoil a person's reputation" (Razmetaeva, 2020: 59). Indeed, the Internet is not designed to forget, but to store our "digital footprints" almost permanently: "Although a permanent, easy-to-access archive of nearly all information ever published has its virtues, it also has potential vices. When it comes to personal information, the Internet that never forgets may forever accentuate the worst or most embarrassing moments of a person's life" (Lee, 2016: 1021). Search engines play a particular role in this respect, as they help users retrieve online information about individuals, regardless of whether it is still relevant, correct, or not harmful for the person involved (Van Hoboken, 2013: 4). Due to search engines, nowadays remembering has become easy and inexpensive, whereas forgetting may turn out difficult and costly (Forde, 2015: 83), thus disrupting the natural cognitive capability of human beings to forget, which can act as a vehicle to maintain dignity and privacy (Criscione, 2020: 319).

Historical memory is antagonistic to the correct exercise of the RTBF, as it prevents updating or deleting facts and events that, even if true, the subject would like to conceal. Nevertheless, oblivion and memory share the same goals, namely the correct and truthful representation of facts and people and the protection of the personal identity and dignity (Bianca, 2019: 26–27). The struggle between oblivion and memory, from which the RTBF emerges, "has also been influenced by changes in the concepts of "time" and "data" in the all-digital age. Information is now stored over an indefinite period but found and disseminated instantly. It is as if we perceived time in two forms at the same time – as an instant and as an eternity" (Razmetaeva, 2020: 65).

Therefore, new concerns are rapidly arising; new demands deriving from this long-lasting digital footprint issue require the implementation of new rights, among which is a "right to digital identity," understood as the right of the individual to obtain the rectification, contextualization, updating, and, in some cases, even de-indexing and cancellation of one's personal data from the Internet, in order to ensure a reliable representation of one's own identity. Therefore, the idea behind the RTBF is to provide a legal claim such that everybody is granted an actual representation of their personal identity by obtaining the erasure of their past "digital traces" left online (Pollicino & Bassini, 2014: 642).

The RTBF is related to concepts such as dignity, reputation, and privacy, being part of the right of personality, meant as the protection of the moral and legal integrity of a person (Weber, 2011: 121) in situations where certain information has lost most of its significance, while continuing to have a negative impact on the privacy of the person involved (Weber, 2015: 7). It is composed of various rights, such as to change one's mind regarding previously disclosed data, to have personal data deleted when no longer required to be kept, not to be permanently reminded of one's past and not to let it disproportionately harm the future, and to obtain de-referencing of data by tackling the power of Internet search engines (Forde, 2015: 101–102). Because of its multifarious features, the term "right to be forgotten" may be perceived as ambiguous and misleading, being normally used to address different situations that sometimes overlap and can be confused with one another, such as the fact "that a historical event should no longer be revitalized due to the length of time elapsed since its occurrence"—which should be more appropriately defined "right to forget"—or "the claim of an individual to have certain data deleted so that third persons can no longer trace them" (Weber, 2011: 120–121; Weber, 2015: 2). With reference to this latter meaning, a further distinction has to be drawn up between the claim for "dignitary privacy" (i.e., the right to be respected in one's own private and family life, home, and communications, envisaged in Article 8 of the *European Convention for the Protection of Human Rights and Fundamental Freedoms* and in Article 7 of the *Charter of Fundamental Rights of the European Union*) and for "data privacy" (i.e., the right to maintain control over the circulation of one's personal data, envisaged in Article 8 of the *EU Charter of Fundamental Rights*) (Post, 2018: 990–995). Indeed, the right to data protection incorporates elements that are distinct from the components of the RTBF, such as "a right to withdraw previously given consent to process data; the right to object to data processing; the duty to delete or anonymize data once the purpose has been achieved and the right to erase data where its processing is noncompliant with protection requirements" (Forde, 2015: 102).

Over the years, the conflict between privacy and freedom of expression has been the source of countless legal battles, in which European courts have generally made an effort to reach a fair and careful balance between these two competing rights. From a European point of view "the right to be forgotten is a response to the echo of totalitarian record keeping, an assertion against governments, and, as time has evolved, non-government entities" (Kampmark, 2015: 5). This approach is different from the American one, which protects freedom of expression to the extent that it almost constitutes a right to remember (Guadamuz, 2017: 61–62). In fact, there is no general data protection law in the USA and, furthermore, the *Communications Decency Act*, dating back to 1996, legally protects intermediaries from all liability for the postings of third parties (CDA, Section 230). "In Continental Europe the ideas of autonomy, self-determination and the right to be secure in one's own reputation from intrusion by others play a key constitutional role; in contrast, American law (mainly the First Amendment to the US Constitution) reflects the traditional distrust of centralized power" (Weber, 2015: 6). The result of this attitude is that American courts adopt an exceptionally strong presumption in favor of allowing the circulation of information, whereas the RTBF is considered a much-diminished tort, deserving protection only in extreme circumstances (Post, 2018: 1061). It is not surprising, then, that many US scholars consider the RTBF "a formidable global threat to freedom of expression" (Nunziato, 2018: 1012) and an example of data imperialism by which the EU is trying to assert its own ideologies on other nations (Criscione, 2020: 353–354). Nonetheless, these concerns probably ought to be debunked: while criticism has been raised at the "imperialist" attitude of EU data protection law, claims to digital sovereignty are emerging also in illiberal regimes around the world, endangering the protection of fundamental rights online; to counter-balance this attitude, the development of transnational legal frameworks among democratic regimes seems to be a necessary measure (Fabbrini & Celeste, 2020: 64).

Shaping the RTBF in the European Union: From *Google Spain* to Article 17 GDPR

For the first time in the landmark case *Google Spain SL v. Agencia Española de Protección de Datos*[1] the CJEU recognized the right to be forgotten, deriving it from Article 12(b) of the Directive 95/46/EC (the so-called *Data Protection Directive*, hereinafter DPD) that established the right of the data subject to obtain "the rectification, erasure or blocking of data the processing of which does not comply with the provisions of this Directive, in particular because of the incomplete or inaccurate nature of the data." Under this rather "creative" ruling, the CJEU granted individuals the right to request search engines to remove links to online content containing

[1] Court of Justice of the European Union, Case C-131/12, 13 May 2014. A summary of the case can be found here: https://globalfreedomofexpression.columbia.edu/cases/google-spain-sl-v-agencia-espanola-de-proteccion-de-datos-aepd/

personal information that are "inadequate, irrelevant or excessive in relation to the purposes of the processing" or "not kept up to date" or "kept for longer than is necessary" (CJEU, *Google Spain*, 92–94). However, this decision is considered rather controversial for various reasons, as many commentators did not fail to point out.

First of all, the CJEU did not clarify for what precise reasons the data subject was entitled to removal of the links to the articles published by the Spanish newspaper *La Vanguardia*, concerning his past financial problems. Indeed, the Court did not explain whether the contested information was inaccurate, inadequate, irrelevant, excessive, not updated, or simply too old (Lee, 2016: 1022, 1033); it simply held that violations of the DPD did not require any showing of prejudice to the data subject (Post, 2018: 998). However, without a conception of harm it is very hard to reconcile the RTBF with the democratic function of public discourse (Post, 2018: 1009), given that the public has a fundamental interest in maintaining the integrity of the structure of communication that makes public discourse possible (Post, 2018: 1015).

Secondly, the CJEU has created a split decision, as the news articles containing the old information of the applicant's debt were not found to conflict the DPD, differently from the Google search results of Costeja's name that produced links to those articles (Lee, 2016: 1031). This difference was justified (CJEU, *Google Spain*, 85–86) by the fact that search engines and publishers may have different interests in deciding whether to accept a person's claim of a right of rectification and may fall under different derogations: in particular, only publishers may be granted the exemption "for the processing of personal data carried out solely for journalistic purposes," as stated by Article 9 DPD. The Court found that a search engine like Google, which stores, organizes, discloses, or makes personal data available, was not to be considered a neutral intermediary, but corresponded to the notion of "data controller" under Article 2(b) DPD, since it was in a position to determine the purposes and means of the data processing. However, Google's interest being solely economic (selling of advertising space), it could not rely upon the "journalistic exemption" under Article 9 DPD (CJEU, *Google Spain*, 56).

The position of the CJEU, however, was opposite to that expressed by the Advocate General Niilo Jääskinen (submission of June 25, 2013), who observed that search engines had a mere intermediary function—providing links to information previously published by third parties, without verifying whether it is legal and legitimate for the DPD purposes and without even distinguishing between personal and other data—and could not be equated to data controllers. Indeed, by providing increased access to the flow of information, search engines play an important role in promoting the transparency of information, which is essential in an open democracy. For this reason, allowing a data subject to obtain a restricted dissemination of personal data from search engines would have a distorting effect on the freedom of expression. Therefore, the Advocate General pleaded for the execution of an appropriate balancing test between conflicting rights—data protection and freedom of expression—concluding that the latter is to be considered generally prevailing (Weber, 2015: 6).

To this respect, the most important question raised by the CJEU in *Google Spain* is whether Google has become, like the modern newspaper, an essential component of the communicative infrastructure necessary to sustain the public sphere (Post, 2018: 1016). The approach of the Court, however, did not support this assumption: Google was considered only as a commercial company asserting its own economic interest, without serving journalist purposes. Indeed, the CJEU failed "to recognize that the circulation of texts of common interest among strangers makes possible the emergence of a "public" capable of forming the "public opinion" that is essential for democratic self-governance" (Post, 2018: 981).

Thirdly, the Court failed to clarify the cases and circumstances in which the preponderant public interest would require permanent access to information and when, instead, the information is no longer relevant (Forde, 2015: 107). The CJEU explained that the balancing between the RTBF and the public interested in the contested information requires case-by-case assessment—considering the type of information in question, its sensitivity for the individual's private life, and the interest of the public in having access to the relevant information—without, however, defining which criteria and procedures are to be followed to carry it out (Lee, 2016: 1034–1035).[2] Nevertheless, the Court seemed to lean toward the prevalence of individual privacy over the collective right to freedom of expression, although this presumption was mitigated by the possibility of some circumstances—particularly the public role of the data subject—that could make the disclosure of information relevant. In other words, this would mean that the extent of the RTBF can be determined by the public relevance of the data subject rather than the public interest in information (Stradella, 2016: 11).

Fourthly, considerable discretion and authority seem to have been delegated to search engines, which, in first instance, carry the primary responsibility to define the contours of the RTBF (Lee, 2016: 1035). Thus, private entities such as search engines have been made "judge, jury, and executioner" of the RTBF, thus taking the role of publishers in assessing the legitimacy of published information, which could lead to the possibility of censorship by a private party (Forde, 2015: 110–113). Moreover, transparency in how Google is currently dealing with delisting requests is problematic, and many have pointed out that the takedown process is operated on a quite arbitrary basis, remains obscure, and does not allow the data subject to have an effective cross-examination (Chenou & Radu, 2019: 89; Guadamuz, 2017: 66–68; Lee, 2016: 1035–1044; Leiser, 2020: 4–5; Post, 2018: 1069).[3]

[2] Actually, a list of 13 of 13 criteria European data protection authorities should take into consideration (on a case-by-case basis) when handling complaints is contained in the Guidelines on the Implementation of the Court of Justice's *Google Spain* judgment issued on November 26, 2014, by the EU's Article 29 Working Group (an advisory body composed of all the Data Protection Authorities in the European Union). Regarding the content of the guidelines, see Leiser, 2020: 5–7).

[3] Chenou and Radu (2019) highlight the emergence of transnational quasi-monopolistic private intermediaries in digital markets, due to a hybridization of governance entailing the transformation of both state and nonstate actors. Since Google exercises quasi-lawmaking, quasi-adjudicative, and quasi-enforcement powers in implementing the RTBF in the EU, it can be conceived as a private

Lastly, it has to be highlighted that even after de-indexing, the content remains on the original page and, although links are no longer displayed if the search is conducted by the name of the person, they can still be found using other relevant search terms (Forde, 2015: 117; Globocnik, 2020: 380). Moreover, even after the search engine has deleted the contested links from all its European domains, the information is still available and can be retrieved either through google.com or any other search engine (Forde, 2015: 112; Weber, 2015: 6), although the guidelines produced by the EU Article 29 Data Protection Working Party within a few months of the *Google Spain* decision determined that de-referencing decisions were to be implemented globally, and not just on search engines' EU domains.

This encouraged the French Data Protection Authority—*Commission Nationale de l'Informatique et des Libertés* (CNIL)—to make an attempt to require Google to implement the RTBF across all of Google's domains, including Google.com (Nunziato, 2018: 1033–1040; Reymond, 2019: 87–90). Nevertheless, in *Google v. CNIL* (24 September 2019, case C-507/17), the CJEU opted for EU-wide de-indexing, concluding that currently there is no legal obligation under EU law for search engines to carry out de-referencing on all their language versions, since the scope of the EU Regulation 2016/679 does not go beyond the territory of the Member States. However, the Court also noted that while EU law does not require de-referencing on a global scale, it also does not prevent national authorities from adopting such a practice. Therefore, after weighing the data subject's right to privacy and the collective right to freedom of information against each other, national authorities remain competent to order search engines, where appropriate, to carry out a worldwide de-referencing, although the court failed to offer a legal basis or guidelines for the execution of such practice, leaving its implementation to Member States (Criscione, 2020: 321–325, 332–334; Globocnik, 2020: 385–387).

The *Google Spain* ruling obviously had an influence on the drafting of the General Data Protection Regulation (EU) 2016/679, which entered into force in May 2018 (GDPR). The result was that the original title of Article 17, referring only to the right to erasure, was supplemented by a reference in brackets to the RTBF. Apart from being mentioned in the title of Article 17 and in the *Whereas* no. 65 and 66 (in both cases as a synonym of the right to erasure), the RTBF is not explicitly explained or regulated by the GDPR, whose Article 17 simply defines the pre-requisites for exercising the right to erasure, already provided by the DPD. The relationship between the right of erasure and the RTBF is not clear, the latter conceived as a mere extension of the first.

In fact, Article 17 GDPR does not establish any new rights but limits itself to specifying the conditions with greater detail and precision, under which data subjects can obtain the erasure of their personal data. The right to de-indexing, as "created"

administrative agency administering the RTBF, which raises serious concerns for democratic accountability and due process (Lee, 2016: 1066). The same opinion is expressed by Leiser (2020: 8–15), who underlines the need for a new public model for resolving international disputes about the implementation of the RTBF.

by the *Google Spain* ruling, is not explicitly envisaged, although it seems to be implicitly enshrined in par. 2, which requires the data controller to inform other controllers that are processing personal data of the fact that the data subject has requested the erasure of any links to, or copy or replication of, those personal data. However, it is not clear which data controller is meant to be the one primarily in charge of informing others: whether the search engine, which should inform publishers and/or other search engines of the data subject's requests for erasure or de-indexing, or the original publisher of the information to which the data subject has requested the erasure.[4] In any case, this provision does not seem to be strictly compulsory since it is explicitly meant to be dependent on the available technology and the cost of its implementation and does not indicate any sanctions in case of noncompliance.

Pursuant to Article 17(1), personal data shall be erased promptly by the data controller upon request by the data subject, when the latter withdraws his or her consent or objects to the processing, or when the personal data are no longer necessary or have been processed unlawfully, or their erasure is demanded for compliance with a legal obligation. This "classic" claim to the cancellation of personal data can be made against any data controller, namely the subject that determines the purposes and means of the data processing. This right is grounded on a proprietary conception of the right to privacy, as a property right exercised on personal data, which would allow the data owner to revoke the authorization for their dissemination issued to the data controller. The scope of the provision of Article 17 GDPR is considerably broader than the right to de-indexing outlined by the CJEU in the Google Spain CJEU case: it is not restricted to search engines, covers all personal information, not only the name and surname, and provides protection not only in cases of loss of interest in past, irrelevant information, but also in other situations, such as unlawful processing or withdrawal of consent (Ovčak Kos, 2019: 202).

The right to erasure can be limited in certain circumstances, the most relevant of which is the possible conflict with the exercise of the freedom of expression and information (Article 17, 1.a). More specifically, Article 85 explains that the right to protection of personal data must be reconciled with the right to freedom of expression and information; therefore, when personal data are processed for journalistic, academic, artistic, or literary purposes, exemptions or derogations from the general legal framework may be provided. However, some aspects of the Regulation—the requirement that the data controller take down personal data without undue delay, the "necessity" caveat on the freedom of expression defense,[5] the burden of proof

---

[4]The *Whereas* no. 54 simply explains that to "strengthen the right to be forgotten in the online environment, the right to erasure should also be extended in such a way that a controller who has made the personal data public should be obliged to inform third parties."

[5]Pursuant to Article 17, par. 1.a, the data controller can refuse the erasure (or de-indexing, in case of search engines) of personal data if these are still necessary in relation to the purposes for which they were collected or otherwise processed. However, Post (2018: 1047–1050) contends that purposes of search engines consist of providing the public the means of acquiring information, knowledge,

placed on the data controller that the data subject's requests are manifestly unfounded or excessive (Article 12), the exorbitant financial penalties for noncompliance, and the absence of an opportunity to be heard for publishers or speakers whose content has been erased or de-referenced—are likely to skew the balance in favor of the data subject's removal rights and against the data controller's right to freedom of expression (Nunziato, 2018: 1056–1057). On the contrary, it can be argued that the public should be somehow legally protected in case of erasure of information, as this interferes with the right to know and to access information (Ovčak Kos, 2019: 203).

The RTBF in the Case Law of the ECtHR and a Final Brief Comparison with a Recent Decision of the Italian Court of Cassation

Neither the *Google Spain* ruling nor the GDPR has defined specific and precise criteria for the practical implementation of the RTBF. Moreover, in shaping the scope of the RTBF, the CJEU in *Google Spain* did not clarify its relationship with the European Convention for the Protection of Human Rights and Fundamental Freedoms (hereinafter Convention) and the ruling of the ECtHR, although all EU Member States are bound to the Convention as signatories (Ovčak Kos, 2019: 200). As the *Google Spain* decision is inconsistent with the principles enshrined in the case law of the ECtHR, it may lead to uncertainties regarding the interpretation of European legal systems and contribute to raising concerns about the scope of the RTBF (Szeghalmi, 2018: 268). Nevertheless, the CJEU's and ECtHR's decisions lie on different grounds: the theoretical framework of the ECtHR's reasoning focuses on guaranteeing a balance between the right to public debate and the damages caused by publication, where the seriousness of the harm caused to the individual concerned constitutes a relevant factor; on the contrary, in *Google Spain*, the CJEU assumed that the RTBF could be granted regardless of the damage suffered, revolving the reasoning around the legitimacy of the data processing (Szeghalmi, 2018: 260–261).

In *Węgrzynowski and Smolczewski v. Poland* (2013),[6] the ECtHR examined the request of two lawyers for the deletion of an allegedly defamatory article published on the website of a Polish newspaper. In fact, although the authors of the article and the newspaper's editor-in-chief had been found liable of defamation, the online version of the article had remained accessible, and the Warsaw Regional Court

---

education, experience, and entertainment, which are incompatible with the idea of the removal of information. Moreover, one may argue derogations provided in par. 3.d (when data processing is necessary for archiving purposes in the public interest, scientific or historical research purposes, or statistical purposes) may apply to search engines as well.

[6]ECtHR, Fourth Section, *Węgrzynowski and Smolczewski v. Poland*, Application no. 33846/07, July 16, 2013.

had refused its removal because this remedy would amount to censorship and rewriting history. In highlighting the need of a fair balancing between the right to respect for private life (Article 8 of the Convention) and the right to freedom of expression (Article 10 of the Convention), both of which require equal respect, the ECtHR stressed the substantial contribution made by Internet archives to preserving and making news and information available, and reiterated that news archives "constitute an important source for education and historical research, particularly as they are readily accessible to the public and are generally free."[7] It also explained that, while the primary function of the press is to act as a "public watchdog," online archives had a valuable secondary role in maintaining and displaying previously reported news, which should prevent judicial authorities from engaging in rewriting history by ordering the removal of publications. Therefore, the Court concluded that there had been no violation of Article 8 of the Convention, although it would have been desirable—if only the applicants had requested such remedy—to add a comment to the online article informing the public of the outcome of the civil proceedings in the earlier libel case regarding the printed version of the article.

A few years later, the ECtHR dealt with the RTBF again in *Fuchsmann v. Germany* (2017).[8] The applicant complained that national courts had refused the erasure or at least the anonymization of an online newspaper article published in the past although there had not been sufficient public interest to justify mentioning him by name, and the article contained mere speculations but no proven facts. He also alleged that the reasoning of the CJEU regarding the RTBF and the right to de-indexing should be transferred to his case. However, although the ECtHR did not address this latter demand specifically, it substantially agreed with the conclusions of the German Court of Appeal, namely that (1) the article contributed to a debate of public interest, including the fact that the applicant was mentioned by name; (2) the article was based on sufficiently credible sources and was free from polemic statements and insinuations; (3) before the publication of the article, the journalist had contacted the applicant, who had not replied to the journalist's questions; (4) the applicant had provided no information in his submissions regarding any efforts made to have the link to the article removed from online search engines; and (5) finally, and most significantly, Internet archives constitute an important source for education and historical research and their function deserves protection. Therefore, the Court concluded that there had been no violation of Article 8 of the Convention.[9]

[7]Already in *Times Newspapers Ltd (Nos 1 and 2) v. The United Kingdom*, Application nos 3002/03 and 23,676/03, March 10, 2009, the ECtHR had noted that Internet archives, including those maintained by the press, are protected by the right to freedom of expression under Article 10 of the Convention.

[8]ECtHR, Fifth Section, *Fuchsmann v. Germany*, Application no. 71233/13, October 19, 2017.

[9]The Court also identified the following relevant criteria in the context of balancing competing rights: 1) the contribution to a debate of public interest; 2) the degree to which the person affected is well known; 3) the subject of the news report; 4) the prior conduct of the person concerned; 5) the

Lastly, in *M. L. and W. W. v. Germany* (2018)[10] the ECtHR examined the request of anonymization of personal data contained in newspaper articles published many years ago and still stored in the media outlets' digital archives. Notably, the applicants, convicted for murder, had not asked for the removal of the reports in question but only for their anonymization – a less restrictive measure in terms of press freedom than the deletion of published articles – claiming that their availability in online archives had the effect of permanently stigmatizing them, even though they had served their sentences and were prepared for their reintegration into society. However, the German Federal Court of Justice had refused the requested remedy, observing that (1) reports concerning criminal offenses were part of contemporary history, which the media had a responsibility to report on; (2) in the case of reports on topical events, the public's interest in being informed generally takes precedence over the right of the person concerned to protection of his or her personality; and (3) the public had a legitimate interest not only in being informed about current events, but also in being able to research past ones. The ECtHR shared the same opinion and concluded that there had been no violation of Article 8 of the Convention, as in that specific case the reports still available online continued to contribute to a debate of public interest which had not been diminished by the passage of time. In the Court's view, while the primary function of the press is that of disseminating information and ideas, playing a vital role of "public watchdog," its secondary but nonetheless valuable role consists of maintaining archives of reported news and making them available to the public. Although convicted persons have an interest in no longer being confronted with their past acts, with a view to their reintegration in society, and although rendering a report anonymous is certainly less detrimental to freedom of expression than its entire deletion, the Court maintained that journalists are free to decide what details ought to be published in order to ensure an article's credibility, provided that their choices are based on their profession's ethical rules and codes of conduct. Therefore, the Court found the applicants had only a limited legitimate expectation of obtaining anonymity in the reports. As for the possibility of being granted the RTBF (de-indexing of the reports by search engines), the ECtHR did not analyze this issue in detail, but limited itself to affirming that because of their amplifying effect on the dissemination of information and the nature of the activity underlying the publication of information on the person concerned, the obligations of search engines may differ from those of the entity which originally published the information. It can be concluded, therefore, that in the case of online media archives a significant limitation to the RTBF is represented by the passive aspect of the right to freedom of expression and information (protecting the public's interest in accessing information) and that this limitation is less relevant with respect to search engines.

---

method of obtaining the information and its veracity; and 6) the content, form, and consequences of the publication.

[10] ECtHR, Fifth Section, *M. L. and W. W. v. Germany*, Applications nos. 60,798/10 and 65,599/10, September 28, 2018.

Quite surprisingly, the following year, in a very similar case the Italian Court of Cassation (Italy's highest court) came to an opposite conclusion.[11] The case, decided in July 2019, dealt with the legitimacy of the re-publication of a newspaper article already published in 1982, concerning a murder committed many years before: the applicant, who had already fully served his sentence, complained that re-publication, in addition to having caused him profound anguish and prostration, had exposed him to a new media pillory, when he had already managed to rebuild a new life. The premises of this case, however, were partly different from the ECtHR's judgment, as they did not concern the permanent availability of past publications in online archives, but the re-publication of an old press article in a paper journal.

After examining the relevant Italian and European case law on the balance between the right to report and the RTBF, the Court concluded that reproducing already published news after a long period of time did not fall under the right to report but merely constituted a historical re-enactment of past events. Given that a historiographical activity cannot enjoy the same constitutional guarantee provided for the press, it is necessary to verify the persistence of public interest case by case in knowing details (such as name and personal image) related to the protagonist of the story. In the Court's opinion, the general principle to be followed in case of purely historiographical activity is that the individual right to anonymity must prevail over other interests, especially when the person's dignity and honor are compromised, unless there is a renewed public interest in the story, or the protagonist has held or holds a public position. In other words, in historical re-enactment individual rights prevail over the journalistic right to disclose personal information, unless the public role played by the person justifies the publication of such information (in line with the CJEU's outcomes in *Google Spain*).

Conclusions

Despite any effort of analysis, the RTBF still appears a very elusive object. It is composed of different elements—control over personal data, claim for privacy and reputation, harm suffered by the data subject, passage of time, right to report, public interest in the dissemination of information, contextualization of news, and role played by online media archives and search engines—that national and European courts weigh, compare, and balance with divergent outcomes. Current European legislation does not contribute much to clarity: the RTBF is not explicitly explained or regulated by the GDPR in force since May 2018, being seemingly conceived as a mere extension of the right to obtain the erasure of personal data (Article 17) and hardly distinguishable from the latter.

[11] Corte di Cassazione, S. U. civ., July 22, 2019, no. 19681. Comments to this case: Colaruotolo, 2019, Peron, 2019, Sicuro, 2019.

In *Google Spain* (2014), the CJEU proved to be extremely creative, sanctioning an unprecedented right to request the search engine to interrupt the connection between the name of the data subject and the links to information published online and no longer of public interest due to the passage of time. However, this ruling has raised a lot of criticism for several reasons, such as the lack of an explanation about the precise reasons behind the granting of the RTBF in that particular case, the different treatment between search engines and publishers in terms of legitimacy of data processing and recognition of possible exemptions from the general discipline, the obscurity regarding cases and circumstances in which the public interest would require permanent access to information, the excessive discretion and authority delegated to search engines, and the absence of an opportunity to be heard for publishers whose content has been erased or de-referenced. All considered, the Court seemed to favor the prevalence of individual privacy over the right to freedom of expression, although this presumption was mitigated by the possibility of some circumstances—particularly the public role of the data subject—that could make the disclosure of information relevant.

On the contrary, the ECtHR, in the cases examined in this chapter, has constantly given greater relevance to freedom of information and right to report than individual expectations of privacy. The positions of the two European courts are not easily reconcilable with each other, where the ECtHR is inclined to consider the seriousness of the harm caused to the individual by the information published online, while the CJEU is rather indifferent to the damage suffered by the data subject, revolving its reasoning around the legitimacy of the data processing. Moreover, the ECtHR has considered the position of search engines only in passing and marginally, limiting itself to affirming that because of their amplifying effect on the dissemination of information, the obligations of search engines toward the person claiming for the RTBF may differ from those of the original publisher of the information.

These diverging opinions do not contribute to clarifying the nature of the RTBF and the conditions for its recognition. It is not surprising, therefore, that national courts may come to unusual outcomes, an example of which may be represented by the decision of the Italian Court of Cassation examined in the final part of this chapter, which drew a line between the right to report and the right to carry out historical re-enactment of past events: in this last case, the individual's right to anonymization was considered prevailing over the public interest in being informed.

The problem, unsolvable for the moment, is that the RTBF is recognized mainly at the jurisprudential level, in the absence of a suitable regulatory basis to define its contours.

References

Bianca, M. (2019). Memoria ed oblio: due reali antagonisti? *Medialaws. Rivista di diritto dei media, 2*, 23–36.

Chenou, J. M., & Radu, R. (2019). The "right to be forgotten": Negotiating public and private ordering in the European Union. *Business & Society, 58*(1), 74–102.

Colaruotolo, A. (2019, December 19). Il passato che non passa. La parola delle Sezioni Unite sul delicato rapporto esistente tra memoria storica, cronaca e oblio. *Diritto Mercato Tecnologia*. https://www.dimt.it/la-rivista/articoli/sezioni-unite-memoria-storica-cronaca-oblio/

Criscione, H. (2020). Forgetting the right to be forgotten: The everlasting negative implications of a right to be dereferenced on global freedom in the wake of Google v. CNIL. *Pace International Law Review, 32*(2), 315–358.

Fabbrini, F., & Celeste, E. (2020). The right to be forgotten in the digital age: The challenges of data protection beyond borders. *German Law Journal, 21*, 55–65.

Forde, A. (2015). Implications of the right to be forgotten. *Tulane Journal of Technology & Intellectual Property, 18*, 83–131.

Globocnik, J. (2020). The right to be forgotten is taking shape: CJEU judgments in GC and others (C-136/17) and Google v CNIL (C-507/17). *GRUR International, 69*(4), 380–388.

Guadamuz, A. (2017). Developing a right to be forgotten. In T. E. Synodinou, P. Jougleux, C. Markou, & T. Prastitou (Eds.), *EU internet law. Regulation and enforcement* (pp. 59–76). Springer.

Kampmark, J. (2015). To find or be forgotten: Global tensions on the right to erasure and internet governance. *Journal of Global Faultlines, 2*(2), 1–18.

Lee, E. (2016). Recognizing rights in real time: The role of Google in the EU right to be forgotten. *UC Davis Law Review, 49*(2), 1017–1095.

Leiser, M. R. (2020). "Private jurisprudence" and the right to be forgotten balancing test. *Computer Law & Security Review, 39*, 1–15.

Nunziato, D. C. (2018). The fourth year of forgetting: The troubling expansion of the right to be forgotten. *University of Pennsylvania Journal of International Law, 39*(4), 1011–1064.

Ovčak Kos, M. (2019). The right to be forgotten and the media. *Lexonomica, 11*(2), 195–212.

Peron, S. (2019). Il difficile bilanciamento tra il diritto di cronaca e il diritto all'oblio: la soluzione delle sezioni unite. *Rivista di diritto dei media, 3*, 203–213.

Pollicino, O., & Bassini, M. (2014). Reconciling right to be forgotten and freedom of information in the digital age. Past and future of personal data protection in the EU. *Diritto pubblico comparato ed europeo, 2*, 641–662.

Post, R. C. (2018). Data privacy and dignitary privacy: Google Spain, the right to be forgotten, and the construction of the public sphere. *Duke Law Journal, 67*(5), 981–1072.

Razmetaeva, Y. (2020). The right to be forgotten in the European perspective. *TalTech Journal of European Studies, 10*(1), 58–76.

Reymond, M. J. (2019). The future of the European Union "right to be forgotten". *Latin American Law Review, 2*, 81–98.

Sicuro, F. (2019). Libertà di informazione e diritto all'oblio. *Dirittifondamentali.it, 1*, 1–28.

Stradella, E. (2016). Cancellazione e oblio: come la rimozione del passato, in bilico tra tutela dell'identità personale e protezione dei dati, si impone anche nella rete, quali anticorpi si possono sviluppare, e, infine, *cui prodest*? *Rivista AIC, 4*(2016), 1–29.

Szeghalmi, V. (2018). Difficulties regarding the right to be forgotten in the case law of the Strasbourg Court. *Athens Journal of Law, 4*(3), 255–270.

Van Hoboken, J. V. J. (2013). *The proposed right to be forgotten seen from the perspective of our right to remember freedom of expression safeguards in a converging information environment*. Publications Office of the European Union.

Weber, R. H. (2011). The right to be forgotten: More than a Pandora's box? *Journal of Intellectual Property, Information Technology and E-Commerce Law, 2*(2), 120–130.

Weber, R. H. (2015). On the search for an adequate scope of the right to be forgotten. *Journal of Intellectual Property, Information Technology and E-Commerce Law, 6*(1), 2–10.

Maria Romana Allegri, graduated cum laude both in humanities and in law, is now an associate professor in Public Law at the Department of Communication and Social Research, Sapienza University of Rome, where she has previously worked as a researcher since 2001. In the last few years, she has focused her research on the legal aspects of the Internet and social networks. Among her most recent publications: *Il futuro digitale dell'Unione europea: nuove categorie di intermediari digitali, nuove forme di responsabilità* (Riv. It. Inf. Dir., 2021); *Il diritto di accesso a Internet: profili costituzionali* (Riv. Dir. Media, 2021); *Oltre la par condicio. Comunicazione politico-elettorale nei social media, fra diritto e autodisciplina* (Milano, FrancoAngeli, 2020); *Ubi social, ibi ius. Fondamenti costituzionali dei social network e profili giuridici della responsabilità dei provider* (Milano, FrancoAngeli, 2018).

Chapter 16
Countering "Surveillance Capitalism." The Intertwining of Objective and Subjective Factors

Emanuela Susca

Introduction

Although the social sciences have been dealing with surveillance at least since the seminal studies of Michel Foucault, globalization and the development of new digital media have obviously profoundly changed both the reality and the content of theorizing on this subject. Hence the centrality of a new type of surveillance that has captured the attention of scholars and observers appears unprecedented for two main reasons. First, the asphyxiating control is not exercised over openly exploited and annihilated subjects but over users who are commonly supposed to be accomplices who are unaware of the surveillance or, in other words, unwitting victims who actively collaborate with their controllers by sharing, posting, or even simply surfing the Internet. Second, states seem to have largely abandoned their previous prerogative of monitoring citizens, contenting themselves with delegating surveillance, now more capillary than ever, to the great economic powers of the new digital capitalism.

Striving to some extent to query certain assumptions or *clichés*, the following pages attempt to answer a fundamental question: why do users generally pay little attention to the serious threats to their privacy inherent in new communication technologies? In other words, why do they continue to leave traces of themselves that make it possible to profile them and even to a certain extent determine their behaviors?

To provide at least some sort of answer, among the not insignificant number of views on surveillance, I choose two approaches that, in addition to being highly successful among epigones and nonspecialists, seem to be complementary in providing space almost exclusively to subjective factors (the first approach) and

E. Susca (✉)
Department of Economics, Society, Politics, University of Urbino 'Carlo Bo', Urbino, Italy
e-mail: emanuela.susca@uniurb.it

F. Comunello et al. (eds.), *What People Leave Behind*, Frontiers in Sociology and Social Research 7, https://doi.org/10.1007/978-3-031-11756-5_16

objective factors (the second). I refer to Zygmunt Bauman's now classic view, focusing on the general need for visibility felt by subjects in a liquid society, and Shoshana Zuboff's more recent but already well-known analysis of "surveillance capitalism." I will try to show that both approaches are extremely interesting but that they do not seem entirely convincing in their depictions either of the user or of the responsibilities they attribute to states.

Thereafter, I propose broadening the theoretical framework that is helpful in thinking about surveillance by taking into account the strong symbolic power exercised by charity. Indeed, as scholars of "philanthrocapitalism" have critically remarked, the most important tycoons of information capitalism are also the undisputed and visible protagonists of a new kind of philanthropy that is radically changing both global power relations and our ways of thinking and feeling. Therefore, I will put forward the hypothesis that, on closer inspection, the nonchalance of users of new technologies and social networks can be more fully understood by taking into account the trust that can be generated by such ostentatious prodigality. Since ordinary people see the alleged generosity of the owners of Microsoft, Amazon, and Facebook widely publicized, it may be reasonable to suppose that they are unconsciously predisposed to think that those "modern-day heroes" are offering their services for free to everyone for the common good.

However, as I will briefly state in my conclusion, it is not essential to assume that users are totally unsuspecting. They may be at least partially aware of the dynamics entrapping them but nonetheless accept that involvement by grasping aspects of it that are not entirely negative or that are even desirable. This is not necessarily related to a selfish drive for self-representation or self-assurance but could be linked to the idea or hope of a better future for all. It is difficult to keep one's guard up when facing someone who is universally regarded as selfless.

Bauman and the Need for Visibility in a Liquid Society

Having spent many years painting a picture of ways of life in a liquid society, Bauman could deal only with surveillance. However, as a scholar of both Baumanian themes and surveillance itself righty observed (Lyon, 2010), he did so starting with *Legislators and Interpreters* (Bauman, 1987) and *Freedom* (Bauman, 1988), both written before the mass spread of the Internet and social networks. It is not surprising, then, that in that period, his attention, far from being devoted to communication techniques or the digital revolution, was directed more generally toward the central issue of all his sociological research: the transition from classical modernity to liquid modernity. In that context, he spoke of a shift from the old centrality of the Panopticon model, so significant from Bentham to Foucault, to postpanoptic forms of control, in which surveillance was, so to speak, "privatized." While modernity's maniacal need for order had given life to forms and techniques of coercion and regimentation, Bauman saw an epochal change driven mainly by the seductive power of consumerism. Since people's "conduct is made manageable, predictable and hence non-threatening, by a multiplication of needs rather than by a tightening of norms" (Bauman, 1987: 168), the old repression was becoming superfluous or even counterproductive. Ordinary people themselves did the dirty work of maintaining the ranks, made docile by their unquenchable desire to buy ever newer goods and services and to become full citizens of the new society. The privatization of surveillance seems, in short, to be directly linked to the privatization of the fight against ambivalence themed in an exemplary way in the second part of *Modernity and Ambivalence* (Bauman, 1991). Ultimately underestimating the power still held in many ways by states to label people and induce conformity (Susca, 2021b), Bauman saw a world where no authority wanted or was able to enforce anything anymore. As a result, masses of people were forced to seek direction and answers within themselves.

Subsequent works have offered a number of interesting considerations of such self-monitoring, in particular linking it to the exclusionary policies and growing inequalities that have emerged with globalization. Bauman famously saw a deepening gulf: on the one hand, the privileged who have full access to increasingly satisfying consumption and, on the other hand, the masses of the excluded, the refuse of our opulent times, or at best useful servants for the comfort of the wealthy. Surveillance techniques allow the former to move, pay, and live in general without complications and, for this reason, seem to represent the perfect reversal of the previous control that strictly circumscribed the range of action of the subjects. The prophecy or dystopia of George Orwell was thus overturned: "Today's Big Brother is not about keeping people in and making them stick to the line, but about kicking people out and making sure that when they are kicked out that they will duly go and won't come back" (Bauman, 2006: 25).

Guaranteed by increasingly sophisticated techniques, the mobility of the most fortunate appears to be a nonstop journey from one city to another and from one experience to another. Additionally, technologies themselves have made it possible to exclude people cut off from the circuits of well-being because they are undesirable and, especially after September 11, even banned from proper civilian life because they are labeled potential terrorist threats.

The work by Bauman most directly concerned with my present topic appeared a few years later under the title *Liquid Surveillance* (Bauman & Lyon, 2013) and is both an interview and a dialogue with David Lyon, a scholar of communication, particularly surveillance. Lyon urged his illustrious interlocutor and, to a certain extent, his teacher to provide a full account of the social consequences produced by technology itself, which are even more evident when possibilities are made available on a large scale that upsets the daily lives of millions, if not billions, of subjects. In contrast, Bauman preferred to speak of two concomitant drives:

> I believe that the most remarkable feature of the contemporary edition of surveillance is that it has somehow managed to force and cajole oppositions to work in unison, and to make them work in concert in the service of the same reality. On the one hand, the old panoptical stratagem ("you should never know when you are being watched in the flesh and so never be unwatched in your mind") is being gradually yet consistently and apparently unstoppably brought to well-nigh universal implementation. On the other, with the old panoptical

> nightmare ("I am never on my own") now recast into the hope of "never again being alone" (abandoned, ignored and neglected, blackballed and excluded), the fear of disclosure has been stifled by the joy of being noticed (Bauman & Lyon, 2013: 23).

Rather than factors that produce or at least accelerate change, Bauman saw the new techniques as deadly weapons of control at the disposal of the powerful but also, and above all, tools that responded to an insatiable need experienced firsthand by users themselves, hence an apparent paradox that broadens the idea of self-surveillance mentioned above. The real protagonists and culprits of the change taking place are not so much privileged people who enjoy the unprecedented possibilities offered by globalization, but ordinary people who collaborate incessantly and even enthusiastically in surveillance in order to not feel alone and have the illusion of living in meaningful bonds. They make themselves everlastingly observable and traceable by continually putting themselves "in the shop window" for fear of being relegated to insignificance, almost obeying a sort of law formulated earlier by Bauman himself: "Whether in their consciousness or their subconscious, men and women of our times are haunted by the spectre of exclusion" (Bauman, 2004: 47).

While there is no doubt that Bauman's focus is definitely on subjective factors, and more precisely on the motivations of individuals, we can rightly speak of a substantial indifference to technology as an objective driving factor. Deliberately ignoring the peculiarities of digital tools, Bauman was certain that people practice self-promotion through social media simply because social media exist and are available. That is why he fully endorsed the words of a digital creative director of an advertising agency: "The Internet doesn't steal our humanity, it reflects it. The Internet doesn't get inside us, it shows what's inside us" (Bauman & Lyon, 2013). In a society without Facebook or similar possibilities, we would all find other means to behave in the same way and achieve the same results.

At the root of it all, then, is complicity, but this kind of complicity concerns only vain and insecure users, while it has practically nothing to do with the possible relations between the "old" political power and the new power, economic and otherwise, of the digital megaindustries. Nor is this actually surprising. Bauman probably viewed with indifference states and governments that do little or nothing to protect the autonomy and privacy of their citizens owing to the simple fact that he interpreted that passivity as one of the manifestations of liquidity. According to him, such capitulation is a much more general issue, and one that concerns the overriding political inability to direct people by organizing their existences from both a material and symbolic point of view.

Zuboff and the Rise of Surveillance Capitalism

The first striking aspect of Zuboff's research on surveillance capitalism (2019) is probably the great commercial success it has achieved. However nonchalantly willing to put everything about themselves on show in order to promote themselves as merchandise, ordinary users may not infrequently be concerned to learn more about the logics in which they are embedded. This may not in itself be decisive or politically mobilizing, but it can hardly be considered counterproductive that people are increasingly becoming aware of the immense power placed in the hands of those who drive the new digital economy. The latter are individuals whom no one has chosen, let alone voted for, but who increasingly decide our lives.

Strictly examining the issue of surveillance, Zuboff wants above all to make us understand that digital megacorporations are not simply able to know everything about us and predict our future behavior. Rather, they are able to *determine* our future, making us do more or less exactly what is most useful to further increase their immense profits. As shocking as her remarks on control and monitoring may seem, they are only one part of her argument. Viewed as a whole, her research aims above all to make manifest the economic principles and laws that tend to remain hidden behind the scandal of the violation of privacy and the disasters represented by the threat to individual autonomy and democratic coexistence. All this is based on the conviction that capitalism has made a real evolutionary leap owing to the exploitation of areas and possibilities that have suddenly become available.

Therefore, she presents her research project by talking not only about lucrative "extraction" and "prediction" operations but also about a process of "construction and elaboration of *means of behavioral modification*" that is inextricably linked to the artificial intelligence of machines and has become a fearsome "*instrumentarian power*" (Zuboff, 2019: 67, *italics in original*). However, there is no concession to a more or less revisited Luddism. As she frankly admits, and as her intellectual itinerary testifies, her point of view is that of a scholar who has scrutinized and in some respects continues to scrutinize the revolution in progress without preconceived hostility and even with a certain amount of cautious optimism (Zuboff, Möllers, Murakami Wood, & Lyon, 2019: 265). Not only does she believe in the emancipatory potential of the new techniques, but she still appears convinced that things are not as they are through some necessity or iron law (which of course also means that things could be different).

In any case, what is more important for my argument is to clarify the relation in which Zuboff places subjective factors (users' propensities) and objective factors (technology above all). Does she see a real intertwining of the two sides? Or does she allow one to prevail, leaving the other in the shade? As I will try to explain in a moment, and reasoning as a whole, it is difficult to deny that she shifts the focus toward objective factors: the economy and above all technology, the latter conceived as the truly decisive factor in the emergence of a dangerous variant of information capitalism.

However, my statement certainly needs to be better specified, especially with regard to the relationship between economics and technology and the related question of how far technology itself can be considered neutral or inherently responsible. These are two points on which Zuboff herself seems extremely clear:

> Surveillance capitalism is a market form that is unimaginable outside the digital milieu, but it is not the same as 'digital' [...] the digital can take many forms depending upon the social

> and economic logics that bring it to life. It is capitalism that assigns the price tag of subjugation and helplessness, not the technology (Zuboff et al., 2019: 15).

As I have just pointed out, arguing against any demonization of technology and of the Internet and the digital in particular, Zuboff wants to highlight the responsibilities of capitalism as it is reconstructed today. It is in this sense that she stresses that surveillance capitalism "is a logic in action and not a technology" (ibid.).

While the digital itself is not to blame, the focus is on capitalism or, more specifically, on those degenerations that make information capitalism responsible for new liberticidal dynamics. Nonetheless, despite her assertion above and similar ones, Zuboff ultimately does not conceive of technology as a mere means but rather as a necessary infrastructure that is coming or has already come to act as a largely autonomous driving factor or even, as it were, as a soul. This means not only that without the technology to collect and process immeasurable amounts of data, surveillance capitalism would not even exist but also that the technology itself tends to behave increasingly less as a mere means. In this regard, we may consider her description of how giants such as Google and Facebook are now obliged to strengthen the deregulation that allows them to freely mine and then exploit data:

> It is important to understand that surveillance capitalists *are impelled* to pursue lawlessness by the logic of their own *creation*. Google and Facebook vigorously lobby to kill online privacy protection. Limit regulation, weaken or block privacy-enhancing legislation, and thwart every attempt to circumscribe their practices because such laws are existential threats to the frictionless flow of behavioral surplus (Zuboff, 2019: 105, *emphasis added*).

In short, one could say that "creation" has come to life and is taking possession of its creator. However, as illustrated especially in the third chapter of *The Age of Surveillance Capitalism*, this perverse dynamic did not apply from the very beginning and *en bloc* to all new technologies. In particular, as is fairly well known, Zuboff attributes to Google a pioneering role in terms of its ability both to produce algorithms capable of learning to understand and predict and to translate innovations into a model of targeted advertising. Once invented and established, Google's standard would have imposed itself on its competitors, leading the way and outdoing any alternative that was more creative or even simply less harmful to users' privacy; hence, the idea that the other main Internet companies (i.e., Amazon, Facebook, Microsoft, and especially Apple) found themselves in the unenviable position of having to follow, even at the cost of betraying their own ideal vocations or abandoning, at least in part, other innovations or possible uses they were working on.

Ultimately, while I would not speak of a true technological determinism in this regard, and while I am aware that Zuboff considers the goals that someone assigns to technology from time to time important, I think that in her approach, it is the technology itself, neutral or not, that truly governs. Nor should it be surprising that she insists that the culprit is not the medium itself but the way in which some capitalists have appropriated it. In addition to explaining and disclosing the facts and their connections, Zuboff clearly intends to fight the possible resignation of users and to expose the responsibility of the real culprits who make extraordinary profits and their various accomplices. If what is happening is not the inevitable effect of innovations that are inherently endowed with deadly power, then the megacompanies that produce our behavior cannot claim innocence; at the same time, states, governments, and even citizens cannot wash their hands of responsibility.

Compared to the role played by objective factors, the weight of subjective factors is frankly much less important. According to Zuboff, ordinary people, i.e., citizens who are mere users, are, or have been until now, unconscious and powerless victims of sophisticated technological manipulations; hence, what could be defined as her pedagogical vocation, which leads her to inform and warn readers so that they can react by interacting with states and governments, asking them for adequate political decisions and new rules, including supranational and global ones. In contrast, her discourse toward the states is markedly different, as she basically holds them jointly responsible both for the deception and exploitation suffered by ordinary citizens and for the far from remote danger of a substantial failure of democracy. Therefore, like Bauman, Zuboff speaks of complicity but traces it back to a distorted or frankly pathological relationship between the new powers of the digital industry and the various nations. If the former have collected almost all the profits of the current exasperated version of information capitalism, the latter are at least guilty of letting themselves be carried away by credulity or disastrously wrong calculations. In a completely unfair quid pro quo, states are said to have ceded to private actors surveillance power that has subsequently grown out of all proportion and to have gained above all a helping hand against the threat of global terrorism. The commercial exploitation of everybody's data seemed a reasonable price for neutralizing certain malign actors and saving democracy, but in the long run, it would strike a mortal blow against democracy itself.

The Almost Irresistible Fascination of Generosity

Zuboff has the merit of focusing on the role played by states, thus somewhat objectively filling a gap in Bauman's approach. However, the picture she proposes does not seem entirely realistic. Can we truly think that states have surrendered to digital megacompanies purely through stupidity or short-sighted calculation? Are they truly powerless? Despite the fact that more than a few theorists of postmodernity have held the opposite opinion, states (or at least some states) continue to hold enormous power, in some respects even greater than in the past. In particular, the USA, the veritable vanguard of surveillance capitalism, holds global supremacy both politically and economically. It is true that its dominance finds objective limits in some protagonists of international politics, above all China, but is it plausible to think of it as surrendering to the web giants? Can one truly think that the USA imposes ridiculously low taxes on Microsoft or Facebook merely through silliness or impotence?

Zuboff's remarks on subjective factors seem no more convincing, particularly with regard to the idea of unsuspecting users. The impression, far from superficial, is that what one may call the "ideological" power of the new surveillance is in her view underestimated or overlooked. In fact, surveillance is highly seductive, being ultimately capable of producing acceptance even at the expense of sensible reasoning. This means that, in general, people are not necessarily unaware that someone or something is constantly watching them and deeply influencing their lives. Rather, they seem to deliberately pretend to ignore surveillance, as if persuaded that it exists as a harmless or even beneficial project.

It may therefore be necessary to explain the reasons for what seems to be neither a simple unconscious error (Zuboff) nor merely the effect of an eagerness to appear (Bauman), i.e., the trust placed in technologies that are known to be responsible for serious limitations of individual freedom or even the decay of traditional democracy. Although users may well be thought to willingly shed important aspects of their autonomy, this does not necessarily mean that they do so out of fear of being alone. Rather, they may consider what they rely on desirable in itself, or at least the lesser evil. The reason may be that technology presents itself to them in the guise of familiar and good, or at least far from bad, faces. To name just a few of the best known, these faces include Bill Gates, who has long supported a wide range of health and educational projects; Jeff Bezos, who recently topped the list of benefactors; and Mark Zuckerberg, who celebrated the birth of his daughter by donating lavishly to build a better world.

In brief, I think one can better understand the reasons for the success of surveillance by taking into account studies and perspectives that have little direct connection with what technologies allow us to do or how we specifically use social media and devices. I am referring in particular to a very extensive bibliography of studies dealing with the social and economic impact of new forms of charity, among which there are fortunately some general introductory works (Callahan, 2017; Dodgson & Gann, 2020; Jung, Phillips, & Harrow, 2019; Maurrasse, 2020; Reich & Cordelli, 2016; Vallely, 2020). Nor, of course, should one neglect studies devoted more specifically to so-called philanthrocapitalism, the neologism with which some authors, mostly but not always critical and pessimistic, indicate the extension of market logic to fundamental sectors such as health, food, environmental protection, and education (Bishop, 2013; Bishop & Green, 2008; Dentico, 2020; Edwards, 2008; McGoey, 2021).

I can say only a few words about it here, but the change that charity has undergone is so important and consequential that it can without exaggeration be called epochal. The increasing process of institutionalization has become an essential tool for the reorganization processes of mature capitalism and has, moreover, affected in various ways all the areas of the world where industrial development is most intense. Indeed, one often speaks of the West and the USA in particular, where the all-Protestant asceticism conceived by Max Weber (1930) seems to stay more alive than elsewhere and even to have been radicalized into extreme forms such as the "prosperity theology" (Lee, 2007; Wrenn, 2021). However, it would be wrong to think that this issue concerns only the USA and its culture, which is supposedly more inclined to conceive of the restitution of part of one's possessions as a means of flaunting one's wealth and feeling righteous at the same time. Often little observed and even less regulated by the European Union and its members, the change is also affecting Europe as a whole (Carnie, 2017) and even countries where asceticism or even civic-mindedness does not seem particularly present, such as Italy (Caroli & Bulgari, 2014; Piaggio, 2019). Nor should one forget Asia and, in particular, the extremely interesting case of the People's Republic of China (Andornino & Wang, 2021). In the latter, the general tendency to give to charity has always been deeply rooted, and after a phase of state repression followed by some years of substantial disinterest, the political authorities have tried, with some success, to regulate the phenomenon by combating possible abuses while safeguarding the freedom and the right to donate.

In general, while trying to do good to others seems to be a universal impulse and in itself not blameworthy (Wiepking, 2021), gifts are less free than they seem when generosity is organized from the point of view of financial return. The new institutionalized charity is not simply a way to obtain substantial tax advantages or even lucrative tax avoidance but also and above all a method of making huge economic, symbolic, and political profits. Practiced according to a market logic but also relying on the rhetoric of altruism (Arrigoni, Bifulco, & Caselli, 2020), philanthropic activity acts as an extension of entrepreneurial action and ensures, along with often significant profits, public acclaim and consent. Nor is it surprising that this symbolic return benefits those figures who have become extremely wealthy through surveillance since they are generally also those most engaged in this current type of charity. After all, by putting their wealth at the service of global good causes, and of course duly publicizing their goodness, the new tycoons of the digital society are not just testimonials to enrichment and free enterprise. They make us all see the best face of surveillance, that of a project or a reality that seems basically good and, in any case, seems capable of showing the way and providing smart answers at a time when traditional politics appears impotent and obtuse.

This is a crucial point. Whether one calls it new altruism or philanthrocapitalism, the new philanthropic activity has some politically relevant effects, the first of which is well illustrated by the case of US private education. Private educational institutions have been targeted by a huge mass of philanthropic investment (Baltodano, 2017), with consequences that make it far from desirable for a similar situation to happen in Europe (Susca, 2021a). The sudden and disproportionate enrichment of the private supply has inevitably led to an impoverishment of the public sector from both a material and a symbolic point of view. If what a state can offer is or seems to be paltry and increasingly unattractive, it is not surprising that public opinion does not tend to call for an increase in public spending. Why should one demand more taxes for the rich or the middle class if the super-rich can spontaneously do better than both politics and democracy (Reich, 2018), moreover almost for free or else in exchange for some of our data?

Second, and as a further factor in the crisis of democracy itself or in the drive toward "post-democracy" (Crouch, 2000, 2005), the ability of citizens to direct and control has been weakened. While voters can influence the decisions of their governments and representatives, the new billionaires and mega-charitable foundations are exempt from any accountability. They are actors who operate on an altruistic impulse, i.e., on something that is and should remain inherently free, which puts them in a position to exercise enormous and unquestionable power.

Third, one must take into account the relationship between the ruling classes and the leading philanthropists, which is so close and particular that it seems to extend far beyond the impotence taken for granted by Bauman or the obtuse delegation of surveillance envisaged by Zuboff. The public sphere declines to regulate the activities of the private sector, if only because the latter are so valuable in a context of cuts in the welfare state and budget austerity. Moreover, however undesirable or regrettable it may be, it is more than understandable that members of the political classes as well as those of the bureaucratic apparatus tend to be subjugated on what can be called a psychological level. Whether they are right-wing or left-wing, and however seriously they may take their jobs, they are likely to be in a state of inferiority in comparison to figures who embody the characteristics and values of winners: "smartness," self-fulfillment, creativity, and, above all, the propensity to do good to the less fortunate.

Finally, at least one other aspect must be taken into account, namely, the danger, far from remote and indeed already present, of a further weakening of democracy in the world. The protagonists of the new philanthropy are increasingly dealing on an equal footing with global powers such as the UN, IMF, or WTO. This means that any effort to reduce inequality between countries must contend not only with the selfishness or arrogance of the richest countries but also with the interference of new players who are in a position to act arbitrarily.

There is enough evidence to rethink, at least partially, the new surveillance. Questionable gratuitousness and altruism are extraordinary means of lowering the users' defenses and gaining their trust. If the mission of giving becomes an inseparable part of both entrepreneurial action and the public image of the digital masters, how can one exactly establish the borderline between what is given for free and what is paid for in a more or less hidden way and perhaps even at a very high price? It is probably not sufficient to issue a warning with the adage "If you don't pay for it, you are the product." Even partially selling oneself may seem acceptable if, in addition to supporting us in doing things and having company, those who actually buy (or manufacture) our lives do so with an overall benevolent and socially responsible design.

Conclusions

Obviously, the above considerations are not meant to deny that awareness of the dangers of surveillance needs to be raised. A better understanding of the extent to which both the independence of individuals and democratic coexistence are threatened can encourage appropriate responses, not only in terms of individual strategies but also in the sphere of collective action. As Zuboff also points out, states and organized political parties should remain or return to being non-occasional interlocutors for certain crucial demands: regulations that effectively defend privacy while imposing more transparency on the uses of personal data, more adequate taxation of the rich emperors of surveillance, and an agenda that clarifies what each politician and party is willing to do to concretely counter the abuses that have become possible. Nor should such claims neglect the supranational and global levels, which are even more important given the disproportionality between the megacompanies and most of the world's states. Before us, in short, is a political challenge in the broadest sense of the term. To understand why it is so difficult to respond adequately, it is not enough to refer generically to depoliticization or to the strength of neoliberalism. After all, as I have tried to show, surveillance can be accepted and embraced not only for what it promises to the individual but also for what it gives or promises to give to our society.

Ultimately, the very image of consumers/users is also at stake. Perhaps we should stop thinking of them as selfish idiots who agree to become commodities to appease their insecurities or out of indifference. The subjects who allow themselves to be captured by leaving traces are neither totally unaware nor necessarily disinterested in their surroundings. Rather, they might even reasonably expect to surrender autonomy in exchange for a better world that, while continuing to reward individual success, is finally able to become more organized and equitable. If this is the case, the emphasis and warnings of critics should be directed not against individualism or the alleged new slavery but toward the ways in which real change for the benefit of the majority can be engineered.

From this perspective, analyzing philanthropy can also be of some use. It is a question of building on a tradition of studies already well established in the social sciences, although newer in sociology in a strict sense (Barman, 2017). This may not be the easiest task since it requires going beyond the usual distinction between public and private, and above all beyond an idea of "gift" that is now perceived as classic (Mauss, 1924) and moreover has been revisited by a perspective that has become a point of reference for many scholars (Caillé & Grésy, 2014; Godbout & Caillé, 1992). However, it may be worthwhile to contribute to counter the surveillance or, rather, the capitalist uses of surveillance itself.

I conclude with one final brief remark. The hypotheses that I have put forward about the almost irresistible fascination of generosity are waiting to be put to the test with new research focused on common sense and the prevailing representations of users. To move beyond seductive reconstructions such as Bauman's and richly documented analyses such as Zuboff's, perhaps we still need to try to better understand how and why individuals bring technology into their daily lives in infinite ways. Whether they are aware of it or not, they sign or renew a contract every time they press a button. It would not be strange if, after all, they entered into those contracts with people they trust.

References

Andornino, G., & Wang, Q. (2021). Philanthropy and social innovation in China. In D. Gosset (Ed.), *China and the world: The long march towards a community of shared future for mankind* (The role of business) (Vol. 2, pp. 23–34). Il Mulino.

Arrigoni, P., Bifulco, L., & Caselli, D. (2020). Perché e come studiare la filantropia. Appunti per un'agenda di ricerca. *Quaderni di Sociologia, 82*(64), 3–23. https://doi.org/10.4000/qds.3651

Baltodano, M. P. (2017). The power brokers of neoliberalism: Philanthrocapitalists and public education. *Policy Futures in Education, 15*(2), 141–156. https://doi.org/10.1177/1478210316652008

Barman, E. (2017). The social bases of philanthropy. *Annual Review of Sociology, 43*, 271–290. https://doi.org/10.1146/annurev-soc-060116-053524

Bauman, Z. (1987). *Legislators and interpreters*. Polity Press.

Bauman, Z. (1988). *Freedom*. Open University Press.

Bauman, Z. (1991). *Modernity and ambivalence*. Polity Press.

Bauman, Z. (2004). *Identity*. Polity Press.

Bauman, Z. (2006). *Liquid fear*. Polity Press.

Bauman, Z., & Lyon, D. (2013). *Liquid surveillance. A conversation*. Polity Press.

Bishop, M. (2013). Philanthrocapitalism: Solving public problems through private means. *Social Research, 80*(2), 473–490.

Bishop, M., & Green, M. (2008). *Philanthrocapitalism: How giving can save the world*. Bloomsbury: Pub Plc USA.

Caillé, A., & Grésy, J.-É. (2014). *La révolution du don. Le management repensé*. Seuil.

Callahan, D. (2017). *The givers: Philanthropy, power and democracy*. Alfred A. Knopf.

Carnie, C. (2017). *How philanthropy is changing in Europe*. Policy Press.

Caroli, M., & Bulgari, M. (Eds.). (2014). *Per una nuova filantropia. Riflessioni ed esperienze dal Primo Forum italiano della Filantropia*. FrancoAngeli.

Crouch, C. (2000). *Coping with post-democracy*. Fabian Society.

Crouch, C. (2005). *Post-democracy*. Polity Press.

Dentico, N. (2020). *Ricchi e buoni? Le trame oscure del filantrocapitalismo*. Emi.

Dodgson, M., & Gann, D. (2020). *Philanthropy, innovation and entrepreneurship. An introduction*. Palgrave Macmillan.

Edwards, M. (2008). *Just another emperor? The myths and realities of philanthrocapitalism*. Demos: A network for ideas & action, The Young Foundation, USA.

Godbout, J. T., & Caillé, A. (1992). *L'esprit du don*. La Découverte.

Jung, T., Phillips, S. D., & Harrow, J. (Eds.). (2019). *The Routledge companion to philanthropy*. Routledge.

Lee, S. (2007). Prosperity theology: T. D. Jakes and the Gospel of the almighty dollar. *CrossCurrents, 57*(2), 227–236.

Lyon, D. (2010). Liquid surveillance: The contribution of Zygmunt Bauman to surveillance studies. *International Political Sociology, 4*, 325–338. https://doi.org/10.1111/j.1749-5687.2010.00109.x

Maurrasse, D. J. (2020). *Philanthropy and society*. Routledge.

Mauss, M. (1924). Essai sur le don. *L'Année Sociologique, 1*, 30–186.

McGoey, L. (2021). Philanthrocapitalism and the separation of powers. *Annual Review of Law and Social Science, 17*, 391–409. https://doi.org/10.1146/annurev-lawsocsci-120220-074323

Piaggio, C. (2019). Il terzo settore e la filantropia nel panorama italiano. In P. Pierri (Ed.), *Filantropia. Attori, caratteristiche e prospettive in Italia* (pp. 31–56). AIPB.

Reich, R. (2018). *Just giving. Why philanthropy is failing democracy and how it can do better*. Princeton University Press.

Reich, R., & Cordelli, C. (Eds.). (2016). *Philanthropy in democratic societies: History, institutions, values*. University of Chicago Press.

Susca, E. (2021a). Philanthropy and education. An alternative between generosity and democracy? In *Proceedings of the 2nd international conference of the journal Scuola Democratica "Reinventing education"* (Citizenship, work and the global age) (Vol. 1, pp. 249–257). Associazione "Per Scuola Democratica".

Susca, E. (2021b). Ambivalence beyond modernity. Rationalization and morality in Bauman's social theory. *The Lab's Quarterly, 23*(4), 59–82. https://doi.org/10.13131/unipi/1724-451x/nt6p-my35

Vallely, P. (2020). *Philanthropy: From Aristotle to Zuckerberg*. Bloomsbury.

Weber, M. (1930). *The protestant ethic and the spirit of capitalism* (T. Parsons, Trans.). London: Allen & Unwin (Original work published 1904–1905).

Wiepking, P. (2021). The global study of philanthropic behavior. *VOLUNTAS: International Journal of Voluntary and Nonprofit Organizations, 32*, 194–203. https://doi.org/10.1007/s11266-020-00279-6

Wrenn, M. V. (2021). Selling salvation, selling success. Neoliberalism and the Us prosperity gospel. *Cambridge Journal of Economics, 45*(2), 295–311. https://doi.org/10.1093/cje/beaa048

Zuboff, S. (2019). *The age of surveillance capitalism: The fight for a human future at the new frontier of power*. Profile Books.

Zuboff, S., Möllers, N., Murakami Wood, D., & Lyon, D. (2019). Surveillance capitalism: An interview with Shoshana Zuboff. *Surveillance & Society, 17*(1/2), 257–266. https://doi.org/10.24908/ss.v17i1/2.13238

Emanuela Susca lectures in General Sociology at the University of Urbino "Carlo Bo." Her research interests mainly focus on social theory, the history of sociological thought, and processes of socialization, with particular attention to issues concerning childhood and the construction of gender identity. In addition to several articles and book chapters, she is the author of *Nuovi media, comunicazione, società* (2007); *Pierre Bourdieu: il lavoro della conoscenza* (2011); *Per una sociologia che comprende* (2012); and *Pierre Bourdieu. Il mondo dell'uomo, i campi del sapere* (ed., 2017).

Part IV
Traces as Strategic Research Materials

Chapter 17
Traces and Their (In)significance

Gabriella Rava

Traces: Some Theoretical Premises

The concept of *trace* belongs to the same semantic field as *footprint* or *index*. The question of the differences and distinctions between these concepts is part of the discussion on the classification of signs or, as pointed out by Umberto Eco, the classification of the different ways of producing signs (Eco, 1975). The footprint as described by the Italian semiotician shares many of the characteristics of the index, the second in the typology of three types proposed by Charles Sanders Peirce, along with the symbol and the icon. Both footprints and indexes are based on a relation of *contiguity* between the sign and the corresponding object, meaning a supposed direct and causal connection. The complicated issues, which arise around the definition of indexicality and, more generally, around the problem of classifying the types of signs, will not, however, be taken into account here. What is relevant for the present analysis is rather to consider the meaning of contiguity in terms of a metaphysics of the relation between the sign and the object. This is where discussion of the trace first appears, entailing how traces have traditionally been conceived.

In his *De la grammatologie*, Derrida conducts a long examination of the "blame" attributed to writing compared to the "innocence" of the spoken word, from the famous accusation of Plato to the anthropological essays of Claude Lévi-Strauss, reading in these denunciations the specter of a metaphysics based on the privilege of the *phonè* on the *graphein* (Derrida, 1967). The voice, and by extension the oral expression, which Plato dignified above all in the form of the dialogue, based on the presence (the *présence*) of the interlocutors, was indeed considered to be closer to the Truth. In a philosophical system centered on the quest for authentic being, of which the matter is supposed to be merely a reflection, oral communication was considered to be a better vehicle for reaching the "essence" of reality. By its very nature, the

G. Rava (✉)
Charles University, Prague, Czechia

F. Comunello et al. (eds.), *What People Leave Behind*, Frontiers in Sociology and Social Research 7, https://doi.org/10.1007/978-3-031-11756-5_17

phonè is founded on the principle of proximity, between the interlocutors but primarily in terms of a presence with oneself, or self-identity; as Derrida puts it, this phono-logocentric regime of truth is based on presence grounded in the voice. Like the effect of naturalness induced by indexes, the spoken word promises to reveal a definitive presence in the form of an origin to which it is closer than the written record. A similar effect is produced by the enunciation in the text.

Paola Sozzi (2015) considers a possible association between indexes and what semiotics calls enunciation, the mechanism of producing a text or a discourse. In her article, the author distinguishes between three types of enunciations, even if the one proposed by the semiotician Greimas, partly derived from the works of the linguist Émile Benveniste, seems to be the richest in terms of its theoretical consequences. According to Greimas, a text/discourse is produced through an operation that he defines as *débrayage*, whose result is a projection of another time/space from that of the "original" act supposedly lying at its basis. The latter can potentially "re-appear" in the text, fictionally, through some traces which barely play the role of a simulacrum of the original act of producing the text/discourse (an operation the semiotician defines as *embrayage*). These traces/marks inscribed in the text are what the supposedly original enunciation has left of that founding act, a fictitious source of the text that carries on the narrative play. As Sozzi outlines, the Greimasian theory states that there is an unbridgeable distance between the act of enunciation and the final statement, the first one being even beyond the domain of semiotics. Any possibility of an ultimate reference to the origin of the text, i.e., the enunciation, is thus denied except as a simulacrum. This understanding is nevertheless comprehensible considering that Greimas was almost exclusively interested in written rather than oral texts; his theory of enunciation shares the same rejection of an alleged source of the text/discourse *De la grammatologie* is based on. Derrida underlines how the same fallacy was at the core of the privilege of the letter as *phonè* over the letter as *graphein*, as the second has long been perceived to be a mere copy of the first, in turn already a duplication - but a degree closer to a desired "origin." Demystifying the metaphysics implied by the values of presence and proximity, the notion of trace in Derrida reactivates the consciousness of the artificial (i.e., cultural) nature of any text/discourse produced. In his theory, the trace does not point toward some imagined lost unity or ultimate truth; instead, it activates that process the philosopher calls *différance*. Untranslatable into English, *différance* means both difference (*différence*) and deferment, the latter implying a process considered by Derrida as potentially infinite, a regression to an origin which is never reached because ultimately it does not exist. Following this theoretical reasoning, the distinction between *phonè* and *graphein* loses its relevance - since if there is no possible ultimate origin, no sign can claim a closer relation to the Truth.

Derridean *différance* reflects the complex notion of *unlimited semiosis* derived from the semiotics of Peirce, offering a particularly fruitful theoretical basis for a further elaboration of the semantic potential the notion of trace can disclose. Derrida's understanding of the latter in fact implies the issue of the reception and interpretation of the text, as well as calling into question the alleged role played by the author as its "authentic producer." Similar to unlimited semiosis, *différance* thus opens up a dialogue between text and reader, somehow releasing the former from the exclusive property of the author and reinserting it into what can be called the community's work of interpretation. To understand the concept of trace within this theoretical framework means taking a fundamental step toward the weakening of the author's intention, a text no longer being read as the exclusive result of the unique meanings imposed by the producer or the source of a "truth" to be revealed.

Intention and Intentionality

To conceive the trace as not strictly dependent on a specific intention is a crucial point. Traces can work as significant elements if they are caught by someone and thus firstly *recognized*. Following the suggestions of Umberto Eco, three kinds of signs are liable to a process of recognition, to be understood as the act instituting them as signs, as actually significant: these are the footprint, the clue, and the symptom. Because of its isomorphism, meaning that the object shares the shape of its imprinter, traces have mainly been considered a kind of footprint, and specifically a footprint already recognized as a sign, or eventually a kind of clue in some particular cases (Mazzucchelli, 2015; Sozzi, 2015; Violi, 2016). This act of recognition is defined by Eco as an example of abduction[1]; only after the sign has been recognized as such is it eventually possible to name it *trace*, as Patrizia Violi (2016) suggests. This means that whoever leaves the footprint/clue is moved by an unintentional force; yet, when observed, the footprint/clue seems to retain a certain degree of intentionality for a receiver who would eventually be able to impose on it a meaning or function. Nevertheless, the question remains problematic - as the distinction between the sign emitted and the sign received is technically possible only on a theoretical basis. By contrast, the specific processes of signification and communication work in a different way. The relationship between the emission and the reception of the sign can be rethought in terms of a potential significance that the act of recognition then turns into an actual sign. Usually conceived as unintentional, footprints and clues reveal in this way a virtual *intentionality*.

The meaning of intentionality here should be understood according to the definition by Greimas and Courtés in their *Sémiotique: dictionnaire raisonné de la théorie du langage*, where the concept is compared to that of *intention* (Greimas & Courtés, 1979). If the latter entails a certain degree of voluntariness or consciousness, the concept of intentionality is, in contrast, more nuanced, yet preferred by the authors as the condition of possibility for the enunciation. Not entirely identifiable with the notion of motivation nor with that of purpose, intentionality eventually subsumes both, inscribing the act in a tension between the potentiality and the realization thereof. The concept of intentionality can thus be adopted as a preferred

[1] Umberto Eco took the concept of *abduction* from Peirce's semiotic theory. In a very simplistic way, abduction can be defined as a kind of syllogism partially based on a certain probability.

foundation of the significant potential triggered by the trace. Based on the considerations made in the previous paragraphs, the trace can then be regarded as the actual realization of the semantic potential of a footprint/clue, i.e., a genuine sign. Still maintaining a causal and "physical" relation to the object it denotes, the trace, like footprints and clues, can be regarded as an example of index, or, better said, of a predominately indexical sign.[2]

Traces, and more generally indexes, have mainly been studied in relation to the spatial dimension, as outlined by Sozzi (2015), since it seems that space is directly involved in their processes of signification. Nevertheless, the theory of trace in Derrida, insisting on the ghost of an origin or source, embraces the dimension of time along with that of space, as the idea of *différance* involves a complete rethinking of an entire tradition centered on imagining time as a linear progression. The redefinition of temporality compared to the previous strict separation of past, present, and future has been instrumental in the development of the semiotics of memory, where traces as present remains of the past problematize the notion of temporality. The trace points in fact to another time as well as another space, both playing a central role in establishing and triggering memories or practices of remembrance. The promise of revealing a lost past or an ideal totality with which the trace is charged has thus been dismissed as the remains of that metaphysics of presence which privileges the ideas of origin and truth over those of absence and finitude. It seems to find confirmation in Umberto Eco's provocative definition of semiotics as the theory of what can be used to lie (Eco, 1975), with all its implications for a semiotic approach to the trace in relation to its supposed values of authenticity and credibility.

Meaninglessness Vs Insignificance

The definition of intentionality given by Greimas and Courtés (1979), a communication driver that does not imply actual consciousness, will be here assumed as the basis of the processes of signification. Even signs which are not recognized as such in previous theories, because of their lack of a proper intention, are in this view virtually motivated by a different sort of intentionality. Eco's *A theory of semiotics* (Eco, 1975) offers the distinction between intentional and unintentional signs, the former constituting signs in the strict sense and the latter bare *signals*. These include specifically the aforementioned footprints, clues, and symptoms, whose significance is dependent on the receivers' willingness to recognize them as signs. Even if not driven by a proper intention, a certain amount of meaningfulness lies virtually in them, ready to be activated at any time. Otherwise, it would be necessary to imagine the trace as a thing turning into a sign after having been recognized as such by the

[2] "Pure" indexes are in fact only possible on a theoretical basis, as the actual processes of signification generally show a much more heterogeneous nature.

community, thus drastically changing its status. Eventually, what the real processes of signification reveal about the trace is its promising significance lying "suspended," waiting for someone to interpret it. This virtual "suspension" of sense can last indefinitely, thereby keeping the trace semiotically "inactive."

Such an eventuality constitutes the core of Massimo Leone's recent book on insignificance in our post-material society (Leone, 2020). The author imagines the case when, mainly due to a lack of cultural knowledge or experience, someone fails to recognize the meaningfulness of an object/act, thus interpreting it as simply meaningless. Usually, the gaining from experience or the correct interpretation of previously unknown habits leads to their status as signs being acknowledged, turning them into meaningful elements. Specifically, the author identifies three different types of *meaninglessness*: undecipherability, incomprehension, and uncanniness. The first type is realized when the receiver apprehends the object/act as a sign, but cannot decipher it; the second type occurs when he/she guesses its significant character despite feeling a certain alienation (normally because of a lack of deep knowledge of the local culture or habits); finally, the last case happens when the object/act is not immediately recognized as a sign, and only after repeated exposures is the receiver eventually able to grasp its sense.

After listing a series of examples of meaninglessness, Leone suggests yet another possible experience of the lack of sense in our lives, something rooted in the daily routine of our existences. It is the more radical feeling of insignificance, not just mere meaninglessness:

> Insignificance is something else. A sign can be meaningless because one fails to access its semantic content, pragmatic functioning, or both. But a sign cannot be insignificant. That would be a contradiction in terms. In order for a sign to be insignificant, it should deny itself, that is, it should deny its own nature of sign. [...] An insignificant sign is a sign that stands for nothing, to nobody, in no respect or capacity. It is a non-sign. It is a thing (ibid.: 12).

Given that the question of intentionality/unintentionality is an important variable in the classification of signs and the way they are "produced," the issue of their possible insignificance is extremely relevant, especially when it comes to indexical signs like traces, usually perceived as "closer to things" when compared to icons and symbols. In fact, the concept of insignificance is described by Leone in terms of second nature, or a set of habits already solidified, and consequently no longer recognized as meaningful by a growing portion of mankind. This state of existence characterizes in particular what the author calls the *post-material* age, the contemporary and mainly digital era in which Western countries are immersed. However, the question that arises here concerns the actual possibility of imagining a "pure" insignificance in the terms stated by Leone. Namely, can a sign really deny itself in any respect or capacity, standing indefinitely for nothing and to nobody? Obviously, it is not the purpose of this article to give a definitive answer to the problematic suggestions offered by Leone, and the following analysis will be limited to a single case study among the different ones examined by the author.

From a semiotic perspective, the notion of a "pure" insignificance presents a paradoxical scenario where signs are no longer significant entities, but are instead things, predictable gestures, missing acts, persisting in their lack of sense despite any attempts to interpret them differently. It has been assumed that signs are the product of a process which implies their recognition from a hypothetical receiver; their significance is not automatically given by the act of emission or production thereof. On a theoretical basis, it is possible to imagine a sort of hiatus between the latter and the moment in which the significance of something is grasped by someone: the prolongation of the hiatus has the effect of meaninglessness as a temporary state, while its virtual persistence has a more radical effect of insignificance. The latter is a permanent condition of existence, unsolvable by any alternative interpretations or imaginary scenarios, where the sense is turned into a thing persisting as a thing: a drastic lack of sense, where the process of signification is interrupted and the act/gesture/signal "falls into the void" of a muted existence. This same schema can alternatively work when imagining the potential significance of the sign unable to turn into an actual one, the sense lying persistently suspended or inactive; in this scenario, the trace remains just a simple remainder, an unacknowledged mark randomly left by an invisible agent, and thus powerless to undermine the apathy triggered by the emptiness and absence it stands for.

This self-denial of the sign proposed by Leone is a strong position, even when applied to certain situations characteristic of the post-material societies the author describes, where feelings of loss and privation are increasing. Leone's proposal is however extremely interesting - as it raises the question of the possibility of a paradoxical semiotics not centered on the sense, but, on the contrary, on the lack of sense, or even, more radically, on a possible semiotics of "nothing." This scenario will be tested only through a very limited example from the digital arena, arguably the sphere most affected by that sense of existential emptiness on which insignificance is grounded. In fact, the realm of digital traces represents the perfect case study for an analysis of the possible emergence of a sense of insignificance - but more generally, it is the very notion of trace, with its fragility, that is suitable for a reflection on the threat of insignificance.

Something similar to a paradoxical semiotics of nothing has been suggested by Susie Scott in a recent work which elaborates a possible sociology of nothing, meaning a sociology not interested in understanding human acts of doings and beings but, on the contrary, states of *non-doings* and *non-beings* (Scott, 2018). The main purpose of the article is to show how even what is deemed to be *nothing* produces, often despite itself, some recognized meaning, at least for an unexpected receiver. In particular, Scott analyzes two different situations in which a sense of nothingness can arise on a social level: through what she calls *acts of commission* or through *acts of omission*. The first are not particularly interesting for the purpose of this paper, as they refer to acts done consciously, such as when someone decides not to do or not to be something; consequently, they are the product of a precise choice, i.e., intrinsically meaningful. More interesting are the acts of omission, not driven by a specific choice or by consciousness; they also include failures, both in acting and in properly assessing a certain phenomenon. These acts can appear as intrinsically insignificant to the person who unconsciously commits them, someone who, unaware of the possible relevance of his/her own gestures, is not even pushed to search for this relevance. This is what distinguishes the state of meaninglessness from the state of insignificance, as described by Leone. Scott, however, suggests that even acts of omission imply the formation of more or less imaginary alternatives, i.e., other possible courses of action, again unintentionally arising in opposition to the actual state derived from not having done or been something.

More precisely, what Scott underlines is that our acts always fall into a social dimension, since people and their behavior are read and interpreted just like any other texts (to be understood in semiotic terms). Even the most radical eventuality of a lack of sense unable to trigger the creation of alternative scenarios could always potentially be forced into being interpreted by someone as a significant act. Silences, the absence, the void, all are open to being converted into traces of something which was or may have been there, testifying to the difficulty of avoiding the dimension of sense. Scott recalls how the concept of nothingness has always intrigued philosophers, scientists, and artists, not to mention mathematicians. *Nothingness* has traditionally been associated with the idea of zero, not known as a number until its introduction into mathematics by the Arabs, despite being already in use among Indian mathematicians. From a semiotic perspective, *zero* has been described by Brian Rotman (1987) as the equivalent of nothing. Specifically, "the semiotic formula given of zero, that is a sign for the absence of other signs, [...] more importantly explicitly invokes and indeed *constitutes itself* in terms of the logocentrically tainted opposition of absence/presence" (*ivi*: 104; author italics). Absence cannot but be *traced* through the convention of zero and, more importantly, all the other numbers come to life as a consequence of zero: they exist precisely because they are not zero, they mean something instead. This fact, as the author remarks, has led to an understanding of zero as the origin, even if a relative one: not only the origin of the other numbers, but also the origin of sense. Zero is thus not a simple sign, but a *meta-sign*, as it is the sign stating the absence/presence of other signs. It is therefore possible to conclude that even *absence* and *nothingness* leave traces, to the extent that they can be detected, read, and interpreted as such - since some sense may always arise from them.

The case study presented in the following paragraphs will offer an opportunity to reflect on another possible manifestation of insignificance in the digital arena, where a different sense of nothingness is expressed.

Case Study. Digital Traces: Trolling

Described as what is left behind on the Internet after digital activities, actions, and searches (but also after deliberate acts of interaction with other users), digital traces can be intentional as well as unintentional (Hepp, Breiter, & Friemel, 2018). According to the distinction made in the previous paragraphs between intention and intentionality, it is preferred here to distinguish between traces left consciously and those left unconsciously, thus never being properly unintentional. As Alexandre Serres (2012) notes, the *trace numérique* is always intentional, in the sense that it is already expected, pre-inscribed in the digital apparatus. This is true for both interactional systems like social media, where the freedom to express our ideas and feelings is inscribed in a pattern which has not been designed by ourselves, as well as for more complex systems, like those behind the collection of cookies when surfing online, considering that these data are collected and stored for specific purposes by a preordained system of traceability. This remark is important in order to reinforce the concept of intentionality introduced above.

In the frame of the conventional opposition between intentional and unintentional digital traces, trolling is usually read as an intentional decision to leave traces of one's own online activities, mainly on social platforms like Facebook or Twitter. Leone has underlined how this phenomenon shares some characteristics with other genres of discourse like provocation and joke. Just as these latter need a "victim," trolling is all about provoking someone, on any possible subject. The difference with provocation lies in the fact that trolling does not really concern the topic being discussed. Trolling is largely indifferent to content, as its real goal lies precisely in the act of provoking the victim, so that the purpose of trolling is accomplished when "the emotional tone of conversation becomes the main focus of conversation itself" (Leone, 2020: 23). This also marks the difference with jokes, as the latter acquire their sense only after being revealed as jokes, meaning that they can be played up to a certain limit, beyond which they fail to be perceived as such. Trolling, however, is totally indifferent to this limit: it appears as an almost endless joke, with no other purpose than, as Leone states, to "make fun *of* someone" (*ivi*.: 24; author italics).

Sharing the same need of digital traces on social media for a public space to appear, i.e., the digital arena, trolling also requires anonymity in order to function; however, the question of identity in this case remains problematic. In fact, it is true that trolls behave as anonymous actors when engaged in a public discourse on a digital platform, but this does not mean that it is impossible to detect some kind of identity, at least a social one, through which they can be categorized. Recently, research on trolling has been developing new methods for understanding the role and behavior of trolls. In a paper dedicated to the analysis of the digital activity of Russian trolls on Twitter, the authors demonstrate how comments and tweets left by trolls can lead to different troll identities being categorized, and then profiled accordingly (Kim, Graham, Wan, & Rizoiu, 2019). Their idea is based on the thesis developed by Latour and other scholars, known as the *actor-network theory* (ANT), stating that the identity of an actor can be described in terms of his/her network; when applied to the digital environment, this amounts to the collection of traces left behind by the online activities of that actor (Latour, Jensen, Venturini, Grauwin, & Boullier, 2012). The individuality of a single identity comes from the sum of the attributes or items that are possible to add to it; the more numerous these are, the more that identity can consequently be shaped in detail.

More precisely, the very act of searching for someone or something on the Internet "creates" the identity of the actor, as the digital traces available online can be combined through the searches, despite the fact that a total, definitive identity is, according to the authors, never achievable. Even if the actor-network theory has been mainly formulated with consideration to online profiles, whose data are deliberately made available and public to other users, its approach can also be applied to trolling. As shown in the aforementioned study analyzing the behavior of Russian trolls, even fake or anonymous profiles can be categorized and identified by users by means of the tweets left behind, namely their digital traces. This way of understanding the phenomenon implies the treatment of the traces as meaningful signs and not just the effect of a very complex system. They are viewed as semantic information by the large companies, which are highly interested in them (Breiter & Hepp, 2018); these companies collect this information in order to model identities, to be meant mainly as social and public identities, which are then adopted in a commercial and marketing context. In this case, and probably the same can be said about the traces left by trolls, the concept of identity is related only to a public dimension, not to a singular one. A similar process happens within particular places that, in some respects, can be regarded as the precursors of the digital platform, which are the so-called non-places (*non-lieux*) already described by Marc Augé in the 1990s (Augé, 1992). The non-places are specific spaces, like airports, supermarkets, shopping malls, or highways, characterized by the fact of being devoid of any historical extent, as they are only places of transition (and transactions). Unable to integrate preexisting spaces, non-places tend, nonetheless, to point to an elsewhere, specifically in the form of advertisements, following the logic of the marketing. Moreover, they are intrinsically meta-descriptive, as they tend to turn themselves into texts, to produce a textual and visual apparatus that talks about them. Exactly like digital traces, non-places can be described as a network; if every trace is a remainder of its producer and consequently always points to it, the same happens inside a non-place. Nevertheless, the crucial issue is how identity is conceived and handled in these spaces. In order to access the non-places, a person is required to give his/her particulars, in the forms of passports, identity cards, or payment transactions, which can all be read as traces left behind, more or less related to the personal data of the passenger/customer of the service offered/requested. These traces are what is needed to "grant" and pay for entering the subsequent state of anonymity that marks these spaces, where the person finds himself/herself lost in the crowd. Traces are there given both consciously (in the case of passports, for example) and semi-unconsciously (payments, data accessed through Wi-Fi connection), similarly to what happens in cyberspace. It should be noted that the kind of identity the non-places require is not an intimate one, as it could be on Facebook's posts, but a legal identity, not concerning the singularity of the individual. The traces left in the non-places function thus in the same way as digital traces work in their logic of collecting data from users: their target is the "average man," possibly a consumer, whose behavior is detected and subsequently solicited through messages and advertisements. Every individual must be reduced to a consumer model - as the trace here is not meant to lead to the singular identity Latour and the other scholars describe in their aforementioned theory, but to an individual already socialized, thus fostering the sense of anonymity of the man lost in a multitude of individuals similarly lost in the same habits and actions.

This sense of anonymity offered to users after their entry into non-places prefigures the feeling of invisibility which characterizes the digital arena. When trolls make fun of other users, they experience an intensified impression of being lost in the mass of online identities, taking advantage of this status. The condition of anonymity is what makes it possible for trolls to play their game, as Leone (2020) suggests, and not only because of the feeling that their individual responsibility is weaker in the digital arena, but also because their concealed identity reinforces their position toward the victim and the sense of confusion derived from it. Leone reads this factor, as well as trolls' indifference toward the content of their posts, as an example of the emergence of insignificance in the digital sphere. In fact, trolls' discourses usually display a notable discrepancy between the expression and the content of the message, something the author understands as a mark of an almost total indifference toward the topic discussed by the other users. Yet, to interpret the digital traces left by trolls as insignificant remains problematic: it is true that the feeling of confusion and frustration they create often leads to the inability to distinguish between real criticism or simple mockery, or between true and false information, but this is frequently part of a strategy. The aforementioned study dedicated to the Russian trolls is aimed not only at proposing a possible categorization of different groups of trolls, but also at showing how the apparent contradictory nature of their posts is a well-planned strategy for destabilizing Western democracies.

Fostering a sense of uncertainty and suspicion through disinformation is an orchestrated project that is anything but insignificant. Furthermore, besides these more specific cases, in which the significance of trolling is easily predictable, even ordinary (and more "innocuous") users deploy some strategy in their digital behavior. Firstly, Leone himself recognizes that certain topics of discussion are especially good for trolling, for example when the topic "entails a potentiality for contrasting opinions" (Leone, 2020: 28). The awareness showed by trolls in this regard is possibly understandable in terms of a programmed strategy, as they seem to know which discussions are likely to become "hot" and inflame an emotional tone in the conversation, and consequently how to keep this up. The preference for certain topics and a certain strategic behavior allows trolling to be considered a fully significant phenomenon. Secondly, as already noted by Leone, trolls tend to communicate their messages in a manner which is (and aims to be) explicitly inaccurate, both on the level of the grammar/syntax and on that of the content expressed, which is frequently illogical or openly contradictory, as the study on Russian trolls underlines. Even this second aspect should, however, be taken as relevant and worthy of significance: again, it is plausible to interpret it as a strategic technique used to decrease the quality and intelligibility of the discourse, aiming at confusing the interlocutors.

Finally, it is important to consider how the other users react to trolling, meaning how they understand the phenomenon and interact with it, emotionally and cognitively. The traces left by trolls' activity are now almost immediately recognized by experienced users, who can, in revenge, turn the situation to their own advantage, becoming the ones who make fun of the trolls or eventually decide to play the same game. This prospect arises from the effect of familiarity with the phenomenon over time, when it is no longer perceived as an oddity: in short, an effect of *acquaintance*, meaning the recognition of a pattern which is identified as significant. In the case of the traces left by trolls, these are read and acknowledged by other users as a sign of trolling, i.e., of a specific behavior in the digital arena. These traces are thus no longer simple signals, according to Eco's terminology, since the effect of acquaintance they unconsciously give rise to turns them into proper signs, a significant pattern for other digital subjects.

Final Remarks: A Possible Paradigm of the Trace

Concluding his study with the affirmation of the insignificance of trolling in an already insignificant digital reality, Leone denounces the phenomenon as the symptom of a crisis of mainstream language and morality. This analysis has tried to deny this conclusion, proposing instead the meaningfulness of trolling, and more generally of the wider concept of a digital trace. The (partial) conclusions that can be drawn lead to the proposal of a paradigm in which the concept of trace could be inscribed. On the basis of the notion of intentionality as described above, it is possible to state that every trace is intentional, since even the ones that users leave unconsciously during their digital activities are always part of an established system that collects and processes those same traces. Intentionality (not to be confused with the close notion of intention) is consequently fundamental for any paradigm of the trace, and for any semiotics of the digital.

The second concept to be taken into account is the aforementioned notion of acquaintance. A trace is never recognized in isolation, since it is reminiscent of some pattern, be it an identity, a past event, or a no-longer-existent entity, so that its full "truthfulness" is revealed by an act of acknowledgment, i.e., it requires the receiver to become acquainted with its recurrence. Lastly, the third element of the suggested paradigm can be summarized by the concept of *circumstance*. The abovementioned actor-network theory applied to digital traces by Latour and the other scholars (Latour et al., 2012) clearly affirms that an identity is the product of the sum of the traces that may be collected and assembled when searching for someone/something on the Internet. This approach centers on the idea of a context, given in the shape of a network, since each trace is related to another one and cannot be considered fully significant unless in relation to other traces. This context is referred to here as the circumstance ("what stands around," etymologically), liable to modify the meaning of the single trace, a fragmentary sign if taken in isolation. Moreover, a trace always points at something, missing or definitely lost, so that the circumstance in which it is caught is highly significant also in this regard. The hypothetical paradigm proposed, in which the trace can be inscribed, consists thus of the three elements of intentionality, acquaintance, and circumstance, all corroborating its significance.

The analyzed case study of trolling can be read through this paradigm, considering the intentionality behind trolls' traces, the effect of acquaintance they give rise to in digital communication, and, lastly, the circumstance in which they are received. The latter is intended as both the specific context of the digital arena with its communicative conventions and the network in which each trace is linked with the previous or following ones. On the basis of the suggested paradigm, an insignificant trace would mean one devoid of any possible intentionality, standing for nothing in any possible circumstances and unable to develop any sort of acquaintance in the digital audience. On the contrary, the examined case of trolling, according to Leone an example of loss of meaning, cannot escape the "holding" of sense, and thus proves to be a fully significant (and hence semiotically analyzable) phenomenon. For this reason alone, the province of meaning must be expanded to include the trace and other quasi-signs that might otherwise be placed beyond the scope of semiotic interest. Following from this, the possibility of insignificance is highly problematic, and it seems (in Leone's perception) to be strictly related to the crisis of values and beliefs sustaining Western (and democratic) discursive practices. Trolling can only and eventually be regarded as an expression of insignificance from such a narrow perspective, and according to a very specific ideological standpoint. The existential, rather than cultural, nuance with which the concept of insignificance is charged, contrary to the one of meaninglessness, seems to disclose in the end a partial outlook on the emergent trends within digital communication.

References

Augé, M. (1992). *Non-Lieux; introduction à une anthropologie de la surmodernité*. Le Seuil.

Breiter, A., & Hepp, A. (2018). The complexity of datafication: Putting digital traces in context. In A. Hepp, A. Breiter, & U. Hasebrink (Eds.), *Communicative figurations. Transforming communications in times of deep mediatization* (pp. 387–405). Palgrave.

Derrida, J. (1967). *De la grammatologie*. Éditions de Minuit.

Eco, U. (1975). *Trattato di semiotica generale*. Bompiani.

Greimas, A. J., & Courtés, J. (1979). *Sémiotique: dictionnaire raisonné de la théorie du langage*. Hachette.

Hepp, A., Breiter, A., & Friemel, T. N. (2018). Digital traces in context. An introduction. *International Journal of Communication, 12*, 439–449.

Kim, D., Graham, T., Wan, Z., & Rizoiu, M. A. (2019). Tracking the digital traces of Russian trolls: Distinguishing the roles and strategy of trolls on Twitter. *ResearchGate*. Online publication. https://www.researchgate.net/publication/330439433_Tracking_the_Digital_Traces_of_Russian_Trolls_Distinguishing_the_Roles_and_Strategy_of_Trolls_On_Twitter

Latour, B., Jensen, P., Venturini, T., Grauwin, S., & Boullier, D. (2012). 'The whole is always smaller than its parts' – A digital test of Gabriel Tardes' monads. *The British Journal of Sociology, 63*(4), 590–615.

Leone, M. (2020). *On insignificance. The loss of meaning in the post-material age*. Routledge.

Mazzucchelli, F. (2015). Abiti di pietra. La memoria architettonica tra indici, impronte e 'invenzioni' del passato. *Rivista italiana di filosofia del linguaggio, 0*(2). Online publication. http://www.rifl.unical.it/index.php/rifl/article/view/312

Rotman, B. (1987). *Signifying nothing. The semiotics of zero*. Stanford University Press.

Scott, S. (2018). A sociology of nothing: Understanding the unmarked. *Sociology, 52*(I), 3–19.
Serres, A. (2012). Problématiques de la trace à l'heure du numérique. *Éditions de l'Association Paroles | «Sens-Dessous», 10*, 84–94.
Sozzi, P. (2015). L'indice in Peirce: alcune riflessioni tra spazio ed enunciazione. *Rivista italiana di filosofia del linguaggio, 0*(2). Online publication. http://www.rifl.unical.it/index.php/rifl/article/view/297
Violi, P. (2016). Luoghi della memoria: dalla traccia al senso. *Rivista italiana di filosofia del linguaggio, 00*. Online publication. http://www.rifl.unical.it/index.php/rifl/article/view/365

Gabriella Rava is a PhD student at Charles University (Prague), Faculty of Humanities, in Semiotics and Philosophy of Communication. She is currently working on her doctoral thesis which analyzes the contemporary political murals in Northern Ireland as representations of collective memories between sectarianism and transnationality. In 2021, she published her first articles in international and peer-reviewed journals and participated in two international conferences. She has been hosted as visiting PhD student (February–May 2022) by the Universidade Católica Portuguesa in Lisbon, Portugal.

Chapter 18
Traces and Algorithms as Socio-digital Objects

Enrica Amaturo and Ciro Clemente De Falco

Introduction

Traces and algorithms have become privileged objects of study to understand many dynamics of contemporary digital culture. Their constant presence in everyday processes makes them a pillar of the digital society.

Actor-network theory (ANT) (Latour & Woolgar, 1979; Callon, 1984; Law, 1992) is a promising approach for studying these objects[1] because it considers the social, material, technological, and scientific domains are intertwined and the role of nonhuman actors, the actants, within the social processes. For ANT, actors are not those who act intentionally but those that modify status quo by making a difference (Latour, 2007).

From an ANT perspective, digital traces and algorithms are a product or an effect of a heterogeneous entanglement of constantly shifting relations between human and nonhuman actants (Latour, 2007; Halford et al., 2010). Lupton (2016) talks about digital data-human assemblages to underline how humans only represent a node of an extensive network composed of nonhuman actors, defined as socio-digital devices. We speak of socio-digital objects to underline the strong intertwining between the social world, made up of norms, economics, politics, and the digital world, formed by material and technological objects. The social and digital worlds influence each other in a dynamic in which they are inextricable.

Digital traces and algorithms may be understood as socio-digital objects because the way they are collected, catalogued, and used is not neutral but results from social,

[1] Waldherr et al. (2019) highlighted that this approach has been handy in fields such as education (Fenwick & Edwards, 2010; Fenwick & Landri, 2012), journalism (Primo & Zago, 2015), marketing (Shim & Shin, 2016), and linguistics (Kelly & Maddalena, 2016).

E. Amaturo (✉) · C. C. De Falco
Department of Social Science, University of Naples Federico II, Naples, Italy
e-mail: amaturo@unina.it; ciroclemente.defalco@unina.it

F. Comunello et al. (eds.), *What People Leave Behind*, Frontiers in Sociology and Social Research 7, https://doi.org/10.1007/978-3-031-11756-5_18

economic, and political interests. Moreover, in socio-digital assemblages, actions and interactions of individuals produce digital traces and are shaped by these.

There is a continuous and deep intertwining between human actors and socio-digital devices. For example, wearable devices such as self-tracking and self-monitoring devices (rings, watches, glasses, etc.) illustrate how these traces can modify people's behaviors and actions. It is possible to use this large amount of digital data generated by these objects for multiple purposes: users can track their health, marketing companies can make a profit, they serve as navigational tools, and they are helpful for location-based services (Murero, 2020).

Algorithms play then a central role in these transformations as they collect, classify, and analyze these traces, thus creating dynamics that impact on the behavior of individuals.

This article aims to identify the features that allow us to frame traces and algorithms as socio-digital objects. We rest on concepts borrowed from the ANT, such as opacity, authority, and autonomy. The following section describes how these objects exercise authority and have consequences over individuals. We will also depict the logic of their functioning and how they are gaining autonomy from human actors in the socio-digital assemblage. In the final section, geographical traces are used as an example to discuss the features of socio-digital objects.

Emerging Features of Socio-digital Objects

There are three main features of algorithms and digital traces as socio-digital objects. The first one is the ability to influence individual and collective action, the second refers to the opacity of their operating logic, and the third is the ability to establish relationships autonomously.

Latour identifies two kinds of figures in the assemblages: the intermediary and the mediator, i.e., those who can convey a meaning or a force and can be both human and nonhuman elements. The difference between intermediary and mediator is in the capacity of transformation. The former is a mere carrier of a social meaning created elsewhere, whereas the latter is an actual social meaning-maker (Latour, 1993; Latour, 2007). So, in the intermediary's case, the output will be predictable when the input is known. In mediator's cases, the output will be unpredictable.

Algorithms presented as neutral intermediaries are instead mediators. We cannot consider algorithms as "neutral entities" (Airoldi & Gambetta, 2018) because critical algorithm studies have highlighted that the algorithms incorporate their creators' social, political, and economic interests (Seaver, 2017). Furthermore, algorithms implement "creative, performative, generative and provocative" processes (Muniesa, 2011), which makes them mediators that actively participate in the process of construction of information (Neresini, 2015).

The new relevance of algorithms arises as a response to the rapid development of the datafication process (Amaturo & Aragona, 2019). Prosumerism and neoliberalism accelerated the transformation of social and individual life into digital traces, which generates new needs for data extraction, identification, and classification. The processing and the ordering of these large numbers of digital traces are algorithms' tasks. For this reason, they acquire an essential role in the new data-human assemblages. This importance also emerges in how algorithms impact the processes of individual and collective action in the digital world.

Rogers (2013) wrote about the "algorithmic authority" for describing how the search engines are authentic epistemological machines that exercise power over sources considered necessary. Cheney-Lippold (2011), on the other hand, speaks of the "soft power" of algorithms to refer to their influence on the existential possibilities of individuals. Many empirical pieces of research highlight the authority of algorithms in the fields in which they are applied (Haimson et al., 2021; Graham & Rodriguez, 2021; Gorwa et al., 2020; Campbell-Verduyn et al., 2017). Among these, we can mention Ma and Kou (2021) research in which emerges that the algorithm underlying the moderation of YouTube's content can orient not only the individual and collective action of YouTubers but also their feelings of insecurity and precariousness. In their work, the two authors pointed out that the interviewees perceive a strong feeling of precariousness because they do not know how the demonetized system works. The inability to understand how the moderation algorithm works causes this feeling.

This inability to access the algorithm's code described by the authors is not an isolated case but rather a constitutive feature of algorithms. To describe this feature, we usually use the concept of opacity. Opacity means that algorithms are sometimes actual black boxes whose functioning is almost impossible to decode (Pasquale, 2015). Cybersecurity positively considers opacity because it allows the defense of information flows from hacker attacks. However, it can have adverse effects on individuals and the community. Burrell (2016) identifies three kinds of opacity:

1. intentional corporate or institutional self-protection and concealment and the possibility for knowing deception;
2. the result of specialistic and technical skills;
3. the mismatch between mathematical optimization in a high-dimensionality characteristic of machine learning and the demands of human-scale reasoning and styles of semantic interpretation (pag. 4).

The last type of opacity would characterize algorithms as socio-digital tools. Machine learning algorithms are an example. According to Burrell (2016), "When a computer learns and consequently builds its representation of a classification decision, it does so without regard for human comprehension. Workings of machine learning algorithms can escape full understanding and interpretation by humans, even for those with specialized training, even for computer scientists" (pag. 10).

This unprecedented type of opacity that characterizes algorithms operating in the digital world with large amounts of data makes complex to control any bias embedded in the process. Socio-digital devices, in fact, by creating their own rules of classification, also tend to create a space of autonomy within the logic embedded in the code. Autonomy is the salient aspect of digital devices' third feature, and sociological studies still little explore this field.

Socio-digital objects are starting to implement the possibility of establishing relationships autonomously. This feature is salient because it allows nonhuman actors to attain their sense autonomously. In ANT, the sense of a nonhuman actor was instead realized only in the relationship with a human actor. So, the socio-digital objects are progressively learning to establish relationships and communicate autonomously with each other. The result is an ecosystem that allows people and smart objects to interact within a social structure of relationships (Baskiyar & Meghanathan, 2005). This new feature of socio-digital objects is the main interest of the Social Internet of Things (SIOT), a new concept merging the Internet of Things and the social capabilities of the modern Internet.

The SIOT works on protocols for digital devices to make them act independently in the network, allowing them to choose which devices to connect to and which kind of data they can request or exchange. We can find examples of interconnected socio-digital devices in individual or community service. Digital devices communicate to identify and manage problems in real time in personal care services or smart cities. It is interesting to point out that a sociological concept such as trust plays a crucial role in SIOT. Firstly, it affects how devices decide to connect, and, furthermore, it configurates the overall assemblage and the outcomes. Thus, the algorithms that will attribute trust to the other actors' network play a key role.

Digital Geographic Traces as Socio-digital Objects

Geographical traces are a very good example of digital traces. These traces are crucial for many geolocalization services, and public bodies and private companies' investments in these services are increasing.

With the spread of Web 2.0 and GPS technologies, two primary sources of digital geographic traces arose. Goodchild (2006) define the first as "volunteered geographic information" (VGI) to describe the use of the web to generate, process, and disseminate geographic information provided by individuals voluntarily. Campagna et al. (2015) define the second as "Social Media Geographic Information" (SMGI). The difference between the two sources is the voluntariness in providing geographic information. In the SMGI the spread of geographic information is not the final purpose of production (Stefanidis et al., 2013). Locative media (Wilken & Goggin, 2015) feed both sources, enabling the process of geomediatization (Fast, 2018). We can extract digital geographic traces from both sources through geocoding, geoparsing, and geotagging.

As Middleton et al. (2018) noted "geocoding is the act of transforming a well-formed textual representation of an address into a valid spatial representation, such as a spatial coordinate or specific map reference. Geotagging assigns spatial coordinates to media content items, typically by building statistical models that, given a piece of text, can provide an estimate of the most likely location (spatial coordinate) to which the text refers. Geoparsing does the same for unstructured free text and involves location extraction and location disambiguation before the final geocoding" (pag. 2).

In the digital society, geographic information allows the citizen to use a variety of services, such as the possibility of obtaining road information, traffic information, information on the closest activities and services, and the evaluation provided by other users. This information is also used in businesses (Pick, 2008), by researchers (De Falco et al., 2022), as well as by governments for multiple purposes, including organizing rescue during environmental disasters (Joseph et al., 2018) or spatial planning (Poser & Dransch, 2010).

Geographic traces acquire social science researchers' attention as socio-digital objects because their creation, collection, and processing are far from neutral processes. Locative media and these traces result from social, cultural, technological, and commercial rationality (Fast et al., 2019). For Thielmann (2010), the adoption of "locative media" was mainly born to respond to the cultural, social, and political crisis introduced by global warming. Furthermore, the production of traces by users derives from social logic, such as identity formation and demarcation between social classes (Lindell et al., 2021).

Regarding the "collection", users do not intentionally produce all traces, and the possibility to use these large amounts of geographical data is allowed by privacy rules. Public and private companies take much information on the users' location without their explicit consent (Obermeyer, 2007). In addition, the algorithms that govern geoparsing operations are blackboxed. Dewandaru et al. (2020) said: "the geoparser does not know anything about the event structure or semantics; the event coding system simply attaches the coordinate of the detected, resolved toponym to the event's location" (pag. 3).

Specific criteria guide user information processing in each place. For instance, "a calculative spatiality that prioritizes economic interactions" (Luque-Ayala & Neves Maia, 2019) characterizes the maps produced by Google Maps. Hence, the algorithms that underlie the mapping app processes possess high authority in defining how users perceive the space and their mobility (Wagner et al., 2021). We are used to imagining the world as represented by maps, but those maps represent only a Cartesian space, while other spaces such as social or cultural space exist (Ferretti, 2007). According to Ferretti (2007), this consideration nourished a debate within the world of GIS (Geographic Information System). The GIS is the adopted standard for map creation and works primarily on a Cartesian concept of space (Goodchild, 2006). For this reason, the algorithm defines the space and the way the user perceives it and how he can move within it.

The consequences of the algorithms influence on how users experience urban spaces are manifold and related to phenomena that have extreme sociological relevance, such as for example gentrification (Jansson, 2019). In a different way, the geomediatization process is shaping the digital economy (McQuire, 2019).

Finally, the increasingly widespread use of geo-data in SIOT is another example of how geographical traces and the algorithms that analyze them have effects on users' behaviors. They are used for developing disaster detection algorithms based on social media data such as Twitter (Bhuvaneswari & Valliyammai, 2019). These systems can identify geographical events and enrich them with photos through the interaction between platforms and data. Other applications concern using geographical and temporal information to model the users' emotional states with cluster analysis (Hu et al., 2019).

As socio-digital objects, geographic traces may represent a fascinating and promising field of investigation for unfolding the dynamics of digital society. Approaching traces and algorithms as socio-digital objects can help us to understand the role they have in influencing individual behavior, human not-human interaction, and information processes. However, much remains to be done, and more empirical studies are needed. To this end, from our point of view, it is crucial, first of all, to work on the operationalization of socio-digital objects' characteristics and then on the creation of research protocols to analyze their production and use.

References

Airoldi, M., & Gambetta, D. (2018). Sul mito della neutralità algoritmica. *The Lab's Quarterly, XX*(4), 25–45.

Amaturo, E., & Aragona, B. (2019). Per un'epistemologia del digitale: note sull'uso di big data e computazione nella ricerca sociale. *Quaderni di Sociologia, 81*(81-LXIII), 71–90.

Baskiyar, S., & Meghanathan, N. (2005). A survey of contemporary real-time operating systems. *Informatica, 29*(2), 233–240.

Bhuvaneswari, A., & Valliyammai, C. (2019). Social IoT-enabled emergency event detection framework using geo-tagged microblogs and crowdsourced photographs. In A. Abraham, P. Dutta, J. K. Mandal, A. Bhattacharya, & S. Dutta (Eds.), *Emerging technologies in data mining and information security* (pp. 151–162). Springer.

Burrell, J. (2016). How the machine 'thinks': Understanding opacity in machine learning algorithms. *Big Data & Society, 3*(1). https://doi.org/10.1177/2053951715622512

Callon, M. (1984). Some elements of a sociology of translation: Domestication of the Scallopsand the fishermen of St Brieuc Bay. *The Sociological Review, 32*, 196–233. https://doi.org/10.1111/j.1467-954X.1984.tb00113

Campagna, M., Floris, R., Massa, P., Girsheva, A., & Ivanov, K. (2015). The role of social media geographic information (SMGI) in spatial planning. In G. Stan, J. Ferreira, R. Goodspeed, & J. Stillwell (Eds.), *Planning support systems and smart cities* (pp. 41–60). Springer.

Campbell-Verduyn, M., Goguen, M., & Porter, T. (2017). Big data and algorithmic governance: The case of financial practices. *New Political Economy, 22*(2), 219–236.

Cheney-Lippold, J. (2011). A new algorithmic identity: Soft biopolitics and the modulation of control. *Theory, Culture & Society, 28*(6), 164–181.

De Falco, C. C., Crescentini, N., & Ferracci, M. (2022). The spatial dimension in social media analysis: Theoretical and methodological characteristics. In G. Punziano & A. Delli Paoli (Eds.), *Handbook of research on advanced research methodologies for a digital society* (pp. 488–509). IGI Global.

Dewandaru, A., Widyantoro, D. H., & Akbar, S. (2020). Event Geoparser with pseudo-location entity identification and numerical argument extraction implementation and evaluation in Indonesian news domain. *ISPRS International Journal of Geo-Information, 9*(12), 712.

Fast, K. (2018). A discursive approach to mediatisation: Corporate technology discourse and the trope of media indispensability. *Media and Communication, 6*(2), 15–28.

Fast, K., Ljungberg, E., & Braunerhielm, L. (2019). On the social construction of geomedia technologies. *Communication and the Public, 4*(2), 89–99.

Fenwick, T., & Edwards, R. (2010). *Actor-network theory in education*. Routledge.
Fenwick, T., & Landri, P. (2012). Materialities, textures and pedagogies: Socio-material assemblages in education. *Pedagogy, Culture & Society, 20*(1), 1–7.
Ferretti, F. (2007). La verità del suolo: breve storia del Critical GIS (1983-2007). *Storicamente, 3*. http://www.storicamente.org/02_tecnostoria/strumenti/ferretti.html.
Goodchild, M. F. (2006). GIScience ten years after ground truth. *Transactions in GIS, 10*(5), 687–692.
Gorwa, R., Binns, R., & Katzenbach, C. (2020). Algorithmic content moderation: Technical and political challenges in the automation of platform governance. *Big Data & Society, 7*(1), 1–15. https://doi.org/10.1177/2053951719897945
Graham, T., & Rodriguez, A. (2021). The Sociomateriality of rating and ranking devices on social media: A case study of Reddit's voting practices. *Social Media + Society, 24*(4), 942–963. https://doi.org/10.1177/20563051211047667
Halford, S., Pope, C., & Carr, L. (2010). A manifesto for Web Science. J. Erickson, & S. Gradmann, (eds.), *Proceedings of the WebSci10: Extending the Frontiers of Society On-Line, Raleigh, United States, 25–26 Apr 2010*, pp. 1–6.
Haimson, O. L., Delmonaco, D., Nie, P., & Wegner, A. (2021). Disproportionate removals and differing content moderation experiences for conservative, transgender, and black social media users: Marginalization and moderation gray areas. *Proceedings of the ACM on Human-Computer Interaction, 5*, 1–35. https://doi.org/10.1145/3479610
Hu, T., She, B., Duan, L., Yue, H., & Clunis, J. (2019). A systematic spatial and temporal sentiment analysis on geo-tweets. *IEEE Access, 8*, 8658–8667.
Jansson, A. (2019). The mutual shaping of geomedia and gentrification: The case of alternative tourism apps. *Communication and the Public, 4*(2), 166–181.
Joseph, J. K., Dev, K. A., Pradeepkumar, A. P., & Mohan, M. (2018). Big data analytics and social media in disaster management. In P. Samui, D. Kim, & C. Ghosh (Eds.), *Integrating disaster science and management: Global case studies in mitigation and recovery* (pp. 287–294). Elsevier.
Kelly, A. R., & Maddalena, K. (2016). Networks, genres, and complex wholes: Citizen science and how we act together through typified text. *Canadian Journal of Communication, 41*(2), 287–303. https://doi.org/10.22230/cjc.2016v41n2a3043
Latour, B. (1993). *We have never been modern*. Harvard University Press.
Latour, B. (2007). *Reassembling the social: An introduction to actor-network-theory*. Oup Oxford.
Latour, B., & Woolgar, S. (1979). *Laboratory life: The social construction of scientific facts*. Sage Publications.
Law, J. (1992). Notes on the theory of the actor-network: Ordering, strategy, and heterogeneity. *Systems practice, 5*(4), 379–393.
Lindell, J., Jansson, A., & Fast, K. (2021). I'm here! Conspicuous geomedia practices and the reproduction of social positions on social media. Information, Communication & Society, 1–20. https://doi.org/10.1080/1369118X.2021.1925322
Lupton, D. (2016). Digital companion species and eating data: Implications for theorising digital data–human assemblages. *Big Data & Society, 3*(1), 1–5. https://doi.org/10.1177/2053951715619947
Luque-Ayala, A., & Neves Maia, F. (2019). Digital territories: Google maps as a political technique in the re-making of urban informality. *Environment and Planning D: Society and space, 37*(3), 449–467.
Ma, R., & Kou, Y. (2021). "How advertiser-friendly is my video?": YouTuber's socioeconomic interactions with algorithmic content moderation. *Proceedings of the ACM on Human-Computer Interaction, 5*, 1–25.
McQuire, S. (2019). One map to rule them all? Google maps as digital technical object. *Communication and the Public, 4*(2), 150–165.

Middleton, S. E., Kordopatis-Zilos, G., Papadopoulos, S., & Kompatsiaris, Y. (2018). Location extraction from social media: Geoparsing, location disambiguation, and geotagging. *ACM Transactions on Information Systems (TOIS), 36*(4), 1–27.
Muniesa, F. (2011). Is a stock exchange a computer solution?: Explicitness, algorithms and the Arizona stock exchange. *International Journal of Actor-Network Theory and Technological Innovation (IJANTTI), 3*(1), 1–15.
Murero, M. (2020). Wearable internet for wellness and health interdigital territories of new technology. In B. Warf (Ed.), *Geographies of the internet* (pp. 334–350). Routledge.
Neresini, F. (2015). Quando i numeri diventano grandi: che cosa possiamo imparare dalla scienza. *Rassegna italiana di sociologia, 56*(3–4), 405–432.
Obermeyer, N. (2007, December). Thoughts on volunteered (geo) slavery. In *Workshop on volunteered geographic information, Santa Barbara, CA.*
Pasquale, F. (2015). *The black box society: The secret algorithms that control money and information.* Harvard University Press.
Pick, J. B. (2008). *Geo-business: GIS in the digital organization.* John Wiley & Sons.
Poser, K., & Dransch, D. (2010). Volunteered geographic information for disaster management with application to rapid flood damage estimation. *Geomatica, 64*(1), 89–98.
Primo, A., & Zago, G. (2015). Who and what do journalism? An actor-network perspective. *Digital Journalism, 3*(1), 38–52. https://doi.org/10.1080/21670811.2014.927987
Rogers, R. (2013). *Digital methods.* Mit Press.
Seaver, N. (2017). Algorithms as culture: Some tactics for the ethnography of algorithmic systems. *Big Data & Society, 4*(2), 1–12. https://doi.org/10.1177/2053951717738104
Shim, Y., & Shin, D.-H. (2016). Analyzing China's fintech industry from the perspective of actor–network theory. *Telecommunications Policy, 40*(2/3), 168–181. https://doi.org/10.1016/j.telpol.2015.11.005
Stefanidis, A., Crooks, A., & Radzikowski, J. (2013). Harvesting ambient geospatial information from social media feeds. *GeoJournal, 78*(2), 319–338.
Thielmann, T. (2010). Locative media and mediated localities: An introduction to media geography. *Aether the Journal of Media Geography, 5*, 1–17.
Wagner, B., Human, S., & Winkler, T. (2021). Bias in geographic information systems: The case of Google maps. In *Proceedings of the 54th Hawaii International Conference on System Sciences| 2021.* Hawaii International Conference on System Sciences.
Waldherr, A., Geise, S., & Katzenbach, C. (2019). Because technology matters: Theorizing interdependencies in computational communication science with actor-network theory. *International Journal of Communication, 13*, 3955–3975. 1932–8036/20190005
Wilken, R., & Goggin, G. (2015). *Locative media.* Routledge.

Enrica Amaturo is full Professor of Sociology at the Department of Social Sciences of the University of Naples Federico II, where she teaches Methodology of Social Research in BA degree in Sociology and Critical Epistemology in MA in Digital Sociology and Web Analysis, of which she is President. She is Coordinator of the Doctorate in Social Sciences and Statistics. She was Dean of the Faculty of Sociology and Director of the Department of Sociology and of Social Sciences at the same university. She was President of AIS - Italian Association of Sociology from 2016 to 2020 and, in the same years, Director of the Italian Sociology-AIS journal of Sociology, Egea, Milan. She recently published: *Critical Optimism: A Methodological Posture to Shape the Future of Digital Social Research.* Italian Sociological Review, 11, 2021 (with Aragona B.); *Digital Methods and the Evolution of the Epistemology of Social Sciences.* Data Science and Social Research II. DSSR 2019. Studies in Classification, Data Analysis, and Knowledge Organization, Springer, 2021 (with Aragona B.); *Per una epistemologia del digitale: note sull'uso di big data e computazione nella ricerca sociale.* Quaderni di Sociologia, 81, 2019 (with Aragona B.).

Ciro Clemente De Falco, PhD in Social Sciences and Statistics, is a research fellow at the Department of Social Sciences, University "Federico II" of Naples. He is member of F.A.S.T Observatory (Future, Algorithms, Society and Technology). His main scientific interests range around digital methods, ecological analysis, electoral behavior, and algorithms. He recently published: *Digital Mixed Content Analysis for the Study of Digital Platform Social Data: An Illustration from the Analysis of COVID-19 Risk Perception in the Italian Twittersphere.* Journal of Mixed Methods Research, 2022 (with Punziano G. and Trezza D.); *The Spatial Dimension in Social Media Analysis: Theoretical and Methodological Characteristics.* Handbook of Research on Advanced Research Methodologies for a Digital Society, IGI Global, 2022 (with Crescentini N. and Ferracci M.); *Tra geografia delle narrazioni e geografia dei contagi in Italia: il contributo dell'analisi spaziale e del contenuto dei tweet alla comprensione della pandemia.* Sociologia e Ricerca Sociale, 125, 2021 (with Punziano G. and Trezza D.).

Chapter 19
"Personal Influence" and Influencer Logic: A Theoretical and Methodological Comparison

Barbara Sonzogni

Digital Sociology

The changes that we have been witnessing for several decades are remarkable, starting with the birth of the Internet in 1969, going through the formation of the World Wide Web in the 1990s, to the mid-twenty-first century, which saw the birth of the first social networks, up to the consolidation of the so-called Web 2.0.

These developments have affected a wide range of scientific fields, and social sciences have also been called upon to face major challenges from an epistemological, theoretical and methodological standpoint (Savage & Burrows, 2007; Ciotti & Roncaglia, 2008; Ruppert et al., 2013; Mayer-Schönberger & Cukier, 2013; Kitchin, 2014a, 2014b; Marres & Gerlitz, 2016; Agnoli, 2016; Conte, 2016; Salganik, 2018). This led to the first articles and texts dealing with issues and topics specific to digital sociology (Wynn, 2009; Neal, 2010) until its academic institutionalisation in 2013 with the curatorship of Orton-Johnson and Prior entitled *Digital Sociology: Critical Perspectives* (2013). The expression "digital sociology" has now become part of the cultural lexicon as well as being specific to the discipline, which, as a branch of culture, communication and media sociology, is attracting a growing interest in the international context (Marres, 2012, 2017; Lupton, 2014).

Digital sociology is oriented towards considering two complementary aspects: examining the digital sphere not only as an object or technology but also as a field of study, considering what is happening as a real paradigm shift (*digital turn*) that the social sciences must take on as part of their purview (Caliandro & Gandini, 2019, pp. 17–18). This is an expression that has become increasingly used to indicate the new directions of sociological research towards digital technologies, which has

B. Sonzogni (✉)
Department of Communication and Social Research, Sapienza – University of Rome, Rome, Italy
e-mail: barbara.sonzogni@uniroma1.it

F. Comunello et al. (eds.), *What People Leave Behind*, Frontiers in Sociology and Social Research 7, https://doi.org/10.1007/978-3-031-11756-5_19

focused its attention on the implications of technology on what happens in our lives, with interest in the effects on, among other things, the relational dynamics of social life, behavioural models, the creation and definition of the self, the spread of forms of online social interaction and how social relations, consumption practices and inequalities change; the contexts in which they are used are also increasingly wide-ranging, e.g. consumption, work, local transport (Uber), hospitality (Airbnb) and industry.

It is not our intention here to reconstruct the rich debate that has developed on these issues but to highlight just a few elements that are useful for the discussion. In this context, it is a shared opinion that since then, people have really started to talk about big data, digital research and web social science, and, from then on, many have become interested in and expressed their views on this epochal change. The changes and challenges that scientific research has undergone and continues to undergo today have highlighted how, on the one hand, the empirical opportunities have increased and, on the other, the risks have increased as well. The reactions—as Veltri (2021, pp. 1 et seq.) summarises—can be identified with two prevailing positions: scepticism and enthusiasm. More specifically, the first position dealt with arguments about data quality, access and ownership, as well as the integration of online and offline data; the second position focused mainly on the fact that the wide availability of digital traces represented a breakthrough in the increasingly difficult collection of data. In addition to these two positions, there was also an intermediate proposal, somewhere between the two. A shared fact is that digital data has changed the way of doing science and research, so much so that even researchers who welcomed the shift from analogue to digital data with an initial enthusiasm related to the great potential were later involved in a reflection on research methodology.

The approach to the digital domain as a field of study arises primarily as a methodological question, in relation to the large amount of data available. An important issue here is the value of data. Its increasing obsolescence, caused by the rapidity of the whole research process, has meant that it has become cheaper, and, consequently, there has been a decrease in the quantity of data required for the planning and preparation phases of the analytical strategy.

The issue soon became also theoretical—as mentioned above—in the sense of an overall approach to the study of the digital sphere. Today, in fact, social action is closely interconnected and integrated with digital technology, so much so that digital contexts have become real social places from which society can be observed and measured (Marres & Gerlitz, 2016). A multitude of the social relationships in which we are involved take place in or are mediated by digital contexts. In this way, digital sociology has developed itself not only on methodological and theoretical levels but also on epistemological ones. From this last standpoint—as suggested by Caliandro and Gandini (2019, p. 20)—there are three relevant issues: the need to add to the media-centric perspective of cultural and media sociology a perspective that puts the social actor at the centre (see Jurgenson, 2011), the rejection of the conceptual and epistemological opposition between online and offline and the rejection of a technical-deterministic conception of digital media. From this perspective, studying the digital society means conceiving digital media and the social relations that take place in them in a unified framework, in a mutually inclusive vision, researching technology and society in a unified vision.

The perspective proposed by digital sociology stands as an alternative to the traditional dichotomy of qualitative and quantitative approaches (Natale & Airoldi, 2017), but not in terms of opposition but rather of complementarity, since it is "capable of supporting, triangulating and completing the study of social action in the Internet age" (Caliandro & Gandini, 2019, p. 15). The Internet is an object of analysis and a source of methods (Rogers, 2009).

Digital Methods

It is within the context of the debate outlined above that, starting from the well-known work of Richard Rogers *Digital Methods* (2009), digital methods (which traditionally straddle different disciplines, including media studies, digital humanities and social sciences) assert themselves as approaches, tools and methods suitable for studying digital environments with the aim, not so much of virtualising traditional research methods by adapting them to the virtual world and understanding how much culture and society are present online but, by overcoming the real-virtual dichotomy, of going beyond the study of online culture to study sociocultural changes using the Internet. In this regard, it is Rogers himself who indicates the importance of immersing oneself in the digital world under observation, "following the medium", following the technical strategies that the same environment uses in order to collect, organise, examine and structure the communication data flows of which it is made up. In this regard, digital methods should be considered as approaches, tools and methods suitable for studying digital environments in a "native" mode, which refers precisely to the natural way in which digital data is organised and which the researcher can use to study the social relations of the digital environment, the ways in which they are formed, maintained or ended, as well as the social and semantic structures that denote them (Caliandro & Gandini, 2019, p. 12). The researcher who moves in the digital world and with digital methods must bring to light networks of meaning (Geertz, 1973) and sociality that social actors and digital devices weave, for example, within social media around a specific object (brand, political issue, celebrities, etc.). Therefore, he or she must be oriented not so much towards identifying an online community but rather mapping the practices through which users and devices construct social formations around a moving object (Büscher & Urry, 2009).

The debate on the changes that characterise social research with the widespread use of the Internet, in general, and with the availability of so-called big data, in particular, has been open for many years now. Big data has gradually been defined in different ways and among the characteristics associated with it there are certainly the well-known "3vs" (Laney, 2001; Zikopoulos et al., 2011; Lombi, 2015): volume, which corresponds to the amount of data generated; variety, which concerns the diversity of formats and also refers to their possible lack of structure (different documents, social networks, microblogging platforms, etc.) and different sources (automatically generated, user-generated, etc.); and velocity, the speed with which data is made available. Big data can also be distinguished by further characteristics: exhaustiveness, which has to do with the difficulties of selecting a sample and its true representativeness; high resolution, resulting from the combined use of more defined visual data and the processes of indexing and tracking people and objects; relationality, the opportunity to link and aggregate data in order to create an amplifying effect (see Crampton et al., 2013); and flexibility, which refers to its adaptability and is considered by many to be the most interesting characteristic from a social science perspective (Aragona, 2016, pp. 44–45).

In the light of this, it can be argued that the characteristics of digital data have drawn attention to the need to use analytical approaches other than those defined as conventional in social sciences. Among quantitative analyses of digital data, three types can be identified: statistical methods of reducing the dimensionality of data, quantitative methods of analysing relational data (network analysis) and quantitative methods of analysing texts as unstructured data (including sentiment analysis). Finally, it should be pointed out that the focus on these categories of quantitative analysis does not mean that conventional descriptive and inferential techniques are no longer used; what is being pointed out is the fact that the nature of digital data makes these three techniques more common (Veltri, 2021).

With what has been said so far, the foundations have been laid for the development of the dialogue that lies at the heart of this intervention: the dialogue between modernity and tradition. Starting from the computational approach mentioned earlier, we have seen that three types of analysis have been identified. Two of these (sentiment analysis and network analysis) are those that will be compared with a proposal from the traditional theoretical landscape of social sciences (the themes of "personal influence" and the "two-step communication flow" theory).

Social Network Analysis

The *social network analysis* (SNA) originated with Jacob Levi Moreno's graph theory (1953). It stands as a variant of structural sociology that considers networks (relationships made up of contacts and exchanges), looking at the non-episodic relationships between social persons they delimit or create action opportunities for individuals.

The measurement of networks gives rise to data that is different from that of other social sciences and therefore a set of methods for its analysis has emerged (Barabási & Posfai, 2016), which has found wide application in the field of digital research; closely linked to this is the issue of reconstructing the networks generated by the use of social media. To this end, the footprints that each individual leaves behind are of the utmost importance, since it is possible to reconstruct links and identify strategic nodes from these; in fact, with the disclosure of one's opinions on the web, a mass of data (big data) has been created that is useful from various points of view (of institutions, political figures, brands, etc.) because of the impact it can have. In this regard, the usefulness and applications of SNA are many: reputation; perception of brands, characters and products; measurement of social media marketing activities; degree of satisfaction; improvement of services and products; prevention and management of online crises; identification of competitors; and identification of influencers.

It is clear that the research methods used in digital social research are not exclusive to SNA, but the same plays a very important role. Similarly, the analysis of online networks does not coincide with the study of social media, since not only the data that can be deduced from the latter, but all that corresponding to our digital traces (telephone calls, commercial transactions, movements signalled by GPS, etc.) can be analysed in the form of networks, and they represent an epistemological approach that is well suited to understanding a hyperconnected world (Easely & Kleinberg, 2010; Riva, 2011; Kramer et al., 2014). As Veltri (2021, pp. 125–127) suggests, at the basis of network analysis, there is an important change of perspective compared to what is usually done in social and behavioural sciences, where we are used to dealing with data by arranging them in matrices of cases by variables, assuming the independence of observations on individual units; therefore, data for different subjects does not depend on each other. This orientation, which is typical of methodological individualism, contrasts with that adopted by network analysis, namely, the constructivist-relationalist approach; in fact, SNA is interested precisely in the interrelationship between individual units, i.e. the relationships between subjects. Network-based theories conceive units as elements that do not act independently but influence each other; to test these theories, the measurement of networks is based on the use of structural or relational information.

Web Sentiment Analysis

In this context, one of the analysis tools that have become more widespread with the massive extension of social media is the "sentiment analysis" (Pang & Lee, 2008) (also called "social media analysis" or "web sentiment analysis") (SA), which is now being studied in both academic and commercial contexts. In this respect, it should be pointed out that SA is part of the more general content analysis (*text mining*) and that there are both qualitative and quantitative forms of content analysis. Specifically, it concerns the platforms, the expression of users' judgements and the computational analysis of feelings and opinions expressed within texts generated on the network by the interactions between users, concerning a product, a service, an individual, an event, etc., in a given space and time frame.

If we think about the era in which we live, the era of digital data, we all know that the texts generated by each user are growing by leaps and bounds and this presents a challenge in terms of the ability to analyse these quantities, which requires a combination of computational and conventional textual analysis methods. SA has found a certain application in the social sciences, becoming an interesting field of study, and its diffusion is closely linked to the availability of digital data in relation to opinions, assessments and judgements; one need only think of social media platforms, blogs and everything else that represents a vast source of data relating to people continuously expressing opinions on people or objects of the most varied kinds. On the one hand, it is a very widespread tool, just think of the numerous applications for its implementation made available by social media themselves (Facebook Insights, TweetStats, Google Analytics, etc.), as well as the availability of paid platforms offering this type of service/analysis (Talkwalker, Digimind, etc.). On the other hand, the methodological soundness of this type of analysis is frequently questioned, especially when compared to traditional (textual and other) analysis tools and techniques, such as telephone surveys and focus groups. Criticism and diffidence have mainly focused on the context, emotional ambiguity, sarcasm and the polysemous nature of language, and although the algorithms underlying the tests have not been able to predict with very high accuracy the feelings associated with people (Saif et al., 2013, 2014; Bravo-Marquez et al., 2014; Vora & Chacko, 2017), this is a field that is finding wide application and growth in many areas.

This issue has recently been addressed in the literature of the sector, which, besides having dealt with some methodological issues concerning the use of digital footprints and the data provided by them (accessibility in view of commercial and/or legal limitations, ethics in their free use, representativeness), has highlighted how the two perspectives (traditional and modern), instead of being opposed, can be used in an integrated manner.

Tradition and Modernity. Comparing Perspectives

"Personal Influence"

In this framework, a further element of interest, which is the focus of this contribution, concerns the comparison between the scenario offered by the analysis of digital footprints through the above-mentioned network and sentiment analysis and the well-known "two-step communication flow theory". Expounded for the first time in 1944 by Paul Lazarsfeld and subsequently revised with Elihu Katz in 1955, this theory addresses the methodological, as well as substantive, problem of studying the effects of mass media, investigating both the effect of communication *between* people and *on* people. In addition to proposing a revision of the approach to mass media that takes into account the individual, the web of ties that he or she weaves, the small groups in which he or she participates and the social conditioning on the existential dimension of the subject, the study goes further, offering fundamental contributions regarding the pervasiveness of conditioning, the network structures of such conditioning, highlighting the subtle tools that it uses and the strength of the drive that it has towards the internalisation of values (Ferrarotti, 1968, pp. VII et seq.).

The expansion of mass media (TV, cinema, radio, press) described by Katz and Lazarsfeld refers to technical innovations affecting the specific sphere of culture; it is analogous to the industrialisation process affecting the economic and labour spheres. Both contexts are thus involved in a process of rationalisation. However, while the phenomenon of industrialisation is structurally oriented and therefore outlines linear research vectors, on the other hand, the role played by mass media is placed at a superstructural level and, by virtue of its greater complexity (influences intersect with action, full of stimuli and proposals), leads to more complex methodology issues (Ferrarotti, 1968, p. IX).

The aim of the research is to understand the effects of mass media, measuring their influence on people's behaviour and psychology. Specifically, there were two directions followed in the research of the time: the first was typical of public opinion surveys and was characterised by the search for correlations between social factors and changes in circulation; the second was the search for "pure" *effectiveness*, the ideal flow from the media to the public, directing its opinions. It is clear that the critical debate on this last approach has been and still is full of doubts and stimuli, especially in the direction of the actual feasibility of an intent such as that just described.

One of the central points, in terms of its originality, of the research proposed by the authors of *Personal Influence* is the role accorded to the small group, placed between "communication" and "mass", with the web of interpersonal relations that constitute it. In this sense, both from the point of view of theory and research, attention is drawn to the connection between the study of the informal group and the study of the effects of mass communication (Statera, 1968, p. XXX). The orientations within the study of the effects of mass media in those years were characterised by two opposing positions: those who saw them as a democratic instrument giving everyone equal access to information and those who saw them as diabolical agents aiming at the destruction of democracy. Far from being in contrast—as Katz and Lazarsfeld point out in the beginning of their book—the two conceptions of the function of mass media actually have the same image of the mass communication process: "a new kind of unifying force" that extends and reaches out to every individual "in a society characterised by a scarcity of interpersonal relationships and an amorphous social organisation" (1955, p. 4).

Precisely interpersonal relations have been accorded such centrality that someone has spoken of the "discovery of 'people'" (Katz & Lazarsfeld, 1955, pp. 11 et seq.), attributing to interpersonal relations the role of a variable intervening in the mass communication process. Research shows that opinion formation and possible change are linked to a specific factor: *personal influence*. Individuals are subject to the influence of the people they come into contact with in small groups (family, colleagues, friends, etc.), among whom some are characterised as *opinion leaders*; the latter, in turn, are influenced by mass media to a greater extent than non-leaders. From this dual process comes the idea of the *two phases of the communication flow*. "In short: ideas seem to pass *from* the radio and *from* the press *to* the opinion leaders and *from* them *to* the less active sectors of the population" (Katz & Lazarsfeld, 1955, p. 16).

In this framework, we outline how opinion leaders are present in all social and economic strata and how they are an integral part of the interaction that takes place on a daily basis in personal relations; therefore, interpersonal relations are potential communication networks within which the opinion leader, as a member of a group, plays a fundamental role of communication towards the other members with whom he or she is in contact.

The research project carried out by the two authors is a complex one, which is why we have chosen to deal here only with those topics that are relevant to what we intend to discuss. The definition of communication flow networks has highlighted some important concepts that—as will be shown later—are well connected to some tools used in the field of digital methods and mentioned above. To this end, and in addition to what has already been said, it is worth drawing attention to the fact that, in the work plan drawn up by Katz and Lazarsfeld, space was devoted to an in-depth examination of the structural connections inherent in the social ties between individuals and how they influence interpersonal communication. In this intention to delve into interpersonal transmission models, the reference to Moreno's sociometric technique (1953) is made explicit directly by the authors. A subsequent step is aimed at identifying strategic transmission roles in the interaction with others and at this point of the work Leavitt's concept of "centrality" (1952) is recalled to describe the degree of access of a subject to all the other subjects in the group, linking it to the role of leader.

Moreover, it should be pointed out that the two American authors were specifically interested in the analysis of political propaganda and commercial advertising; digital methods are also said to have originated as a qualitative-quantitative approach mainly functional to the study of political issues emerging on the web (Rogers, 2013). However, beyond the investigated phenomenon, it has been seen that the research highlighted a structure of the influencing process, which we defined above as the ideal flow *(effectiveness)* going from the media to the public and directing their opinions. Over the years, this proposal has had a rich series of applications and revisitations (Postmes, 1997; Liu, 2007; Park, 2018), among which we specifically mention Jensen's (2009).

As can be seen from the figure below, the proposal draws a parallel between the two-step model of 1944 and its 2009 version. The latter is clearly a modern adaptation to the specific context of digital social networks, which are really the third step added to the original version. What changes further are the individual contacts with the opinion leaders: while in the original model these are undirected contacts, in the revised version, they are not only directional but even two-way (Fig. 19.1).

Katz and Lazarsfeld proposed a two-step communication pattern that was witnessed in different contexts (industrial, urban community, etc.). That model, in a version adapted to digital communication, is still present and valid today, with a few additions. In short, we could say that the medium has changed and the modes have adapted: in the past, the conditioning of opinions took place through traditional media, such as TV; today the stage has changed to social media. In this respect, it is

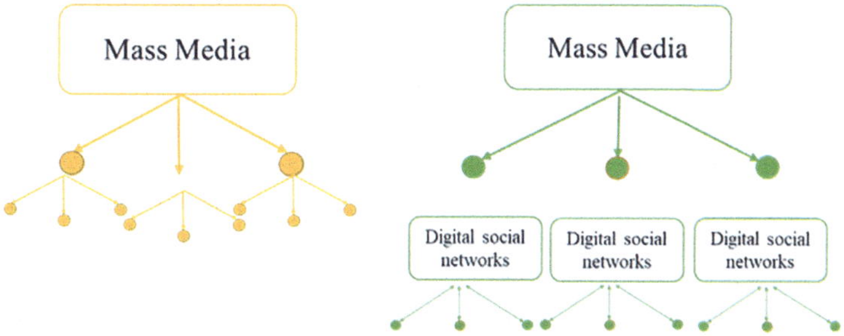

Fig. 19.1 Two-step flow (Lazarsfled et al., 1944) and three-step flow (Jensen, 2009) comparison

fair to note that the changes in communication modes offer a much more interesting panorama in some respects.

Influencer Logic

Although the expression "digital society" refers to a vast complex of relations, objects, environments and actors and although social media are not an exclusive part of the analysis of the ways in which social actors act in forms mediated by technology, it has been said that social media, as social spaces, represent one of the primary objects of interest of digital sociology (Caliandro & Gandini, 2019, p. 20) and within them the activity of figures identified as "influencers" takes place. Whereas in the past, speakers, communicators, political figures and leaders used the streets and then the traditional means of communication—those studied by Katz and Lazarsfeld, for example—to speak to the masses, today's influencers use social media.

At this point in the work, we could say that "the concept of opinion leader and that of influencer are not far apart", aware that this would provoke a not very positive reaction, not to say disconcertment. Well-aware of the importance of the Katz-Lazarsfeldian tradition and of the undeniable disruption with which modernity pervades our lives, as individuals and as researchers, we cannot deny—even though some scholars consider it lacking in scientific depth—the notion, the figure and the role that influencers play nowadays. As a first step, we would like to draw attention to the fact that when we talk about influencers, a variety of people who have become known through social media come to mind, and very often we think of people who are the object of the most disparate criticism, on the one hand, and of the most total veneration, on the other. In this respect, however, it is worth emphasising that this ambivalent figure has a central role and exerts its presence with respect to a plurality of interests (such as the political sphere, the measurement of reputation, the assessment of marketing activities) and in a variety of contexts (tourism, fashion, sports, food, etc.) (Senft, 2008; Ejarque, 2015; Viviani, 2017; Del Franco García & Segado

Sánchez-Cabezudo, 2016; Olietti & Musso, 2018; Braves et al., 2019; We are social, 2022).

In the virtual world, one can most often read and listen to opinions on this subject, and many times—whether rightly or not is not for us to determine here—other issues are called into question (sexism, minorities, power, etc.). The debate is mostly characterised by regarding the word "influencer" as a synonym for stupid, superficial; to call someone an influencer is to mock them and belittle what they do. Someone else countered by saying that this happens "since this is an activity in which women are on average more successful". Others point out that, in reality, influencers require more skills than one imagines: a good knowledge of marketing, video-photographic skills, writing and storytelling abilities, as well as qualities such as empathy and the ability to create a bond with the audience, continuous updating and constancy.

First of all, however, it should be borne in mind that influence is a complex phenomenon closely linked to cultural, psychological, economic, communicative, political and social aspects. In the age of digital media, studying and understanding influence and how it works has become increasingly complex. In such a framework, the issue of digital influence, taking into account the various points of observation, has been the subject of in-depth studies that have led to numerous studies and theorisations on the subject, at the centre of which is the figure of the influencer (Polesana & Vagni, 2021), which, therefore, leads to the creation of a true "influencer logic".

But what is the meaning of the word "influencer"? Actually, influencers are those who have a large following on social media, regardless of the topics they talk about (make-up, sustainability, science), and, unlike any other user, influencers are able to influence their numerous followers with their opinions, generating strong opinion trends, so much so that the opinion of an influencer cascades over a number of other online users who largely align themselves with their point of view. For example, influencer marketing uses this effect to give maximum visibility to a brand or product, accompanying it with a halo of acceptance. Having an influencer who speaks well of a product means gaining the interest and attention of at least one segment of followers, who will be inclined to perceive and/or evaluate the brand or product in a positive way precisely because the influencer has pointed it out and spoken positively about it.

Are there any characteristics that make it possible to identify an influencer? The main ones are five:

(a) High number of followers. There are different classifications of influencers based on the number of fans, one of which, by way of example, which is considered valid in the Italian context, classifies them into micro influencers (from 5000 to 20,000 followers), middle influencers (from 20,000 to 150,000 followers) and top influencers (above 150,000 followers). Niche areas, such as those with a strong technical and scientific characterisation, should be excluded from these groupings, for which the numbers are certainly lower.

(b) Original and relevant content. Influencers are characterised by publishing valuable content with a certain ability to address topics and an approach strongly characterised by a personal style, clarity, incisiveness and empathy.
(c) High engagement. One of the main characteristics that distinguishes an influencer is the ability to dialogue and interact with the audience, so as to be a reference point for the latter in creating opinions. This can be detected through some typical social traits, such as instant interactions (likes, tweets), shares, comments and replies to comments.
(d) Charisma and identifiability. The influencer is distinguished by being a person with a strong character who makes the way something is said almost more important than the content itself.
(e) Ability to persuade. A characteristic trait is to be able to induce followers to follow one's suggestions. An influencer differs from a simple columnist in that he or she does not just give advice or propose ideas but is able to influence the choices and actions of followers, inducing a positive reaction in terms of adherence (comments, reactions).

The above characteristics should be understood in combination with each other. Thus, for example, any classification of influencers based solely on the number of followers is not effective; it is necessary to consider the type of relationship, the level of consideration that followers have for the influencer. Furthermore, with regard to engagement, a post addressed to a pool of tens of thousands of users may receive no reaction, which denotes little influence on followers, while a post that receives many comments but no counter-response from the influencer indicates a lack of relational availability, which in turn implies a lower capacity to influence. For this reason, many companies relying on influencer marketing increasingly prefer to focus on micro influencers, who have a smaller number of followers but are still able to interact directly with them. This is the reason why companies often prefer these influencers, because they are more likely to create a network of direct relationships. Therefore, they are characterised by greater credibility and, consequently, their ability to influence users' decisions is greatest. On the other hand, influencers with a large number of followers most likely will not be able to relate directly to their fans, thus losing their persuasive effect.

Concluding Remarks: Personal Influence vs Influencer Logic

In the digital age, there are an increasing number of areas where the footprints we leave behind (voluntarily or not) become relevant for the use (legitimate or not) that can be made of them, creating new broad scenarios of analysis in different fields of interest: politics, stock markets, communication and marketing, sports and medical and natural sciences. By surfing the web from any device (mobile phone, tablet, personal computer), each of us now leaves footprints. As explained above, this changing landscape has posed and continues to pose challenges for social sciences,

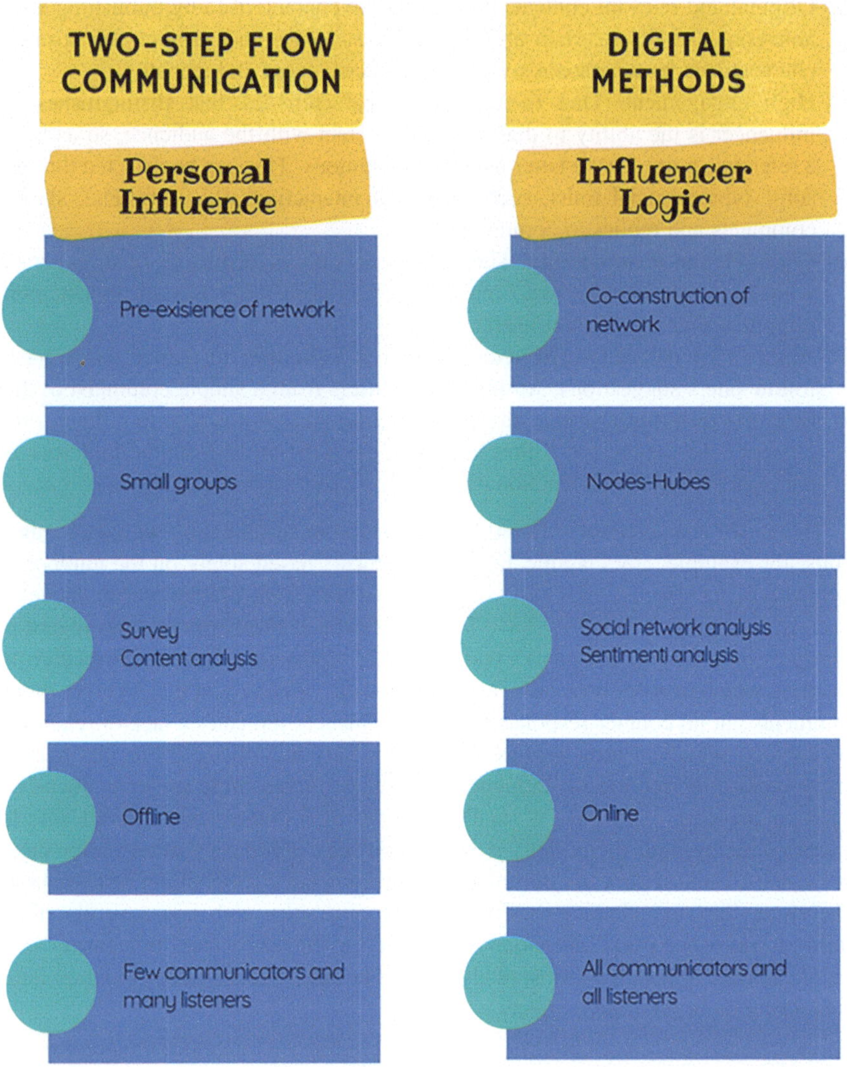

Fig. 19.2 A theoretical and methodological comparison between personal influence and influencer logic

which are called upon to reflect on new issues from both a theoretical and empirical perspective. In this regard, the use of research tools, such as those discussed in this paper, poses many questions to the researcher regarding their robustness, also in comparison to traditional research methods and techniques. The diagram in the figure represents the central focus of this exposition (Fig. 19.2).

What has been discussed so far lays the groundwork for the comparison announced at the beginning of this paper between the proposal of the Katz-

Lazarsdelfian tradition of the notion of *personal influence* and the one of *influencer logic*. Starting from this comparison, the question is whether what is happening in the field of the analysis of the big data provided by the spread of the digital footprint is capable of adding some new element to what has already been highlighted by the "two-step communication theory", or whether it simply represents its explication. Is something happening that Katz and Lazarsfeld predicted? Or do the analyses of networks and feelings even conflict or contradict the two authors?

Pre-existence of Networks and Co-construction of Networks A first point for reflection is that the underlying logic is not dissimilar: the 1944 proposal placed at the centre of the process of influence that the media exerted on the population the figure of the opinion leaders who, through their personal influence, played a strategic role in the dissemination of opinions among opinion followers; today influencers exert their influence in the dissemination of opinions through digital channels by creating contacts with their followers. However, while the concept of "personal influence" presupposes the existence of networks and influence that pre-exist the communication flow, the concept of "influencer" seems to allude to the fact that nodes are, in some ways, created by the very use of communication, in a logic of co-construction of networks.

In this respect, we recall that unlike virtual methods (Hine, 2005), which involve adapting methodological strategies developed offline to digital environments, digital methods use the nature and affordances of online environments to understand how digital devices (search engines, social platforms, functions such as retweeting) structure communication and interaction flows on the Internet (Caliandro & Gandini, 2019, pp. 38–39). Close attention should be paid to the "structuring" concept. The inspiration comes from the well-known *action-network theory* of Bruno Latour (1988) and Michel Callon (1986), a theoretical and methodological approach that investigates the network of relations between human beings and material objects and the consequent co-construction of social reality resulting from their interaction. Digital users and devices, human and non-human actors, are "co-authors of social research, as they provide the researcher with the so-called 'naturally digital methods' necessary for the analysis of digital life forms and the emic categories for their interpretation" (Caliandro & Gandini, 2019, p. 39). From this perspective, social media represent such a fluid and dynamic reality that social formations are to be considered as a result of the activity of actors, rather than a starting point for analysis (Postill, 2016).

Small Groups and Nodes-Hubs Of course, the nature of the contacts between the two compared situations is not the same, the former involving face-to-face contacts, the latter virtual contacts. In this regard, let us return for a moment to Katz and Lazarsfeld's proposal, to recall that one of the central points to which they turn their attention in their model of communication flow and to which they also devote a paragraph in Chap. 2 was "The 'rediscovery' of the small group", "highlighting how they reached the idea that primary interpersonal relations could be an important intervening variable in the process of mass communication" (Katz & Lazarsfeld, 1955, p. 17). The authors thus explore different contexts in which this rediscovery can be witnessed: the industrial context, the armed forces, the urban community context, specifying "the common elements in this pattern of rediscovery".

Well, what does this have to do with influencers, if some claim that "social media makes us more lonely" (Turkle, 2011)? It should be remembered—as mentioned in the first part of the paper—that the epistemological perspective underlying digital sociology rejects the techno-deterministic perspective; from this standpoint, it is therefore the way in which people nowadays live their online relationships that makes the difference. The technological medium does not come between the interacting parties; it is used for and is part of the interaction itself.

This is not the place to provide a complete picture of SNA, but it is interesting to highlight which key concepts are relevant to the parallel we are presenting between "modernity and tradition". Even those who have little knowledge of SNA know that when analysing networks we are dealing with *actors* (also called *nodes*) and *links* (between these actors). There are some concepts that highlight the connection between the SNA and the perspective of Katz and Lazarsfeld. Among the basic metrics used in network analysis, we find the concept of *centrality* and, specifically *degree centrality*, which can indicate how easily actors with another *out-degree centrality* can exchange information with others or quickly spread it to many; this is the case of highly influential nodes-actors (Veltri, 2012); *betweenness centrality* measures the degree to which a node is connected to other nodes that are not connected to each other, i.e. the degree to which a node acts as a bridge. Nodes-actors with a high value of this measure can have considerable influence within a network by virtue of the control they have over the passage of information between others (Veltri, 2021, pp. 135–137). Furthermore, among the types of networks, we identify the *ego network*, which is based on a model in which there is a subject (*ego*) and all the people with whom he or she has a social link *(alter*) who are arranged in a series of four or five inclusive groups (circles), depending on the strength of their social links (Veltri, 2021, pp. 138–139). Finally, among the properties of networks, based on the structure and model of the network, the so-called *scale free* network, characterised by the fact that the number of links from a given node, shows a distribution that follows the power law (*power low distribution*), which results in many actors-nodes with few links and few actors (the *hubs*) with a large number of links (see Barabási & Albert, 1999), hence, the ability of these *hub* actors to greatly influence other hubs because they are connected to so many people that the likelihood of them being connected to others who are easily persuaded is high (Veltri, 2021, pp. 142–144).

Survey, Content Analysis and Social Network Analysis and Sentiment Analysis As with the previous point, from a technical-methodological standpoint, a change in the context and the way our lives and the interactions that take place in them are carried out is followed by an adaptation of the investigation tools and methods. Thus, whereas Katz and Lazarsfeld's research used questionnaire surveys and content analysis, in social media social, we use network analysis and sentiment analysis.

From Offline to Online but with the Same Need to Belong and Assert One's Identity This is evident, for example, when it comes to consumption. Let's try to think about the concept of fashion as it has changed over time. In the 1960s mini-skirts were worn and were also a symbol of women's emancipation, and in the 1970s the hippies chose a certain type of clothing as a sign of non-conformity; today there are punk and hipster styles. All these people share a claim to their freedom, a common need. Why should the 4.0 consumer be just a puppet at the mercy of good social marketers? Is it not the case that today, as in the past (if not even more so than in the past), the weakening of traditional ties has led to a landscape in which collectivity has been replaced by individuality but in the end the need to feel part of a community, to feel the strength of ties, the belonging to an identity has become urgent?

The search for an identity, a sense of belonging, leads to a desire for sharing, which often finds a response and space in the virtual community, which is a powerful tool for social representation. One answer—right or wrong—can be found on social channels and in the figures of influencers. Whether or not this is a bluff is not for us to determine. What needs to be emphasised is the fact that, both in sociology's own digital methods and in our own lives, the transition from online to offline life is fluid. Therefore, also as digital social scientists, it is perhaps good to become aware of the changed theoretical and methodological frameworks, in order to be able to make (possibly critical) use of them.

From "Few Communicators and Many Listeners" to "All Communicators and All Listeners" In the days of traditional mass media, most people were spectators and users, playing a passive role in receiving information, and just a few people had a voice. Today more people can speak (potentially everyone), and this also offers more freedom in choosing who to listen to. Therefore, it is not only the role of the communicators that is changed but also that of the listeners/followers.

This links to other crucial issues, such as power and minorities. Power is a privilege, and having access to the media (especially if it is widely distributed) is an opportunity for those who can speak out and a threat for those who would like to control communications in order to choose what is right to convey and what is not. If in the past there was only one story, today there are many stories. Among these stories there are more or less authoritative voices, more or less able to influence, but just as there is freedom to express oneself, there is also the freedom to choose who and what to listen to. That is why it is not so proper to use the word "influencer" with disdain, just because there are people who are more competent or more capable of using digital media to promote battles, themselves, products and why not to sell a powder pink or neon coloured nail polish worn by a man.

References

Agnoli, M. S. (2016). L'arte intellettuale al cospetto dei big data. *Sociologia e ricerca sociale, 109*, 7–17.

Aragona, B. (2016). Big data or data that are getting bigger? *Sociologia e ricerca sociale, 109*, 54–69.

Barabási, A. L., & Albert, T. (1999). Emergence of scaling in random networks. *Science, 286*, 509–512.

Barabási, A. L., & Posfai, M. (2016). *Network science*. Cambridge University Press.

Braves, P. L., Liebers, N., Abt, M., & Kunze, A. (2019). The perceived fit between Instagram influencers and the endorses brand. How influencer-brand fit affects source credibility and persuasive effectiveness. *Journal of Advertisini Research, 59*(4), 440–455.

Bravo-Marquez, F., Mendoza, M., & Poblete, B. (2014). Meta-level sentiment models for big social data analysis. *Knowledge-Based Systems, 69*(1), 86–99.

Büscher, M., & Urry, J. (2009). Mobile methods and the empirical. *European Journal of Social Theory, 12*(1), 99–116.

Caliandro, A., & Gandini, A. (2019). *I metodi digitali nella ricerca sociale*. Carocci.

Callon, M. (1986). Some elements of a sociology of translation domestication of the scallops and the fishermen of St. Brieux Bay. In J. Law (Ed.), *Power, action and belief: A new sociology of knowledge* (pp. 196–229). Routledge.

Ciotti, G., & Roncaglia, F. (2008). *Il mondo digitale. Introduzione ai nuovi media*. Laterza.

Conte, R. (2016). Big data: un'opportunità per le scienze sociali? *Sociologia e ricerca sociale, 109*, 18–27.

Crampton, J., Graham, M., Poorthuis, A., Shelton, T., Stephens, M., Wilson, M., & Zook, M. (2013). Beyond the geotag? Deconstructing 'big data' and leveraging the potential of the Geoweb. *SSRN Electronic Journal*. https://doi.org/10.2139/ssrn.2253918

Del Franco García, M., & Segado Sánchez-Cabezudo, A. D. (2016). Identifying the new influencers in the internet era: Social media and social network analysis. *Revista Española de Investigaciones Sociológicas, 153*, 23–40.

Easely, D., & Kleinberg, J. (2010). *Networks, crowds, and markets: Reasoning about a highly connected world*. Cambridge University Press.

Ejarque, J. (2015). *Social media marketing per il turismo. Come costruire il marketing 2.0 e gestire la reputazione della destinazione*. Hoepli.

Ferrarotti, F. (1968). Prefazione. In E. Katz & P. F. Lazarsfeld (Eds.), *L'influenza personale nelle comunicazioni di massa* (pp. XVII–XXXII). Edizione Rai Radiotelevisione Italiana.

Geertz, C. (1973). *The interpretation of cultures*. Basic Books.

Hine, C. (2005). Virtual methods: Issues in social research on the internet. .

Jensen, K. B. (2009). Three-step flow. *Journalism, 10*(3), 335–337. https://doi.org/10.1177/1464884909102594

Jurgenson, N. (2011). *Digital dualism versus augmented reality. The Society Pages.*. https://thesocietypages.org/cyborology/?s=Digital+dualism+versus+augmented+reality

Katz, E., & Lazarsfeld, P. F. (1955). *Personal influence: The part played by people in the flow of mass communications*. Free Press. *L'influenza personale nelle comunicazioni di Massa* (1968). Edizioni rai Radiotelevisione Italiana.

Kitchin, R. (2014a). *The data revolution*. Sage.

Kitchin, R. (2014b). Big data, new epistemologies and paradigm shifts. *Big Data & Society, 1*(1), 2053951714528481. https://doi.org/10.1177/2053951714528481

Kramer, A. D. I., Guillory, J. E., & Hancock, J. T. (2014). Experimental evidence of massive-scale emotional contagion through social networks. *PNAS, 111*(24), 8788–8790. https://doi.org/10.1073/pnas.1320040111

Laney, D. (2001). 3D data management: Controlling data volume, velocity and variety. *META Group Research Note, 6*. http://blogs.gartner.com/doug-laney/files/2012/01/ad949-3D-Data-Management-Controlling-Data-Volume-Velocity-and-Variety.pdf.

Latour, B. (1988). Mixing humans and nonhumans together: The sociology of a door-closer. *Social Problems, 35*(2), 289–310.

Lazarsfled, P. F., Berelson, B., & Gaudet, H. (1944). *The people's choice*. Columbia University Press.

Leavitt, H. J. (1952). Some effects of certain communications patterns on group performance. In G. E. Swanson, T. M. Newcomb, & E. L. Hartley (Eds.), *Readings in social psychology*. Free Press.

Liu, F. C. S. (2007). Constrained opinion leader influence in an electoral campaign season: Revisiting the two-step flow theory with multi-agent simulation. *Advances in Complex Systems, 10*(2), 233–250. https://doi.org/10.1142/S0219525907001008

Lombi, L. (2015). La ricerca sociale al tempo dei Big Data: sfide e prospettive. *Studi di Sociologia, 2*, 215–227.

Lupton, D. (2014). *Digital sociology*. Routledge.

Marres, N. (2012). The redistribution of methods: On intervention in digital social research broadly conceived. *The Sociological Review, 60*, 139–165.

Marres, N. (2017). *Digital sociology. The Reinvention of social research*. Wiley & Sons.

Marres, N., & Gerlitz, C. (2016). Interface methods: Renegotiating relations between digital social research, STS and sociology. *The Sociological Review, 64*(1), 21–46.

Mayer-Schönberger, R., & Cukier, K. (2013). *Big data: A revolution that transforms how we work, live, and think*. Houghthon Mifflin.

Moreno, J. L. (1953). *Who shall survive? Foundations of sociometry, group psychotherapy and sociodrama*. Beacon House.

Natale, P., & Airoldi, M. (2017). *Web & social media: le tecniche di analisi*. Maggioli Editore.

Neal, R. (2010). *Expanding sentience: Introducing digital sociology for moving beyond buzz metrics in a world of growing online socialization*. Lulu Press.

Olietti A., & Musso P. (2018). Turismo digitale. In viaggio tra i click. .

Orton-Johnson, K., & Prior, N. (Eds.). (2013). *Digital sociology: Critical perspectives*. Houndmills.

Pang, B., & Lee, L. J. (2008). *Opinion mining and sentiment analysis*. Now Publisher.

Park, C. S. (2018). Revisiting the two-step flow model on twitter: Interconnection of self-identified south Korean twitter opinion leadership, news consumption, news links, and news curation. *Association for Education in Journalism and Mass Communication, 13*(2), 63–77. https://doi.org/10.1177/1931243118809780

Polesana, M. A., & Vagni, T. (Eds.). (2021). *L'influenza digitale. Studi, teorie e ricerche*. Guerini Scientifica.

Postill, J. (2016). Researching social worlds. In S. Pink et al. (Eds.), *Digital ethnography: Principles and practices* (pp. 101–122). Sage.

Postmes, T. T. (1997). *Social influence in computer mediated groups*. Universiteit van Amsterdam.

Riva, G. (2011). *I social network*. Il Mulino.

Rogers, R. (2009). *The end of the virtual: Digital methods*. Amsterdam University Press.

Rogers, R. (2013). *Digital methods*. MIT Press.

Ruppert, E., Law, J., & Savage, M. (2013). Reassembling social methods: The challenge of digital devices. *Theory, Culture, & Society, 30*(4), 22–46.

Saif, H., Fernez, M., He, Y., & Alani, H. (2013). Evaluation datasets for twitter sentiment analysis: A survey and a new dataset, the STS-gold. In *1st International Workshop on Emotion and Sentiment in Social and Expressive Media: Approaches and Perspectives from AI (ESSEM 2013)*, Turin, Italy.

Saif, H., Fernandez, M., He, Y., & Alani, H. (2014). *SentiCircles for contextual and conceptual semantic sentiment analysis of twitter*. 11th International Conference on Semantic Web: Trends and Challenges (ESWC 2014), Crete, Greece.

Salganik, M. J. (2018). *Bit by bit: Social research in the digital age*. Princeton University Press.

Savage, M., & Burrows, R. (2007). *The coming crisis of empirical sociology*. SAGE Publications.

Senft, T. M. (2008). *Camgirls: Celebrity & community in the age of social networks*. Peter Lang.

Statera, G. (1968). Introduzione. In E. Katz, & P. F. Lazarsfeld, *L'influenza personale nelle comunicazioni di massa* (pp. V-XV). Edizione Rai Radiotelevisione Italiana.
Turkle, S. (2011). *Alone together: Why we expect more from technology and less from each other.* Basic Books.
Veltri, G. A. (2012). Information flows and centrality among elite European newspapers. *European Journal of Communication, 27*(4), 354–375.
Veltri, G. A. (2021). *La ricerca sociale digitale*. Mondadori.
Viviani, D. (2017). Masterspot. Testimonial and food advertising. *Micro & Macro, 3*, 473–486.
Vora, J., & Chacko, A. M. (2017). Sentiment analysis of tweets to identify the correlated factors that influence an issue of interest. In *2017 2nd International Conference on Telecommunication and Networks (TEL-NET)*, 1–6.
We are social, Hootsuite (2022). Digital 2022. https://wearesocial.com/it/blog/2022/01/digital-2022-i-dati-globali/
Wynn, J. (2009). Digital sociology: Emergent technologies in the field and the classroom. *Sociological Forum, 24*(2), 448–456.
Zikopoulos, P., Eaton, C., De Roos, D., Deutsch, T., & Lapis, G. (2011). *Understanding big data: Analytics for enterprise class hadoop and streaming data*. McGraw-Hill.

Barbara Sonzogni is Associate Professor of Sociology at the Department of Communication and Social Research, Sapienza University of Rome, where she received also her PhD in "Methodology of Social Sciences". Her main scientific interests include sociological historiography, sociology of knowledge, sociology of culture, political sociology, digital social research and, within the methodology, the applications and developments of agent-based social simulation. Her fields of research are deviance, interethnic coexistence, social policies, religiosity, network analysis and lifestyles.

She teaches theory and technique of social simulation at the Inter-University Master's Degree Course in "Sociology: theory, methodology, research" at the University of Rome, and she is a member of the Doctoral Scientific Council in "Communication, Social Research and Marketing" at Sapienza University of Rome.

Her contributions include, for Springer, *An Agent Based Model of Camorra: Comparing Punishment and Norm-Based Policies in Contrasting Illegal Activities* (with Cecconi F., Andrighetto G., Conte R), in A. Herzig, E. Lorini (eds. by), 2015, and *The Cognitive Foundations of Group Attitudes and Social Interaction* (2015). Also, *Improving Social Stability: A Democracy Perception Analysis in the European Area* (with Marconi L., Cecconi F.), in "Sociologia" (2021); *Gli stili di vita: Una prospettiva junghiana* (with D'Ambrosio G.), in Bonolis M. (ed. by); and *Lo "spirito" nell'anima: Indagine sulla spiritualità giovanile* (2020).

Chapter 20
What People Leave Behind Online: Digital Traces and Web-Mediated Documents for Social Research

Laura Arosio

What People Leave Behind (Online)

Individuals and groups leave evidence of their lives when they are engaged in their activities. They move through time and space and modify the environments in which they live, leaving behind signs of their passage. These signs include a variety of materials that differ in content and form, such as written texts, images, material objects, audio tracks, links, maps, metadata and hypertexts. They may relate to personal interests, have to do with larger organizations or be cultural products. This evidence is not created for research purposes, but it can provide a great deal of insight into individual and group behaviours, attitudes and values (Webb et al., 1966).

Leaving behind a sign of one's activities has been part of the human condition since the first appearance of humankind, and it is seen as a necessity for maintaining memory and ensuring the existence of the world in which people live (Gleick, 2011). This process has accelerated in certain historical contexts and because of breakthroughs in communications (such as the introduction of writing, printing and mass media) or even technical progress in the field of manufacturing and transportation.

The creation of a vast amount of documentation, generally in written form, has become a constituent of contemporary societies. We can consider Max Weber's idea of bureaucracy (Weber, 1922) and Jacques Derrida's reflection on writing to be characteristic elements of our age (Derrida, 1967). These materials are thought of as a source of legitimation of the existence of groups and organizations and of the activity of individuals. In this respect, a practice such as photography becomes a tool for people to make everyday experiences "real" (Sontag, 1977). In addition, in contemporary societies, there has been a continuing trend towards the creation and

---

L. Arosio (✉)
Department of Sociology and Social Research, University of Milano-Bicocca, Milan, Italy
e-mail: laura.arosio@unimib.it

F. Comunello et al. (eds.), *What People Leave Behind*, Frontiers in Sociology and Social Research 7, https://doi.org/10.1007/978-3-031-11756-5_20

spread of material objects, whether mass-produced or personalized, that circulate on a planetary level and are charged with meaning for those who produce and consume them (Kopytoff, 1986; Appadurai, 1986).

Today, the advent of new information technologies and the growth of the World Wide Web have encouraged the creation, dissemination and preservation of many different types of materials that people leave behind online. The Web is a place of interaction in which a very large number of people move about, spend time and practice a variety of activities, leaving signs of their passage. In surfing the Net, people produce a large amount of material on different topics. These materials are stored and recorded in different places, such as on personal and institutional devices, in forums and on blogs and social network pages.

With the advent of the Internet, many aspects of social life have been coded and quantified, and these data have been stored and potentially made available to third parties (see the concept of datafication by Mayer, Schoenberger and Cuki (Mayer-Schonberger and Cukier 2013) and its critics (see van Dijck, 2014)). The use of new technologies has introduced a revolution that is not only technological but also social and cultural (among others, see the idea of *documediality* (Ferraris & Martino, 2018) and *self-tracking culture* (Lupton, 2019)). These changes bring a new kind of reflexivity and can be read as opening a new era of social sciences (Boullier, 2015).

The materials that individuals and groups leave behind while performing their online activities can provide much information about their behaviours, values and ways of thinking. Messages, posts, photos, videos, audio files, searches and online activities become persistent data that account for a wide range of experiences. As some scholars have argued, digital data can be seen as a kind of individual and social memory (Hand, 2016) or identity (Reigeluth, 2014; Kneidinger-Muller, 2018). If properly used, these data provide information about experiences, beliefs and values. Even though they were not originally intended as research materials, researchers can use them to study contemporary societies.

Before they are used in research practices, digital data left behind need to be placed in a rigorous theoretical and methodological framework. They cannot be used indiscriminately and without preliminary investigation. The aim of this contribution is to debate what people leave behind (WPLB) online from a methodological point of view, recognizing elements of both continuity and novelty in comparison to other types of data sources. We first connect WPLB online data to the unobtrusive measures framework and point out the major strengths and weaknesses of these data. Then, we propose dividing the broad family of unobtrusive measures collected online into three different categories. This categorization has important implications for research. We then discuss the characteristics that allow us to distinguish different online materials. As a result, the importance of contextualizing (digital) data is emphasized.

WPLB Online as Unobtrusive Measures

From a methodological point of view, WPLB online has a first distinctive feature: it was not produced for the purpose of scientific research. The materials have been created spontaneously by individuals and groups while performing their activities and have not been solicited in a research context. For this reason, WPLB online can be considered to be part of the so-called unobtrusive measures. This term was coined by Webb and colleagues in 1966 (Webb et al., 1966) and refers to data collected through methods that do not require direct elicitation by researchers (Webb et al., 1966, 1981; Kellehear, 1993; Lee, 2000). In unobtrusive data collection, the research team does not interact with the subjects to be studied and does not require active cooperation from them. Therefore, unobtrusively collected data are considered nonreactive: because there is no direct contact between researchers and those observed, the subjects do not alter their behaviours because they do not know that they are being studied (Given, 2008).[1] Unobtrusive measures provide complementary—not alternative—information to be used in conjunction with data collected through direct elicitation methods (Sechrest, 1971).

WPLB online data share the wide potential of traditional unobtrusive measures. They are not reactive and allow hidden populations or practices to be studied (Hine, 2011). They can be used together with data gathered by intrusive methods such as interviews, questionnaires and participant observation. They can encourage integration among methods (Tashakkori & Teddlie, 1998; Creswell & Plano, 2011) and support methodological triangulation (Denzin, 1978; Morse, 1991). Furthermore, the use of unobtrusive data collection online enhances the study of materials such as written texts, images, audio tracks and other data that risk being marginalized by mainstream research. The use of WPLB online can foster imagination and creativity, against the risk of relying excessively on self-reported measures and on the technical requirements of the research process (Mills, 1959). The study of different materials promotes contamination and boundary crossing between academic studies. By emphasizing that every human activity is cultural and full of meaning, WPLB online data promote the Internet as a place for research and the study of online environments as a source of information. WPLB online data welcome the challenge of a "punk" sociology, which is able to consider new methods, new knowledge and new representations of social life (Beer, 2014).

WPLB online data magnify some of the benefits of traditional unobtrusive measures (Hine, 2008; Janetzko, 2017). Worldwide, an increasing number of people with diverse characteristics are currently online, performing a wide variety of activities: they participate in discussion forums, leave opinions and reviews, upload photographs and videos, find a partner, learn and offer skills, make purchases, spend

---

[1] Data collection through direct elicitation methods such as interviews and participant observation is considered reactive methods: researchers can systematically distort their measurements by their presence because the subjects can modify their behaviour in order to provide a desirable picture of themselves—the so-called Hawthorn effect (Mayo, 1949).

their free time and send and receive messages. Unobtrusive data collection online allows us to research a large number of people and facilitate the gathering of a large volume of data, breaking down geographical distances and increasing the speed of communication. Unobtrusive measures conducted online are often cumulative and allow the gathering of longitudinal data. In this respect, WPLB online data can also support comparative studies (Smelser, 2013) of social phenomena. Online data are already registered and stored; they are readily available, inexpensive and easy to access.

WPLB online also present the limitations of unobtrusive measures. Some of these limitations are at risk of being reinforced by the online collection method. Although everything is currently increasingly connected, some activities are not performed on the Internet and therefore do not leave digital evidence. Some data are kept private and are difficult to access. Some are selected for preservation, while others are not. Digital data can be incomplete, inaccurate and dispersed (Pink et al., 2018). As a consequence, some behaviours and opinions can be collected and recorded by unobtrusive methods online, while others cannot (Janetzko, 2017). There are also differences among those who use digital devices in terms of age, gender, socioeconomic condition and geographical area: while some groups are totally confident in utilizing digital tools and create a variety of contents, others are excluded (the so-called digital divide; see, among others, Norris, 2001). While the main disparities between those who have access to digital devices have diminished, there are still deep differences between those who produce content and those who do not (second-level digital divide; see Hargittai, 2002). In many cases, the identity of authors is not known, as they are anonymous or use pseudonyms. People use strategies of identity management online (Janetzko, 2017) and tend to provide wrong or misleading information. Communications can be self-censored because of privacy concerns (Eynon et al., 2008; Joinson et al., 2010). For these reasons, unobtrusive data collected online have limitations in relating content to authors' characteristics. The purposes and recipients of the data may also be unclear. Additionally, there are ethical questions to be considered in using unobtrusive methods online: to what extent can WPLB online be used for research purposes? Should the authors be informed about the use of their data? Should consent be required? Do information and sensitive issues exist that should be protected? (For a wider discussion, see, among others, Johns et al. (2004) and McKee and Porter (2009)).

These first remarks show how WPLB online can be reconnected to the classical methodological framework. It shares the advantages and disadvantages of unobtrusive methods and at the same time poses unprecedented challenges. Moreover, it is clear that WPLB online data cannot be used without first being analysed, examined and interpreted. Their meaning depends on the circumstances of their production, creation and dissemination (Boyd & Crawford, 2012; Leonelli, 2016).

Three Categories of WPLB (Online) Data

Data collected online by unobtrusive methods are often viewed as being undifferentiated and referred to as "traces", which is used as a synonym for "evidence". We believe that this term is inaccurate and does not reflect the complexity and rich variety of digital data. On the one hand, online materials can have different characteristics; therefore, we propose dividing them into three categories of unobtrusive data collected online. On the other hand, the term "traces" has already been used in the methodological literature in a restrictive sense; therefore, we propose a different vocabulary. It is not only a terminological issue but also a conceptual and methodological one. Distinguishing between different categories, as well as indicating them in clear and unambiguous terms, allows us to understand the real nature of the data and their specific contribution to knowledge. It also makes it possible to match the different categories of digital data to the traditional methodological approaches to which each of them belongs. Furthermore, drawing boundaries between different categories of unobtrusive materials online stresses the need to analyse these data before they are used for research purposes.

In their seminal work on nonreactive measures in social research, Webb and colleagues distinguish three types of unobtrusive data: *found data*, *retrieved data* and *captured data* (Webb et al., 1966).

By the term "found data", the authors refer to material inadvertently left behind by subjects and groups as they go about their lives. Found data are defined as the remnants of their passage (pressed grass, discarded items, removed flyers, worn tiles, etc.). They give this type of material the name "traces" (Webb et al., 1966). Traces can be left by erosion or accretion. In the first case, something is removed from the environment (floor wear in the halls of a museum); in the second case, something is added (garbage thrown in the baskets of the halls of the same museum). In these two examples, traces are remnants of visits to the museum that can be used to understand the behaviours, habits and preferences of the visitors.

"Retrieved data" are defined by Webb and colleagues as materials intentionally created by individuals and groups while pursuing their aims. They can be public (laws, regulations, newspaper articles, billboards, songs) or private (family photographs, letters to friends, personal notes). Webb et al. (1966) distinguish "running records", which are archival materials that have a continuous form and cover long periods (data gathered for administrative purposes, actuarial records, sales data, media materials that appear in regular form), from "episodic records", which are discontinuous (a sentence, some letters, a few novels). Retrieved data can take different forms and use different languages. They reveal tastes, attitudes, choices and behaviours and show how events and meanings are socially constructed. It is worth noting that retrieved data correspond to the definition of documents in documentary analysis (McCulloch, 2004; Prior, 2003; Scott, 1990; Scott, 2006). Webb et al. use the term "documents", particularly in relation to personal and episodic records, and the term "archives" for public and running records.

"Captured data" are defined as behaviours and non-verbal cues such as movements, postures, gestures and even conversations "in situ" captured using nonparticipant observation methods, such as simple observation, meaning unobserved, passive, unobtrusive observation (Webb et al., 1966). These are not persistent but ephemeral data that arise during social interactions and vanish in the moment they are realized, so they need to be captured by researchers. Examples are analysing non-verbal behaviours, such as looking, touching and verbal latency, to understand the social dynamics of a group, listening to market conversations between sellers and customers to understand how a product's identity is constructed and studying eye movements to reveal interest or other attitudes (Lee, 2000).

Webb and his colleagues (1966) talk about physical materials and social interactions that occur in face-to-face environments. We believe that this distinction can be adapted for WPLB online. There is a wide family of data collected online by unobtrusive methods. Within this family, we can distinguish three categories: *online found data* (unintentional digital traces/traces in the restrictive definition), *online retrieved data* (web-mediated documents with communicative ends) and *online captured data* (ephemeral behaviours that occur online).

Online Found Data

Online found data are remnants of other online activities produced inadvertently by users while navigating the Internet. Online found data include log file data (i.e. reports of technical operations carried out online generated automatically by computer applications—they can be access log files, request log files or email log files), mouse clicks, search requests, links, cookies and time measurements. Log file data can be used to generate statistics on the number of pages requested, time spent on a particular site and web browsing patterns. Email log files report information on senders, receivers, times and data of messages, disclosing networks of relationships and their characteristics. Cookies can gather information on visits to websites (date and time, action performed). Time measurements capture durations and latencies (for an in-depth presentation, see Janetzko, 2017). Online found data are a residue left unintentionally. According to the more restrictive methodological definition, online found data are digital traces (Lee, 2000). The methodological roots of this approach can be found in classical trace analysis (Webb et al., 1966; Kellehear, 1993).

Online Retrieved Data

Online retrieved data are materials that Internet users intentionally create and upload to the Web. They can be texts, videos, images, audio tracks, and hypertexts. Online retrieved data are created not for research purposes but to achieve the authors' goals (private purposes, administrative aims, communication, artistic expression).

Examples are messages and photographs uploaded to social networks, administrative acts published online, news broadcast on the Internet, movies and songs on personal, institutional and cultural pages. Texts and photographs published on blogs can be used to explore the authors' representations of their lives (Snee, 2013). Online retrieved data have communicative purposes and express the point of view of individuals and groups. Owing to their characteristics, they are web-mediated documents (Arosio, 2010). The methodological roots of this approach can be found in classical documentary analysis (McCulloch, 2004; Prior, 2003; Scott, 1990; Scott, 2006).

Online Captured Data

Online captured data are behaviours, conversations, gestures, non-verbal cues and expressive movements captured simultaneously by observers while people are interacting online. Examples are synchronous interactions taking place in digital contexts such as online conferences, lectures, chat rooms and virtual worlds when actors are simultaneously connected. Online captured data come from nonpersistent social interactions of which no record would remain. They are ephemeral data captured through simple observation (hence the need to record digital field notes, as suggested by Boellstorff et al., 2012). The researcher is either invisible or hidden behind a false identity in order to be unobtrusive.[2] Online captured data refer to the so-called netnography (Kozintetz, 2010; Costello et al., 2017) as far as simple observation is concerned (digital ethnographic research often uses unobtrusive methods in conjunction with direct elicitation methods both because of the centrality of the dialogue with the subjects to be studied and because of ethical issues; see Ugoretz, 2017). The methodological roots of this approach can be found in classical simple observation (Lee, 2000).

Our proposal is summarized in Table 20.1.

How to Operate a Distinction: The Issue of Intentionality

We proposed dividing online WPLB data into three different categories (Table 20.1). On the one hand, online captured data are easy to identify by their very nature: they are social interactions that occur online that researchers can observe as they are in progress. Online found data and online retrieved data are both persistent data stored on the Net that researchers encounter online at a later stage. Online found data and

[2]Covert and passive observation in online environments is also known as "lurking" (Ugoretz, 2017).

Table 20.1 What people leave behind online. *Three categories of unobtrusive digital data: A proposal*

	What people leave behind online		
Category	Online found data	Online retrieved data	Online captured data
Research object	Digital traces	Web-mediated documents	Online behaviours
Main examples	Log files, links, mouse clicks, feeds, search requests, cookies	Images, texts, videos, audio files, hypertexts published online by users	Gestures, behaviours, non-verbal cues, in situ conversations
Nature	Remnants of other activities	Communicative acts	Social interactions
Quality	Inadvertent data	Intentional data	Ephemeral data
Research approach	Online trace analysis (Lee, 2000)	Web-mediated documentary analysis (Arosio, 2010)	Netnography (Kozintetz, 2010; Costello et al., 2017)
Roots in classical methodology	Trace analysis (Webb et al., 1966; Kellehear, 1993)	Documentary analysis (Prior, 2003; Scott, 2006)	Simple observation (Webb et al., 1966)

online retrieved data can easily be mistaken for each other and require an element to operate a distinction. We focus on them.

Following the definition used in section "Three Categories of WPLB (Online) Data", the distinctive element between found data and retrieved data is intentionality. While the former are inadvertent data, the latter are intentional data. Digital traces are left as a residue of other activities; they do not have a purpose of their own. Web-mediated documents are created to achieve a purpose (communication). The element of distinction between traces and documents is intentionality, understood as the will of the subjects to carry out that action, giving it a purpose.

Intentionality is not understood as "awareness", and leaving traces does not necessarily imply lack of awareness. Individuals may be more or less conscious of leaving online traces. Increasing attention to privacy issues and online security discourses has increased people's awareness that online data can be recorded and stored on the Net. Scandals that in recent years have received widespread media coverage have highlighted that major technology companies have access to personal information and may use it for commercial and political purposes, and people have no control over these actions.

We can illustrate these concepts using the example of email, a widespread form of online communication that can be analysed by researchers to gather information about contemporary societies (for a review, see Perer et al., 2006). Whenever email messages are sent, evidence of the activities carried out by individuals and groups is left behind. On the one hand, there are the texts of the emails. These are materials that subjects and groups intentionally create and disseminate for communication purposes. The message contained in the email is the main purpose of the action. They are "web-mediated documents": personal web-mediated documents if sent for private purposes and institutional web-mediated documents if sent for organizational purposes (Arosio, 2010). On the other hand, whenever emails are sent and received,

Table 20.2 Email communications between web-mediated documents and digital traces

Content of email messages	Communicative act	Intentional	Main purpose of the action	Web-mediated documents	Messages and points of view
Email log files	Involuntary remnant	Inadvertent	Leftover of the action	Digital traces	Frequency and directionality of communication

automatic systems generate and store log files that contain information about the sender and the recipient and the date and time of the messages, depending on the protocol used (Janetzko, 2017). Email log files are remnants of another activity because they are not the primary purpose of the action (the subjects sit at a computer to send a message, not to generate log files). Email log files are therefore digital traces (Lee, 2000).

As illustrated in Table 20.2, the aim of email communications is to send and receive the content of the message, and the creation of email log files does not have intentionality, as it is not the main purpose of the action but rather a leftover. Subjects leave traces without attributing a meaning to them. Digital traces and documents are both useful in research; they just have different characteristics and provide different information. Email log files capture the frequency and directionality of communications and allow networks of relationships to be reconstructed. Email texts capture messages and points of view.

Even though intentionality is a central feature in understanding the very nature of data, it cannot always be easily identified. Arosio (2021) discusses the example of self-tracking data, where the level of intentionality is not self-evident. Self-tracking data may be the result of an unintentional action, as in the case of subjects wearing a mobile device with tracking functions enabled by default. In other cases, self-tracking data can have a communicative intent, for example, when data are collected to be shared by subjects on their social networks or even used as a form of artistic expression. On the surface, the data appear to be the same, but in fact, they are very different. In the first case, researchers are dealing with digital traces, and in the second, they are dealing with web-mediated documents. A major work of reconstruction of the context of production and use of (digital) data is therefore required (Arosio, 2021).

Why Operate a Distinction?

Every day, people pass through social environments in living their lives: they work, study, go on vacation, compose songs, take a walk in the park, cook or visit a museum. The same happens for groups and organizations. Each of these activities leaves something behind: an attendance sheet, a legal act, a textbook, a souvenir photo, crushed grass, discarded objects or worn tiles. These are all sources of information that can be used by researchers to understand behaviours, attitudes and values.

Today, due to the widespread use of new communication technologies, many activities are performed in digital environments, and much evidence is left behind online. WPLB online data can offer a relevant contribution to the study of social reality in contemporary societies (among others, see Back & Puwal, 2012; Ruppert et al., 2013; Lupton, 2015). On the one hand, the use of the Internet as a source of information represents a challenge that social researchers need to address to capture the dynamics of social change. On the other hand, there is a need to develop a solid methodological framework before using digital data for social research. The innovative features of these data need to be known, as do the characteristics that connect them to the classical methodological repertoire (see among the others, Amaturo & Aragona, 2021).

This work offers a contribution in this direction. First, it reconnects WPLB online data to traditional unobtrusive measures. Second, it stresses the complexity and varied features of online unobtrusive measures. We focus on the difference among three different categories of online data: online behaviours, digital traces and web-mediated documents. In doing so, investigating the context of production, dissemination and use proved to be a key point. Contextualizing data is not easy, especially unobtrusive measurements and digital data, because unobtrusive measures and online environments reduce the degree to which the researcher has control over the type of data collected (Trochim, 2006). This difficulty does not detract from the need for the nature and limitations of data to be understood before they are used.

Distinguishing different types of online WPLB data is not just a purely terminological issue. Rather, it has important theoretical and methodological implications. Online behaviours, digital traces and web-mediated documents can all provide deep insights into individuals, groups and society. However, they offer different perspectives and different pieces of information. For example, whereas traces are automatically generated by a computer system, online documents are the result of a communicative will. They contain an interpretation, a subjective point of view on reality, which is affected by the author, recipient, purpose and circumstances of sending the message. In this sense, documents should be critically investigated before being analysed (Scott, 1990; Cohen et al., 2000).

The emergence of various categories of digital data calls for reflection on other circumstances. Unobtrusive online collection methods are generally thought of as a source of big data. However, even in this case, digital data can be differentiated. Digital data can be thought of as *big data* (large amounts of data that need to be processed by some kind of data mining/scraping procedures to reveal patterns and trends) or as *small data* (data that are smaller in volume and format and allow for in-depth study).[3] Digital traces, automatically generated by computer systems in

[3]The big data/small data distinction echoes the methodological debate on quantity/quality or correlation/causation. In this context, we cannot address the issue extensively. For a first discussion, see Cowls and Schroeder (2015).

huge quantities over an extended period, can be interpreted as big data. The simple observation of social behaviours on the Net or the analysis of documents such as blogs and social network pages comes closer to the definition of small data (Lindstrom, 2016).

Ethical issues, which are central to the use of unobtrusive online data, as well as key issues such as privacy, informed consent and the use of data for research purposes should also be explored in more detail when considering the three categories of WPLB online data.

Properly identifying the different natures of digital data has many implications. We have mentioned some of them, and many others need to be explored further. Our remarks are intended as a starting point to develop a deeper understanding of WPLB online from a methodological point of view.

References

Amaturo, E., & Aragona, B. (2021). Digital methods and the evolution of the epistemology of social sciences. In P. Mariani & M. Zenga (Eds.), *Data science and social research II. Methods, technologies and applications* (pp. 1–8). Springer.

Appadurai, A. (1986). *The social life of things: Commodities in cultural perspective*. Cambridge University Press.

Arosio, L. (2010). Personal documents on the internet: what's new and what's old. *Journal of Comparative Research in Anthropology and Sociology, 1*(2), 1–16.

Arosio, L. (2021). Between digital traces and documentary analysis: The methodological challenge of self-tracking data. *Journal of Comparative Research in Anthropology and Sociology, 12*(1), 1–10.

Back, L., & Puwal, N. (2012). A manifesto for live methods: Provocations and capacities. *The Sociological Review, 60*(S1), 6–17.

Beer, D. (2014). *Punk sociology*. Palgrave Macmillan.

Boellstorff, T., Nardi, B., Pearce, C., & Taylor, T. L. (2012). *Ethnography and virtual worlds: A handbook of method*. Princeton University Press.

Boullier, D. (2015). Les sciences sociales face aux traces du Big Data. Société, opinion ou vibrations? *Revue Française de Science Politique, 65*(5–6), 805–828.

Boyd, D., & Crawford, K. (2012). Critical questions for big data. *Information, Communication & Society, 15*(5), 662–679.

Cohen, L., Manion, L., & Morrison, K. (Eds.). (2000). *Research methods in education*. Routledge.

Costello, L., McDermott, M. L., & Wallace, R. (2017). Netnography: Range of practices, misperceptions, and missed opportunities. *International Journal of Qualitative Methods, 16*(1), 1–12.

Cowls, J., & Schroeder, R. (2015). Causation, correlation, and big data in social science research. *Policy & Internet, 7*(4), 447–472.

Creswell, J. W., & Plano, C. V. L. (2011). *Designing and conducting mixed methods research*. Sage.

Denzin, N. K. (1978). *The research act: A theoretical introduction to sociological methods*. Praeger.

Derrida, J. (1967). *De la grammatologie*. Ed. de Minuit.

Eynon, R., Fry, J., & Schroeder, R. (2008). The ethics of internet research. In N. G. Fielding, R. M. Lee, & G. Blank (Eds.), *The Sage handbook of online research methods (pp. 22–41)*. Sage Publications.

Ferraris, M., & Martino, V. D. (2018). What is Documediality and why traces, documents and archives are normative. *Law Text Culture, 22*(1), 21–30.
Given, L. M. (Ed.). (2008). *Unobtrusive research. The SAGE Encyclopedia of qualitative research methods.* Sage Publications.
Gleick, J. (2011). *The information: A history, a theory, a flood.* Pantheon Books.
Hand, M. (2016). Persistent traces, potential memories: Smartphone and the negotiation of visual, locative, and textual data in personal life. *Convergence, 22*(3), 1–18.
Hargittai, E. (2002). Second-level digital divide: Differences in people's online skills. *First Monday, 7*(4), 1–16. https://doi.org/10.5210/fm.v7i4.942
Hine, C. (2008). The internet and research methods. In N. Gilbert (Ed.), *Researching social life* (3rd ed., pp. 304–320). Sage Publications.
Hine, C. (2011). Internet research and unobtrusive methods. *Social Research Update, 61*, 1–3.
Janetzko, D. (2017). Nonreactive data collection online. In N. G. Fielding, R. M. Lee, & G. Blank (Eds.), *The Sage handbook of online research methods* (pp. 161–174). Sage Publications.
Johns, M. D., Chen, S. L., & Hall, G. J. (2004). *Online social research: Methods, issues & ethics.* Peter Lang.
Joinson, A., Reips, U., Buchanan, T., & Paine Schofield, C. (2010). Privacy, trust, and self-disclosure online. *Human & Computer Interaction, 25*, 1–24.
Kellehear, A. (1993). *The unobtrusive researcher: A guide to methods.* Allen & Unwin.
Kneidinger-Muller, B. (2018). Self-tracking data as digital traces of identity: A theoretical analysis of contextual factors of self-observation practices. *International Journal of Communication, 12*, 629–646.
Kopytoff, I. (1986). The cultural biography of things: Commoditization as process. In A. Appadurai (Ed.), *The social life of things: Commodities in cultural perspective* (pp. 64–92). Cambridge University Press.
Kozintetz, R. V. (2010). *Netnography: Doing ethnographic research online*. Sage.
Lee, R. M. (2000). *Unobtrusive methods in social research.* Open University Press.
Leonelli, S. (2016). *Data-centric biology: A philosophical study.* Chicago University Press.
Lindstrom, M. (2016). *Small data: The tiny clues that uncover huge trends.* Hodder & Stoughton.
Lupton, D. (2015). *Digital sociology*. Routledge.
Lupton, D. (2019). *Data selves: More-than-human perspectives.* Polity Press.
Mayer-Schonberger, V., & Cukier, K. (2013). *Big data: A revolution that will transform how we live, work and think.* John Murray.
Mayo, E. (1949). *Hawthorne and the Western electric company. The social problems of an industrial civilisation.* Routledge and Kegan Paul.
McCulloch, G. (2004). *Documentary research in education, history and the social sciences.* Routledge.
McKee, H. A., & Porter, J. E. (2009). *The ethics of internet research: A rhetorical case-based process.* McLaughlin.
Mills, C. W. (1959). *The sociological imagination.* Oxford University Press.
Morse, J. (1991). Approaches to qualitative-quantitative methodological triangulation. *Nursing Research, 40*, 120–123.
Norris, P. (2001). *Digital divide: Civic engagement, information poverty and the internet worldwide.* Cambridge University Press.
Perer, A., Shneiderman, B., & Oard, D. W. (2006). Using rhythms of relationships to understand E-mail archives. *Journal of the American Society for Information Science and Technology, 57*(14), 1936–1948.
Pink, S., Ruckenstein, M., Willim, R., & Duque, M. (2018). Broken data: Conceptualising data in an emerging world. *Big Data & Society, 5*(1), 1–13.
Prior, L. (2003). *Using documents in social research.* Sage Publications.
Reigeluth, T. (2014). Why data is not enough: Digital traces as control of self and self-control. *Surveillance & Society, 12*(2), 243–254.

Ruppert, E., Law, J., & Savage, M. (2013). Reassembling social science methods: The challenge of digital devices. *Theory, Culture & Society, 30*(4), 22–46.
Scott, J. (1990). *A matter of record: Documentary sources in social research*. Polity Press.
Scott, J. (2006). *Documentary research*. Sage Publications.
Sechrest, L. (1971). Unobtrusive measures in data collection. *Academy of Management Annual Meeting Proceedings, 1*, 58–66.
Smelser, N. J. (2013). *Comparative methods in the social sciences*. Quid Pro Books.
Snee, H. (2013). Making ethical decisions in an online context: Reflections on using blogs to explore narratives of experience. *Methodological Innovations Online, 8*(2), 52–67.
Sontag, S. (1977). *On photography*. Penguin Books.
Tashakkori, A., & Teddlie, C. (1998). *Mixed methodology: Combining qualitative and quantitative approaches*. Sage Publications.
Trochim, W. M. K. (2006). *Unobtrusive measures*. Retrieved March 31, 2022, from http://www.socialresearchmethods.net/kb/unobtrus.php
Ugoretz, K. (2017). *A guide to unobtrusive methods in digital ethnography*. Retrieved March 31, 2022, from https://www.researchgate.net/publication/331287677_A_Guide_to_Unobtrusive_Methods_in_Digital_Ethnography
van Dijck, J. (2014). Datafication, dataism and dataveillance: Big data between scientific paradigm and ideology. *Surveillance & Society, 12*(2), 197–208.
Webb, E. J., Campbell, D. T., Schwartz, R. D., & Sechrest, L. (1966). *Unobtrusive measures: Nonreactive research in the social sciences*. Rand McNally.
Webb, E. J., Campbell, D. T., Schwartz, R. D., Sechrest, L., & Grove, J. B. (1981). *Nonreactive measures in the social sciences*. Houghton Mifflin.
Weber, M. (1922). *Wirtschaft und Gesellschaft. Grundriß der verstehenden Soziologie*. Mohr.

Laura Arosio, PhD is an Associate Professor in Sociology in the Department of Sociology and Social Research at the University of Milano Bicocca, Italy. She has a PhD in Sociology. Her main interests concern processes of family formation and transformation in contemporary Italy, with a focus on homogamy and social heterogamy, marriage, marital disruption and its consequences. She has worked on rites of passage and divorce ceremonies from a life course perspective. She is interested in the field of methodology and empirical research (both qualitative and quantitative). Her recent methodological studies focus on documentary analysis, unobtrusive measures, digital data and the implications of using the Internet in social research.

Chapter 21
Trace and Traceability in/of the Face: A Semiotic Reading through Art

Silvia Barbotto Forzano

Donde hay orejas pero no hay canto
En este mundo que se desvanece
Y el ser se otorga a quien no lo merece
Soy mucho más mis huellas que mis pasos. (Original text:
"Where there are ears but no song
In this fading world
And being is bestowed on the undeserving
I am much more my footprints than my footsteps.")
(Jodorowsky, 2008: 97)

Prolegomenon

Starting from Peirce's tripartition of signs, we turn our attention to indexes such as those types of signs causally connected with their object (Peirce in Eco, 2016, p. 190). Indexicality opens its territory by expanding the presential option of the object of reference and allowing the introduction of an indirect but imbricated correlation between expression and content: "The presence of the object is not necessary for the sign to signify, although it is required to verify the use of the sign in an act of reference" (Eco, 2016, p. 297).

The *topo-sensitivity* inherent in the indexes highlights the spatial relationship that builds the semantic pathway, which propitiates different directional movements and has various dynamic possibilities. *Chrono-sensitivity*, on the other hand, emphasizes the temporal relation which, as we shall see, can take backward or proximal routes: a trace can therefore be read as a sign that makes it possible to return to the origin or as

This article is part of FACETS: the project has received funding from the European Research Council (ERC) under the European Union's Horizon 2020 research and innovation program (grant agreement No 819649—FACETS, PI Massimo LEONE)

Many thanks to FACETS team NB.

S. Barbotto Forzano (✉)
Department of Philosophy and Education Sciences, University of Turin, Turin, Italy
e-mail: Silvia.barbotto@unito.it; https://silviabarbottof.com

F. Comunello et al. (eds.), *What People Leave Behind*, Frontiers in Sociology and Social Research 7, https://doi.org/10.1007/978-3-031-11756-5_21

an indication yielding a new route. Motivation versus arbitrariness seems to be one of the driving forces behind circumstantial research: the trace as the motivated result of an underlying content, the trace as the motivator of a developing content, ex post facto.

The objective of this text is to work with the *indicative emanations* called traces, the constitutive clues of subjective and collective meaning, which are advanced as a continuous processual configuration in which the hypothetical directions can only be comprised in the *forming formation*, toward the elaboration of a sociopolitical, bio-metaphysical fabric whose semiotic substrate is necessary as well as pertinent. A certain phenomenon, a sign, a set of signs, can constitute not only a model but rather the basis on which a model is established. Approaching the traces implies a prior work of pertinentization and therefore of observation, delimitation, and argumentation; the outcome is a punctilious work of questioning not only the cause-effect linearity but also the logic underlying the sign, i.e., the constitution of a text and of a space.

We actually enter the semiotics of the body as text and archive, as a space of figural memory resulting from a process of synchronic contact and a *diachronic reading* of an echo of matter that refracts on itself and dissipates in the world, of a spongy face imbued with penetrating magnitude. We are in a semiotics of art as a special space of passionate, political, and transhistorical daily experimentation. The underlying anthropological paradigm completes the absolution of being as part of a cosmic and natural organization in which culture is involved: the human face is our spatial situation of analysis. Thinking of the face as a place of discourse, as the writing of a tale and a narrative sign, does nothing other than propose to the analytical gaze an opening *-scopic* inclusive of the stories already experienced, a summing up: "From the perspective of a semiotics of text and discourse, the body is first and foremost a site of meaning, and of a meaning that takes shape from the sensations and impressions that this body experiences in contact with the world."[1] (Fontanille, 2003, p. 3).

We will be providing a general panorama, selecting only a few emblematic art pieces as a reduced corpus that can propitiate a kind of coherence with the entire position, showing how porous contemporary society is: recalling the sign as something that stands for something else, we thus see in otherness the cohesive element and in the intervening spatiality the construction of semiosis.

We will travel between different historical epochs, contextualizing contemporaneity within a necessarily historical marker, and transit geographically between extremes in order to be located in a transversal and multi-situational topographical position where the face has the property of constituting, reinforcing, or dissolving intimate and collective subjectivities.

[1] Original text: "Dans la perspective d'une sémiotique du texte et du discours, le corp est d'abord un lieu de signification, et d'une signification qui prend forme à partir de sensation et impressions que ce corps éprouve au contact du monde."

Phenomenological and ontological references are often necessary to bring attention back to the becoming of material signs, to in situ even if not necessarily analogical incorporation, to the deconstruction of the subject through its traces, and to the constitution of the traced personality. Denuded of the complex machinery that composes our face, expression and name, and vibration and trace, there remains the neutral that is intrinsically expressive versatility, collection of immanent memory, and secularized sediment of inadvertent powers.

We take the artistic paradigm as a model through which reality is approached and treated in accordance with criteria of intuition and freedom and by referring to a specific *modelling system* that is "a structure of elements and rules of their combination, existing in a state of fixed analogy to the whole sphere of the object of perception, cognition, or organization. (. . .) The content of art as modelling system is the world of reality, translated to the language of our consciousness, translated in turn to the language of the given form of art" (Lotman, 2011, p. 250).

Let us consider the traces following three primary, if not exclusive, lines of investigation:

1. Traces emanating from the face
2. Traces on or in the face
3. Traces erased toward new tracks

On the basis of a semiotics of the face in inclusive assonance with a semiotics of the body, according to the idea of the *witness body* (Fontanille, 2003) and elaborating it further in line with our criteria and those of other authors of reference, we can try to understand how these three paradigms integrate specific examples and *sense vectors* built on different semiotic axes. Although we do not intend to reduce the semiotic interpretation to a diagrammatic schematization, we will simplify by pointing out the following characteristics of each in the light of their multidimensional intersection.

The body in movement constitutes itself in a deictically marked path and therefore, at least in part, is recorded, traced; from it derived the first type of emanations, in a sort of enunciation in which the narration of the trace runs along opposite routes in the two cases mentioned. In the artistic case, the trace is contextualized within an aspirational path projected into the future, and the predicative argument underlying it is a discovery rather than a finding. The mode of existence of the new constituted subject is an inventive simulacrum, actualized, and projected.

In forensic cases, however, the trace is contextualized within an aspectual path projected into the past, the basic argument being the backward search aimed at the semantic area of finding again. The body in movement, whose matter degenerates because it is encroached upon by its own wholeness and compactness, blurs into the world: the rediscovery of its parts and above all the reunion with its own origin, as well as the reintegration of the gap previously left, aspires to figurative and formal completeness.

The second model, on the other hand, deals with the face in dialogue first and foremost with its own circumscribed material form, with a well-known syntactical feature: both in the combinations of reading the signs on the face on the basis of physiognomy or other pseudosciences and in the inscription of new signs, the trace is preponderantly an element of memory. Its elements inhabit the organic microcosm which, in the provision of a paradigmatic as well as syntagmatic reading of the figurativeness of the face, is then immersed in the authentication of the evidence of a state, the articulation of the face as witness of contact, enunciated autopoietic resource, and filiation of intimate inscription whose vision and interpretation are crucial.

The act of inscription can be automatic or involuntary but also sought after or propitiated: in the first sphere, we can refer to the signs of time and character (whose reading is attributed to physiognomy and other pseudosciences), while the second sphere comprises those signs caused by accidents or misfortunes. The analyses of physiognomic traces but also of all those linked to the ontologically experienced face are part of the figure of the stratified body, an inhabited archive whose continuous movement becomes a memory in construction: an embodied face whose movement over time sediments, creating forms.

This second group, however, also includes those traces of intentional origin, at the basis of which we usually find aesthetic, political, or cultural motives, as in the case of the street artist involved in our study: "matter is subject to forces, the balance of which gives it form"[2] (Fontanille, 2003, p. 4). The malleable and elastic face takes on new signs symbolizing membership of a tribe, and the face belonging to the so-called fleshly body is materially reshaped through the process of scarring, a figure of reconciled frontier and indelible recision at the same time. The new syntactical marks, with a specific directionality and form, are strictly connected with the semantical vestige of affiliation to a major collectivity: the trace also becomes a symbol for distinguishing group membership.

This brings us to our third tensive band of actorly displacement, which tries to establish a heuristic dialogue between the reference in the natural world and the intelligible sensory inference. It is not a question of corporal inscription in these cases but of textual reformulation with erasure as a supporting strategy: the story written in the traces wants to change "the relationship between the thread—the thread of the story that helps us to orientate ourselves in the labyrinth of reality—and the trace"'(Ginzburg, 2020, p. 7)[3] is broken.

If we think of the following semiotic square from Greimas and Courtes (1982, pp. 308–311. Fig. 21.1), we propose to problematize the relation between permanence and cancellation and underline different strategies of memory fixation through traces.[4] While in the case of Saraji, we will see a strong trace of resemantization through the erasure of faces represented photographically, in that of Janez Janša, it is a matter of cancellation of face traces as bio-political instances (Fig. 21.1).

[2]Original text: "la matière est soumise à des forces, dont l'équilibre lui procure une forme."

[3]Original text: "il rapporto tra il filo—il filo del racconto che ci aiuta a orientarci nel labirinto della realtà—e le tracce."

[4]Semiotic square presented during FACETS program "Chronotopes of the face n. 9": https://www.youtube.com/watch?v=MANCsmJrdz0

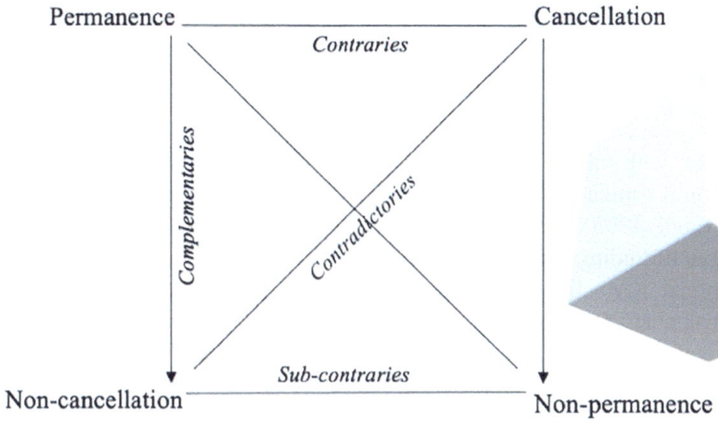

Fig. 21.1 Greimas square

The body emphasizes its subjectivity by following an *a-rebours* path in search of the inscriptions no longer of the ontological and actualized face but of a symbolic and potential face, inscriptions that prove the univocal relationship formed by the face-name isomorphism: all the texts projecting this formation are the basis of the change. The face becomes the spectator of a radical change that sees in the alteration of name a strategy with which the body concurs, in a kind of performance absorbed in the proximal environment.

Perception and action undergo slight *techno-aesthetic* variations, enabling us "to relate interactively with our environment, from which we grasp potentialities that can be elaborated not only on a cognitive-conceptual level, but also, and in a more original sense, techno-aesthetically elaborated, with a view, for example, to the production and use of artefacts" (Binda, 2017, p. 138).

It is precisely these latter works that become meta-witnesses of the witnessing body: identity documents, credit cards, and all those artifacts in which the name appears, often combined with the face photograph, are moments of identity reformulation but also reformulation of the environment. This is, in fact, the resonance of the art pieces of this collective, in which every day technical objects take on a different function, being shown as evidence of a synergic conversion with the environment.

The ontological face and the semiotic face are mainly interdependent to the point of discovering a disciplinary syncretism that focuses on the same conscious function of the passage and its phases.

Traces Emanating from the Face: [Material Turn/Material Split]

Traces have always been an important tool not only in establishing a contract, albeit a provisional one, with missing texts, but also in setting up possible paths on the basis of conjectural similarities. In some cultures, their reading becomes a kind of science or art. Magli (1995) reminds us of the Argentinean *rastreador* mentioned by Borges, in charge of finding lost cattle in the fields, but also presents to us a similar practice widespread in Muslim jurisprudence: "the art called Kiyafa ("to follow", in Arabic), says Fakhr al-Dīn al-Rāzī, is divided into Kiyafat al-athar ("to follow the track") and Kiyafat al-bashar ("to follow the man along a path according to a direction"). "As regards the first type, it consists in knowing how to follow footprints or hoofprints left on sandy paths, which are likely to receive their imprint. (. . .) The second was instead an art that made it possible to discover kinship links. This art was so called because the Kai'f carefully examined the appearance of individuals, the epidermis, the shape of the limbs with particular attention to that of the feet. The consideration of the globality of all these clues allowed him to establish if there were blood ties between two individuals" (Magli, 1995, pp. 47–48).

The experience of unidirectionally matching interpretations and traces requires, first and foremost, a meticulous capacity for observation of the details and the whole in a sort of mereological attitude, but other prerequisites include the recognition of the truthfulness of the gesture of inscription, as well as the ability to decrypt the writing and thus the sign. How are we to follow this path if the signifier is apparently completely free or far from its initial meaning? "It is we, our culture, our arbitrariness, who decide on the status of referentiality of a writing. What does this mean? That the signifier is free, sovereign" (Barth, 1999, p. 29).

In this freedom, the pertinence inherent in the written trace suggests a certain relationship with the object-subject through which it is inscribed. Here then is the possible inverse, inventive process: a construction resulting from the assembly of deconstructed fragments which, allowing a glimpse of connective hints because they are inscribed in the often-invisible residual matter, contain indicative and therefore significant information.

Atmospheric aerosols and droplets[5] are perhaps particularly resonant terms from 2020 onward, the year in which the COVID-19 pandemic takes shape, and we begin to understand that our saying, speaking, and even breathing take place in contact and exchange with the surrounding atmosphere, subtly penetrated by the invisible traces we impalpably emanate. The face, immediately covered by the mask which has been made compulsory in most of the countries involved, has to deal with what it exhales.

Fluid dynamics researcher Lydia Bourouiba has recently been working on detecting (with high-speed cameras and the support of light) the dynamics of pathogen expulsion from the human body. "Slowed down to 2000 frames per

[5] https://www.focus.it/scienza/salute/coronavirus-covid-diffusione-via-aerea

second, the videos and images from her lab show that the fine mist of mucus and saliva expelled from a person's mouth can reach a speed of 160 km per hour and cover a distance of up to 8 meters."[6] Their permanence, however, would depend on specific site conditions, including humidity and temperature.

We become potential transmitters of the virus, occluding ourselves behind our new appearance, often behind the medical masks, creating internal hoods of potentially asphyxiating, stale atmospheres. "The problem of social distancing, a proxemic problem, becomes our magnifying glass with which to observe how our bodies, and above all our faces, change in the days of the pandemic, how they resemantize and transform themselves as the viral emergency spreads" (Gramigna & Voto, 2020, p. 134).

The emission of substances from our faces was already known to us, as was the fact that they contained viruses and bacteria; we understood, too, that there is invisible matter that traces our passage, from a penetrating gaze to the *droplets* of speech. Its possible permanence and active perseverance over time, however, have perhaps been less considered. Indeed, while in forensic science the practice of identifying and reinvigorating traces has always been fundamental, in common knowledge it has so far been sidelined. Despite the fact that tracing is articulated by placing a certain element in retroactive connection with the subject of origin, the motive paradigm of such a path can be very different.

Heather Dewey-Hagborg,[7] for example, works with traces of works of art and, using hair, cigarettes, and chewing gum taken off the street, programs and builds 3D faces through the DNA found in them: characterized by the interpenetration between new media and human physiological nature, her proposal questions the awareness of production emanating from materials which, read backward, can venture into the rewriting of new texts.

The frontiers between biomolecular and indifferent modulation, one's own and others' spatiality, and the intimate and contextual body, blur but still perpetuate. The physical delimitation, which so clearly distinguishes between ipseity (ownness) and otherness, fades away, giving rise to a continuous echo, a constant diffuse mnemonic trace, which interacts with the environment: it may simply merge with it, or instead be considered writing, and thus be read, interpreted, and made pertinent.

The artist in question, for example, calls herself a biohacker; in her project entitled Stranger Vision, she follows these steps:

- Collect hair, chewed gum, fingernails, and cigarette butts from public spaces.
- Extract DNA from them.
- Analyze it computationally through genomic research.
- Parameterize a 3D face based on these traits.
- Print it with a 3D printing machine (Fig. 21.2).

[6] https://www.nationalgeographic.it/scienza/2020/04

[7] https://deweyhagborg.com

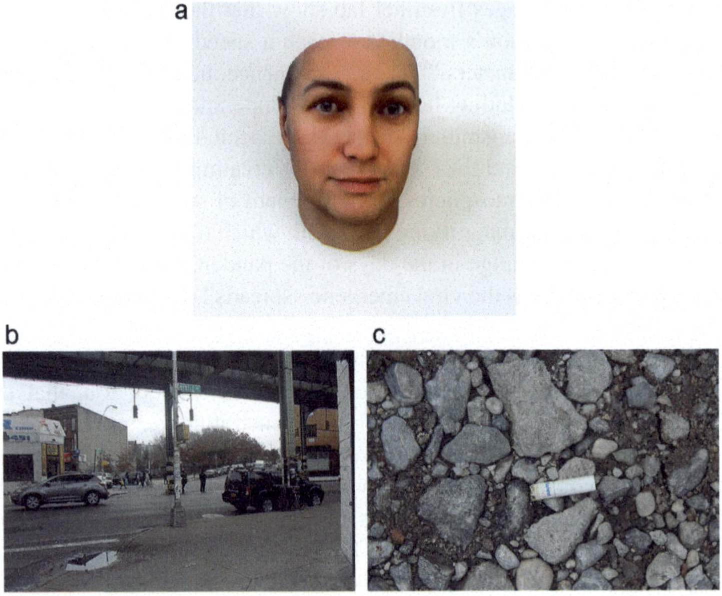

Fig. 21.2 Heather Dewey-Hagborg, *Portrait and samples from New York: Sample 4*. [1/6/13 12: 20 pm, Myrtle ave. and Himrod St. Brooklyn, NY]. Mix media Collection Stranger visions, 2013. Courtesy Heather Dewey-Hagborg and Fridman Gallery, New York

"Initially,—she says—the idea behind the project was to research what I could learn about the people who had dropped them. What I found was that by combining an arsenal of published research, bioinformatics and machine learning tools, I could draw statistical inferences or predictions about what these individuals looked and behaved like, what kind of health conditions they had and even what their surnames were."[8]

In the same article, Dewey-Hagborg criticizes the current use of this practice, appropriated from forensic work that not only constructs typologies but, in some ways, consolidates stereotypes: "The practice of rendering appearance from forensic samples is called 'Forensic DNA Phenotyping' (FDP) or 'molecular photofitting' (...)." While there are some traits such as eye and hair color that can be predicted from DNA with a high degree of certainty, the bulk of FDP is based on algorithmically derived statistical compositions. We tend to look at technical systems as neutral black boxes, but if you open them up and look at the component parts, you find that they reflect the assumptions and motivations of their designers. (ibidem) "Indeed, we have to question how the algorithmic work made automatic is actually the result of lengthy, extensive teaching based on parameters and indications that are already questionable beforehand "to show in practice the fallacy of the myth of algorithmic neutrality, as well as to examine its various discursive facets. In particular, three key

[8] https://thenewinquiry.com/sci-fi-crime-drama-with-a-strong-black-lead/

aspects of the myth will be discussed and problematized (...): firstly, the assumption that no systemic distortions have interfered in the design and/or training phase of the algorithm and that, therefore, the output returns an objective point of view on reality; secondly, the idea that the automation and disintermediation of complex processes are in themselves guarantees of neutrality; thirdly, the claim that the results of algorithmic computation, narrated as accurate and infallible, do not alter reality according to socially, historically and politically determined logics" (Airoldi & Gambetta, 2018, pp. 33–34).[9]

For example, *Parabon Snapshot*[10] elaborates specific personalities by exclusion and predicts physical characteristics including skin pigmentation, eye and hair color, face morphology, sex, and genomic ancestry and identifies distant familial relationships between samples. They define their work in this way: "Using genomic data from large populations of subjects with known phenotypes, Parabon's bio informaticists have built statistical models for forensic traits, which can be used to predict the physical appearance of unknown individuals."[11] But we are able, now, to understand how spurious this prediction may be.

In Dewey-Hagborg's intentions, the possibility of being the precursor of a model later adopted by the laboratories of the judicial police was perhaps not contemplated. And this itinerary is typical of the artistic journey in which the avant-garde of art is a visionary predecessor with respect to future actions, sometimes even misleading in relation to its initial ideals and prerogatives.

The trace emanating from the face is an indication of what has been, an organic remnant of a passage that has taken place whose signs, albeit ephemeral, are installed in a material that preserves them. Some artists work with the materiality of residues, with the emanations and secretions of the body and face but also with the creation of ad hoc traces propitiated by physical contact between the body and other matter. Let us think in this regard of the works of Ana Mendieta, whose naked body becomes a matrix of mold, whose generated fluids become themselves pictorial materials for *printing*: with her blood, she invades her body, which in turn paints her canvases;

[9]Original text: "a mostrare in pratica la fallacia del mito della neutralità algoritmica, cosi come a esaminarne le varie sfaccettature discorsive. In particolare, tre aspetti cardine del mito verranno discussi e problematizzati (...): primo, l'assunto che nella fase di progettazione e/o addestramento dell'algoritmo non abbiano interferito distorsioni sistemiche e che, pertanto, l'output restituisca un punto di vista oggettivo sulla realtà; secondo, l'idea che l'automatizzazione e la disintermediazione di processi complessi siano di per se stesse garanzie di neutralità; terzo, la pretesa che i risultati del calcolo algoritmico, narrati come accurati e infallibili, non alterino la realtà secondo logiche socialmente, storicamente e politicamente determinate" (Airoldi, Gambetta, 2018: 33–34).

[10]https://parabon-nanolabs.com/news-events/2014/12/announcing-parabon-snapshot.html

[11]To emphasize this possibility of error, we again recommend delving into the text by Airoldi and Gambetta (2018: 37–38) who, in a passage devoted to application fallibilities, give the example of the COMPAS software (*Correctional Offender Management Profiling for Alternative Sanctions*) and the dataset used by Wu and Zhang.

with her body[12] she leaves traces after contact with earth or with sand as, for example, in the Silueta Series, Mexico, 1976.

"If a body is capable of preserving, by way of figurative memory, the traces and imprints of its sensory interactions with other bodies, then we can hypothesize that a subject of enunciation that would also be a body is likely to testify to its experiences"[13] (Fontanille, 2003: p. 1). The face that traces, the traced face, involves inscription and possible backward reading: "it is always a question of keeping track of an event, so as to be able, in an act of verification, to return to the origin" (Fontanille, 2003, p. 1).

Traces on or in the Face [Intra-Face: Introspection/Imbrication]

We now move from *extrinsic* traces that are dislocated with respect to the subject to which they belong and eventually return in a sort of spatial adjustment, to *intrinsic* ones that are an integral part of the operational framework of their subject. These kinds of traces can be found and understood mainly through their reading, which can be effected in various ways, for example, through physiognomy. "Physiognomy, the practice of reading the face, dates back to the Paleo-Babylonian period in Mesopotamia. Scholarly references can be found as early as the eighth century BC (Homer) and fifth century (Hippocrates), as can social references: Pythagoras reportedly used it as an interviewing technique, claiming to have his potential students *physiognomized* before agreeing to be their tutor" (Helfand, 2019, p. 153).

It is doubtful that the traces of a delinquent personality are genetically established and therefore transmitted from birth and scrutinized in the face from an early age, but it is probable that cultural, habitual, and event-related traces are decanted into the face. While in the former cases we speak of anthropometry and biometrics, in the latter we are closer to physiognomy and traces in the face as a residual indication.

In addition to distinguishing between types and temperaments physiognomy, as the art of interpretation, is concerned with giving voice to the traces present in the face not only so as to study their origin and thus give them a diagnostic role but also to possibly redeem their predictive role. Among the leading physiognomists, Della Porta certainly stands out, his juxtapositions of man-nature and, above all, man-animal enjoying great success between the middle and the end of the sixteenth century: his studies in the footsteps of predecessors Polemon and Adamantius

[12]To get acquainted with the work of Mendieta, we recommend visiting the page www.guggenheim.org/artwork/5221 or https://www.malba.org.ar/ana-mendieta-alma-silueta-en-fuego-1975/.

[13]Original text: "Si un corps est susceptible de conserver, au titre de la mémoire figurative, les traces et empreintes de ses interactions sensorielles avec d'autres corps, alors on peut faire l'hypothèse qu'un sujet d'enonciation qui serai aussi un corps est susceptible de *témoigner* de ses expériences."

compared the entire human figure and, above all, the face with animals that were similar in figure and character. In his second book, for instance, we find explanatory tables of the details of the mouth in comparison and assimilation to certain animals according to position and form; the author also goes into detail about the lips, mouth, teeth, and tongue; about yearning, sighing, and laughing; about the beard, neck, Adam's apple, and cervical bones; and up to the interpretation of the voice and speaking. Only in book number three is the subject of the eyes the exclusive theme of the entire manuscript, which is characterized by numerous references to the previous studies of Aristotle and Galen: the constitution, size, and shape of the eyes, the consistency of the angles, the upper and lower eyelids, the pupils and their degree of hydration, the color and their location in the facial set, and the attitude to the surrounding space (open, trembling, pleading, oblique, twisted, threatening) are analyzed.

"Laughing eyes, of firm and menacing aspect. But if with a threatening countenance, and with steady eyes they regard, they counsel iniquitous deeds. Adamantius. But Albert. Mainly by these signs the eyelids sometimes draw close, and some separate, there is for sure the sign that they have iniquitous thoughts in their hearts"[14] (Della Porta, 1995, p. 218). He was followed by Petrus Camper, a Dutch naturalist and biologist, and Johann Casper Lavater, who in eighteenth century Switzerland studied and represented human qualities in the form of a map.

The tendency to measure has always been inherent in the perfect geometry of the human being: from the very beginning, exactitude has constituted an ideal to be aspired to (think of Leonardo's Vitruvian man and the harmonious inscription of the details of the body), with indications being proposed concerning supposed normality and certain quantitative parameters within which to fall in order not to be deviant.

Above all, this normalizing determinism, a vocation established mainly in medical and police circles, was based on an arbitrary deliberation of averageness: "Inspired by the writings of Adolphe Quetelet, a Belgian statistician who had introduced in 1835 the concept of what he called *l'homme moyen* (the average man)—a standard-bearer against whom the general population could be effectively compared—the young Bertillon chose to devote himself to the study of a more precise visual observation" (Helfand, 2019, pp. 17–19).

And if in some cases the identification of anomalies could suggest illness, discomfort, or disease, in many cases moving away from established normality meant approaching the suspicious and different otherness often attributed to criminality. Indeed, Bertillon became an expert in the judicial area by coining what was to become known as the *Portrait parlé*, the spoken portrait. Looking at a copy, we can see that it is a file in which, in addition to the photographs (front and profile) of the accused, there is a series of items of information divided into:

---

[14]Literary translation from old Italian. Original text: "Occhi ridenti, di fermo, e minaccevole aspetto. Ma se con volto minaccevole, e con fermi occhi riguardino, consigliano iniqui opere. Adamantino. Ma Alberto. Principalmente sì con quelli segni le palpebre alcune volte li giongono, & alcuni si separano, s'hà per certo segno che hanno nel cuore iniqui pensieri." (Adamantius and Albert where two philosophers with different opinions about laughing eyes.)

- Anthropometric observations (body and head measurements)
- Color information (eyes, beard, hair)
- Descriptive information of profile analysis (contour, forehead, nose, right ear, lips, and chin)
- Descriptive information of face analysis (contour, eyelashes, eyelids, mouth, corpulence, clothing, others)

Each of these categories was in turn subdivided into the articulation of detailed volumetric formulations. A few years later, Sir Francis Galton created an anthropometric laboratory, the purpose of which was "For the measurement in various ways of Human Form and Faculty." Other experts in anthropometry specialized precisely in criminals: Cesare Lombroso and Earnest A. Hooton, for example, shared the idea that one could be a criminal from birth and that this was recognizable from biometric features.

Such pseudoscientific foundations, then as now, incur a number of anthropological, ethical, and semiotic problems. The informativeness of the reading codes established in such practices potentially nurtures racial tendencies and stereotypical extremism. The information conveyed is pre-established by the positional authority of questionable and hierarchical knowledge; in the face would therefore be written what is right and what is wrong in a delicate and imputable axiological line.

With the coming of the world wars and the misuse of information from phrenology and physiognomy for racist speculation, these pseudosciences degenerated almost completely. Both, in fact, initially developed as sciences of facial observation and as integrations of the qualitative aspects aimed at specific reading and interpretation and then became inflections of a limiting tendency more linked to the biology of the face than to the traces of its becoming.

In recent years, however, we seem to be seeing a revival and rapprochement with physiognomy thanks to new technological supports. Going back to the examples given in the first part, we have seen how, to the naked eye, a hair or the residue of lipstick left on a cigarette butt tell us nothing, while the use of technology, hybridizing with human design skills, has made it possible to interpret and decode what in the past could be tackled only by highly specialized observers. There are currently a number of innovative projects concerned with reading what the human eye is not, *or is no longer*, capable of doing.

Numerous apps for smartphones fall into this category, such as Face2Gene which, generated by Boston's FDNA, now seems to be able to recognize genetic diseases such as Cornelia de Lange, Angelman, and Noonan syndromes with relative accuracy (around 65% of correct diagnoses): after uploading a photograph of the patients into the program, phenotypes are extracted that serve to reduce the possibilities of interpretation and offer support to the diagnosis, which will then certainly have to be supplemented and possibly confirmed by targeted DNA tests. So-called deep learning consists of wide-ranging algorithmic teaching: enormous quantities of data are entered into the machines, and consequently the variants resulting from their crossing are also far-reaching (Airoldi & Gambetta, 2018).

Human observation and tactile and presential precision, even in medicine, are rapidly being supplemented and partly replaced by artificial intelligence. Some holistic sciences still use them today to deepen the psychophysical situation and thus facilitate its improvement and rebalancing. Perhaps this inversion is part of the so-called material turn, in which the return to the signs caused by the passage of an energy, or in material connection – albeit indirectly – with other original signs, takes shape and meaning again.

Guglielmini proposes a distinction between fixed and "temporary" traits. The former are "part of the physical constitution and show the genetic heritage inherited from one's family of origin. (...) These permanent traits, such as the shape of the face or the size of the ears, reveal our basic nature; they cannot be changed, they can only be fully developed or repressed" (Guglielmini, 2012, p. 8). The latter "are temporary changes that appear on our face and represent the psychophysical state at a given time in our lives. Once that time has passed, the face resumes its usual appearance. (...) Finally, the 'mobile' features are the most obvious, changing and expressive part of our face. The face contracts and moves incessantly and with its mimicry, conscious or unconscious, manifests the emotions we are feeling" (Guglielmini, 2012, p. 9).

Thinking about the inscription of these signs, but above all their legacy on the face, means considering the presence of absence, a trace that takes on character and expressive features, an attitude made up of sedimented gestures whose material transformation can be examined. It also implies reopening the connective possibilities of epistemological spaces that are distant but ontologically coexistent: semiosis, a kind of bridge between the two foundations, connects existence with knowledge and makes sense of it.

Finally, it is important to remark that the face's organic exteriority, normally contemplated as the skin tissue formed by the outer epiderma and the underlying dermis, is a complex organ and part of the peripheral sensory mechanisms: "The haptic system uses sensory information derived from mechanoreceptors and thermoreceptors embedded in the skin ("cutaneous" inputs) *together with* mechanoreceptors embedded in muscles, tendons, and joints ("kinesthetic" inputs)" (Lederman & Klatzky, 2009, p. 1439).

The traces belong to a haptic influence of two or more bodies that meet and leave the echo of their contact in the form of an aesthetic, narrative, epidermal seal. The physiological role of this layer, as an account of all that surrounds it and the counterpart of what it excludes and that from which it is excluded, is that of a frontier: its elasticity allows the malleability needed in acting as a transition. The cutaneous receptors which densely inhabit the face regulate its sensitivity, temperature, excretion, and absorption. "The body—world open to the world—just as it continually gives off substances of different significance and consistency, also continually incorporates other substances: air, dust, sound, light or shadow. Subjected to the siege of what comes upon it, the body needs the senses so that the absorption is gradual and the world, therefore, is not only bearable but as far as possible physical or at least always significant. Thus, the senses, at the same time as they open the body to the absorption of the world, protect it from it, organize its defense"[15] (Dorra, 2005, p. 107).

The marks on the face, provoked or received without choice, mark a contact with otherness that is solidified not only in action but also in permanence. Jorit is the pseudonym of an Italian street artist known for his monumental graffiti scattered mainly around the city of Naples, where he lives. After travelling to Africa and approaching African culture, he decided to include a sign of recognition of African origin in his hyperrealistic paintings. A trace of pigment in his portraits, the two lines that cross the cheeks of his characters "refer to the African practice of fleshing out, to symbolize the unity of the tribe as opposed to the singularity of the individual."[16] In 2020, the artist decided to make a gesture that was not representative but embodied, having the stripes imprinted on his cheek, in a sort of personified ritualization and subjective identification of the nucleus conveyed by his works: the tribe. This permanent performance resulting in a face engraved forever opens its body to a form of empathizing with its creatures where the trace also becomes a symbol.

Traces Erased Toward New Tracks [Bio-societal Propagation/Recognition]

Assuming the examples shown until now to be part of a polyphonic semiosphere, we can observe how some of them flourish from the tangible but often ignored traces left everywhere by humans during daily life, while others are instances completely imbricated in the face itself. "To move oneself or have self-consciousness is in effect to refer oneself to oneself, to be an origin. Then a subject-origin which is also a subject of flesh and blood becomes problematic. The effort is made to understand it on the basis of an incarnation as an avatar of the representation of oneself, as a deficiency of this representation, the occultation of a translucid and spontaneous consciousness into receptivity and finitude" (Levinas, 2006[1998], p. 78).

Photography, an index by definition, is a trace of the subject filtered and transmitted in the form of light. The portrait, a genre par excellence in which the face is the protagonist, becomes a trace of absence if the face is dulled or even erased. Dondero proposes the analysis of a visual apparatus in term of forces, where it is possible to distinguish intensive and extensive weights: "Here, it is a question of

[15] Our translation from the original text: "El cuerpo—mundo abierto al mundo—así como continuamente desprende sustancias de diversa significación y consistencia también continuamente incorpora otras sustancias: aire, polvo, sonido, luz o sombra. Sometido al asedio de lo que viene sobre él, el cuerpo necesita de los sentidos para que la absorción sea gradual y el mundo, por lo tanto, sea no sólo soportable sino en lo posible fórico o al menos siempre significante. Así, los sentidos, al mismo tiempo que abren el cuerpo a la absorción del mundo lo protegen de él, organizan su defensa."

[16] https://www.napolitoday.it/cultura/jorit-segni-faccia-tatuaggio.html Last consultation on 26th of April 2021.

intensive magnitudes, and the forces which are at play consist in rhetorical operations of subtraction or inhibition. In what concerns extensive forces, it is necessary to be able to conceive of negative space: The negation of a portion of space consists in the suspension of a sensible quality which is normally associated with a certain presence in such space. In other words, negation can manifest itself through a rupture of the dependency between portions of space and sensible qualities" (Dondero, 2020, pp. 40–41).

Numerous artists use the medium of photography and post-portraiture to address, argue, and represent this posture. In Saraí's case, the face made memory through photography is colonized by an invasive, clear-cut, tabula rasa erasure of faces. The contextual traces, which are often still visually present, constitute the foundations for the gaze to still exist despite its absence: the severed faces conceal an intimate conversation within themselves, as if the gaze, previously turned outward, has performed a horizontal rotation of 160 degrees, moving the forces inside and showing us the back. A back that is not the rear portion of the head but a new face: in the white there is absence and infinity, in the negation of the gaze a new imagined density (Figs. 21.3 and 21.4).

In the emerging texture, we cannot avoid the simulacral reference, the cathartic cancellation, and the plasticity of a gesture substituted in a form exemplifying reality. Like a kind of magic, the stroke replaces the action and allows, at least visually, a complete semantic restructuring: "both simulacrum and copying are related to magic, with the only difference being that, in the first case, it is a magic of substitution and in the second, a magic of resemblance" (Stoichita, 1999, p. 33).

Taking as our reference the compactness of the present body but partially emptied of its receptive and productive formal and politico-social accumulation and stratification, in this last part, we deal with the erasure of traces, the backward path whereby from a trace of absence, one can eventually trace a new presence, a significant constitution of the same blood in a new imbricated and shared name.

The Janez Janša artistic collective is surely integrated in a kind of action where traces are emerging as symbolical and pragmatical signs in order to test, destabilize, and reorganize, in an innovative way, parts of the cultural complexity. Composed of three people, the group worked for years on an artistic piece that has gone down in history as emblematic evidence of contemporaneity and has been profoundly explained in a film directed by one of them. "*My Name is Janez Janša* is a documentary film about names and name changes, focusing on one particular and rather unique name change that took place in 2007, when three artists officially changed their names into the name of the Prime Minister of Slovenia, Janez Janša" (Figs. 21.5 and 21.6).[17]

"Jaz sem Janez Janša," the reverberation of the sentence as a mnemonic stabilization of the self, is associated with ancestral practices, in some cultures called mantra: the continuous repetition of certain sounds allows them to be internalized, whether they are morphemic or phonemic sets. A new identity needs to be

[17] https://vimeo.com/46937250

Fig. 21.3 Saraí Ojeda, *Abril del 67* Collection: Donde no puedas verme. Photography intervened. Printing: dye sublimation on cotton paper Dimension: 5 × 9 inches, México, 2018, Courtesy Saraí Ojeda

impersonated by the three protagonists, and the incorporation of the new name is one of the fundamental steps to be carried out. "The name is probably the most important marker of an essential human being, that we have in language. (. . .) There would be other markers, that are not linguistic, in visual language, but in written language and in spoken language, the name is the most important thing" (Catherine M. Soussl in *My Name is Janez Janša*).

Other artists have resorted to executing a similar performance: for example, on 5 October 2007, the artist Kristin Sue Lucas decided to go into what she called "the utmost conversion of myself." The honorable Frank Roesch confirmed that she changed her name in the spirit of "refreshing herself": in effect, the artist waded through a long bureaucratic, political, intimate mechanism to foster a symbolic change and reiterate her own name, thus engaging in subjective linguistic isomorphism and identifying traces.

The Janez Janša go through their autobiographies to rewrite themselves in a collective and constant political act; at the end of the documentary that tells their story, an infinity of people repeats *Jaz sem Janez Janša* in a sort of emphatic process.

Fig. 21.4 Saraí Ojeda, *Junio del 62* Collection: Donde no puedas verme. Photography intervened. Printing: dye sublimation on cotton paper Dimension: 5 × 9 inches, México, 2018, Courtesy Saraí Ojeda

Fig. 21.5 Janez Janša, Janez Janša, Janez Janša, *002199341 (Identity Card),* Print on plastic 5.4 × 8.5 cm, Ljubljana, 2007. Courtesy Aksioma, (www.aksioma.org) Institute for Contemporary Art, Ljubljana

A biography of them has also been written despite the fact that, during the documentary, Caronia tells us that "Biography is a destabilizing colonization operation because it constructs a referent that does not exist. The life of Janez Janša, if I read and try to interpret literally what is written in this book, I will never be able to find the real referent who is a totally imaginary character, whose life derives from the intersection of the three lives of three real characters" (Fig. 21.7).

The writing of the biography can be considered a partial achievement, because it implies that the subject about whom it narrates exists, albeit in symbolic terms: in fact, this subject has been constituted after overcoming an articulated pragmatic narrative program. Interpreted according to generative semiotics, we might think that the constitution of the new hybrid identity can be considered the object of value accomplished. The initially virtual modalities, in which duties and wishes coincided (wanting to change name and therefore having to face a whole series of sociopolitical but also intimate/mathematical vicissitudes), immediately intersected with

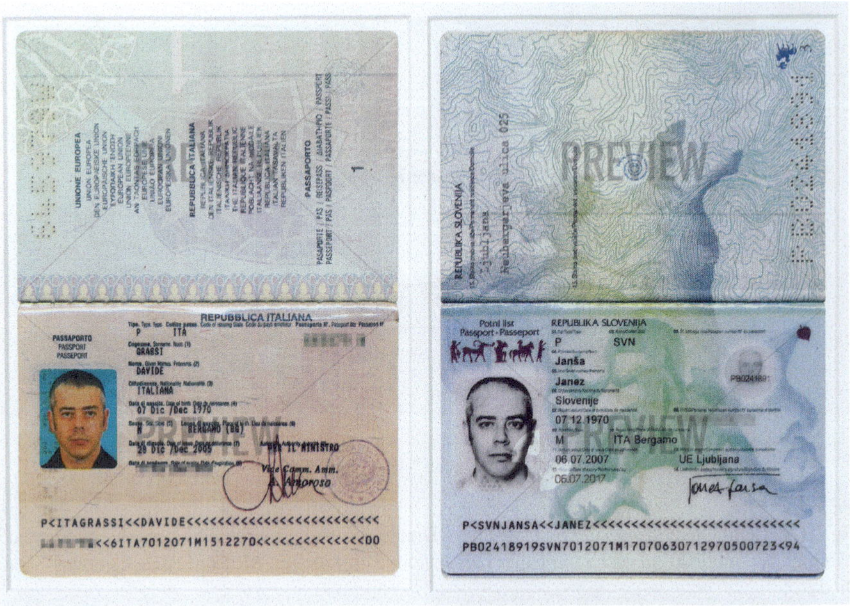

Fig. 21.6 Janez Janša, Janez Janša, Janez Janša, *Work*, (detail) Museum of Modern and Contemporary Art Rijeka, Mali salon, Rijeka, 2013. Curators: Sabina Salamon, Ksenija Orelj. Photo: Robert Sošić. Courtesy Aksioma, Institute for Contemporary Art, Ljubljana

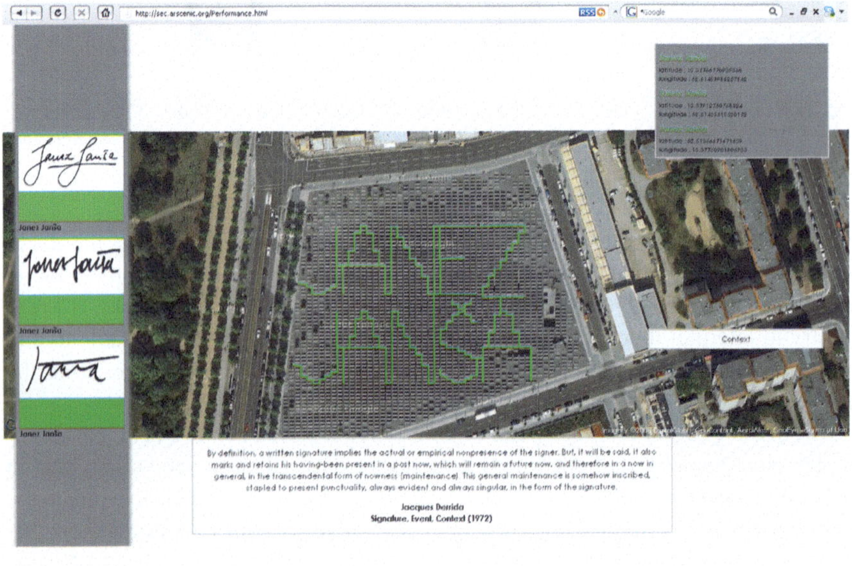

Fig. 21.7 Janez Janša, Janez Janša, Janez Janša, *Signature Event Context,* Berlin, 2008. Performance (screenshot). Courtesy Aksioma, Institute for Contemporary Art, Ljubljana

actualizing modalities. The latter category includes both knowledge (whether intrinsic or acquired along the way) and power (that set of endogenous or exogenous possibilities).

The virtual and actualizing modes can give rise to a third mode, in which the conjunction of the subject with its object of value, the new shared name, is achieved.

Following Steps

"The naive interpreter reads every projection as an imprint, i.e. as a direct transformation from the properties of a real thing; whereas projection is always the result of transformative conventions whereby certain traces on a surface are stimuli that prompt one to transform backward and postulate a type of content where in fact there is only one occurrence of expression. Thus it is possible to project from nothing or from contents to which no referents correspond"[18] (Eco, 2016, p. 370).

It is worth noting that the analysis of single signs is always part of a broader reading in which the crucial factor is the discursive whole, which also includes the ideological and cultural imbrication of the interpretations involved. There thus seems to be a kind of abductive logic in the genesis of the trace: a sign, as index and trace, acts as a mediation between two or more dimensions which, as envisaged by the abductive logic, come together by finding or creating the semiotic thread that sustains them: "at first sight abduction seems more like a free movement of the imagination nourished by emotions (like a vague 'intuition') than a normal process of decoding. (…) But the abductive movement is accomplished when a new sense (a new combinatorial quality) is assigned to each sound (or every kind of sign, note of author) as a component of the contextual meaning of the whole piece" (Eco, 2016, p. 211).

The proposed argumentations are thus also products of a combinatorial positioning that does not appeal to precise codifying rules but rather leverages the continuous performative possibility of form and track: "Underlying and beneath every semiotic impulse is the aesthetic pleasure of discovery" (Leone, 2020, p. 31).

[18]Original text: "The naive interpreter reads every projection as an imprint, i.e. as a direct transformation from the properties of a real thing; whereas projection is always the result of transformative conventions whereby certain traces on a surface are stimuli that prompt one to transform backward and postulate a type of content where in fact there is only one occurrence of expression. Thus, it is possible to project from nothing or from contents to which no referents correspond."

References

Airoldi, M., & Gambetta, D. (2018). Sul mito della neutralità algoritmica. In A. Martella, E. Campo and L. Ciccarese (Eds.) *Gli algoritmi come costruzione sociale* (pp. 25–45). LQ The Lab's Quarterly a.XX.n.4.

Barth, R. (1999). *Variazioni sulla scrittura. Seguite da Il piacere del testo.* Einaudi. (Original work pubblished 1973, Ed. Seuil).

Binda, E. (2017). Interagire con l'ambiente. In S. Capezzuto, D. Ciccone, & A. Mileto (Eds.), *Dentro/Fuori. Il lavoro dell'immaginazione e le forme del montaggio.* Ebook: Il lavoro culturale.

Della Porta, G. (1995). *Della fisionomia dell' huomo.* Bibliotèque numèrique.

Dondero, M. G. (2020). The language of images. The forms and the forces. In A. Sarti (Ed.), *Serie lecture notes in morphogenesis.* Springer.

Dorra, R. (2005). *La casa y el caracol.* Plaza y Valdes Eds.

Eco, U. (2016). *Trattato di semiotica generale.* La nave di Teseo.

Fontanille, J. (2003). *Quand le corps témoigne : approche sémiotique du reportage. Documents de Travail 329.* Università degli Studi 'Carlo Bo'.

Ginzburg, C. (2020). *Il filo e le tracce. Vero falso finto.* Feltrinelli. (Original work pubblished 2006).

Gramigna, R., & Voto, C. (2020). Semiotica, prossemica e contagio. Il senso delle distanze ai tempi del Covid-19. In M. Leone (Ed.), *Volti virali.* FACETS Digital Press, Open Access.

Greimas, A. J., & Courtés, J. (1982). *Semiotics and language. An analytical dictionary.* Indiana University Press. (Original work pubblished 1979).

Guglielmini, A. (2012). *Il linguaggio segreto del volto.* Ebook: Piemme.

Helfand, J. (2019). *FACE. A visual Odissey.* The MIT Press.

Jodorowsky, A. (2008). *La danza della realtà* (M. Finassi Parolo Trans.). Feltrinelli.

Lederman, S. J., & Klatzky, R. L. (2009). Haptic perception: A tutorial. In *attention. Perception & Psychophysics, 71*(7), 1439–1459.

Leone, M. (2020) *Colpire nel segno. La semiotica dell'irragionevole.* I Saggi di Lexia 38: Aracne.

Levinas, E. (2006 [1998]). *Otherwise than being or beyond essence* (A. Lingis Trans.). Duquesne University Press. (Original work published 1981).

Lotman, J. (2011). The place of art among other modelling systems. (in 3rd volume of Trudy po znakovym sistemam, 1967). *Sign Systems Studies, 39*(2/4), 249–270.

Magli, P. (1995). *Il volto e l'anima. Fisiognomica e passioni.* CDE.

Stoichita, V. I. (1999). *Breve historia de la sombra.* (A.M. Coderch Trans.) Madrid: Siruela. (Original work published 1997).

Silvia Barbotto Forzano, PostDoc Fellow FACETS (ERC project headed by Massimo Leone), professor in University of Turin (IT) and Autonomous University of Yucatan (Mx).

PhD in *Art: research and production* (2014, San Carlos, Spain). Graduated in *Communication* (2004, UniTo, Italy).

Now researching in areas as semiotic of face, bodies and cultures, perception and senses, (self)portrait/re(cognition) through art and new media, comparative physiognomic and anthropo-neuro-physiology, Artificial agency and intelligence, Transmedia and digital narrativities, critical anthropocene and heritage. Artist and Yogini, her research join academic semiotic theories and aesthetic/experimental practices.

Open Access: *Forme di vita* (http://hdl.handle.net/2318/1737209), *El rostro enlarvado en el arte contemporáneo* (http://hdl.handle.net/2318/1824192), *I volti di. Quell'anno in cui...*(http://hdl.handle.net/2318/1824191), *Etnografia de un espacio de creaciòn* (http://hdl.handle.net/2318/1823749), *Artificial face and transhumanism in contemporary art* (http://hdl.handle.net/2318/1823765), *Accenni pre-veridici del complotto nel sistema dell'arte e face studies (*http://hdl.handle.net/2318/1784853), *Art, face and breathscape: air is also a cultural issue (*http://hdl.handle.net/2318/1824298), *Semiótica de la fotografía con los ojos de Graciela Iturbide* (http://

hdl.handle.net/2318/1824178), *Della mistica nell'arte. Parallelismi tra autobiografie e autoritratti spirituali (*http://hdl.handle.net/2318/1824300), *Volto di cenere e suono. Cronotopi, semiotica implicata e teatro contemporaneo* (http://hdl.handle.net/2318/1824302). *La multidimensionalité dans la construction du futur: le visage, le désert et les machines* (forthcoming), *Transmedia storytelling, meta-verso(?) e* corpi estesi (forthcoming). One book *Vitàcora. Interferencias cotidianas* (2016) Yucatán: Sedeculta. Member of IASS, SSA, AES, Journalist Board. Works presented in Europe, México, USA, Latin America, India.

Chapter 22
Shameful Traces and Image-Based Sexual Abuse: The Case of Tiziana Cantone

Vincenzo Romania

The Events[1]

I have chosen Tiziana Cantone's case for various reasons. First, it shows the complex interrelationships between technological, relational, cultural and normative frameworks. Second, it enables understanding the role of traces in the transmissibility and transformability of shame in diverse face-to-face and digital contexts. Third, it demonstrates how political and economic actors negotiate the institution of a digital moral order. Fourth, the case played a major role in the redefinition of the normative regulation of pornography and hate cybercrimes.

Let me briefly summarise the main events. Between November 2014 and April 2015, Tiziana Cantone, a 30-year-old woman living in a village near the metropolitan city of Naples, yielded to her partner's request to be filmed while having sex with other men. In total, the couple recorded six videos that, in April 2015, were shared with acquaintances, who apparently disseminated them without their consent to other WhatsApp users. In the shared videos, all the participants' faces were pixeled (obscured) except for Tiziana Cantone's. Within hours, the videos went viral on WhatsApp and were downloaded by several thousand people on their devices. The videos spread mainly in the densely inhabited geographical area where the couple lived, fuelling gossip against Cantone. On April, 2015, the compromising videos were first posted on major pornographic portals, still without any consent from Tiziana Cantone. A little later, some users extracted a scene that would go viral from one of the six videos. The short video excerpt shows Tiziana

[1] Most of the information in this section derives from the Italian newspaper *Il* Post, 2016.

V. Romania (✉)
Department of Philosophy, Sociology, Education and Applied Psychology, University of Padua, Padua, Italy
e-mail: vincenzo.romania@unipd.it

F. Comunello et al. (eds.), *What People Leave Behind*, Frontiers in Sociology and Social Research 7, https://doi.org/10.1007/978-3-031-11756-5_22

Cantone having sexual intercourse with another man and exclaiming as she turns to her partner, "Mi stai facendo il video? Bravo!" [Are you making a video? Bravo!].

This scene would be used in parodic videos and memes that spread very quickly on the main social networks to the point of making Tiziana Cantone a negative icon of collective mockery and shaming. Thousands of social media users participated in this process, including Italian celebrities. In the following days, Cantone's memes were reproduced on t-shirts, mugs and other merchandising items (BBC, 2017), her negative icon utterly commodified. A parody of the unhappily famous scene was also included in the music video of an Italian pop star posted on YouTube in June 2015 and still available on the platform.[2] As I write this article, the music video has collected 28.3 million views.

Tiziana Cantone, the victim of this enormity, took the case to court in May 2015, suing those responsible for the non-consensual dissemination of intimate images and asking the porn websites, social networks and web providers to remove the six original videos and all the derived content. Given the glacial pace of the Italian judicial system, the court reached a verdict only a year later. In the meantime, Cantone requested and was granted a changed surname. She moved away from her usual place of residence and did everything possible to conceal her identity in the offline world.

In the summer of 2016, an Italian court required companies such as Facebook, Twitter, Yahoo, Google and YouTube to remove any post or content directly or indirectly related to Tiziana Cantone. The judge found the platforms guilty of not having timely accepted the woman's request to remove the offending content and their indexing of it. The court recognised Cantone's right to compensation but postponed its determination to a future trial. Meanwhile, Cantone was forced to pay each of the five companies €3655 (for a total of €18,225 + VAT = approximately €22,000) due to formal errors committed by her lawyers. Another relevant aspect of the story with respect to the topics of this article is that Cantone was denied the right to be forgotten because, according to a statement in the verdict, "[The] fundamental prerequisite for the interested party to oppose the processing of personal data, citing the right to be forgotten, is that such data relate to events dating back over time" while, in Cantone's case, "the court did not consider the time elapsed long enough to make the collective interest disappear" (*Il* Post, 2016).

A few days after the reading of the judgement, in September 2016, Tiziana Cantone committed suicide. Judicial investigations of the causes and dynamics of her death are still ongoing. The case has produced a great international impact. Global broadcasters, such as CNN, BBC and the *New York Times* (CNN, 2016; BBC, 2017; *New York Times,* 2016) have covered it. The international debate on this and homologous cases has given rise to calls for legal changes regarding the

[2] I refer to the music video of the song *#fuori c'è il sole* by Lorenzo Fragola, in which the parody of Tiziana Cantone's phrase is at 3′ 57″. https://www.youtube.com/watch?v=1rekwTmhYtQ (accessed: 19 February 2022)

diffusion of leaked private videos and for greater protection for the victims of such cybercrimes (Pavan & Lavorgna, 2021).

A Theory of Digital Shameful Traces

The production and diffusion of a digital shameful trace are a complex social process, and understanding it requires focusing on the elements of a concerted social action. I propose here to divide the phenomenon into five constitutive elements; first, the *ontology* of the symbolic element that becomes the trace and conveys shame; second, the *actors* involved in its production and diffusion; third, the temporal and spatial coordinates of the *diffusion* and the technical or social means employed in it; and finally (fourth and fifth), the cultural and normative *frameworks* constituting the background of the shaming process and enabling the diffusion of shame.

Regarding the ontology of a shameful trace, we must start by deconstructing some commonly understood categories, such as revenge porn, that are often used in media studies to address cases like the one here analysed. That category, as Tiziana Cantone's case shows, is reductive. First, the concept of *revenge* focusses attention on the responsibility of only one offender—the partner who initially disseminates intimate images—while, as we will show, the number of human and non-human actors and audiences involved in the process of shaming is very large, and their conduct and responsibility are highly differentiated but interconnected. Digital shaming cannot be understood as other than a massive sociotechnical process.

Second, the concept of revenge attributes to the male partner a specific and reductive intention: creating awareness of the purported offence of his (ex- or current) partner for relational reasons. However, this is not always the case. In most cases of cyberviolence against women, it is not simply or not only a conscious desire for revenge that motivates men who disseminate intimate images without the consent of their partners. Rather, the situations in which the images are produced and then disseminated, the relationship between the victim and the perpetrator and the states of awareness (Glaser & Strauss, 1968) that characterise all the actors involved in the process are plural and contradictory. Third, focussing on revenge implicitly blames the victim for her relational conduct. Fourth, what becomes a source of shame is not only and not simply pornographic content. It is, rather, an intimate slice of privacy that becomes a source of shame only in given situations and in given cultural and normative frameworks with the participation of given social actors united by a given social bond. Finally, as Tiziana Cantone's case shows, the source of shame may shift from the original content disseminated by a partner to further user-generated by-products.

More neutral categorisations, such as *image-based sexual abuse* (IBSA) (Henry et al., 2020) and *non-consensual dissemination of intimate images* (NCDII) (Maddocks, 2018) may be more useful in reaching a sociological understanding of the digital forms of violence against women enacted through the use of shameful traces. Still, they do not help us understand how shame is culturally and interactionally produced and transmitted, understand the role of social bonds or understand how digital traces transform the overall process of shaming. Let us start with the first dimension.

Shame is a family of social emotions of diverse intensity and expression. Thomas Scheff defines it as “the large family of emotions that includes many cognates and variants, most notably embarrassment, guilt, humiliation, and related feelings such as shyness that originate in threats to the social bond. This definition integrates self (emotional reactions) and society (the social bond)” (Scheff, 2003: 255). Shame, then, depends on social bonds, on role expectations in a social organisation (Goffman, 1956) and, finally, on the contexts of interaction, i.e. situations. The process of shaming typically follows a moral transgression of publicly accepted rules of behaviour/appearance/conduct from the societal side and a sense of inadequacy from the subjective side. As Thomas Scheff brilliantly suggests, shame is our moral gyroscope (Scheff, 2003: 254). Any of our behaviours is preceded and influenced by “a sense of shame” (Scheff, 2000: 96).

Therefore, no trace of a morally reprehensible behaviour/appearance/conduct is in itself a shameful trace. It is so only in latent form (Sabetta, 2018). For a record—such as a memory, text, audiovisual record or any other element—to become an object of shame, it is necessary that it crosses the moral boundaries of specific situations, social bonds and regulatory standards. Actually, a shameful trace is a vector. It transports shame from a spatial context to another, from a temporal context to another. The overall process of shaming is the mediation between something that happened in a context where it was legitimate and its moral condemnation in a different spatial, temporal and social context. Given this consideration, in a digitalised society, intimate shameful traces are more and more important in the spreading of shame.

Indeed, the collective violence perpetrated against Tiziana Cantone depended on the circulation of non-consensual intimate images outside the intimate sphere of the couple. It is necessary to emphasise that it was not the sexual behaviour itself that was stigmatised so much as the fact that a trace of it was spread outside the moral boundaries of her intimacy without the consent of the victim. The shameful trace is an evidence marker (Brekhus, 1998) of the unequivocal existence of a behaviour that goes against the moral standards of the community. In modern Western societies, self-discipline (Elias, 1994), control over of one’s corporeality (Goffman, 1961) and rules of conduct represent essential symbolic means of preserving face (Goffman, 1955). Any dissemination of intimate images, i.e. traces of sexual activity, outside the private sphere is therefore a clear threat to one’s reputation. This is particularly true in an ambivalent technological context in which people are asked to preserve their privacy but also pushed to renounce to it to interact on social media and other platforms that threaten their privacy.

Cuckoldry, Masculine Domination and Shame

Shame based on NCDII is a critical social problem for women, whose sexual freedom is still contested and who are the predominant victims of this kind of cybercrime (Pavan & Lavorgna, 2021). Let us return to Tiziana Cantone's case and to the sexual act she performed together with her partner and others external to the couple to understand how such practices make women's reputations particularly vulnerable.

Cuckoldry is a very old sexual script (Simon & Gagnon, 2003) that has been represented in narrative fiction since the times of Boccaccio and Shakespeare (Alfar, 2017). In the public imagination, it is a typically heterosexual phenomenon. As considered using the concepts introduced by Goffman in *Frame Analysis* (1974), consensual cuckoldry represents a *regrounding* of traditional patriarchal dynamics.[3] During the sexual act, the traditional power inequality between men and women is inverted. The woman enacts a dominant role by flirting or having sex with other men, while the man assumes the role of the humiliated (ashamed, for our theoretical interests). As soon as the performance of cuckoldry ends, however, the masculine domination and the risk of shaming (Bourdieu, 2001) are both against the female partner. The male partner controls the scene, its reproduction and its public dissemination, while the other men participating in the performance[4] control information about their sexuality that could be harmful to both, but that is particularly harmful to women as explained before. Also, cuckoldry challenges the traditional relationship between romantic love and sexual scripts; it is constitutively based on a challenge to traditional norms of shame avoidance.

What has recently changed is the relevance of audiovisual traces produced during this kind of performance. In the past decade (Lokke, 2019), cuckoldry pornography has become very popular on the internet thanks to the proliferation of pornographic portals and forums hosting amateur material and because of the weak normative regulation of this world. While, in classic cuckoldry, the masculine domination (Bourdieu, 2001) was enacted simply by control over the scene, now, as in the case of Tiziana Cantone, it is based on control of the visual traces produced during the cuckoldry and on the ritual degradation of women's reputations enacted by sharing their intimacy with other men and by forcing women to endure any form of public offence to their dignity. In cuckold forums, such as the ones now spreading on Telegram (Semenzin & Bainotti, 2020), NCDII represents a kind of currency in a market of moral degradation (Ziccardi, 2020). The female body is commodified and

---

[3] In Goffman's *Frame Analysis*, regrounding is one of the five categories of essential keys. A *key* is defined as "the set of conventions by which a given activity, one already meaningful in terms of some primary framework, is transformed into something patterned on this activity but seen by the participants to be something quite else" (Goffman, 1974: 43–44). The notion of regrounding, Goffman says, "rests on the assumption that some motives for a deed are ones that leave the performer within the normal range of participation, and other motives ... leave the performer outside the ordinary domains of the activity" (ibid.: 74).

[4] In pornographic slang, these men are called the bulls.

offered to the male gaze as a dematerialised currency exchanged within a wider market of erotic extortion (Kempton, 2020). The participants exchange intimate images of their partners in market-like transactions that fuel both their sexual pleasure and the moral degradation of their partners.

To conclude, the sexual behaviour of the couple becomes an object of possible shame and moral degradation as soon as it is exposed to an audience larger than the couple themselves.[5] Subsequently, audiovisual traces are key elements, and the digital turn of society has made this point more evident than ever before.

Shame, Social Bonds and Communication

Thus, a consideration of the relationship between shame and situation is merited. Applying Thomas Scheff's theory, I first consider the relationship between shame and social bonds. In Section "The Sociotechnical and Normative Frameworks", I focus on the socio-technological and normative frameworks.

The key moments in the dissemination of shameful traces against Tiziana Cantone were as follows:

- First, her partner shared their private videos with a group of acquaintances.
- Second, some of the recipients shared the videos with other WhatsApp contacts who mainly lived in the metropolitan and peri-urban area of Naples.
- Third, someone posted the videos to pornographic portals, sharing them with a potentially vast audience of web users.
- Fourth, by-products of the original videos (shorter clips, memes, parodic videos) were produced and shared on social media among a national audience.

In the first context, the recipients of the videos personally knew the couple and had already interacted with them before the delivery. Therefore, the mediated digital interaction (Thompson, 2020) took place from a sender to a small number of known recipients. The video recordings had a predominantly erotic value. The few male recipients, in fact, represented the audience chosen by Tiziana Cantone's partner to realise his erotic fantasy in front of an audience.

In the second context of shame, Cantone and her partner's acquaintances shared the videos with a larger audience comprising their WhatsApp contacts. These, in turn, transmitted the videos to other contacts, giving rise to a massive, snowballing process of dissemination. Between this stage and the following, over 200,000 users would download Tiziana Cantone's videos on their devices.[6] From a communicative point of view, this is perhaps the most interesting stage. In fact, what happened was neither an interpersonal communication of one to a few defined recipients as in the first stage nor a communication of one to many indefinite recipients as in the typical

[5]Of course, this argument could be extended to other phenomena of IBSA, such as sexting.

[6]These data are mentioned in the judicial ruling published in September 2016 (*Il* Post, 2016).

case of mass media broadcasts (Thompson, 2020). Rather, we are faced with many networked publics (Russel, 2008) that internally shared the videos. Recalling Coleman's boat metaphor (Coleman, 1994), what appears a posteriori as a macro-sociological phenomenon was the sum of many actions in many smaller social circles that shared interpersonal social bonds.

In this second sociotechnical context, the social function of the visual traces changed. They were now vectors of shame and mainly used as a source of gossip, a form of social control that joins the private and public spheres (Scotson & Elias, 1965), and that tends to be violent in its social effects. Significant in this regard is the fact that the videos first spread in the same densely inhabited geographical area where the couple lived. Furthermore, Tiziana Cantone's identity was made easily recognisable. To describe homologous processes, feminist scholars have spoken of *slut-shaming*. As Gong and Hoffman put it, "Women who do engage in sexual activity or are simply perceived to be interested in such activity are [condemned and considered as] bad or dirty" (Gong & Hoffman, 2012: 580).

The third phase is the one where the communication is similar to the forms of mass media broadcasting: from one to many indefinite recipients (Thompson, 2020). Still, even on the most famous pornographic website, the identity of the victim was made recognisable, and this aspect connected the indefinite audience of web users with the local community where Tiziana Cantone lived and where shame kept circulating. Thus, interpersonal social bonds were less evident but still present even at this stage.

Finally, the original shameful traces were transformed in user-generated by-products: shorter non-pornographic captures, memes and parodic videos widely shared on social media. At a national level, the defamation and shaming that befell Tiziana Cantone relied heavily on such secondary, non-pornographic products derived from the original videos. It all began with the publication of a meme that went viral in a very short time. The visual is a capture from one of the six original videos. The text mentions the sadly famous sentence pronounced by Tiziana Cantone to her partner: "You are making a video? Bravo!" She appears confident in performing the sexual activities and in their videotaping. In the eyes of common feeling, she thus demonstrates inappropriateness and naivety, because she is unable to predict the consequences that she would encounter. Soon, the sentence became a catchphrase, a national running joke all over Italy, and Cantone became a negative icon to be publicly mocked. Thousands of web users shared homologous memes and parodies without this being perceived as a morally despicable practice. At the base of these diffusion processes are specific characteristics of this communicative genre, to which it is therefore necessary to turn our attention.

According to the Oxford Learner's Dictionary, *meme* has two meanings, the first being "an idea that is passed from one member of society to another, not in the genes but often by people copying it". This meaning derives from the work of Richard Dawkins, who introduced the term in *The Selfish Gene* in 1976. Etymologically, the term derives from the Greek *mímēma* (imitation). Only in the past decade, first within internet studies and then in the common understanding, has a second meaning emerged that is more appropriate to the case we are investigating: "an image, a video, a piece of text, etc. that is passed very quickly from one internet user to another, often with slight changes that make it humorous" (Oxford Learner's Dictionary).

The definition contains three elements, all pertinent to the Cantone case: social contagion (or imitation), appropriation and humour. That is, virality is not enough for content to become a meme (Börzsei, 2013). It is also necessary for a user to actively transform it into something personal, to appropriate it with humour and bring it closer to her/his own experience (as do others). Memes are indeed hybrid cultural products. They use digital pop culture images to express feelings, moods, stances and relationships. This interpenetration of semantic levels makes them particularly suitable for communicative contexts, such as those of social media, in which the genres of public discussion and interpersonal narration come together.

In conclusion, in all phases of this diffusion of shameful traces, one can observe a connection between various forms of social and emotive bonds: the couple's private sphere, the interpersonal sphere of a given social circle and the wider audience composed of first a local community and then a national community of web users. In each of these contexts, the predominant meaning and function of the trace changed. In successive iterations, it represented erotic content, a virtual currency of moral degradation, a topic of gossip and, finally, humorous content to be shared with social media friends and followers. This shows that shameful traces are plastic signifiers that adapt to the contexts of diffusion and to the actors who appropriate them.

Two crucial elements that we have not yet discussed are the sociotechnical contexts and the regulatory frameworks that constitute the background of the spread of traces. I do this in the next section.

The Sociotechnical and Normative Frameworks

The shaming that affected Tiziana Cantone in 2015 would have had different—probably less cruel—effects in the current sociotechnical and normative context.[7] Since the events, instant messaging platforms, social media networks and pornographic portals have adopted more restrictive policies against NCDII. In 2018, the European General Data Protection Regulation took effect, offering stronger protection of web users' privacy and security. Various countries, such as Australia (2018), Italy (2019) and the UK (2021) as well as 42 states in the USA have introduced new laws to combat IBSA and other forms of cybercrime, but, frankly, the overall regulation of hate speech, IBSA and homologous cybercrimes is not as linear as it may seem.

[7] I use the term sociotechnical to emphasise that, in digital communication, the two levels (social and technological) interpenetrate and interact with each other. In other words, communicative technologies are domesticated in our daily life, reorganising our collective social mindscapes (Zerubavel, 1999).

First, legislatures must achieve the right balance between censorship and freedom of expression. Second, the bargaining power of the big web players is so great that it is most often states that must negotiate the conditions of action within them. Third, a substantial number of xenophobic and/or populist politicians exploit existing normative vacuums to construct a consensus based on symbolic violence. Fourth, the intersection of online and offline worlds often makes it difficult to establish the real jurisdiction of some cybercrimes. Finally, each new legislation collides with the very rapid obsolescence of hardware and software technologies. The more technological change accelerates, the quicker the normative regulation of it becomes obsolete.

Tiziana Cantone's case involved three main sociotechnical frameworks of trace diffusion: WhatsApp, pornographic portals and Facebook. In none of them did censorship stop the circulation of shameful traces (pornographic videos and derived content).

Beginning with WhatsApp, it must be considered that its nature as an instant messaging platform without any official access to users' messages makes the moderation of shared content impossible. When Cantone's videos were disseminated on WhatsApp, the existing procedure made it very quick and easy for users to share content in a few clicks with as many as 256 contacts at a time. This technical capability strongly affected the speed of the diffusion of the shameful traces. Only in 2019, in the face of political and civil pressure to reduce the viral spread of fake news and hate content, was this capacity for mass forwarding removed from the app. Today, it remains possible to share defamatory content with thousands of contacts, but the operation has become far slower and more laborious, as the maximum number of shares each time varies from 1 to 5.[8]

Pornographic websites constituted the second context of defamation and shame. Again, together with the introduction of new laws protecting people's privacy and security, the civil sphere has played a massive role in limiting the circulation of non-consensual intimate images. In December 2020, a New York Times inquiry by Nicholas Kristof denounced the dissemination of content showing sexual abuse or portraying minors or NCDII on one of the major players in this field, Pornhub (New York Times, 2020) and a broad public controversy arose in the USA and around the world. Pornhub immediately banned the uploading of videos to unverified accounts—basically, ones other than those of production companies and actors—and removed the feature that allowed videos to be downloaded. This change in the biggest porn player's policies also affected competing websites, although significant differences still exist between national regulations as well as between the indexed web and the dark web.

[8]This is mentioned in the WhatsApp F.A.Q.: "You can forward a message with up to five chats at one time. However, when a message is forwarded through a chain of five or more chats, meaning it's at least five forwards away from it original sender, a double arrow icon and 'Forwarded many times' label will be displayed. These messages can only be forwarded to one chat at a time, as a way to help keep conversations on WhatsApp intimate and personal. This also helps slow down the spread of rumors, viral messages, and fake news". https://faq.whatsapp.com/general/chats/about-forwarding-limits/?lang=en (Accessed: 12 February 2022).

The last and most complex context is that of social media. Here, shameful traces were of different kinds: video excerpts from the original videos, links to external pornographic and non-pornographic websites, memes and parodic videos. While it is easier to identify and ban explicit pornographic content on platforms such as Instagram and Facebook, only the intervention of the judge in Cantone's case made it possible to remove all the defamatory content of a non-pornographic nature.

Another socio-normative controversy concerns the juridical nature of social media and whether they are more similar to organs of information or to simple containers of user-generated content. From one case to another, the responsibilities and functions of social networks change considerably. In 2016, the Italian Supreme Court, in a judgement concerning a case of insults and defamation (manifested in the form of offensive material published on the platform), clarified that Facebook is not included in the concept of the free press, falling at most in the related category of "any other means of publicity".[9]

Looking again at Facebook, recent research has revealed a poor process of moderation of abusive comments and posts. Matthew Hindman, Nathaniel Lubin and Trevor Davis analysed the 500 US-based pages with the highest average engagement in the summer of 2020, and the preliminary results were published in February 2002 in The Atlantic. As they summarise in the article, "Of the 219 accounts with at least 25 public comments, 68 percent spread misinformation, reposted in spammy ways, published comments that were racist or sexist or anti-Semitic or anti-gay, wished violence on their perceived enemies, or, in most cases, several of the above" (Hindman et al., 2022).

In conclusion, regarding the socio-technological and normative frameworks pertinent to the case, we may observe some points of sociological interest. First, the digital normative order is the product of competing yet linked ecologies (Abbott, 2005), such as government, supranational entities, digital media companies and actors in civil society. Second, the overlap between competing jurisdictions often makes regulatory frameworks opaque and contradictory. In this condition, shameful traces tend to circulate more rapidly, and those who share them or download them on their devices act within hybrid communication frameworks in which the private and public spheres often overlap. Consequently, morally despicable behaviours are not perceived as such. In other words, an "everybody does it" immunity is claimed, and, in highly imitative processes, profiling and indexing algorithms certainly play an important role. The shame projected on the victim subjectively mitigates the shame associated with the denigratory action of the web users.

[9]Judgement n. 4873, Cass. pen., Sect. V, 14 November 2016

Discussion

Shameful traces are the constitutive elements of IBSAs and other, similar forms of cybercrime involving the denigration or stigmatisation of the victim. They move from a communicative and normative ecology to another when specific interactional, sociotechnical and normative conditions occur as demonstrated in the previous two sections. Their high shareability extends the magnitude of the shame over time and space and makes them essentially undeletable, as the reference to the denial of the right to be forgotten in Tiziana Cantone's story shows. Furthermore, they connect the intimate, interpersonal and collective dimensions. Shame is thus expressed in a semi-private and semi-public digital context in which the moral degradation of victims is unconnected to any moral imperative.

To understand this last point, it seems useful in conclusion to propose a comparison between IBSAs and what Harold Garfinkel has defined as successful degradation ceremonies. In Garfinkel's approach, a degradation ceremony could be conceived as "Any communicative work between persons, whereby the public identity of an actor is transformed into something looked on as lower in the local scheme of social types" (Garfinkel, 1956: 420). The perpetrator is a representative of a public authority and an emanation of the social structure. The site and time of the ceremony is separated from everyday life. It is performed because of moral indignation and the danger that the precipitating events pose to social solidarity.

In IBSAs, by contrast, audiences share a common focus of attention (the shameful trace) but in separate and overlapping places and times. The reason for the violence directed at the victim has nothing to do with moral indignation or the reconstruction of some form of social solidarity. No public authority conducts the ceremony. Rather, multiple users stage their own personal or interpersonal degradation ceremonies in their semi-private and semi-public digital spaces.

We are therefore in a rather different situation from the typically Durkheimian one that inspired Harold Garfinkel in the elaboration of his famous theory. Indeed, shameful traces are shared and instrumentally used in various situations of contrasting nature. Compared to the symbolic interactionist perspective and to the ethnometodological perspective, the case I analysed defies the same assumption of a situation as a normative, clearly perceived and operationally defined frame of action.

References

Abbott, A. (2005). Linked ecologies: States and universities as environments for professions. *Sociological Theory, 23*(3), 245–274.

Alfar, C. L. (2017). *Women and Shakespeare's cuckoldry plays: Shifting narratives of marital betrayal*. Routledge.

BBC. (2017). Italy's Tiziana: Tragedy of a woman destroyed by viral sex videos. Retrieved from: https://www.bbc.com/news/world-europe-38848528 (Last accessed: 18 February 2022).

Börzsei, L. (2013, February). Makes a meme instead: A concise history of internet memes. *New Media Studies Magazine, 2013*, 1–28.
Bourdieu, P. (2001). *Masculine domination*. Stanford University Press.
Brekhus, W. (1998). A sociology of the unmarked: Redirecting our focus. *Sociological Theory, 16*(1), 34–51.
CNN. (2016). *Tiziana Cantone's family calls for justice after suicide over sex tape*. Retrieved from: https://edition.cnn.com/2016/09/16/europe/tiziana-cantone-sex-tape-suicide/ (Last accessed: 18 February 2022).
Coleman, J. S. (1994). *Foundations of social theory*. Harvard University Press.
Elias, N. (1994). *The civilizing process*. Blackwell.
Garfinkel, H. (1956). Conditions of successful degradation ceremonies. *American Journal of Sociology, 61*(5), 420–424.
Glaser, B., & Strauss, A. (1968). *Time for dying*. Aldine.
Goffman, E. (1955). On face-work: An analysis of ritual elements in social interaction. *Psychiatry: Journal of Interpersonal Relations, 18*(3), 213–231.
Goffman, E. (1956). Embarrassment and social organization. *American Journal of Sociology, 62*(3), 264–271.
Goffman, E. (1961). *Asylums: Essays on the social situation of mental patients and other inmates*. Doubleday Anchor.
Goffman, E. (1974). *Frame analysis. An essay on the organization of experience*. Northeastern University Press.
Gong, L., & Hoffman, A. (2012). Sexting and slut-shamming: Why prosecution of teen self-sexters harms women. *Georgetown Journal of Gender and the Law, 13*(2), 577–590.
Henry, N., Flynn, A., & Powell, A. (2020). Technology-facilitated domestic and sexual violence: A review. *Violence Against Women, 26*(15–16), 1828-1854.10.1177/1077801219875821.
Hindman, M., Lubin, N., & Davis, T. (2022). Facebook has a Superuser-supremacy problem. *The Atlantic*. Retrieved from: https://www.theatlantic.com/technology/archive/2022/02/facebook-hate-speech-misinformation-superusers/621617/ (last accessed: 18th February 2022).
Kempton, S. (2020). Erotic extortion: Understanding the cultural propagation of revenge porn. *SAGE open*. First published online: 3 June 2020. https://doi.org/10.1177/2158244020931850.
Lokke, G. (2019). Cuckolds, cucks, and their transgressions. *Porn Studies, 6*(2), 212–227. https://doi.org/10.1080/23268743.2018.1555053
Maddocks, S. (2018). From non-consensual pornography to image-based sexual abuse: Charting the course of a problem with many names. *Australian Feminist Studies, 33*(97), 345–361. https://doi.org/10.1080/08164649.2018.1542592
Pavan, E., & Lavorgna, A. (2021). Promises and pitfalls of legal responses to image-based sexual abuse: Critical insights from the Italian case. In *The Palgrave handbook of gendered violence and technology* (pp. 545–564). Palgrave Macmillan. https://doi.org/10.1007/978-3-030-83734-1_27
Il Post. (2016). *Storia di Tiziana Cantone*. Retrieved from: https://www.ilpost.it/2016/09/15/storia-tiziana-cantone/ (Last accessed 15 February 2022).
Russel, A. (2008). *Networked publics*. MIT Press.
Sabetta, L. (2018). *La dimensione latente dell'azione sociale*. Franco Angeli.
Scheff, T. J. (2000). Shame and the social bond: A sociological theory. *Sociological Theory, 18*(1), 84–99. https://doi.org/10.1111/0735-2751.00089
Scheff, T. J. (2003). Shame in self and society. *Symbolic Interaction, 26*(2), 239–262.
Scotson, J. L., & Elias, N. (1965). *The established and the outsiders*. Sage.
Semenzin, S., & Bainotti, L. (2020, October). The use of telegram for consensual dissemination of intimate images: Gendered affordances and the construction of masculinities. *Social Media + Society, 2020*, 1–12. https://doi.org/10.1177/2056305120984453
Simon, W., & Gagnon, J. H. (2003). Sexual scripts: Origins, influences and changes. *Qualitative Sociology, 26*(4), 491–497. https://doi.org/10.1023/B:QUAS.0000005053.99846.e5

The New York Times. (2016). *Viral sex tapes and a suicide prompt outrage in Italy*. Retrieved from: https://www.nytimes.com/2016/09/17/world/europe/italy-tiziana-cantone-sex-tapes-suicide.html (Last accessed: 18th February 2022).

The New York Times. (2020). Opinion. The Children of Pornhub. Retrieved from: https://www.nytimes.com/2020/12/04/opinion/sunday/pornhub-rape-trafficking.html (Last accessed: 19th February 2022).

Thompson, J. B. (2020). Mediated interaction in the digital age. *Theory, Culture & Society, 37*(1), 3–28. https://doi.org/10.1177/0263276418808592

Zerubavel, E. (1999). *Social mindscapes: An invitation to cognitive sociology*. Harvard University Press.

Ziccardi, G. (2020). *Online political hate speech in Europe: The rise of new extremisms*. Edward Elgar Publishing.

Vincenzo Romania is Associate Professor in Sociology at the University of Padua and Invited Professor at the Venice International University. He has been editor of different sociological journals and secretary (2017–2020) of the AIS (Italian Sociological Association) section in Sociological Theory. His main interests are social theory, identity studies and cultural pluralism. His last contributions are "Vilfredo Pareto" in M. Cerulo and A. Scribano (eds.) (2022); *The Emotions in the Classics of Sociology*, London: Routledge, pp. 96–112; "COVID-19 and Transformations of the Interaction Order: patternization and de-ritualization of social interactions", in J. M. Ryan (ed.); and *COVID-19: Volume IV – Individual Rights and Community Responsibilities* (Fall 2022, in press).

The manufacturer's authorised representative in the EU is Springer Nature Customer Service Centre GmbH, Europaplatz 3, 69115 Heidelberg, Germany. If you have any concerns regarding our products, please contact ProductSafety@springernature.com

Printed and bound by CPI Group (UK) Ltd, Croydon, CR0 4YY
30/09/2026
02225493-0014